# DOCUMENTS
# OF
# DIALOGUE

## By HILEY WARD

PRENTICE-HALL, INC., ENGLEWOOD CLIFFS, N. J.

*Documents of Dialogue*

by Hiley Ward

© 1966 by Prentice-Hall, Inc., Englewood Cliffs, N.J.

Library of Congress Catalog Card Number: 66-22100

Printed in the United States of America

T 21695

Prentice-Hall International, Inc., London
Prentice-Hall of Australia, Pty. Ltd., Sydney
Prentice-Hall of Canada, Ltd., Toronto
Prentice-Hall of India Private Ltd., New Delhi
Prentice-Hall of Japan, Inc., Tokyo

*TO:*
LAUREL JANE
who
at two
is moving from monologue to dialogue

BY THE AUTHOR:
Creative Giving
Space-Age Sunday

CONTRIBUTOR:
Reaching Beyond Your Pulpit

## ACKNOWLEDGMENTS

In preparing this manuscript, much is owed to many, first of all, to my wife, Charlotte, for her encouragement and patience, and helpfulness in some of the detailed chores of getting the book together, and to a number of individuals, libraries, and ecumenical centers. The documentation at the end of each chapter is also a special thank you to the nearly 300 sources.

Miss Lillian Block and her staff of Religious News Service were helpful in providing their files in New York for a day-by-day check of inter-Christian activities for the last ten years. At Duquesne University, Pittsburgh, Dr. Leonard Swidler, associate professor of history and theology and co-editor of the *Journal of Ecumenical Studies*, provided contacts with his overseas abstractors.

The directors of various information offices deserve special mention: among them, Erik Modean, of the National Lutheran Council, Fletcher Coates and Bruno Kroker of the National Council of Churches, the Rev. Father Vincent Yzermans, of the National Catholic Welfare Conference Bureau of Information, Mrs. Nancy Robb and Miss Faith Pomponio, of the World Council of Churches, and a dozen denominational press officials.

I am indebted also to the special readers who so kindly reviewed parts of the manuscript and offered their suggestions, particularly the Very Rev. Msgr. William W. Baum, secretary for the U.S. Roman Catholic Bishops' Commission for Ecumenical Affairs, and the Rev. Dr. J. Robert Nelson, former secretary of

the World Council of Churches' Commission on Faith and Order
and professor of systematic theology at the Boston University
School of Theology.

Appreciated also is the help of translators and language advisers, although we elected at last to concentrate the bulk of
the book on the United States situation. A thank you to Dr.
Joseph A. Finn and Dr. Philip Love, of the Department of Modern Languages, University of Detroit, German and French
respectively; Waltrud Woyack, Georgetown (Kentucky) College, German; the Rev. Father George Tavard, Mount Mercy
College, Pittsburgh, and the Rev. Father Charles Boyle, New
Orleans, Louisiana, French; George Buffington, San Francisco,
Japanese; Jack van de Werken, Carpentersville, Illinois, Dutch;
the Rev. Father Julio Mariani, PIME, Queen of Missions Seminary, Oakland, New Jersey, and the Rev. Father Lawrence
Chiesa, director of studies, PIME missionaries, U. S. Province,
Detroit, Italian.

# Contents

# INTRODUCTION

"Every teacher has learned to recognize the sense of awakening that comes to students when for the first time they deal with 'primary sources.' Readers of such sources gain the feeling, quite rightfully, that they are not mere observers of observers. Instead, with a sense of immediacy and participation, they are in a sense 'on the scene' itself, dealing with the traces great events leave.

"Certainly modern ecumenism is a great event. Until now too many people have stood outside, as observers of observers. With this well-introduced collection more of them can become participants, can gain first-hand impressions, and be prepared to speak their own piece and take their own part. A wide range of documents, chosen with originality, are collected here."

So says the Rev. Dr. Martin E. Marty, associate editor of the *Christian Century* and associate professor of church history at the Divinity School, University of Chicago. Upon request Dr. Marty, along with others, graciously offered advance comment on this book after seeing several chapters during the working stages. Dr. Marty's remarks sum up the intent of this book.

For the student, then, as well as for the neighbors on each side of the fence, in the yard, or beside the invisible fences in commercial, social, and church life, this book is intended. For the pastor and the lay leaders of congregations beginning to structure dialogue or looking for excerpts and quotable material for the diocesan or parish paper—this book, we hope, will also be of considerable value. Answers to specific questions, the precise "who, what, where, when, and why" questions, are here. Accounts of dialogue, guidelines, and excerpts of actual services also answer such questions as "how" to go about improving communications and experiences of dialogue between the Christian faiths. (The growing dialogue between Christianity and all the other faiths, even with atheism, continues to be more fascinating by the day, but to get into these other dialogue topics would require other volumes.)

It is as a student researcher, and as a newsman, that my own personal interest in documents developed. My student days introduced me to the exciting lure of voices of the past, long silenced, but speaking directly and clearly through the legacy of documents. As a newsman, my work is with contemporary life, which has introduced the sense that much of the material around us now will be the official documents of the historian of tomorrow. Of course, one cannot act as a historian in the present, but he can sample the Herculean material (made ever so immense by increased leisure, with more time for the layman, for instance, to be involved in such things, and by communications, adding to the incredible bulk of printed matter that emerges in the current popular dialogue). The newsman, whether he likes it or not, has to act as a sort of historian—or selector pro tem—for the documents of the present.

As a student, I experienced the simple joys of handling sources in three seminaries, from the older musty pages of volumes to more modern-day collections such as Bettenson's *Documents of the Christian Church* and the Westminster *Library of Christian Classics*. I remember sampling some of them in the original Greek, particularly the *Didache*, not to mention all those Greek exegetical courses in the Septuagint and most of the New Testament, and some limited Hebrew exegetical work.

As a newsman, sources and documents have not always been as available or as ready to come by as the historical documents and, much of the time, secret sources had to be reconstructed by indirection—by those who had seen and been entrusted with secret documents and who would "fill" one in on the contents. Secrecy in the long run was often discarded, and the sources, awaiting some emendation, were laid out in some way for consultation, whether they be the various documents of the World Council of Churches and its related movements, or the Latin *relatio* and *schemata* of the Second Vatican Council. With the researcher's interest and the newsman's sense of importance for the larger community, we hope these documents, from official pronouncements voted and promulgated in sacred aula to the more private sources, such as letters, will indeed stir, as Dr. Marty suggested, "the sense of awakening" in students of Christianity, young—and old.

We have sought to make the documents not only readable by selection and some editing (deletions), but by the narrative techniques of magazine and news feature writing. Within a reasonable, but not always consistent chronology, we have hitched some documents onto others by topical relation, and in certain cases made clear breaks for contrast purposes, when the new section of material could stand as its own "hook" or readability gauge. This is to say we have aimed for readability and continuity in the presentation, to achieve interesting reading as well as essential reference.

With dialogue becoming accelerated in the last decade, particularly with the appearance of Pope John XXIII in 1958, an overall 10-year time span in which to capture the mood and sources of current change appeared to be quite adequate. Introductory material before each item, however, serves to relate these documents of this significant last decade with earlier roots, particularly with the seeds of the modern ecumenical movement in this century; but obviously since this is a book of documents selected to cover a limited modern period, all the aspects that would be developed in history texts cannot be touched on in this work.

While a book of this sort will include surprises, and documents that perhaps the reader might have overlooked, it will also be minus some documents that various readers would like to have in it. No work could possibly include items to the full satisfaction of each individual.

Facing the growing length of this project, we decided against a final chapter which would have been entitled "Toward One Church," and it is well, for such a chapter would presuppose a church union complex for dialogue whereas dialogue is not always that simple or final. Some of the participants in dialogue today have little interest in organic union (Baptists and Methodists, for example), while others do have ultimate union more clearly in mind. Also there are some good sources available concerning church union progress, namely in *The Ecumenical Review*, and its reprint pamphlets (surveys of church union negotiations can be found in detail in *The Ecumenical Review* issues of April, 1954, p. 300; October, 1955, p. 76; April, 1957, p. 284; January, 1960, p. 231; April, 1962, p. 351) and for those who wish to go further back there are *A Decade of Objective Progress in Church Unity: 1927-1936*, by H. Paul Douglass (Harper and Brothers, New York, 1937), and *Towards Church Union: 1937-1952*, by Stephen Neill (SCM Press, London, 1952).

Also for further background of dialogue related to the inter-confessional church union, as well as the overall scene, there are the four series on *Documents on Christian Unity*, of the late Bishop of Chicester, G. K. A. Bell, from 1924 to 1957 (Oxford University Press). These include not only the denominational church union documents up to that time, but the documents influential in the formation of the World Council of Churches, and occasional Vatican documents. In a way, Bell's effort could be regarded as a sufficient predecessor to this book. Yet this book goes beyond what Dr. Bell would have done for the past decade. For here you have a wide sampling of documents of local dialogue, which have never been compiled in any way before, along with excerpts of the more majestic documents of the World Council of Churches and the Second Vatican Council and other corporate structures.

By documents we mean the official or accepted formulation of policy of a church body, on the one hand, and the concrete statement or expression or account, local or national or international, of some phase of inter-Christian relations on the other.

Dialogue is harder to define. As a starter we can say that dialogue centers in conversation, which is true to the literal root of the word, Gr.: *Logein*, to talk; *dia*, between.

Dialogue, unlike monologue, is never one way. Dialogue is conversation which involves two or more persons or an interper-

sonal relationship with or without persons per se. To engage
in dialogue, one has first to assume relationship. On this basis,
hermits of old, Stylites, St. Maron, St. Acepsimas, in their isolation, appear at first sight not to have carried on dialogue, sitting
alone on top of a pole or alone in a desert or swamp—only monologue. But they, too, carried on dialogue with the Unknown in
their mystic framework.

The difficulty in defining dialogue comes in realizing just what
is "personal" in an age when theologians and philosophers such
as the late Martin Buber, Nicholas Berdyaev, and Teilhard de
Chardin personify the inanimate (as created material fashioned
by God—in nature, or fashioned and imbued by God-created man
—in industry using God-created materials). For Buber, his emphasis on an I-Thou relationship also permitted an I-It concept
of personal proportions; Berdyaev, at war with modern mechani-
zation, could still sense the personal, suffering presence in the
inanimate; for Chardin, all matter had a certain "inwardness."
And thus the mystic hermits of old, alone and isolated with nature and matter, could, even by modern reckoning be said to be
in dialogue.

Dialogue with the world per se has become an important concern of the modern world "coming of age," as Bonhoeffer would
put it. From Baptist Harvey Cox (*The Secular City*) to Pope
Paul VI, who in his coronation speech said he will "listen to
these voices of the world," and the Second Vatican Council's
comprehensive constitution on the Church in the Modern World,
the church's interrelationship with culture is assumed and in-
separable. That move, to be relevant, however, is a dialogue in a
category of its own. It is largely a dialogue between a particular
institution or group and a collective society, a dialogue that must
often be vague although it reflects personal qualities. But in this
book, for the purpose of limitation, the dialogue is parochial
—between parties of religion—and, although it includes dialogue
with and within the world, as the social action projects of the
final chapter will show, the dialogue is primarily between persons of a religious stance within a category of defined relations.
That category is the modern ecumenical movement with the subjects of the dialogue being Orthodox, Protestant and Roman
Catholic Christians.

It is important to note, as we have touched upon in regard to the ascetic mystics, the solitary stance of these hermits implied an unseen party. While their social dialogue with the world was virtually nil (although this could perhaps be challenged, to the degree they influenced thought or served contemporary purposes), the presence of God in their isolated predicaments cannot be challenged. Thus, recognizing the wider implications of the predicament of the hermits in mystical relationships, and the cultural involvement of religion, a third party is often implied in even the simplest of the two-way dialogical conversations. So while this book deals largely with observable dialogue on one plane with two basic poles of reference—Roman Catholic and the Protestant-Orthodox—a third party, deity, and a fourth, the world out there in relation to the other parties, are often if not always implied. Dialogue cannot fully escape the philosophical implications of its activity, which makes it one of the more difficult words to fathom completely.

For our purposes, dialogue will be limited to historical religious subjects, personal and multi-personal, within the human complex, although the common subject matter is often the implied other parties—God and the world. But the dialogue here is not that of a mystic collection nor is it documents of a social manifesto. The dialogue is between churches, however much they may have recourse to the other parties in their conversations.

Dialogue here will have, as most dialogue does, observable points of reference. (Even the mystic dialogue of Scripture between man and God, as a personified being who spoke audibly, had observable points of reference. For example, Adam and Eve, and God, had the apple as a point of reference; Job, and God—possessions; John, and God—a vision of a new Jerusalem.) The early Christians had the Scriptures as a point of reference. "Then Philip opened his mouth, and began at the same Scripture, and preached unto him Jesus," as he interpreted Scriptures for the Ethiopian eunuch (Acts 8: 35). Said John in his Gospel: "Many other signs truly did Jesus in the presence of his disciples, which are not written in this book: but these are written, that ye might believe that Jesus is the Christ, the son of God . . ." (John 20: 30, 31). A dialogue of words presupposes some previous objective content. Therefore, the importance of objective formulations such as documents.

Dialogue originated historically as a literary tool in Greek philosophy and drama. Plato used dialogue for all of his philosophical writings except the *Apology*, which, describing the death of Socrates in the first person, itself has a strong dialogical tone. Plato's dialogues are traceable to the early Sicilian poets who wrote brief mimes or caricatures of real life with only two performers.

In Christian literature, Aristo, in A.D. 140, in Pella, Palestine, (one of the Greek cities that became a refuge for Jerusalem Jews and Christians at the destruction of the Temple in A.D. 70) wrote a *Dialogue of Papiscus and Jason*, a Christian and a Jew. In like vein, Justin Martyr in the second century wrote a dialogue between himself and a Jew named Trypho (a name similar to a well-known rabbi of his time, Rabbi Tarphon). *The Dialogue of Simon the Jew and Theophilus* by the monk Evagrius appeared in the fifth century and the *Dialogue of Papiscus and Philo*, another Jewish-Christian debate using the name of one of Aristo's characters, appeared in the sixth century. Anselm used the technique of dialogue in his *Cur Deus Homo*, a conversation between himself and Boso in the Middle Ages. Philosopher Bishop George Berkeley used the dialogue form in his *Hylas and Philonus* in 1713.

Although dialogue implies a conversation and even a "little drama" in its oldest sense, in Greek etymology it also has a "disputation" connotation (as Plato himself and the later polemical Jewish-Christian dialogues used it). As a verb in the Greek (*dialogizesthai*), it also means to engage in dialogue "to reason," "to settle accounts," "to ponder and consider," and a noun form used in the New Testament (*dialogismos*) means "reasoning," "disputation," "contention," or "doubt," or "hesitation." There is then thought, and reasoning, as well as neutral conversation (if conversation can be neutral) in the meaning of dialogue.

The Rev. Father Edvard Vogt, a Catholic scholar on dialecticism (namely Marxism) and founder of an ecumenical retreat-research center near Bergen, Norway, links dialecticism and dialogue, thus bringing in the dimension of "synthesis" or consensus.

Conflicting views seek an answer. Where there are questions and disagreement, an answer is implied. Dialogue is not mere declaration. (That would be monologue). The direction of dialogue is toward answers or the seeking of answers (even though a "dialogue" may be billed as only a "get-acquainted" session).

Cooperative projects—in areas such as world peace, relief, and race relations—are evidence that dialogue implies answers of some sort on the periphery, if not always at the center of things. Again the activity of dialogue presupposes documents at the other end, not only as points of reference, but as a means of positing its results.

Dialogue is a way, not a state in itself to be desired. Consensus (even union) and cooperative projects result, but they are not to be taken as dialogue per se. One who seeks is in dialogue. He finds answers, but the seeking is the essence; "Ask, and it shall be given you; seek, and ye shall find; knock, and it shall be opened unto you" (Matt. 7: 7), said Jesus. There are always answers yet to come.

Consensus is not theoretically a part of dialogue, for it consummates phases of dialogue. Yet a church consensus or union can be classified as a form of dialogue because it is also a way, a stepping stone into another stage.

When a goal is reached, dialogue does not end. Although it may achieve a peak or impasse, and must descend, the direction can still be ongoing, whether circumventing that peak or going up another. If dialogue leads to consensus and union, it also leads the new embodiment on to other creative heights. Dialogue is like a stream that can be contained for a while, but it has its own force and can change the terrain, either on the surface or from subterranean depths that eventually come into the terrain of life.

In this book are markers in that new torrent of dialogue. Selected words in that ongoing conversation show something of where we are, and help to judge and fathom the course of dialogue. The documents are the dam, the floodgates, the catwalks, and the stepping stones, the solid ground within and toward the future.

Documents of dialogue are a substance of things . . . hoped for.

# one

# Seeds of Change

The seeds of fruitful cooperation between Roman Catholics and Protestants that blossomed in the late 1950's were watered and nourished by many forces and events, all contributing to the growing flower of unity. It was the process of spiritual growth that emerges out of the unpretentious efforts described by St. Paul: "I have planted, Apollos watered; but God gave the increase" (I Cor. 3: 6).

Roman Catholics, with individual exceptions, were largely standoffish in the first half of this century. Even as midcentury approached, the Vatican declined invitations for a few individuals to attend the organizational meeting of the World Council of Churches in 1948. The Vatican went further in that year to issue a *monitum*, or warning, that "mixed meetings" without permission of the Holy See were contrary to canon law. The Vatican, however, had indicated some interest, if not action, by agreeing to a proposal of the Provisional Committee for the World Council of Churches in 1939 "to exchange information . . . on matters of common interest" and "from time to time" have the occasion of "unofficial consultation with Roman Catholic theologians and scholars."

Earlier, Pope Benedict XV gave some encouragement on a very limited scale by increasing ties with Eastern Christianity through a new Congregation for the Eastern Church and the Institute of Oriental Studies in 1917, and he permitted the Malines

1

(Belgium) talks to encourage a reunion of Anglicanism with the
Roman Catholic Church. His successor, Pius XI, continued the
Malines talks but issued in 1928 his *Mortalium animos* encyclical
that warned Catholics of the dangers of eclecticism in such movements as Faith and Order, one of the two parent movements of
the World Council of Churches. Pius XI warned that "it is easy
for many to be misled" even when there was talk of a "hope of
a union apparently consonant with the wishes of Holy Mother
Church, whose chief desire it is to recall her erring children and
to bring them back to her bosom. In reality, however, these fair
and alluring words cloak a most grave error, subversive of the
foundations of the Catholic faith. . . ." It remained for the
Protestants and the Orthodox to develop the spirit of ecumenism,
a coalescing which was really essential in the first place, for in
the converging Protestant-Orthodox movements, there emerged
the more general groupings necessary for serious, more equitable
conversations.

The Faith and Order (or theological unity) movement of the
Protestants and Orthodox was set in motion early in the century
by a missionary-minded bishop interested in union, the Rt. Rev.
Charles Henry Brent, a Protestant Episcopal bishop assigned
to the Philippines and later to Western New York. His suggestion for a theological meeting in cooperative Christianity followed
the widely representative World Missionary Conference of Protestant Missionary Societies in Edinburgh in 1910. (Actually, to
go back further in modern times, William Carey, the "father of
modern missions" who went to India, had suggested in 1806 that
there be "a meeting of all denominations of Christians at The
Cape of Good Hope somewhere about 1810." It took nearly a century for such a meeting to be realized, but by the end of the
nineteenth century the competition and overlapping of the mission societies was beginning to be felt. There was injected also
the note of urgency as a result of growing new ideologies in the
industrial age and the new realism that was born in World
War I.) The 1910 meeting was not the first such world gathering
of mission leaders. In 1888 in London 1,500 were present for an
international mission gathering, and in 1900 a larger meeting
was held in New York. Billed as an Ecumenical Missionary Conference, it introduced into modern times, for Protestants at

least, the word "ecumenical" (see glossary). Catholics had had
their 20th Ecumenical Council (First Vatican) in 1869-70, and
the word "ecumenical" was not entirely strange.

Giving further ecumenical impetus to the Protestant churches
at the turn of the century was the interdenominational YMCA
organized in 1878, followed by the World Student Christian
Federation organized by a United States Methodist layman John
R. Mott, in 1895. And on the United States scene itself there was
the formation of the Federal Council of Churches of Christ in
1908, with 30 denominations, later to become the National Council of Churches in 1950, with the purpose: "To express the fellowship and catholic unity of the Christian Church" and "to bring
the Christian bodies of America into united service for Christ
and the world."

Bishop Brent's proposal for friendly talks on church unity,
with strong encouragement from a U.S Protestant Episcopal
Faith and Order commission, found quick support among the
churches, but it was nearly ten years before he could get together
the representatives of the 69 commissions appointed by the
churches. They held a preparatory meeting in Geneva in 1920.

In the same year, the Eastern Orthodox patriarchate of Constantinople, a group of Orthodox prelates acting in the name of
the Ecumenical Patriarch, which position was vacant at that
time, said in an encyclical "to all the churches of Christ who-
soever they be" that "our church is of the opinion that a closer
intercourse with each other and a mutual understanding between
the several Christian churches is not prevented by the doctrinal
differences existing between them. . . ." They proposed a "league
of churches," comparable in the life of the church to the League
of Nations, the first official proposal in modern times for a permanent organization of the various churches.

Faith and Order finally convened officially on a full scale in
Lausanne in 1927, showing that various churches or communions
could converse on doctrinal issues, although talks centered
largely in a comparison of views. The second conference on Faith
and Order, in 1937 in Edinburgh, underscored the sin of disunity and found new lines of agreement among the churches.
Here it proposed the formation of a World Council of Churches,
into which it was eventually absorbed at the founding of the

WCC in Amsterdam in 1948. Future conferences of Faith and
Order, now a "wing" or commission of the WCC, were held in
Lund, Sweden, in 1952, and in Montreal in 1963. Lund saw a
going beyond comparing faiths into a "new methodology," assuming an existent unity in Christ and emphasizing that all
churches stand in the light of the final judgment. Emphasis was
not on creating a unity, but in discovering the unity that exists.
Montreal dealt again in specifics, but did not show consensus on
important issues.

While Faith and Order was developing, so was the Life and
Work movement. The key man here was the Lutheran archbishop
of Upsala, Sweden, Nathan Söderblom, who proposed a meeting
of the faiths to promote principles of Christ in the life and work
of Christians. He made his suggestion at a meeting of the World
Alliance for Promoting International Friendship through the
churches in The Hague in 1919. The first assembly of Life and
Work met in Stockholm in 1925, and stated: "We believe that
there is a longing on the part, not merely of the trusted servants
of the Church, but of all followers of our Lord and Master, to see
Christendom so far united as to be able to work together in applying the principles taught by Him to the problems which con-
front us both in national and international life. . . ." Here representatives of the Eastern Orthodox participated in a modern
ecumenical gathering for the first time.

Christians at Stockholm from 37 countries authored a prayer
for unity, praising God "for sending us Christ our Lord, he who
is our Peace, he who wishes to reconcile us with each other and
to make us, through the Cross, one single body. . . ." Life and
Work met again at Oxford in 1937, and like the Faith and Order
movement in the same year, agreed to join in forming the World
Council of Churches, an action that was to be postponed for 11
years because of the war.

In 1961, the International Missionary Council, the oldest of
the twentieth century ecumenical movements, merged with the
World Council of Churches, as Faith and Order and Life and
Work had done in 1948. Founded in 1921 in Lake Mohonk, New
York (although planned at Edinburgh in 1910), and a successor
to earlier cooperative mission efforts, the IMC met in Jerusalem
in 1928; Tambaram, India, in 1938; Whitby, Canada, in 1947;

Willengen in 1952, and Ghana in 1957. The merger of the IMC with the Council in 1961 united a concern for witness with unity.

The World Council of Churches and the Roman Catholic Church, if they were to take unity seriously at all, could now hardly escape one another. The 550 million Roman Catholics and the 200 million members of the WCC were ready to communicate on a greater plane of consensus; for Catholics, undergoing more subtle winds of change, came up with a great gust of renewal consciousness in the brief papacy of Pope John XXIII. The change in Catholicism would, however, have remained largely meaningless, or at best a monologue, if it were not for the developments within Protestantism in the World Council of Churches, which indeed complemented if not motivated, along with other causes, modern Roman Catholic ecumenism.

1. A statement adopted by the Executive Committee of the World Council of Churches, meeting in Odessa in 1964, sums up the accumulative experience of the WCC and its constituent groups concerning ecumenism and the new twentieth century image of the Protestants and Orthodox that greeted their Roman Catholic brethren:

> In the World Council all member churches have the same privileges; all participate in the elaboration of the common policies, statements or practical decisions and in the choice of officers or members of the responsible organs. In the fellowship which the Council seeks to establish, churches are involved in multilateral relationships with each other, and this is expressed in the structure of the Council. Each church is free to take whatever initiative it desires in the sphere of inter-church relationships, but the Council as such acts only on the basis of the common consent of its members.
>
> The World Council seeks therefore to promote a conversation within a fellowship which has become a new experience in the life of the churches as they have shared in prayer and action. This experience has led to a dialogue between churches which recognize one another as confessing the same Lord, sharing the same baptism and participating in a common calling to the glory of the one God, Father, Son

and Holy Spirit. Although the churches may have reservations concerning one another's ecclesiological position, they
are ready to engage in this conversation on equal terms.
It is a conversation in which all are expected to listen as
well as to speak, to receive as well as to give, and in which
existing differences and tensions are frankly faced.

The churches in the World Council believe that the member churches should recognize their solidarity with one another, render assistance to each other in case of need, and
support one another in their witness to Christ and in their
evangelistic and missionary task, and wherever it is possible
to do so, take common action and render common witness
on the basis of consultation and agreement with one another.

2. In a far-reaching action, in 1961, the General Assembly of
the World Council of Churches voted 383 to 36 (7 abstentions) to
accept a new basis of membership that underscores the Lordship
and divinity of Christ and the Trinity. The new "basis" gave the
WCC more than an organizational image, and placed it in line for
theological dialogue, namely with Rome. Leading church ecumenist, Presbyterian Eugene Carson Blake said in the debate in New
Delhi that the new "basis" makes "clear to some churches outside our fellowship that it is not 'mere togetherness' which is
the foundation of the ecumenical movement but an authentic
Christian confession based upon the Scriptures."
    The new "basis" of the WCC says:

The World Council of Churches is a fellowship of churches
which confess the Lord Jesus Christ as God and Saviour
according to the Scriptures and therefore seek to fulfill together their common calling to the glory of the one God,
Father, Son and Holy Spirit.

3. The Third Pan-Orthodox Conference at Rhodes formulated
a policy on November 13, 1964, concerning dialogue with Rome
and other Christians, a reflection of the earlier desire of the
ecumenical patriarch of Constantinople joined by other Greek
metropolitans in 1920. While the Third Pan-Orthodox Conference
at Rhodes presented a modest declaration, it did crystallize a call

for "preparations" for a fruitful theological dialogue long in the making:

> (1) Our holy Orthodox Church proclaims that she has always wished to be on good terms with all the Churches and Christian confessions to build the unity of Christians in the One, Holy, Catholic and Apostolic Church of the Lord, according to his word: "That all may be one" (John 17: 21).
>
> (2) In this spirit the first Pan-Orthodox Conference of Rhodes has expressed favor on keeping a good rapport with the other Christian communities, in Christ's charity; and the second conference has decided as first objective to propose, on basis of equality, a dialogue with the Roman Catholic Church.
>
> (3) This conference takes up this desire, already expressed by the Orthodox Church about this matter and, after having considered the matter on its own, she believes that, as an initial fruit of a practical theological dialogue, one must make adequate preparations and create favorable conditions.
>
> (4) This does not mean that every Church is not free to continue to have fraternal relations with the Roman Catholic Church, but each one can act in its own name and not in the name of the entire Orthodox Church, in the hope that in this way they may gradually overcome the difficulties which still remain.
>
> (5) To this end and for a better realization of this holy cause, the Third Pan-Orthodox Conference extends an invitation to all the Churches to study, each one on its own, this area of the dialogue from the Orthodox viewpoint, exchanging among themselves the findings of their studies and any other information on the matter.

4. A similar desire to move out of isolation and recall primitive church alliances was developing among the other Eastern Christian bodies. (Again, the interest was not new. Emperor Haile Selassie I of Ethiopia recalled in a visit to the WCC Ecumenical

Center in Geneva, November 3, 1965, that in his first trip to Europe in 1925, he had discussed Christian unity with Nathan Söderblom, archbishop of Sweden.) The leaders of five ancient Eastern churches that grew up independently of Rome and Constantinople met in Addis Ababa, Ethiopia during January 1965, for the first time since the Council of Chalcedon met across the straits from modern Istanbul, Turkey, in 451. Traditionally self-sufficient, and thoroughly isolated from the rest of Christendom during the height of Islam, the patriarchs of these Eastern Christian groups, now in the Space Age, turned their eyes specifically outward. The declaration of the five Oriental churches (Armenian, Coptic, Ethiopian, Indian, Syrian) dealt with relations with other groups, along with other topics of world responsibility. (Originally considered "Monophysite," or believers in the one nature of Christ as against the divine and human nature of Christ defined at Chalcedon, the distinction between these five and the Orthodox is more academic than clear-cut today). They attributed their greater sense of oneness partly to participation in the WCC. The Oriental Orthodox said in their statement in Addis Ababa:

> ... Though in our concern for the reunion of Christendom we have in our minds the reunion of all churches, from the point of view of closer affinity in faith and spiritual kinship with us we need to develop different approaches in our relationship with them. This consideration leads us to take up the question of our relation with the Eastern Orthodox Churches as a first step. We shared the same faith and communion till the Council of Chalcedon in 451, and then the division took place.

> Concerning the Christological controversy which caused the division, we hope that common studies in a spirit of mutual understanding can shed light on our understanding of each other's positions. So we decide that we should institute formally a fresh study of the Christological doctrine in its historical setting to be undertaken by our scholars, taking into account the earlier studies on this subject as well as the informal consultations held in connection with

the meetings of the World Council of Churches. Meanwhile, we express our agreement that our churches could seek closer relationship and cooperate with the Eastern Orthodox Churches in practical affairs.

With the Church of Rome also we shared the same faith and communion till the Council of Chalcedon in 451, and then the division took place. We rejoice about the new awareness which the Roman Catholic Church has begun to show of the need on its part for recognizing the other churches, particularly the Orthodox Churches of the East. With this new spirit in view, we suggest that we should be willing to enter into conversation with the Roman Catholic Church with a view to closer understanding. In our relationship with it the principle of dialogue on the level of churches must be adopted. In this connection, we should ask the Roman Catholic Church to reconsider its theory and practice both of maintaining uniate churches and of proselytizing among members of our churches.

We are happy to note that the Eastern Orthodox Churches have also expressed a positive attitude in regard to establishing a dialogue with the Roman Catholic Church, and we hope that it will be possible for our churches to proceed in this direction in collaboration with them.

With the non-Orthodox member Churches of the World Council of Churches we have cordial relations through it and we hope and pray that God will open the way for our mutual understanding and cooperation wherever possible. Of these churches, the Old Catholic Church and the Anglican Churches must be considered in a special way. The Anglican Churches, for instance, have always shown appreciation for the Orthodox Churches of the East, and we trust that this will lead to a fruitful dialogue between them and our churches. Our churches have also been in contact with the other member churches of the World Council of Churches. In our mutual relationship there have been, and still there exist, difficulties which arise from certain attempts at proselytism made by some of the Protestant Churches. We hope that such attempts will cease. We believe that God, who has brought our churches and the other member churches of the World Council of Churches together into friendly relations through that Council, will help us to grow in fellowship with one another and restore us all into fulness of unity in his own time and in the manner he ordains.

Before we conclude, we would like to express a genuine appreciation of the whole ecumenical movement such as that made manifest through the World Council of Churches. The new spirit of fellowship, mutual understanding and cooperation fostered by the ecumenical movement has had beneficial effects in the life of all the churches involved.

We hope and pray that God will strengthen every effort made for the progress of the ecumenical movement to enable the churches to fulfill their mission through common and concerted efforts in ever greater faithfulness to our common Lord Jesus Christ.

5. The move of the Russian Orthodox to join the World Council of Churches growing out of years of negotiations delayed by cultural, if not ideological differences, brought a new bridge between the predominantly Protestant WCC and the Roman Catholic Church. The historic letter in 1961 signifying the Russian Orthodox decision to join the WCC described the bridge-making role of the Orthodox which share concepts of the church and sacraments with Roman Catholics. Now the "catholic" tradition was evident in the WCC. The letter from the patriarch of Moscow said:

> The General Secretary
> Dr. W. A. Visser 't Hooft
> Geneva
>
> My dear General Secretary,
>
> On behalf of the Holy Synod of the Russian Orthodox Church I send you the following declaration concerning tho

entrance of our Church into membership of the World Council of Churches.

We declare our agreement with the Basis of the World Council of Churches as expressed in paragraph one of its Constitution.

We declare that the Russian Orthodox Church corresponds to the criteria of independence, stability, size and the requirements concerning mutual relationships with other churches, which are required according to the constitution of the World Council of Churches. . . .

The Russian Orthodox Church has always attached the utmost importance to the problems of mutual rapprochement between all Christians, the deepening of mutual understanding among committed Christians and the strengthening of universal brotherhood, love and peace among the nations on the basis of the Gospel.

In this respect we count on the efforts made by the World Council of Churches to strengthen the spirit of ecumenical brotherhood as well as the contacts with the Russian Orthodox Church. Believing in the One, Holy, Catholic (Sobornaia) and Apostolic Church and being herself an integral part of that Church, the Russian Orthodox Church has not only always prayed and continues to pray for the welfare of the Holy Churches of God and the union of all, but is fully determined to make her contributions to the great task of Christian Unity on the lines of the previous movements of "Faith and Order," "Life and Work" and "International Friendship Through the Churches" which now find their common expression in the different forms and aspects of the activities of the World Council of Churches, all of them being directed towards the realization of the aims mentioned above.

In the love of Christ,

*Signed* Patriarch Alexi
Patriarch of Moscow and All Russia

6. What the World Council of Churches means by "unity" was sketched out at St. Andrews, Scotland, in 1960, and with some changes in the preliminary statement, restated and affirmed at the General Assembly of the WCC in New Delhi in 1961. (The St. Andrews and subsequent WCC statement at New Delhi represents a rewriting of a similar statement in a book, *One Body, One Gospel, One World*, by the Rt. Rev. J. E. Lesslie Newbigin, bishop of the Madras diocese of the Church of South India and at that time secretary of the International Missionary Council.) Some have seen the St. Andrews-New Delhi statements as committing the World Council to more interest in local cooperation and federation rather than constituting a churchly entity; others, including the Rev. James E. Wagner, former president of the Evangelical and Reformed Church, saw in the St. Andrew's report a renewed emphasis on union and reunion. Perhaps both views are justified. But the statement introduces a certain tangibility or objective quality of the church in the use of the words "visible" and "place"; the use of the word "fellowship" eliminates concepts of parochial boundaries in the church; the emphasis is on a common baptism, an important premise in all ecumenical discussions, recognizing a certain validity of the status of those baptized in other faiths (see Chapters III, IV, and V).

The statement on unity as adopted (based on Bishop Newbigin's paragraph and St. Andrew's statement) by the WCC at New Delhi:

> We believe that the unity which is both God's will and his gift to his Church is being made visible as all in each place who are baptized into Jesus Christ and confess him as Lord and Saviour are brought by the Holy Spirit into one fully committed fellowship, holding the one apostolic faith, preaching the one Gospel, breaking the one bread, joining in common prayer, and having a corporate life reaching out in witness and service to all and who at the same time are united with the whole Christian fellowship in all places and all ages in such wise that ministry and members are accepted by all, and that all can act and speak together as occasion requires for the tasks to which God calls his people.

7. Great names played a significant role in twentieth century ecumenism. At the top has been, on the Protestant side, the Rev. Dr. Willem Adolf Visser 't Hooft, who for ten years headed the provisional committee preceding the WCC in 1948, and for the next eighteen years headed the WCC as its first general secretary. There were men, already mentioned, such as John R. Mott; Archbishop Nathan Söderblom, head of the church of Sweden 1914-1931; Archbishop William Temple, of York and Canterbury, who was called the "perfect president" of the 1937 Faith and Order Conference at Edinburgh; J. H. Oldham, a pioneer of the IMC; Archbishop Yngve Brilioth, of Upsala; Bishop Anders Nygren, of Lund; Archbishops Chrysostomos of Greece and Germanos Strenopoulos, of Thyateira; Bishop V. S. Azariah, of Dornakal, South India; Marc Boegner, of France; Hendrick Kraemer, first director of the Ecumenical Institute of Bossey, and many others. An Episcopal layman, Robert R. Gardiner, from Maine, head of the Episcopal commission on Faith and Order, in 1910 paved the way for Faith and Order conferences (and the WCC) with others; first order of business at the first Faith and Order conference was a tribute to this layman who had died three years previously in 1924.

On the Roman Catholic side, personalities were equally important, but their roles were largely in isolated capacities away from official Rome (an exception: D. J. Cardinal Mercier, of Malines), in the retreat and study centers and the monasteries (see Chapter II), but no less effective than their Protestant and Orthodox counterparts in more official capacities. Pope Pius XII, on the day after his election in 1939, turned his thoughts to "all who are outside the fold of the Catholic Church . . . we beseech the all-bounteous and almighty God to grant them His divine assistance," but most of the talk was of "tolerance" rather than active humility in search for unity. Pius XII's 1957 letter marking the fiftieth anniversary of the eight days of prayer for unity (see Chapter VI), spoke in terms of all returning "as soon as possible to the indestructible Rock of the Prince of the Apostles" and saw the week of prayer, January 18-25, as enabling the "separated brethren" to "happily return to the bosom of the Catholic Church" (*Unitas*, IX, No. 4, Winter, 1957, p. 259).

And then in the papacy itself came a personality that cap-
tured the imagination of individuals of all faiths for unity. A
new pontiff, taking the name of John, apostle of unity, looked
toward unity. Angelo Roncalli, on October 28, 1958, said:

> We love the name of John, so dear to us and to all the
> Church, particularly because it was borne by two men who
> were closest to Christ the Lord, the divine Redeemer of all
> the world and Founder of the Church: John the Baptist,
> the precursor of our Lord. He was not indeed the Light, but
> the witness to the Light. And he was truly the unconquered
> witness of truth, of justice and of liberty in his preaching,
> in the baptism of repentance, in the blood he shed. And the
> other John, the disciple and Evangelist, preferred by Christ
> and by His most Holy Mother who, as he ate the Last Sup-
> per, leaned on the breast of our Lord, and thereby obtained
> that charitable love which burned in him with a lively
> apostolic flame until great age. . . .
>
> My children, love one another. Love one another, because
> this is the greatest commandment of the Lord. Venerable
> brethren, may God in His mercy grant that, bearing the
> name of the first of this series of supreme pontiffs, we can,
> with the help of divine grace, have his sanctity of life and
> his strength of soul, unto the shedding of our blood if God
> so wills.

8. Pope John, who had been in the papal chair for only a
matter of weeks, was inspired in December 1958, to call an ecumenical council, the first in nearly 100 years. He coupled his announcement of the Council with an announcement of a Roman
Diocesan Synod which was to be held Jan. 24-31, 1960. Discussion at the synod was limited, most of the time taken up with the
reading of 755 new statutes proposed by a diocesan committee,
and five talks by Pope John. Nevertheless, there was the hint of
concern with world issues and the conviction that there could
be some positive accommodation with the world no matter how
adverse the situation. Pope John outlined his plans to 17 Roman

cardinals on Jan. 25, 1959, in the cloister of the Benedictine Monastery next to the Basilica of St. Paul Outside the Walls:

> Grave obstacles arise to confront the Church and her children in her fight against errors which, throughout history, have always brought about fatal and evil divisions, spiritual and moral decay, and the destructions of nations.
>
> This most disheartening sight has caused this humble priest (whom Divine Providence singled out, although unworthy, for the exalted mission of the Supreme Pontificate) to make a decision intended to recall certain ancient forms of doctrinal affirmation and of wise arrangements for ecclesiastical discipline. These forms, in the course of Church history, have yielded the richest harvest of results because of their clarity of thought, their compactness of religious unity, and their heightened flame of Christian fervor, which we acknowledge (with reference to our temporal welfare, too) as abundant wealth 'de rore coeli et de pinguedine terrae' (Gen. 27: 28—'Dew of heaven, and of the fatness of the earth').
>
> Venerable Brethren and beloved sons! Trembling a little with emotion, but with humble firmness of purpose, We now tell you of a two-fold celebration: We propose to call a Diocesan Synod for Rome, and an Ecumenical Council for the Universal Church. We also will tell you why We propose this action.
>
> To you, Venerable Brethren and beloved sons, We need hardly elaborate on the historical significance and juridical meaning of these two proposals. They will lead to the desired and long awaited modernization of the Code of Canon Law, which is expected to accompany and to crown these two efforts in the practical application of the rules of ecclesiastical discipline, applications the Spirit of the Lord will surely suggest to Us as We proceed. The coming promulgation of the Code of Oriental Law foreshadows these events.

> Let it suffice for today that We made this announcement to
> those members of the Sacred College who are present; We
> intend to communicate it to the other Cardinals who have
> already returned to their various episcopal sees, spread all
> over the world.

9. True to one of his namesakes, the Apostle John, Pope John
XXIII cited John's words of unity as he discussed the forthcoming council in his first encyclical, *Ad Petri Cathedram*. His first
Christmas message of December 23, 1958, also quoted and emphasized Jesus' words, "There shall be one fold and one Shepherd" (John 10:16). From *Ad Petri Cathedram*, June 29,1959:

> In the words of God our Savior, "there shall be one fold and
> one shepherd."
>
> This fond hope compelled Us to make public Our intention
> to hold an Ecumenical Council. Bishops from every part of
> the world will gather there to discuss serious religious
> topics. They will consider, in particular, the growth of the
> Catholic faith, the restoration of sound morals among the
> Christian flock, and appropriate adaptation of Church
> discipline to the needs and conditions of our times.
>
> This event will be a wonderful spectacle of truth, unity, and
> charity. For those who behold it but are not one with this
> Apostolic See, We hope that it will be a gentle invitation to
> seek and find that unity for which Jesus Christ prayed so
> ardently to His Father in heaven.

10. To the diocesan presidents of Italian Catholic Action, August 4, 1959, Pope John explained the "sudden flowering" of his
council idea:

> The Ecumenical Council will be a demonstration, uniquely
> far-reaching in its significance, of truly world-wide cathol-
> icity. What is happening is proof that the Lord is assisting
> this salutary plan with his holy grace. The idea of the Coun-
> cil did not come as the slowly ripening fruit of long delib-

eration but was like the sudden flowering of an unexpected spring. . . . By God's grace, then, we shall hold this Council; we shall prepare for it by working hard at whatever on the Catholic side most needs to be healed and strengthened [according to the teaching of our Lord.] When we have carried out this strenuous task, eliminated everything which could at the human level hinder our rapid progress, then we shall point to the Church in all her splendor, *sine macula et ruga*, and say to all those who are separated from us, Orthodox, Protestants, and the rest: Look, brothers, this is the Church of Christ. We have striven to be true to her, to ask the Lord for grace that she may remain forever what he willed. Come; here the way lies open for meeting and for homecoming; come; take, or resume, that place which is yours, which for many of you was your fathers' place. O what joy, what a flowering even in civil and social life, may be looked for by the whole world if we once have religious peace and the re-establishment of the family of Christendom!

11. In an apostolic letter in June 1960, Pope John established the preparatory Secretariat for the Promoting of Christian Unity, which later was to become a permanent secretariat:

As a clearer expression of Our love and good will toward those who bear the name of Christian but are separated from the Apostolic See, and to enable them to follow the Council's activities and thus find it easier to discover the path that will lead them to the unity that Jesus Christ sought from the Heavenly Father with fervent prayers, a special committee or secretariat, headed by a cardinal to be chosen by Us and set up in the same way as the commissions mentioned above, is hereby established.

12. To the 35 Protestant and Orthodox observers gathered in the Vatican's Consistory Hall two days after the start of the Council, Pope John, sitting humbly in an armchair on the same level as his guests, said:

Gentlemen, today's most welcome meeting, friendly and confidential in tone, is to be marked with respect and simplicity as well. The first word which rises up in my heart is a prayer taken from the 67th psalm, which has a lesson for all: *Benedictus Dominus per singulos dies: portat onera nostra Deus, salus nostra.* Blessed be the Lord day after day: God, our salvation, bears our burdens (Ps. 67: 20)! ...

Without wishing to encroach upon the future, let us content outselves today with stating the fact. *Benedictus Deus per singulos dies!* Yet, if you would read my heart, you would perhaps understand much more than words can say.

How could I forget the ten years spent in Sofia? Or the ten more at Istanbul and Athens? They were twenty happy and satisfying years, during which I became acquainted with venerable persons and with young people of great generosity. I looked upon them with affection, even though my work as representative of the Holy Father in the Near East was not explicitly concerned with them.

Then again at Paris, which is one of the crossroads of the world—and was especially so immediately after the last war—I had frequent meetings with Christians of various denominations.
Never, in my knowledge, was there confusion among us over principles, nor any disagreement on the plane of charity in the common work of helping those in need, which the circumstances of the time made necessary. We did not haggle, we talked together; we did not have arguments, but bore each other good will.

Your welcome presence here and the emotion of my priestly heart—the heart of *episcopus Ecclesiae Dei* [a bishop of the Church of God], as I said Thursday before the Council assembly—the emotion of my fellow workers and, I am certain of it, your own emotion too, prompt me to confide to you that there burns in my heart the intention of working and sacrificing to hasten the hour when for all men the prayer of

> Jesus at the Last Supper will have reached its fulfillment.
> But the Christian virtue of patience must not hinder the
> equally fundamental virtue of prudence.
>
> And so I say again: *Benedictus Deus per singulos dies:*
> Blessed be God day after day. For today, let that suffice. . . .

13. When Pope John died, June 3, 1963, Protestants and other
non-Roman Catholics remembered the gentle peasant pope who
gave a new life and hope to Protestant-Catholic relations. Presbyterian Robert McAfee Brown, professor at Stanford Univer-
versity, and an observer later at the Second Vatican Council,
paid one of the most eloquent tributes:

> Pope John XXIII will be remembered for many things. His-
> torians will remember him for convoking the Second Vati-
> can Council, Catholics will probably remember him chiefly
> for the truly pastoral quality which emanated from his per-
> son and his office. Most of us who are non-Catholics will re-
> member him as the pope who set a new tone in the Catholic
> church's approach to the non-Catholic world.
>
> Pope John did not initiate the ecumenical concern for the
> rest of Christendom that has become so widespread in Cath-
> olic life today. But he gave his blessing to the forces that
> were already tentatively at work, encouraging them, sup-
> porting them, and (through the creation of the Secretariat
> for Christian Unity) placing them centrally within the
> structure of Catholic life. He gave currency to the phrase
> "separated brethren," to describe those who are outside the
> visible structure of the Roman Catholic Church, and for him
> the noun was basic rather than the adjective. To him we
> were first of all "brethren" and only secondarily "sepa-
> rated." That so much has happened in so little time to im-
> prove the climate of understanding between Catholics and
> Protestants is something we must attribute to the initiative
> and leadership of Pope John—though to be totally accurate
> we would have to assign the reason for this, as he would
> have done, not to himself but to the Holy Spirit.

He beckoned the Catholic church to move out toward the
"separated brethren" as far as she could, in fidelity to her
own convictions, and to engage in that renewal which is always the church's task, and the task in which Christendom
is always most loathe to engage. It must therefore be our
prayer that the concerns of Pope John, so manifest through
the first session of Vatican Council II, will be brought to
fruition when the Council reconvenes under the order of
Pope John's successor. He has led the way, and the completion by his fellow bishops of that which he initiated will
be the most signal mark of honor his own church can bestow
upon him. . . .

In him we have heard the voice of the Good Shepherd, solic-
itous for those outside as well as inside the sheepfold. Catholics have lost a pope; we have lost a friend and brother.

So we share with our Roman Catholic brethren in their sorrow, for it is also our sorrow. And it is assuaged only by the
recognition that the forces Pope John unleashed within his
brief pontificate will be the dominant forces in the future of
the church he served, as the influence and impact of this man
of God are extended across the weeks, months, years, and
centuries in which his name will be accorded reverence and
honor, and will be uttered with love.

14. Giovanni Battista Cardinal Montini, of Milan, elected
pontiff on June 21, 1963, took the name of Paul VI after the first
great Christian missionary, St. Paul. His choice of name showed
a cognizance of the church's mission and outreach in a hostile
world, a concern also close to the heart of Protestant ecumenists.
(The World Council of Churches had, in fact, in its concern for
the worldwide mission and witness of the church, merged with
the International Missionary Council two years before in New
Delhi.) The new pope continued the council. His opening speech
was marked with a willingness to accept guilt in the church's
divisions. (He expressed similar sentiments 18 days later as he
received 65 non-Roman Catholic delegates from 22 churches in

his private library.) To the observers in the Council he said, on
Sept. 29, 1963:

> We speak now to the representatives of the Christian de-
> nominations separated from the Catholic Church, who have
> nevertheless been invited to take part as observers in this
> solemn assembly. We greet them from Our heart. We thank
> them for their participation. We transmit through them Our
> message—as father and brother—to the venerable Christian
> communities they represent.
>
> Our voice trembles and Our heart beats the faster both be-
> cause of the inexpressible consolation and reasonable hope
> that their presence stirs up within Us, as well as because of
> the deep sadness We feel at their prolonged separation.
>
> If we are in any way to blame for that separation, we
> humbly beg God's forgiveness and ask pardon too of our
> brethren who feel themselves to have been injured by us.
> For our part, we willingly forgive the injuries which the
> Catholic Church has suffered, and forget the grief endured
> during the long series of dissensions and separations. May
> the heavenly Father deign to hear our prayers and grant us
> true brotherly peace.
>
> We are aware that serious and complicated questions remain
> to be studied, treated and resolved. We would wish that this
> could be done immediately on account of the love of Christ
> that "urges us on." But We also realize that these problems
> require many conditions before satisfactory solutions can be
> reached—conditions which are as yet premature. Hence We
> are not afraid to await patiently the blessed hour of perfect
> reconciliation.
>
> Meanwhile We wish to affirm before the observers here
> present some points in Our attitude toward reunion with
> Our separated brethren, with a view that they may com-
> municate then with their responsive Christian communities

May Our voice also reach those other venerable Christian communities separated from Us, that did not accept the invitation freely extended to them to attend the council. We believe these points are well known, but it is useful to repeat them here.

Our manner of speaking toward them is friendly, completely sincere and loyal. We lay no snares. We are not motivated by temporal interests. We owe our Faith—which We believe to be divine—the most candid and firm attachment.

But at the same time We are convinced that this does not constitute an obstacle to the desired understanding with our separated brethren, precisely because it is the truth of the Lord and therefore the principle of union, not of distinction or separation. At any rate we do not wish to make of our Faith an occasion for polemics.

Secondly, we look with reverence upon the true religious patrimony we share in common, which has been preserved and in part even well developed among our separated brethren. We are pleased to note the study made by those who seek sincerely to make known and to honor the treasures of truth and of genuine spirituality, in order to improve our relations with them.

We hope that just as they are desirous to know more about our history and our religious life, so also they would wish to make a closer study of our doctrine and its logical derivation from the deposit of Divine Revelation.

Finally, We wish to say that, aware of the enormous difficulties still in the way of the desired union, We humbly put our trust in God. We shall continue to pray. We shall try to give better proof of our efforts of leading genuine Christian lives and practicing fraternal charity. And should historical reality tend to weaken our hopes, we shall try to recall the comforting words of Christ: "Things that are impossible with men are possible with God" (Luke 18: 27).

15. A spirit of nonchalance, if not indifference, was abroad, and winds of change though they met brief obstacles soon had broad lands to sweep across. The call to the Vatican Council found Roman Catholics generally unready, not only for the Council which had not occurred before in the lifetime of any of them, but also for the by-product of dialogue with their neighbors. As the cardinals reportedly sat dumbfounded at Pope John's announcement of the council, so were United States Catholics reluctant to hail a Council or the spirit of change, though their very indifference made it generally easy for new attitudes to find root. Observed the late Gustave Weigel, S.J., in 1959:

> At the present moment, the American Catholic Church is neither a harassed minority nor a belligerent group. It is more prone to conservatism than radical change. Its tendency is toward American chauvinism rather than anything anti-American. It is rather contemptuous of what is foreign, even when visible in the Catholic church elsewhere. Its generosity, activism and optimism are probably more American than Catholic.
>
> One thing American Protestants must recognize though they are slow to do so, is that American Catholics are no threat to them, nor do they wish to be. The diminution of Protestant power understandably makes Protestants nervous, but there is no ground in Catholicism for their nervousness.
>
> The American Catholics do not consider Protestantism as their great preoccupation nor do they pay much attention to it. They arrange their own affairs and conversations with little or no concern for the Protestant dimension of our country.

16. Preparation for dialogue came about through interfaith programs in the arts. In dialogue with the world of the arts and with the world in general, the churches were also talking with one another. In Fargo, North Dakota, and Moorhead, Minnesota, in 1964, a massive program of dialogue with the world sug-

gested by preliminary efforts in Brookings, South Dakota, in
1963 was launched in the theaters, on television, and over radio.
Leading scientists, businessmen, theater and nightclub enter-
tainers, clergy, psychologists and others took part in the discussions. (A similar project followed in 1965 in Duluth, Minnesota,
only, unlike the others it had Jewish as well as Protestant and
Catholic support.) The Fargo dialogue came about because:

> There are many reasons why the church today should be
> engaged in serious conversation with the world. Some are
> very ancient, but others are of modern origin. Some of these
> reasons are to:
>
> —provide an educational experience for the laity— dram-
> atizing the significance of their ministry of daily life. . . .
>
> —respond to the needs of the community thereby dem-
> onstrating the interest and concern of the church in assist-
> ing those facing the difficult social issues of today. By
> identifying with human problems the church bears witness
> to the compassion of Christ. . . .
>
> —help the churches discover that as they move out from
> their individual sanctuaries into public life they, like other
> community groups, must work and live together and can do
> so without losing their own distinctive witness. . . .
>
> —dramatize to the church the opportunities for witness
> in the world by uncovering questions and issues being asked
> there. The world set the agenda for this "meeting." This is a
> painful but healthy experience for churches which too long
> have been preoccupied with their own institutional con-
> cerns. . . .
>
> —provide a platform for the discussion of issues within
> the community which provides an occasion for witnessing to
> the Christian faith. . . .
>
> —undertake a "scouting" expedition to chart the terrain

of contemporary society and to report back to the church so that she may understand more clearly the character and urgency of her mission.

—avoid cheap and easy answers from either the church or the world to the issues of life. Both are confronted in this program with the important realities that each brings to the dialogue. The message of the Gospel must be spoken through and to the actual conditions of the day. The community's reflection upon basic issues should not be deprived of the resources of the Gospel. . . .

17. In the South, churchmen, spurned by greater involvement in the secular sphere (Supreme Court anti-school-segregation ruling, growing integration and civil rights ferment, a shrinking world geographically and economically), began discovering with greater frequency new motifs of unity in God's word. Sunday-school lessons espoused the meaning of the group and fellowship. Presbyterian lesson writer Ernest Trice Thompson said in 1961:

*"Let the word of Christ dwell in you richly, as you teach and admonish one another in all wisdom, and as you sing psalms and hymns and spiritual songs, with thankfulness in your hearts to God."* [Col. 3:16]. The main point here is that Christians grow through the mutual support which they receive from one another. The world of Christ bears its full fruit in our lives only as we teach and admonish *one another* and as we sing *together* our hymns of praise. The Christian life cannot mature in isolation. Attend one of those rare religious services where the congregation sings wholeheartedly and you will recognize the power there has been, and may be again, in Christian hymnody.

The final rule which Paul gives us for the realization of the Christian ideal is, *"And whatever you do in word or deed do everything in the name of the Lord Jesus."* [Col. 3: 17].

18. Hostility brought churches together. The most extreme case was China, where differences were forceably obliterated.

a A study periodical published by the interdenominational Christian Study Centre on Chinese Religion and Culture, in Hong Kong, said:

> Question. Circumstances on the China mainland forced on the church an outward unity. There are, for example, four Protestant churches in Peking, one for each sector of the city. Preachers are rotated, or denominations rotate in conducting the services. Such a pattern is either forced directly by the government or indirectly by the Three Self Movement. In Hong Kong there is no such compulsion to be united. Is it possible that we have placed too much stress on the individual at the expense of the life of community? In the West the desire to be a "true Christian," or to attain some standard of perfection, has often meant that the idea of community has been lost sight of.
>
> Reply. No Christian can ever claim to be perfect. One who matures in the Christian life is more sensitive to the need for God's forgiveness. A distinction between the individual and the corporate is false. When we are in fellowsip with God and involved in the community of the spirit, we ought no longer to think of ourselves as individuals, but as part of the church which is both worldwide and eternal. These two dimensions of the church are like the two dimensions of the cross. When we are truly in the Fellowship of Saints of all ages we just can't think in terms of salvation of the self alone.

b. A Red Chinese directive to the churches bound them together in persecution and obliterated signs of denominational vestiges:

> All former governing committees and boards shall be abolished; there shall be no preaching of the last days or the vanity of the world—instead we will emphasize dignity of labor which is the dividing line between right and wrong; belief and unbelief shall not be made an issue of marriage; the Salvation Army shall give up their uniforms; the Seventh-day Adventists shall abolish morning prayers; the YMCA secretaries shall be assigned to productive labor.

19. Pope Pius XII had cited indirectly the contribution of the Church's adversaries in a modern society to dialogue between the churches in his Encyclical *Sempiter Rex*, Sept. 8, 1951. He asked "Christian forces to immediately close ranks and fight under the one and only standard of Christ against the fierce attacks of the enemy from hell." Events of reaction against Communist rule have also been cited for their contribution to dialogue. The Hungarian revolt against the Soviets in 1956 was called an "ecumenical event" by Msgr. Bela Varga, archdean of Veszprem and a former president of the Hungarian parliament in an interview. The Catholic prelate noted 50,000 martyrs of all faiths perished together for a common cause. Similarly, Auxiliary Bishop Fulton J. Sheen, of New York, national director of the Society for the Propagation of the Faith, attributed a degree of the dialogue to the equalizing forces of world movements such as Communism:

> I think sometimes when I look at the hammer-and-sickle on the red flag of Communism that the hammer represents the cross of Christ and the sickle the crescent of Islam, being drawn together by the sea of blood of the victims of atheist persecution.

> When the White Fathers first went to Africa, they reported pessimistically that it would take 100 years to make a single Moslem convert. Now Moslem parents are eager to send their children to our schools.

> The ecumenical movement has been greatly helped by the Communists, although they never intended that it should be.

20. A popular French Protestant communal movement, the Taizé brothers, who live on a small village hill overlooking castles and vineyards, have elicited a new spirit of poverty of spirit and goods—a reminder to Catholics (21 Latin American bishops visited them in 1965) as well as to Protestants, to seek a more common and less ornate existence. The Taizé prior, Roger Schutz, said:

These Protestants know that the possessions of the Church of certain Protestant communities weigh heavily on them and are today a stumbling block which makes the indifferent fall. Deploring an unacknowledged need for temporal power which exists in certain of their institutions, these Protestants wish that the Catholic Church, too, might appear more and more as being firstly the church of the humble, the oppressed, the hungry. In effect the Virgin Mary could proclaim that, by the coming of Christ, the humble would be elevated and the powerful be humbled.

It would seem that the richness of the Catholic Church might be more apparent than real. But if temporal power or richness are no more than a facade, Protestants who love this Church wonder if it would not be essential to sacrifice such an appearance . . .

In this respect, how significant is the gift of great estates, property of the Church, made by the Catholic bishops in Brazil. Certain attitudes of simplicity of Pope John XXIII find also a very favorable echo.

21. Affluence, as well as hostility, proved a leveler in religious differences. The Rev. Father Walter J. Ong, S. J., in an article for the National Conference of Christians and Jews, noted: "It appears that Catholic and other groups, religious or secular, are more considerate of one another in an economy of abundance than in an economy of scarcity."

Concern for a common good paralleled national efforts for "new frontiers," "great societies," "socialization" (to use a term in translation of Pope John's encyclical, *Mater et Magistra*). Reinhold Niebuhr revised his views on the involvement of man in immoral societies, noting his own "increasing devotion to the principles of religious pluralism in an open society which allows the various religious faiths and traditions to contribute their treasures to our common fund. . . . " (*Man's Nature and His Communities* New York: Charles Scribner's Sons, 1965, p. 27). Protestant and Catholic thought had evolved from concern with the special community (e.g., Clarence Jordan's isolated Protestant Koinonia Farm in Americus, Georgia) to a "common front" or "common good," terms once shunned, now revamped to indicate Christian concern in the total world. The late John LaFarge, S.J., leading ecumenist and associate editor of *America*, after whom the John LaFarge Institute, an ecumenical center, New York, is named, at a conference sponsored by the Anti-Defamation League and Assumption College, Worcester, Massachusetts, in 1959 stated:

> A mere fellowship of strategy and defense is not enough. Nor is a mere outpouring of kindly feelings enough. . . . Rather, the pressure that rests upon all of us to find ways and means out of such an impasse should be the occasion for a deeper search into a real and profound community of interest: a search for the basis of that community. So that quite regardless of the issue of defense against communism we would be seeking to construct, as far as is humanly and practically possible, the concept of our common good. Outrageous crimes are committed in the name of the common good, it is true: the inverted concept of the common good, the good of the Communist state, the supposed good to which all individual and lesser goods must be sacrificed. But the very fact that the crimes are committed in the name of the common good is all the more reason for not shunning the inquiry and taking refuge in a willful individualism. Rather, they call for an intense investigation of the genuine notion of what may be conceived as our common interests, with the hope that thereby we may push further and further toward the notion of the common good itself. . . .

> The all-pervading image industries have made us image-conscious. Hence it is no idle speculation, but a matter of most practical importance, to consider the relation of man himself, as man, to the profound determinant of the Common Good.

> For the Common Good is not a mere abstraction. Metaphysics, noisily ushered out of the front door of public discussion, returns quietly by the back door of our basically meta-

physical perplexities. Man as a mere abstraction is intolerable, as a being who falsely apes the angels. But it is the all-precious gift of man's own intellect that reveals the human image in its breadth, height, and depth; its openness of being and its call to fellowship with the Creator. The task of the modern intellect is to re-discover man's true dignity as expressed in the new terms of the dynamism of this new and still mysterious and perplexing age; and thereby peer deeper into the reality of our common good.

22. The youth were heard and they met together for interfaith rallies and workshops at the University of Detroit and St. John's Episcopal Church, Royal Oak, Michigan, for instance. A statement circulated by the Catholic Youth Organization said:

Ecumenism is a newly popular word for an oddly unpopular commandment: Love ye one another. And, as in the words of the old minstrel song, everyone talking about ecumenism isn't practicing it. Hence, the timeliness of the theme of the 1964 National Catholic Youth Week: Truth in Love—Bond of Union.

This is where young people have tremendous advantages: they aren't grooved into set patterns and reactions; they are willing to take a chance, in a good sense, with something new and a little bit different.

23. There was a rediscovery of early roots of unity.
a. Disciples of Christ recalled their early philosophy forged out in the Kentucky log cabins at the end of the Revolutionary War. Said a writer, Hampton Adams, in *The Christian-Evangelist*:

We believe that Christian unity must be a primary concern of the Disciples of Christ as long as we are separated from any body of Christian people, for we came into existence to make the prayer of Jesus for the unity of His church our plea.

We do not believe that the fellowship of the Disciples of Christ is so right about all things that we can be smug in this rightness and wait for other communions to join us. We do not believe that any denominational church is in that position. We believe that all churches are awaiting today that further truth about Christian unity into which the Holy Spirit will have to lead.

"When the Holy Spirit is come. . . . " This we believe is essential. The Holy Spirit, the Spirit of God, the Spirit of Christ, must come in increasing power; and then the way of Christian unity, that is far from clear now, will be made clear.

What does the Spirit wait upon? Faith, faith in Christ.

b. Minnesota Presbyterians marking a centennial recalled the unity of the old frontier, a unity which they recommended as applicable on "new frontiers," too. A "message" from the "moderator," Hugh B. Jones, of the Synod of Minnesota, said:

Two things impress me in the early history of our church. One is that the movement for Christian churches in this area was a movement sparked by laymen. . . .

The second element is the sense of unity which moved and ever moves within the church, even in times of apparent diversity. Individual Christians on the frontier felt that their lives were inadequate until they had organized churches in which the sense of Christian fellowship could be expressed. Then these churches could not remain as separate entities. They must needs unite as Presbyteries and as a Synod. And in their union Presbyterians of the Old School and New School found their lives bound together by a common loyalty to Jesus Christ. The same forces are at work today. Our laymen in ever-increasing numbers are accepting their responsibilities in a church that proclaims the "priesthood of all believers." And more and more throughout

the church there is the conviction that we shall not be far
from one another if we love the Lord Jesus Christ and seek
to know and to do His will. May the sense of oneness in
Christ be with us as we commemorate our Centennial. . . .

24. Various new philosophies, of a non-institutional variety,
were heard, namely existentialism and personalism. (Though
singular in emphasis, they nevertheless paved the way for the
"participatory democracy" of which Harvey Cox of Harvard,
talks—namely the individual in an anonymous city exercises a
wide range of choices, all of which can be directed to and realized
in a common good.) Personalism and varieties of existentialism
were espoused not only in individual Protestantism but also in
Catholicism. From Jean Mouroux's new catechism book, *From
Baptism to the Act of Faith* (which talks about "individual
singularity" in faith and making Christ's redemptive act one's
own) to the United States bishops' statement of 1961 (which
says "we must show the reality of personal responsibility")
there could be seen the themes of recent philosophical thought.
This development was evident even in the new decree on priestly
training proclaimed by Pope Paul at the Second Vatican Council
on Oct. 28, 1965, it is said that besides traditional training the
seminaries are to take "into account the philosophical investiga-
tions of later ages."

A Catholic, the Rev. Father Alfred B. Fellows, J.C.L., speaking before the annual workshop of the Protestant Church-owned
Publishers' Association, in Kansas City, in 1965, said:

> The scholasticism propounded by the followers of St.
> Thomas Aquinas has had its unique part to play in the de-
> velopment of Roman Catholic thought. But now in the midst
> of the 20th century, because of the urgency of contemporary
> life, because of the great forces at play within our world
> and because of the unbelievable speed with which the move,
> it has become necessary to approach reality from a slightly
> different standpoint. The existentialism presented by
> Kierkegaard which has played so vital a role in the de-
> velopment of modern Protestant thought has found its way
> into the writings, the thinking, the theologizing of all sig-

nificant Roman writers. The infusion of the existentialist vision has then given birth to a new development, that of the personalist concern. St. Paul, St. John were personalistic in their writing, in their thinking.

25. Augustin Cardinal Bea, of the Secretariat for the Promoting of Christian Unity, urged an understanding of philosophical language, which is also a concern of modern linguistic and analytical philosophers who have been active in Protestantism (for example, Willem Zuurdeeg, Paul M. van Buren). Said Cardinal Bea in a letter to the Sister formation section, National Catholic Educational Association, April 25, 26, 1962, meeting in Detroit: "How can we understand one another on the level of confessional differences, unless we first know the language of others, and, more important, the mentalities that are expressed in these languages?" The newly expressed systems were not necessarily a negation of traditional Christian forms. Upon Theologian Paul Tillich's death in 1965, the Rev. Father Avery Dulles, S.J., was quoted in the NCWC news service as saying Tillich's "theology of symbolism" was very useful in understanding religious language and sacramental theology. "He was anxious constantly to preserve the Catholic substance of Christianity, subjecting it to the criticism of what he called the 'Protestant principle,' and therefore he tried to retain a great deal of Catholicity in his Protestantism," said Father Dulles.

The philosophical and theological developments, including those of the popular sometimes called, inadequately, "death of God" young men (van Buren, who disowns the term, William Hamilton of Colgate Rochester Divinity School, Thomas J. J. Altizer, of Emory, and Gabriel Vahanian, of Syracuse among others) who obliterate some traditional differences by calling an end to certain terms of the faith, among them concepts of God, in favor of more relevant, experiential and verifiable terms, such as the personal elements in faith in Christ, were reflected in the seminaries, particularly in Protestantism. Gone was the easy faith. The neat "three-story universe" and formulas were set aside, thanks to many, among whom are aging exegete Rudolf Bultmann of the University of Marburg, Anglican Bishop John A. T. Robinson of Woolwich, and the literary influence of Albert

Camus, approximating Christianity without assimilating it.
Transient Abraham is a new archetype, according to Dr. Calvin
H. Reber, professor of missions to the incoming class of United
Theological (EUB) Seminary, Dayton, Ohio, in 1964:

> Whatever orientation Abraham may have had, it never made
> him feel at home. The promised land through all his life
> was a strange land. His journey all his life was like that of
> Graham Greene when he followed the bush paths of the in-
> terior of Liberia. It was, to use the title of Greene's book,
> "a journey without maps."
>
> If this is how it was with Abraham, it just might be that
> way with us. It may be that orientation will not do what we
> wish it to do because by the nature of the experience, the
> whole seminary time is a journey without maps. Still more,
> it may be that seminary which is expected to be an orienta-
> tion to the whole ministry will not serve that expected pur-
> pose because all of life is a journey without maps.
>
> In these rapidly changing times when there seem so few
> certainties, this suggestion is not good news. After un-
> settling times like college, we want assurances and answers.
> We don't want to go wandering on without a map. We want
> to know whether the road is good, where there are gas
> stations, and how far it is to the next good restaurant. If it
> can be arranged we would prefer to have a motel reserva-
> tion for the night's stop. We not only want a map. We want
> touring service.
>
> This is what we want, but in honesty we must face the fact
> that neither seminary, nor life, nor the Christian ministry
> can be so nicely arranged.

26. Great frequency of meetings, made possible by greater ease
in travel and other socio-economic changes, increased larger understanding. The *Lutheran World* (Vol. 2, 1955-56, p. 50) noted:
"An interesting fact within our [Lutheran World] Federation is
that we now are 'at home' with one another as we meet, that is,

we have become so well acquainted with each other as individuals representing various churches that we have gone far beyond the first attempt in trying to make friends and are now able to speak as brethren as equals."

Politicians created images of oneness. President Johnson, a former Baptist, now a Disciples of Christ member received communion in both the Disciples' church and St. Mark's Episcopal, Washington, where his wife, a former Methodist, is a member. His daughter, Luci, is baptized a Catholic, and married a Catholic in the summer of 1966. Special calls for church unity by national leaders had their affect.

a. In the Congo, Premier Moise Tshombe said:

> We shall get nowhere unless there is true and honest reconciliation and unless justice is done in this country. We must remember the words of Jesus Christ: "Love one another." If we Congolese love one another and form one body, trying to lay aside everything that would divide us, if we consider one another as brothers . . . then our country will enjoy peace. There is only one force which can help us, and that is the Divine Force.
>
> I beg you to pray for the Congo. Our country needs this strength, this Divine Force. I think the time has come for all Christians to be conscious of their strength so as to combat our common enemy, Satan. But Satan is working among brothers, among sons of this country. We witness corruption. For the sake of money, thousands of innocent people are being killed.

b. In Egypt, President Nasser of the United Arab Republic laying the cornerstone for a new Coptic Orthodox cathedral in Cairo, said:

> Islam has recognized Christians as brothers, both in the sphere of religion and in the nation. With regard to the religions, our revolution is based on charity, fraternity, and equality. Our aim is a healthy society which rejects sectarianism and fanaticism and recognizes only nationalism.

c. In Ethiopia, Emperor Haile Selassie I addressed the Conference of Heads of Oriental Churches meeting in Addis Ababa (see also section 4):

> It is therefore with great joy that we welcome Your Holinesses to our land and to our Church. Your Holinesses bring with you sacred memories from the ancient past. Your presence here is a pledge and token of the desire of all Christians to be one.
>
> Ever since we ascended the historic throne of Ethiopia, we have considered it our duty to call for a meeting of the churches who belong to the same fold. We were praying to God for His help in achieving this holy purpose, so that He may grant it to us to see this event. In ancient times the Byzantine emperors used to summon the councils. Our sincere wish from the very beginning was to see these churches meeting to discuss their common interests and decide on their common problems. This wish is in actual fact fulfilled today, and we are happy to witness it. Therefore, we thank Almighty God first because He has enabled us to properly fulfill our clear duty and, secondly, because our long cherished desire has now met with fulfillment. Henceforth the matter will demand the spiritual unity and hard work of Your Holiness. For strength can be achieved through unity, and success is the fruit of cooperation. There is no doubt that work done through a cooperative spirit shall meet with success. . . .

27. Endorsing the United Nations underscored a general appreciation of one another's views and motivated dialogue. Leaders of six faiths (three Christian bodies—Protestant, Roman Catholic and Eastern Orthodox—and Judaism, Buddhism, and Islam), with 2 billion followers, issued calls of support for world peace and joint efforts for pursuing spiritual values. Those of the Christian faith represented at the special convocation marking the twentieth anniversary of the United Nations in a ceremony at the Cow Palace, San Francisco, were Bishop Prince Taylor, president of the Methodist Council of Bishops; Archbishop

Martin J. O'Connor, president of the Pontifical Commission for Social Communications at the Vatican, and Archbishop Iakovos, a member of the Holy Synod of the Patriarchate of Constantinople [not the American Greek Orthodox primate].

a. Archbishop O'Connor read a message from Pope Paul VI:

> How truly right and proper it is that a religious convocation has been included among the commemorative ceremonies. . . .
>
> Peace, which according to St. Augustine is the tranquillity of order and the work of justice, is likewise a gift of God and the fruit of good will among men. God has created the world to be a sojourn of peace.
>
> If therefore peace is desired, faith in God must be nourished and our prayer must be directed to Him, the giver of every good: "grant peace in our days, O Lord." Then not hate but love must be encouraged, not indifference but solidarity, not the race to arm but to disarm, not the first to dominate but to serve.

b. Archbishop Iakovos proposed a new United Religious organization:

> While religions throughout the world have come a long way toward realization, they have done very little to date in the direction of condemning or abolishing war and establishing peace. . . .
>
> It would be ideal if the UN organization could be implemented by a United Religions organization, in order that thus fulfilled, it might be able to serve the cause of true peace more effectively.

c. Bishop Taylor said:

> The purposes of the UN charter and the programs of the UN agencies reflect the saying of the prophets and apostles.

The UN's works of mercy toward the poor, the sick, the il-
literate, the shelterless, and the refugees are to us manifestations of the spirit of Jesus Christ.

We Christians, accepting the political implications of the
fatherhood of God and the brotherhood of man, cannot accept any nation or group of nations as our inevitable enemy.

28. The ecumenical movement emerged, according to Greek
Orthodox scholar John S. Romanides, as a historical force:

One can distinguish four types of Ecumenical movements
today. The one is represented by Communism which seeks
political and religious dominion of all peoples. The second
is represented by the Christian Ecumenical Movement which
seeks religious union alone. The third form is represented
by the United Nations which seeks political cooperation at
the international level. And the fourth type of Ecumenical
movement is represented by such groups as the National
Conference of Christians and Jews, and the Pro Deo Movement which seek the cooperation of Christian, Jewish and
other religions for the common good.

The Ecumenical Movement among Christians has two aspects: the one inherited from her primitive history, the
other inherited in the form of her most serious problem from
the fifth, eleventh, and sixteenth centuries. From primitive
Christian times the Church believed herself to be the New
Israel, the New Zion and the New Jerusalem. Old Israel
according to the flesh and New Israel by spiritual adoption
were believed by Christians to be one single universal nation created by God with the mission of uniting humanity
in the true worship and service of Himself. The Church was
by her very nature an Ecumenical Movement with an Ecumenical mission.

29. The Japanese "non-church" movement was revived and
stirred interest among scholars and ecumenists, among them the
late Carl Michalson, professor of systematic theology at Drew

University and visiting professor at Tokyo Union Theological Seminary, Tokyo, and Aoyama Gakuin University, Tokyo:

> By its acts of interpretation, the theological mind of Japan has bridged the gap between Jerusalem, Rome, Wittenberg, and Geneva on the one side, and Tokyo on the other. That is an enormous chronological distance, but it shrinks to nothing in the face of such responsible Christian understanding. Time is easier to collapse than space, however. There is unilateral character to the interpretation of the past. The historian can grasp the past somehow without the past's consent and make it his own. Overcoming spatial distance, however, such as the distance that exists in the present between the traditional churches of the West and the younger churches of the East, requires bilateral encounter. The Japanese have served their apprenticeship at learning their lessons from the West. If Christian history as an ecumenical actuality is to persist in the future, the West must take up its side of the theological partnership and converse with the East. . . .
>
> How can a theology that is so deliberately dependent upon the existence of the church avoid endorsing denominationalism? According to [Yoshitaka] Kumano, it is impossible for theology to be undenominational. Tradition as history (*dento*) includes the fact of the plurality of churches. To say that if theology were based on the Bible, there would be only one theology and one church is a most abstract way of thinking. The way to save theology from being denominational is precisely to know how one's denomination has originated from within the Catholic tradition. Rather than calling upon the denominations to dissolve themselves, Kumano is urging them to go behind their traditions as history (*dento*) in order to recover the tradition as witness (*densho*) that originally gave rise to their churches.

30. Over all, a deep sense of guilt for the divisions of Christianity, perhaps occasioned by the anxieties of the times and needs for conscious organismic factors in life, among other forces, un-

derscored Christian thinking; evidenced, for instance, in the Tokyo Ecumenical Group, organized in Japan in 1962. The group brought together the whole spectrum of Christianity, from Southern Baptists to Roman Catholics with Mennonites, the Church of the Brethren, Lutherans, Anglicans, the United Church, and the Orthodox also included. Special speakers ranged from Professor Hromadka from Czechoslovakia to theologians visiting from West Germany with opposite views. The deep sense of guilt that marks much of Japanese (and other) thinking on church unity is noted by Hiroshi Hirata, writing in Japanese in the *Japan Missionary Bulletin*, a Catholic publication in Tokyo:

> The other day a non-Christian said to me, "We have no complaints about what Christianity has to say; but when we see it split into so many sects, with all of them criticizing each other, we just can't believe in it." No need to tell us this—for we are often aware that Christianity is divided into Catholics and non-Catholics. Actually isn't it true that people have even come to think of it as the normal thing— that they do not even question it? But we Catholics who believe in the Son of God and who have made the Last Supper, which is the Mass, the center of our spiritual lives, cannot forget the prayer of our Lord, the Christ, which He made at that Last Supper—"that all become one as we are one . . ." (John 17 : 21). . . . "Love one another as I have loved you"— (John 13 : 13). That was the new law which our Lord gave His disciples at that time. And after that our Lord, by the love which gave of himself completely, made His disciples into one unified group. And the fact that these splits exist even now, after so many centuries have passed, is a deep shame to the Christian believer. "Look! How they love one another!" exclaimed the pagans at the unity and love of the First Century Christian. What would the pagans say if they could see the deep rifts between modern Christians?

31. The Freedom Movement was a cause that led to overcoming theological differences in practicalities. (It was also an effect of ecumenism—see Chapter VII.) According to J. Oscar Lee, asso-

ciate director, National Council of Churches Commission on Religion and Race:

> The Freedom Movement speaks to the churches in no uncertain terms. It says, "Physician heal yourself . . ." Race blemishes the Church by the deep divisions it creates in the Christian community. This movement bids the Church to witness in its life and work that it is a community of fellow believers —a community which exhibits internal bonds of fellowship and unity because in its behaviour it gives practical expression to the belief that Christ died for all men. It lifts up the fact that the Church cannot be truly ecumenical as long as churches anywhere allow themselves to be divided by race, language, ethnic origin or any social factor which perpetuates injustice, denies dignity, and withholds freedom.

32. Among those who helped to bring about dialogue, there is agreement that God Himself had planted the seed, and the Holy Spirit was causing the *aggiornamento,* or renewal, that John XXIII had talked about.

a. Said Joseph Cardinal Ritter, of St. Louis, in a speech at Eden (United Church of Christ) Seminary, Webster Groves, Missouri:

> There are those in every tradition who see in the ecumenical movement a banding together of the churches against the threat of atheism or communism. Fear is undoubtedly a powerful factor in human affairs, but it surely would be an unworthy motive for action by the Church.
>
> Still others see the ecumenical movement as the establishment of a cordial fellowship involving some sociological cooperation and unimpeded by doctrinal differences. This again falls short of genuine ecumenical aspirations.
>
> It is the more general belief of those committed to the ecumenical movement that we have been led by God to a pain

ful awareness of our estrangement from each other, and
to the desire to move toward the unity willed by Christ
through more faithful discipleship.

b. Said the six presidents (and honorary president J. H.
Oldham) of the World Council of Churches in their Pentecost
message for 1965:

God has never cancelled the promise or withdrawn the gift
he gave at Pentecost. That power is always available to the
church which wants it enough to pay the price. The price
is to be made utterly one with the Lord Jesus Christ—one
with his humiliation in order to be one with his victory.
The power is power to believe and to help others to believe,
power to hope without wavering to the end, power to love
to the limit, power to make peace, to work for justice and
reconciliation between men. It is the power of the coming
Kingdom, given to us now. It is the pledge of glory. And it
is offered to all who ask.

We ask you, then, to join with us at this season of Pentecost, in praying the Lord to fill the whole Church afresh
with the power of His Spirit, so that it may be His witness
to the ends of the earth.

## REFERENCES

### Chapter I

1. Ecumenical Chronicle, *The Ecumenical Review*, XVI, No. 3 (April,
   1964) 325, sections 8, 9, 10.
2. Willem A. Visser 't Hooft, ed., *The New Delhi Report* (New York: Association Press, 1961), p. 152.
3. "Dichiarazione Dinale della Conferenza Panortodossa di Rodi," in
   *L'Oriente Cristiano*, Caminao Como, ed., IV, No. 4 (Oct.-Dec., 1964), 22.
4. Text courtesy of Mr. Seifu Metaferia, secretary-general, of the Interim Secretariat of the Conference of the Heads of the Oriental Orthodox Churches, Addis Ababa, Ethiopia.
5. *The Ecumenical Review*, XIII, No. 4 (July, 1961), 514, 515.
6. Visser 't Hooft, *The New Delhi Report, op. cit.*, p. 116.
7. "Vocabor Ioannes," John XXIII, to the College of Cardinals, Oct. 28,
   1958, *The Pope Speaks*, V, No. 2 (Spring, 1959), 134.
8. An address of Pope John XXIII to the Roman Cardinals, "Questia
   festiva," Jan 25, 1959, English translation, in *The Pope Speaks*, V,
   No. 4 (Autumn, 1959), 400, 401.

9. Encyclical, *Ad Petri Cathedram*, English translation, *ibid.*, pp. 368-9.
10. Address to the diocesan presidents of Italian Catholic Action, Aug. 4, 1959, in *Discorsi, messaggi, colloqui del Santo Padre Giovanni XXIII.* (Citta del Vaticano: Tipografia Poliglotta Vaticana) 1960, I, 709, 710.
11. Motu Proprio: *Superno Dei Nutu*, English translation, in *The Pope Speaks*, VI, No. 3 (summer, 1963), 242.
12. Address to observer delegates to the Council, Oct. 13, 1962, English translation, in *The Pope Speaks*, VIII, No. 3 (1963), 225-227.
13. *Presbyterian Life*, July 1, 1963, p. 25. Used by permission.
14. English text by National Catholic Welfare Conference, Sept. 29, 1963.
15. Gustave Weigel, S. J., "Inside American Roman Catholicism," *Christianity and Crisis*, XIX, No. 10 (June 8, 1959), 90.
16. "Faith in Life" section, in *Sunday Fargo Forum*, Sept. 20, 1954, p. 3, "Why Dialogue?"
17. Ernest Trice Thompson, "Growth in Christian Relationships," Sunday-school commentary, for Oct. 22, 1961, in *Presbyterian Outlook*, Oct. 9, 1961, p. 14.
18. a. Chiu Teng-kiat, "Is the Chinese Church Maturing?", in *Ching Feng*, VIII, No. 1 (Winter, 1964, published by the Christian Study Centre on Chinese Religion and Culture, Hong Kong), 25, 26.
    b. From a Chinese government 1958 order aimed at Christian churches, quoted by Tracey K. Jones, Jr., executive secretary of the Board of Missions, The Methodist Church, "What Happened to the Chinese Christians?", in *Together*, June, 1961, pp. 17, 18.
19. Bishop Fulton Sheen, at the annual meeting of the Mission-Sending Societies, Religious News Service, Sept. 29, 1959.
20. Roger Schutz, from a document he gives to journalists who visit Taizé and ask him of the Council, "Le Concile et Notre Sereine Attente," a mimeographed document.
21. John LaFarge, S. J., keynote address, The Institute on the Person and the Common Good, May 9, 1959, Assumption College, Worcester, Mass., in co-operation with the Anti-Defamation League of B'nai B'rith.
22. Floyd Anderson, director, press department, National Catholic Welfare Conference, editorial, "Truth in Love—Bond of Union," distributed by the National CYO Federation.
23. a. Hampton Adams, "What We Believe—About Christian Unity," in *The Christian-Evangelist*, July 18, 1956, p. 10.
    b. Hugh B. Jones, moderator, Synod of Minnesota, "A Message From Our Moderator," *The Minnesota Presbyterian*, I, No. 1 (Sept., 1957), 1.
24. Alfred B. Fellows, J.C.L., moderator of the Pope John XXIII Foundation, Kansas City, in a speech before the annual workshop of the Protestant Church-Owned Publishers' Association, in Kansas City, "Roman Catholic Theology Today and Tomorrow," *National Catholic Reporter*, Mar. 10, 1965, p. 7.
25. Calvin H. Reber, "A Journey Without Maps," *United News*, Bulletin of the United (EUB) Theological Seminary, Dayton, 1964, LXIII, No. 5, 5.
26. a. Congo Mission News, quoted in *Presbyterian Survey*, Vol. V, No. 2, (Feb. 1965).
    b. *Ecumenical Press Service*, No. 27, July 29, 1965, p. 9.
    c. Text courtesy of Interim Secretariat of the Conference of the Heads of the Oriental Orthodox Churches, Addis Ababa.
27. *Chicago Tribune*, June 28, 1965, "Leaders of Faiths Ask Spiritual Revival," by Seymour Korman, p. 4.

28. Rev. John S. Romanides, "An Orthodox Look at the Ecumenical Movement," *The Greek Orthodox Theological Review*, X, No. 1 (Summer, 1964), 7.

29. Carl Michalson, *Japanese Contributions to Christian Theology* (Philadelphia: The Westminster Press, 1960), pp. 60, 61, 62. Used by permission.

30. Hiroshi Hirata, "Ecumenism," in *The Japan Missionary Bulletin*, XVIII, No. 1 (Jan., Feb., 1964, pub. by Oriens Institute for Religious Research), 53.

31. J. Oscar Lee, "The Freedom Movement and the Ecumenical Movement," *The Ecumenical Review*, XVII, No. 1 (Jan., 1965), 23. Cf. also Robert W. Spike's *The Freedom Revolution and the Churches* (New York: Association Press, 1965).

32. a. Joseph Cardinal Ritter, at Eden Seminary, Webster Groves, Mo., June 4, 1965, supplied by the Bureau of Information, Archdiocese of St. Louis, news release, June 1, 1965.

    b. Pentecost Message, 1965, signed by the presidents of the World Council of Churches—J. H. Oldham, honorary president; Archbishop of Canterbury, Arthur Michael Ramsey; Archbishop Iakovos, New York; Sir Francis Ibiam, Enugu; David G. Moses, Nagpur; Martin Niemoeller, Wiesbaden; Charles Parlin, New York. World Council of Churches release, New York office, Nb/18-65; PC: 1.

# two

# Getting Acquainted

The biggest hurdle in dialogue—whether between boy and girl, neighbors, professors and students, or even between churches or with divine subjects—is to get acquainted. At the start of the decade 1956-1966, churchmen were hardly speaking to each other. Most contacts between Catholic and Protestant were personal encounters among scholars. For example, Yves Congar, the Catholic Dominican, often visited Lutheran scholar Oscar Cullmann at his forest retreat at Chamonix, France, in the Alps near Mont Blanc; the saintly Abbé Paul Couturier, of Lyon (died in 1953), who developed the Week of Universal Prayer (see Chapter VI), inaugurated talks between Catholics and the Reformed theologians and made introductions of Catholics to the World Council of Churches.

The warnings against ecumenism (*Mortalium animos*) by Pope Pius XI lingered in Europe, and in the United States there were the fresh memories of a pastoral letter by the late Cardinal Stritch forbidding Chicago Catholics to go near the Second Assembly of the World Council of Churches meeting in 1954 in Evanston and in Chicago's Soldier's Field. But the barriers began to fall during the decade 1956-1966, and the rival factions became acquainted again.

33. The first contacts came largely through a host of study and retreat centers, often connected with monasteries. Although

these were the quietest occasions of dialogue, some of the most
intense and fruitful have been among the monasteries and special
centers. In Europe, the Protestant monastic movement in Taizé,
France (and its counterpart for women in Areuse, Switzerland,
the *Communauté féminine de Grandchamp*), the Iona Community on a tiny island near Scotland, and the Methodist Sisters of
Darmstadt (Ecumenical Sisterhood of Mary), are centers for
contacts between the faiths. Most recently, in 1966, there were
the first efforts of structuring monastic life together. Two Swedish Lutheran monks joined six Roman Catholic monks (in a ten-
year-old community following the Benedictine rule), and formed
an "ecumenical monastery" at Erlach, Upper Austria. The
bishop of the Evangelical Church in Austria, said: "It is our conviction that Protestant monks can live together with Roman
Catholic monks in one monastery just as well as marriage partners of different confessions. They can have spiritual fellowship
as long as none of them denies the special heritage of his own
confession, but endeavors to share it without endangering the
other's freedom of conscience."

Among monastic and retreat movements, Paris had a special
attraction for ecumenical centers, largely as a result of the in-
flux of Russian Orthodox refugees after the Russian revolution.
Pope Pius XI, hoping to convert some of the Orthodox refugees
for vocations, set up a seminary of the Eastern rite in 1923
under the Dominicans at Lille. But the Orthodox proved more
durable than the pope, once a nuncio in Poland, had thought.
The seminary had practically no students. The interchange between Roman Catholics and the Russian Orthodox developed,
and the seminary project in 1927 turned into a study center,
"Istina," which means "truth" in the Slavonic languages. The
Rev. Father C. J. Dumont, O.P., came in 1932 and promptly
closed the ailing seminary and concentrated on the center with its
ecumenical dimensions. Moving to the Paris suburb of Boulogne-
sur-Seine in 1936, the center publishes a quarterly "Istina," and
has broadened its interest to encourage unity among all Christians—not exclusively among Orthodox and Roman Catholics.
In Paris also, is the Paris Diocesan Secretariat for Christian
Unity, which runs an ecumenical information office and holds
discussions at St. Severin's Community Center. And Pastor

Hebert Roux heads a *Commission des Relations avec le Catholicisme* (Commission for relations with Catholicism) of the Protestant Federation to structure dialogue.

Also pioneering with ecumenical centers, the Catholic Monks of Chevetogne, Belgium, and the Society of Christ the King, of German martyr Father Max Metzger were among those who made the earliest efforts in this century for bringing reconciliation among the Christian faiths. The Chevetogne Monks began with the Monks of Union founded in 1925 at Amay-sur-Meuse by Dom Lambert Beauduin at the suggestion of Pius XI, under the inspiration of Russian Metropolitan Szeptickyj, archbishop of Lwow. Chevetogne, to which the monks moved in 1939, was described in the monastery journal *Irénikon* in 1951 (p. 33) as welcoming outsiders: "Hostelry, refectory, oratories for the different rites, libraries, rooms for meetings, gardens that invite encounter—everything is designed, in harmony with the pattern of life of its inhabitants, to make Chevetogne a hospitable resting-place on the road to Union; an Emmaus where together we can listen to the wishes of the Master."

Father Metzger, jailed three times before his death in 1944 at the hands of the Nazis, also formed (in 1939) the Una Sancta Brotherhood from the Una Sancta movement, a previous, uncorrelated group which had brought Catholics and Protestants together informally. The spirit of the movement has been continued by Archbishop Lorenz Jaeger, of Paderborn, West Germany, in his efforts to bring Catholics and Protestants together. Current headquarters for Una Sancta is the Bavarian Abbey of Niederaltaich. Archbishop Jaeger also founded the Adam-Moehler Institute in the Paderborn Seminary to train specialists on Lutheran and ecumenical questions.

Various study and lay academies were effective in developing ecumenism. There were, for example, the Ecumenical Center of Utrecht, The Netherlands, under Bernard Cardinal Alfrink; the World Council of Churches Ecumenical Institute in Bossey, near Celigny, Switzerland; the Evangelical Academy, Bad Boll, Germany; the "Church in the World" movement in Horst-Driebergen, Germany; the Lutheran Foundation for Interconfessional Research, in Strasbourg; and Gossner-Haus in Mainz-Kastel, West Germany.

In Rome, on a back street off the expansive, quietly lit Navona Square, is a door that leads through a long corridor and elevator to the office and tenant rooms of an ecumenical rooming house (once a palace for Renaissance nobility) and center, Foyer Unitas, under the quiet guidance of the Ladies of Bethany, who conduct this "half-way hostel" principally for non-Roman Catholic guests in Rome. There you can meet a cardinal or lesser prelates one or several nights a week as they are called in to address predominantly Protestant or interfaith gatherings. Cardinal Rugambwa and English and Indian archbishops came to honor non-Catholic artist Frederick Franck, whose free-lance sketches of the Council had universal appeal. Franck himself, a non-Catholic, has built a chapel out of an old grist-mill near his country home near New Milford, New York, and dedicated it to Pope John. A report of Foyer Unitas gives a glimpse of the variety of ecumenical endeavors:

Among . . . things we remember:

—The agape in January in the Roman Institute for Social Studies, where Cardinal Bea, in front of hundreds of guests, kindly and calmly made his pioneering speech about freedom of conscience and where one of our guests, an American Congregationalist missionary in India, gave her personal testimony about truth and love;

—The gathering in our living-room on Maundy Thursday, when we listened together to the words of the high-priestly prayer in which our Lord prayed for unity, and recited together the Lord's Prayer, each in his own language;

—The common joy about the new Pope, elected by the Conclave, Paul VI, who, in 1950, together with Father (Charles) Boyer, S. J., took the initiative in the founding of the Foyer Unitas;

—Receptions during the autumn: A group of Orthodox theologians and teachers from Greece, to whom we could only speak the language of cordiality and hospitality.

34. In the United States, centers of Catholic-Protestant exchanges have included Packard Manse, Boston, a United States counterpart of retreats held at Taizé; the Anglican Benedictine St. Gregory's Priory in Three Rivers, Michigan; the Institute for Advanced Pastoral Studies, Bloomfield Hills, Michigan; Holy Cross Monastery, West Park, New York; Parishfield, near Brighton, Michigan (a counterpart of Bad Boll, Germany); the Spiritual Life Institute of America at Holy Cross Chapel, Sedona, Arizona; and the World Center for Liturgical Studies, Boca Raton, Florida.

In Canada, Mother Françoise de la Visitation organized a prayer meeting at her convent for the success of the Fourth Faith and Order Conference in Montreal, in 1963. She invited the Anglican Sisters of St. Margaret to join with five congregations of Catholic nuns in prayer for the Montreal Faith and Order meeting and for the eventual achievement of unity. Also the Roman Catholic Centre in Montreal has launched a study-retreat house on Lake Memphremagog.

In Oxford, Michigan, the Rev. Arthur Kreinheder, the lone Lutheran monk who runs St. Augustine Retreat house on a quiet hill, is often found at the St. Benedict Sylvestrine (Catholic) Monastery, down the road, and the Benedictines, two dozen of them, can often be found on a Sunday morning sitting around a circle talking at the St. Augustine (Lutheran) House. In North Palm Beach, Florida, the Passionist Fathers were host to 40 Protestant ministers in Our Lady of Florida Retreat House on Lake Worth. And the exchanges of the Convent of St. Helena (Anglican), Newburgh, New York, with Roman Catholic neighbors have reached a rapid tempo:

> Our contacts with Roman Catholic communities have been numerous, happy and quite informal. They have been for the most part, casual visits, invitations to conferences, participation in educational programs. Both colleges in Newburgh, the junior college of the Sisters of the Presentation and the four-year college of the Sisters of St. Mary, Dominican, have offered us courses for training our novices if we wish to send them. We sent one professed sister to Mary-

knoll College for missionary training before she was sent to
our convent in Liberia.

We have not worked out any program for dialogue. We just
meet casually and talk. One contact came through a basket
of fruit delivered to us rather than to St. Joseph's. I have
found the sisters more than willing to listen, to learn, to ask
questions and answer them. Almost all of our encounters
have been pleasant. Two of our sisters will be visiting Protestant and Roman Catholic communities in Europe this
summer. . . .

35. Sister Mary Luke, superior general of the Roman Catholic Sisters of Loretto, and the first American woman auditor at
the Vatican Council, outlined recent happenings in ecumenism
and the role of the nun, in this address given to the American
hierarchy and Council observers in Rome on Nov. 4, 1964:

One of the hopes dearest to sisters as women alive to the
interests of the Church is that of Christian unity. . . . The
Council Fathers have said that the restoration of unity is
a matter for the whole Church, and that it affects everyone
according to his age, profession, circumstances and talents.
Sisters, along with all those seriously seeking unity, are
eager to implement the schema on ecumenism. How will
they begin? It is my firm conviction that the effectiveness
of the apostolate of sisters is directly related to the excel-
lence of their formation period. In regard to ecumenism,
attention and emphasis must be given to the cultivation of
positive attitudes toward the beliefs and practices of others.
These attitudes will be reflected in their whole future apostolate, both in the home missions and the missions overseas.
With authoritative impetus given to ecumenical endeavor, I
would like to suggest some possible paths open to sisters.
First, on a specialized level, there will be a select group
of highly qualified sisters who can meet our separated
brethren on a theological footing. Although presently few
in number, this group is gradually increasing. Secondly,
initial but firm contacts are being established with sisters

of other churches. And thirdly, ecumenical horizons are being broadened because of the expanded apostolate of sisters within the Church itself. . . .

As educators, sisters might well explore another new avenue and that is, seeking help from other Christian educators in such areas as effective methodology in teaching religion. I know that excellent work has been done in this field by Protestant research, and I believe that we should make more use of the results. Concentration on our mutual efforts to spread the Gospel cannot but be conducive to genuine unity in Christ. . . .

I would like to cite the work being done by the Sister Formation Conference, a committee of the Conference of Major Superiors. With proper ecclesiastical approval from the Sacred Congregation of Religious, the local ordinaries concerned and the Conference of Major Superiors, this committee has been working for several years to foster meaningful contacts with various communities of Anglican sisters. A number of Episcopalian communities now receive Sister Formation literature and attend meetings sponsored by that committee, including institutes for superiors and workshops in spirituality. In addition, the personal and written contacts made with members of the Episcopal hierarchy have had a wholesome and enriching effect on all concerned. Howsoever modest, this rapprochement is meaningful, and points the way to further developments.

36. A "nun-for-a-day" movement has become popular among a group of Protestant women in the Denver, Colorado, area. Called the Fransisters, after St. Francis of Assisi who is appreciated by Catholic and Protestant alike for his compassion for humanity, the group seeks to give the average housewife that special day away from it all with the spiritual blessings found by the full-time contemplative. The women, wearing a simple white habit for the day, meet in a retreat mountain home 12 miles west of Littleton, Colorado. Founded in 1957 by a Denver study group and chartered in 1909, they have been encouraged by

Catholic religious orders, among them the Poor Clare Sisters of Roswell, New Mexico. Sister Mary Francis, abbess of the Poor Clare Monastery, invited the Fransisters to observe the investiture of a new sister from Littleton, and later wrote her visitors: "More and more, I cannot imagine there was ever a time when we did not know and love you."

a. The Fransister's purposes are three-fold:

The first purpose is to fill the devotional need of every woman, to love and be loved, and to learn to look to a Spiritual Source for her inner strength and peace. This can be achieved through a daily quiet time in which her emotional nature is cleansed and fed.

The second purpose of the Fransister Movement is to make retreats possible so that every woman may have at least one day of quiet each month in which she can find herself and become whole. This is especially needed by young mothers, and women who serve as teachers, clerks, office or factory workers, nurses, professional women, ministers' wives —all women.

The third purpose of the Fransister Movement is to recognize the similarities in all religions, respect those who worship in the way they have chosen, and "love one another."

b. The Fransister's rules and intentions:

(1) To be joyous, kind and grateful, these three aspects of a whole which is love.

(2) To have reverence for all life, human, animal and plant.

(3) To accept all people as children of God and all forms of worship as acceptable for those using them; if in acting upon them the devotee grows "better than he is," more helpful, more forgiving, more loving, then his form of worship is right for him.

(4) To make Free Time each day in which to "Talk to the Father, and wait upon His answer in her heart."

(5) To accept the Poverty of Indulgence. (Living in the world, it would be difficult to renounce "things," but we can regard ourselves as custodians and see that all things are rightfully used. And we *can* renounce harmful and destructive thoughts, emotions and words, and overcome wrong habits.)

(6) To believe that "The main purpose of living is to find and know God, for without that there can be no happiness, and life without happiness is futile."

(7) To offer herself, her day, and every task and problem and joy to God to use, "For the glory of Life, the benefit of all mankind and the fulfillment of her own divine nature."

37. The men were not inactive either when it came to ecumenical projects, and their church clubs met together. In Dearborn, Michigan, in 1965, the Cherry Hill United Presbyterian Men's Club and the Divine Child Dad's Club held a banquet together, and couples' groups met ecumenically. Seventeen couples from St. James' Episcopal Church, Mesilla Park, New Mexico, held a weekend retreat at the Holy Cross Retreat of the Franciscan Fathers, near Las Cruces, November 6-8, 1964. In the next year, of 40 persons making the same retreat, one couple was Roman Catholic and two couples were mixed, Episcopalian and Roman Catholic. Both the rector of St. James', the Rev. Konrad Kelley Jr., and the Franciscan retreat master, the Rev. Father Brice R. Moran, alternated as retreat and meditation leaders. Father Kelley describes the retreat:

The beginnings of this retreat lay with the laymen of my parish. It was they who made the initial contacts with the Roman Franciscans; it was they who arranged the conference that we had with Bishop Metzger of El Paso, and it was they who handled publicity and registrations. For my part, I was concerned with the theological and pastoral aspects of the retreat. One of the interesting aspects of these ecumenical years in the Roman Church has been an openness of all kinds of conversation. We were able to sit quietly and to discuss the differences between Anglicans and Romans and come to terms not only on the mechanical aspects, but also on those areas in which as brothers we would have to agree to disagree. I offer you two examples of this: the Episcopal Church does not accept the doctrine of Transubstantiation, yet it does teach the doctrine of the Real Presence of Christ. Our Roman brothers were well assured that we had a respect for their feelings and that we would respect their reservation of the sacrament upon the altar, so we were permitted the use of the chapel for our meditations. We were able to agree that in the meditations themselves, neither the Roman nor the Episcopalian Retreat Masters would be required to compromise any position of their respective Churches for the sake of a "harmony" that could not be real. What we did agree to do was to say, "this is what the Roman Church holds" at this point, or "this is what the Episcopal Church teaches." We felt that honesty demanded such an approach. The laymen who came asked for explanations of some of these differences in the open discussion periods which were scheduled in the retreat, and both the Roman and Episcopal priests replied candidly. This was the working relationship which made this retreat possible.

38. A series of top level encounters began late in 1960, with the announcement from Lambeth Palace, London, that Geoffrey F. Fisher, archbishop of Canterbury, would visit Pope John, the first meeting between the heads of Anglicanism and Roman Catholicism since the parting of the ways four hundred years earlier.

A number of others made the same courtesy call—among them, the Rev. Archibald Craig, moderator of the Church of Scotland; Orthodox Metropolitan Damaskinos, of Volos, Greece; Greek Orthodox Metropolitan Meliton, of Heliopolis, a member of the Holy Synod in Istanbul and president of the Third Pan-Orthodox Conference; Chrysostomos, of Myra, secretary of the Pan-Orthodox Conference; the Rt. Rev. Arthur C. Lichtenberger, presiding bishop of the Protestant Episcopal Church in the U.S.A.; Methodist Bishop Fred Pierce Corson, of Philadelphia; the Most Rev. Joost de Blank, archbishop of Capetown and presiding bishop of the Anglican Church in the Union of South Africa;

the Rev. Dr. Joseph H. Jackson, president of the National Baptist Convention in the U.S.A., Inc.; the Rev. Dr. Eugene Carson Blake, at that time, stated clerk of the United Presbyterian Church in the U.S.A.

Metropolitan Athenagoras (English Orthodox primate, not to be confused with Patriarch Athenagoras) told a London University audience of his visit to Pope Paul VI. "When I saw the humble man, how he greeted me, and then arranged a chair for me, I was moved to tears."

a. About the event that started this series of visits to Rome, the Lambeth announcement said, in guarded understatement:

> The Archbishop of Canterbury plans to leave London Nov. 22 for Jerusalem where he will be the guest of the Anglican archbishop in Jerusalem . . . His Grace will visit the holy places and call on the Orthodox patriarch of Jerusalem and the heads of other churches in the Middle East. . . . On his way back the archbishop hopes it will prove possible for him to call at Istanbul to visit His All Holiness Athenagoras, the first ecumenical patriarch of the Orthodox Church.
>
> After Istanbul the Archbishop of Canterbury proposes to spend a few days in Rome in the course of which he will pay a visit of courtesy to Pope John XXIII. The archbishop will return to the country Dec. 3.

b. The first formal, personal contact between Canterbury and Pope, beyond that of a courtesy call, occurred in March, 1966, when Arthur Michael Ramsey, archbishop of Canterbury, met with Pope Paul VI for a series of talks and together joined in public prayers in the Basilica of St. Paul Outside the Walls. In their concluding joint statement, calling for more serious efforts in dialogue, they said:

> In this City of Rome, from which St. Augustine was sent by St. Gregory to England and there founded the Cathedral See of Canterbury toward which the eyes of all Anglicans now turn as the center of their Christian communion, His

Holiness Pope Paul VI and His Grace Michael Ramsey, Archbishop of Canterbury, representing the Anglican communion, have met to exchange fraternal greetings.

At the conclusion of their meeting they give thanks to Almighty God who by the action of the Holy Spirit has in these latter years created a new atmosphere of Christian fellowship between the Roman Catholic Church and the churches of the Anglican communion.

This encounter of the 23rd [of] March, 1966, marks a new stage in the development of fraternal relations, based upon Christian charity, and of sincere efforts to remove the causes of conflict and to re-establish unity.

In willing obedience to the command of Christ who bade his disciples love one another, they declare that, with His help, they wish to leave in the hands of the God of mercy all that in the past has been opposed to this precept of charity, and that they make their own the mind of the Apostle which he expressed in these words:

"Forgetting those things which are behind, and reaching forth unto those things which are before, I press towards the mark for the prize of the high calling of God in Christ Jesus."

They affirm their desire that all those Christians who belong to these two communions may be animated by these same sentiments of respect, esteem and fraternal love, and in order to help these develop to the full, they intend to inaugurate between the Roman Catholic Church and the Anglican communion a serious dialogue which, founded on the Gospel and on the ancient common traditions, may lead to that unity in truth, for which Christ prayed.

The dialogue should include not only theological matters such as scripture, tradition and liturgy, but also matters of practical difficulty felt on either side. His Holiness the

Pope and His Grace the Archbishop of Canterbury are, indeed, aware that serious obstacles stand in the way of a restoration of complete communion of faith and sacramental life; nevertheless, they are of one mind in their determination to promote responsible contacts between their communions in all those spheres of church life where collaboration is likely to lead to a greater understanding and a deeper charity, and to strive in common to find solutions for all the great problems that face those who believe in Christ in the world of today.

Through such collaboration, by the grace of God the Father and in the light of the Holy Spirit, may the prayer of our Lord Jesus Christ for unity among his disciples be brought nearer to fulfillment, and with progress toward unity may there be a strengthening of peace in the world, the peace that only He can grant who gives "the peace that passeth all understanding," together with the blessing of Almighty God, Father, Son and Holy Spirit, that it may abide with all men forever.

39. Official invitations went initially to approximately 45 non-Roman Catholics to participate in the Second Vatican Council as observers. There had been some precedent. Luther almost came to a Council, the Council of Trent, which stretched from 1545 to 1563 and spanned the lives of five popes. Protestants were invited to all three periods but attended only the second session of Trent. Luther's associate, Melanchthon, was on the way after Luther's death to the second convocation when it was dissolved at the impending war between the emperor and the Duke of Moritz.

In 1868, on the eve of the First Vatican Council, an apostolic letter from Pope Pius IX went to all the bishops of the Eastern churches not in communion "with the Apostolic See:" "We beseech, admonish, and pressingly exhort you to come," the letter said. But it fell into hands of journalists before it was delivered, and the Patriarch of Constantinople, offended by the lack of protocol and disagreeing with what he considered a paternalistic attitude in the letter, rejected the invitation forthwith, and there were no observers at the First Vatican Ecumenical Council, 1869-70.

The invitations to the Second Vatican Council in 1962 had for the most part been initiated by the Vatican, although there were several "hospites," who not representing any organization officially had come for the most part at their own suggestion as personal "guests" of the Secretariat for Promoting of Christian Unity. In this category was the Rev. Dr. Joseph H. Jackson, of Chicago, who said that he was personally invited orally by John XXIII during a papal audience. Another personal guest, Baptist Stanley Stuber, head of the Missouri Council of Churches at the time, said he had asked to go to the Council.

A year previously, five Roman Catholics were observers at the Third Assembly of the World Council of Churches meeting in New Delhi. (Roman Catholic observers had accepted invitations to send four observers to the Edinburgh Faith and Order Conference in August, 1937 and the Vatican had sent three observers to the Faith and Order Conference in Lund, Sweden, in 1952.)

Now the Vatican's guests in 1962 were to be a who's who of Protestantism and Eastern Christians—among them heads of denominations, bishops, and World Council officials.

a. Typical of the Vatican II invitations to observers is this one to the Lutheran World Federation:

SECRETARIATUS AD CHRISTIANORUM UNITATEM FOVENDAM
PRAEPARATORIUS CONCILII VATICANI II

E Civitate Vaticana, die
20th June, 1962

Dr. Kurt Schmidt Clausen
General Secretary of the Lutheran World Federation
17, Route de Malagnou
Geneva, Switzerland.

Dear Sir,

In the name of His Holiness, Pope John XXIII, who has demonstrated so much good-will toward Christians who are not in communion with the Holy Apostolic See, our Secretariat, after coming into contact through its Secretary,

Msgr. J. G. M. Willebrands, with the competent authorities
of your Federation, has the honor to invite the LUTHERAN
WORLD FEDERATION to send to the Second Vatican
Council in the capacity of Delegated Observers two or three
church representatives or theologians in whom you have
confidence.

We would be grateful to you if you could let us know the
names of the Delegated Observers by July 31, 1962. When
we have been informed of these names, we shall send to
you without delay our consent and the necessary information, with the request that you pass them on to those concerned.

Enclosed are the guide-lines for the Delegated Observers,
in which the rights of the latter are precisely laid down.
Our Secretariat will take care to send to them all information which might be to your interest.

It is our hope and prayer before Our Lord that the presence
of these observers may be an efficacious contribution to an
ever increasing understanding and esteem between all those
who have been baptized in Christ, our common Lord and
Master.

United in prayer and faith to Our Lord Jesus Christ, God
and Saviour.

> Yours,
> + Aug. Card. Bea
> Willebrands, Secr.

b. These are the "rules and regulations regarding delegated observers" which Cardinal Bea enclosed in his invitation to
the Lutherans:

(1) In order that Christians who are separated from
the Apostolic See may be better informed on the work of
the Second Vatican Council, the Holy See invites them to
send Delegated Observers.

(2) The Observers are entitled to be present at the Public Solemn Sessions and at the closed General Assemblies where the schemata of the Council are presented for open discussion. They are not entitled to observe, generally, the Work-Sessions of the Commissions, unless special circumstances warrant this and permission has been obtained from the competent authority.

(3) The Observers are not entitled to speak or to vote at the discussions and sessions of the Council.

(4) It is the task of the Secretariat for Promoting Christian Unity to mediate between the organs of the Council and the Observers whatever information is necessary for following more easily and completely the work of the Council.

For this, the Secretariat can hold special sessions for the Observers, in order to discuss with them the deliberations of the Council. To such sessions competent people, including Fathers of the Council, can be invited, in order that the Observers are exactly informed on the themes discussed in the Council.

c. Kurt Schmidt-Clausen replied:

THE LUTHERAN WORLD FEDERATION
Executive Secretary: Dr. Kurt Schmidt-Clausen

Geneva,
Route de Malagnou 17
August 4, 1962

To the President of the Secretariat for Promoting
    Christian Unity
H. E. Cardinal Bea
Rome
Citta dell' Vaticano

Your Eminence,

It is an honor and a joy for me to answer your letter of June 20, 1962, in which the Lutheran World Federation was invited to send Delegated Observers to the Second Vatican

Council. The responsible organs of the Lutheran World Federation have taken note with gratitude of the letter of invitation, and have carefully examined the question of sending Delegated Observers. The President of the Lutheran World Federation has now authorized me to inform you that the Lutheran World Federation will be glad to send Delegated Observers to Rome. At the same time he asks me to express to you the thanks of the Lutheran World Federation for the invitation which was extended.

The Lutheran World Federation names as its Delegated Observers:

(1) Professor Dr. Kristen Einar Skydsgaard, Professor of Systematic Theology at the University of Copenhagen, Director of the Special Commission on Inter-Confessional Research of the Lutheran World Federation. Address: Copenhagen, St. Kannikestr. 11.

(2) Professor Dr. George Linbeck, Professor of Historical Theology at Yale University, New Haven, Conn., U.S.A., at present Research Professor for the Special Commission on Inter-Confessional Research of the Lutheran World Federation. Address: at present: Copenhagen, Vodroffsvej 8.

Since both gentlemen will not be in the position to remain continually in Rome until the end of the Council, it will be necessary—as has been previously discussed with Msgr. Dr. Willebrands—to replace them with alternates when they are not present. We ask you to inform us if you agree to this. We would then send you the names of the alternates so that the necessary formalities could be carried out quickly and without difficulty.

May God guide the deliberations of the Second Vatican Council to the honor of His Holy Name.

Your most sincerely,
Dr. Kurt Schmidt-Clausen
Executive Secretary of the
Lutheran World Federation.

40. Similar correspondence went to the World Council of Churches, The WCC explained why it was accepting and sending at the outset, Lukas Vischer, research secretary for the WCC Department Faith and Order:

> The reasons why the Executive Committee feels that the invitation should be accepted are the following: This is the first time in history that observers from so many confessions are invited to follow the proceedings of a Council of the Roman Catholic Church. This new departure is not unrelated to the rise of the modern ecumenical movement. The World Council which has ever since its first Assembly invited Roman Catholics to attend its main meetings as observers should use this opportunity to become better acquainted with developments in the life of the Roman Catholic Church. The observers may also have opportunity to explain informally what the World Council stands for and to forward a true conversation between the Roman Catholic Church and the Churches in the WCC. The observers will have no authority to speak officially for the WCC nor to engage in any negotiation. The acceptance of the invitation is to be seen wholly in the light of the purposes of the WCC and especially of its task "to draw churches out of isolation into conference in which none is to be asked to be disloyal or to compromise its convictions, but to seek to explain them to others while seeking to understand their point of view" (Faith and Order Constitution).

41. The Orthodox Ecumenical Patriarch Athenagoras I, who was expected to recommend sending observers, decided otherwise at the last minute. Greek primate Chrysostomos was especially opposed to developing contacts with Rome. However, the Russian Orthodox, expected to stay at home, in a late hour decision decided to come. Here is a summary of that involved negotiation, told by Vitaly Borovoy, University of Leningrad professor and representative of the Moscow patriarchate at the World Council of Churches:

> We knew that Monsignor Willebrands had been to see Patriarch Athenagoras at Istanbul and had brought him an

invitation. We also knew that Monsignor was again in the East in May and had visited all the Church heads with the exception of the Russian Orthodox. We knew that the Greek Patriarch Athenagoras was joyfully prepared to send delegates to the Council. We too followed with great interest. In fact, as we have affirmed, Patriarch Athenagoras sent us a report of his conversation with Monsignor Willebrands, but there was not a syllable about an invitation.

Monsignor Willebrands came to Geneva in the spring and addressed a meeting of the Confessional World Association. I was there, but I was not approached since we Orthodox are a Church and not a confessional association. I waited in vain.

Monsignor Willebrands and I met again at a meeting of the Central Committee of the World Council of Churches in Paris in August. This time I served as an interpreter between him and our Archbishop Nikodim, the director of the Foreign Office of the Moscow Patriarchate. We made Monsignor Willebrands understand that if he desired our presence in Rome, he would have to invite us personally. We honor the Patriarch of Constantinople (Istanbul) in everything, but we are an independent Church. Monsignor Willebrands asked if his visit in Moscow would be welcomed, and we answered that whenever he would like to come, he would always be cordially welcomed. We waited. August went by and almost the whole of September without hearing a word. Suddenly on the 26th a telegram came announcing that the Monsignor would be in Moscow on the next day. I was called in especially from Leningrad to speak with him.

*But why wasn't the Patriarch present?*

At that very moment the Patriarch was in his summer residence at Odessa. Why should he bestir himself to come to Moscow? After all Monsignor Willebrands is a simple prelate like my colleague and myself! . . .

Monsignor Willebrands remained with us for six days. He even spoke about inviting some members of the holy synod. But he did not have an invitation with him. He explained that before issuing the invitation he had to know whether we would be willing to accept his invitation. Whereupon we explained to him that we could make no decision before we had the invitation in our hands. The Monsignor completed some unfinished business and left, promising to give us exact information from Rome. . . .

Constantinople knew about them [the negotiations] in August. On October 6 we received a telegraphed inquiry from Athenagoras asking what we were planning to do. But all we could answer was: "We have nothing new to communicate." We had not yet received any news from Rome. The official invitation came one day before the opening of the Council. The holy synod immediately held a meeting at which it was decided to send two observers. We announced this on the same evening. We were convinced that we would also find the observer of the Greek Patriarchate in Rome. You can imagine our disappointment to find ourselves alone here. . . .

Athenagoras, nevertheless, has declared that he decided *not* to send an observer "after consultation with all Orthodox Churches." How does that coincide with everything else?

At any rate he didn't consult with us. He wired us his decision on October 10. But this declaration reached us after we ourselves had already announced the dispatch of two observers and they could no longer be withdrawn. We were speechless over Athenagoras' measure for the very reason that before this he had so openly evidenced his sympathy for the Council—so much so, that the first person to receive his telegram could not believe his eyes and gave it to another person who knew Greek better, for translation. So you see if there was a committee of Orthodox Churches, in which all the autocephalous Churches of the Orthodox faith were represented, as was decided in Rhodes, such a misunderstanding could not have occurred. All information and opinions would immediately be discussed among the members. We are always pressing for the foundation of such a committee, but Athenagoras has not yet acted.

42. A general proposal to enter a two-way dialogue with Rome sometime following the end of Vatican II, submitted by Ecumenical Patriarch Athenagoras was unanimously approved at a Pan-Orthodox Conference of ten Eastern Orthodox churches in Rhodes in 1964. About his decision, Athenagoras said:

> We are coming out of our isolation and in coming out, we are opening the doors which imprison us. Catholics and Greek Orthodox have much in common; traditions, dogmas, sacraments, the catacombs and the common blood of the martyrs. We have decided to engage in a dialogue. Isolation is a disgrace and aloneness is isolation.

43. Pope Paul VI gave the Orthodox encouragement as they examined the possibility of formal discussions. He sent this message to the Third Pan-Orthodox Conference in Rhodes, held November 1-15, 1964:

> From the depth of our heart we send you our fraternal greetings. In this moment in which your brothers of the Roman Catholic Church, gathered together in the Council, are looking for the road that must be followed in applying faithfully God's will for the Church, in this era so rich in opportunities, but also of temptations and trials, you, too, in answer to the Lord's will, are preparing to reflect over the same problems.
>
> Fully aware of the importance of your holy meeting, we invoke over it with a fervent prayer the light of the Holy Spirit. Let us see to it that the Blessed Virgin, our common Mother to whom we pray with the same fervor, intercede for our growth, wholly and always, in the love of Her Son, our Savior and only Lord. Let us see to it that love, drawn at the Lord's table, lead us in order that we might keep more every day "the unity of the Spirit of peace." (Eph. 4:3.)

44. Pope Paul enhanced cordial relations when he called other Christian groups, "churches," instead of separated brethren in his Holy Thursday week message, March 26, 1964. (Later in the same year, the new Decree on Ecumenism contained a chapter entitled "Churches and Ecclesial Communities Separated From the Roman Apostolic See," although the decree does employ the term "separated brethren" on occasion.) Pope Paul, however, reverts to the less desirable term, "separated brethren" in his Easter message of the same year. The Holy Thursday message, however, was significant, for by his terminology Pope Paul recognized that non-Roman Catholics had churchly structures and essence, too. He said:

> We send our well-wishing Easter salute . . . to the Oriental churches disjointed from us at present but already together with us in faith. Greetings and peace to all the Anglican church, while with sincere charity and equal hope we trust to be able to see it one day recomposed honorably in the unique and universal fold of Christ . . . to all the other Christian communities derived from the Reform of the 16th century and who are separated from us.

45. A dramatic encounter between Pope and Patriarch occurred when Pope Paul VI met with Patriarch Athenagoras I on January 6, 1964, in Jerusalem. It was the first confrontation of patriarch and pope since the "paper" council of Florence worked out a union of Eastern and Roman Christians. That abortive union, that never found support in the East, was tentatively agreed on July 6, 1439, in the presence of Pope Eugenius IV, Patriarch Joseph of Constantinople, and the archbishops of Ephesus, Nicaea and Kiev.

In the recent meeting, Patriarch Athenagoras and the Roman Pontiff exchanged the kiss of peace during the forty-minute encounter on the Mount of Olives, and issued this joint communique:

> At the end of their meeting in Jerusalem, the Holy Father Paul VI and the Ecumenical Patriarch Athenagoras, in agreement with his Holy Synod, have together acknowl-

edged the great significance of this event and have given
thanks to Almighty God, Father, Son and Holy Spirit, who
has guided their steps to the Holy Land where our common
Redeemer, Christ our Lord, lived, taught, died, rose again,
and ascended into heaven, whence He sent down the Holy
Spirit upon the infant Church.

This meeting cannot be considered otherwise than as a fraternal gesture inspired by the charity of Christ, who left
to His disciples the supreme commandment of loving one
another, of forgiving offenses even to seventy times seven,
and of being united one with another.

The two pilgrims, with their eyes fixed on Christ, the Ex-
emplar and Author with the Father of unity and peace,
pray to God that this meeting may be the sign and prelude
of things to come for the glory of God and the illumination
of His faithful people.

After so many centuries of silence they have now come together in the desire to realize God's will and to proclaim
the age-old truth of His Gospel entrusted to the Church.

These common sentiments are manifested to all the members of their respective hierarchies and to all the faithful
so that they too may participate in them and offer to God renewed prayers that the truth of the one Church of Christ
and of His Gospel, light and salvation of the world, may
shine with ever greater brightness in the sight of all Christians.

46. In another historic confrontation, Augustin Cardinal Bea,
of the Vatican's Secretariat for Promoting Christian Unity, met
with French Pastor Marc Boegner, a past president of the World
Council of Churches and a pioneer in the development of the
ecumenical movement, and the WCC general secretary, Willem A.
Visser 't Hooft. The confrontation on February 18, 1965, provided the means to confirm agreement to begin official dialogue

between Geneva and Rome through the formation of a Joint
Working Group ("Committee of 14"):

    a. Said Dr. Boegner:

> Anyone who has lived during the last 55 years [since the
> Edinburgh Conference of Protestant missionary societies
> in 1910] realizes what a prodigious achievement this visit
> is. [It will] strengthen the atmosphere in which will ripen
> the fruits of mutual understanding, of mutual respect, of
> joint theological study in search for the truth of Christ,
> which brings with it all promise and all demands of love.

    b. Dr. Visser 't Hooft said:

> Your Eminence, President Boegner, Representatives of the
> Churches, of the Diplomatic Corps and of the Government
> of Geneva, Ladies and Gentlemen:
>
> It is indeed a joy and an honour for the World Council of
> Churches to receive at its headquarters two men whose
> names are indissolubly linked both with the past history
> and with the present development of the ecumenical move-
> ment. The fact that we welcome at the same time His Emi-
> nence Cardinal Bea, director of the Secretariat for the Pro-
> motion of Christian Unity, and President Boegner, one of
> the founders of the World Council of Churches, speaks vol-
> umes in itself. And the moment at which we do so, namely
> a few months after the promulgation of the Vatican Coun-
> cil's decree on Ecumenism and a few weeks after the decla-
> ration made by the Central Committee of our Council
> concerning the further pursuit of conversation with the
> Roman Catholic Church—this moment is singularly ap-
> propriate. . . .
>
> I should like to emphasize two things which seem to me of
> special importance.
>
> The first is the clear statement in the decree that the future
> progress of ecumenism depends upon the renewal of the
> life of the Church, a renewal understood as an ever-grow-
> ing faithfulness to her vocation. . . .

In the second place, we are glad to find that the decree rejects any notion of "ecumenical confusion," and describes the ecumenical quest as a "loyal dialogue" in which genuine differences are taken with full seriousness.

Allow me at this point a remark concerning terminology. I have been struck by the fact that the decree so often uses the words "nevertheless" (*nihilominus*) or "however" (*atamen*). And I think that this is good. For true ecumenism is indeed an attitude characterized by these two words. We do not minimize our differences, nor do we yet see how they could be reconciled. . . .

The fact that we are now preparing to set up a working party, composed of representatives of the Roman Catholic Church and of the WCC, means that we wish to engage in a common exploration of the ways in which we can contribute to the establishment of closer relations with one another. It is not the role of the WCC to engage with the Roman Catholic Church upon negotiations concerning church union, but there are plenty of important questions which we could and should study together in order that we may give a positive direction to the development of ecumenism. We are thinking here both of these questions which have caused, and do still cause, severe tensions between the churches, and also of matters in which there is a real possibility of working together in the practical field. . . .

Your Eminence, M. Boegner, we thank you with all our hearts for the honour that you have done us by paying us this visit, and we wish to express to you our respect and our brotherly greetings. Our good wishes go with you personally and with your service of the ecumenical cause.

c. Cardinal Bea said:

Most dear Brothers in Christ, I do not think I could use a more appropriate expression or name in greeting you at this moment which we can tranquilly call a solemn one and a great gift made by the Lord of the Church to all of us. . . .

The term "brothers in Christ" epitomizes the deepest things which, as a consequence of our baptism, we have in common, by which we are rooted and founded in charity and thus in Christ (cf. Eph. 3: 17). The name "brothers in Christ" moreover sums up the spirit in which we must and we wish to meet, no matter what our creed may be. Lastly, this term expresses our aim; we desire, that is, to be brothers in Christ in a perfect way and therefore to be perfectly united in the manner in which he wishes us to be united.

(1) What is to be the first idea expressed in this greeting, if not that of *joyful gratitude to God,* the Giver of every good, for this hour, for this meeting in itself and for what it signifies and promises? . . .

That which chiefly emphasizes the importance of today's meeting and gives it much greater significance is, as it were its *actual historical context.* In reality, there is question here of a meeting preceded by long preparation, not so much technical as of a psychological nature, that is, the whole series of contacts made and developed in these last five years since the Foundation of the Secretariat for Unity, both with many of the Churches which are members of the Council and also with the World Council as such through its directive organ here in Geneva. The most important and deep-rooted among these contacts were those which were prolonged during the three sessions of the Second (Vatican) Ecumenical Council. There is question here, moreover, of a meeting which receives a very particular light from the Decree on Ecumenism finally approved and promulgated by the Vatican Council last November. . . .

(2) Seen in this concrete context of a Conciliar decree based on the experience itself of the Catholic hierarchy, today's meeting is also a *symbol of fruitful prospects for further developments.* . . .

The Holy See greets with joy and fully accepts—and I am particularly happy to be able to communicate this fact officially on the present occasion—the proposal made by the

Central Committee of the World Council of Churches in Enugu last month, that is, to set up a mixed committee, composed of eight representatives of the World Council of Churches and six of the Catholic Church to explore together the possibilities of dialogue and collaboration between the World Council of Churches and the Catholic Church. As we all know, the task of this Committee is not that of making any decisions, but merely that of exploring what the principles and methods of a possible dialogue and collaboration can be. The results of the Committee's work will be submitted for further examination and decision to those responsible on both sides. I do not doubt that this step which corresponds so well to the letter and the spirit of the Decree on Ecumenism will give excellent results, both in the field of mutual collaboration for the solution of the great and urgent problems of our day and also in that of dialogue properly so-called.

(3) What I have said regarding the historical importance of today's meeting and of the fruits which it will bring, does not at all signify that we are unaware of the *mountain of obstacles and difficulties* which still rise up in our path. . . . Difficulties, of whatever kind they may be, are by no means a reason for causing brothers to withdraw diffidently from contact one with another. Our fraternal charity and love of unity will rather give us the courage for an open dialogue even on difficult questions. This holds also in the case of conversations in the most delicate field, namely that of doctrine. For this we all have a basis in common: the word of God in Holy Scripture, bearing in mind also its concrete expression in the writings of the ancient Fathers of the East and of the West. . . .

We shall not then look at one another with diffidence, or in a spirit of criticism, but rather with incitements to charity and to acts of piety (cf Hebr. 10: 24).

47. On the local level, in equally dramatic though unheralded ways, the faithful of various backgrounds became acquainted.

Marie Killilea wrote of an interfaith hospital drama in *Guide-posts* Magazine (Vol. 16, No. 9), involving members of different faiths learning to pray for one another. A *Christian Herald* survey on ecumenism on the local level turned up, among others, these comments that illustrate the types of movements, and attitudes toward one another that exist on the local level.

From Salem, Wisconsin: "While my wife was teaching Bible school three Catholic ladies came in to look over our new Lutheran church and to compliment us on it. One of the ladies later sent two bouquets for our altar on Sunday."

From Washington . . . a reader who felt there had been a noticeable gain in friendliness in his community, but who thought union would be undesirable, commented: "A local priest was given a reception on his 90th birthday, and I saw almost as many Methodists there as there were members of his own parish. He has been pastor here for the last 30 years."

From Illinois: "A year ago last winter, four young people of our city (two Lutheran, two Catholic) were killed in a plane crash in Florida. Tragedy did more than anything to unite the city. Our pastors attended the Catholic funeral and the priests and nuns attended the one in our church."

From Ohio: "I am an Episcopalian but I frequently go to Roman Catholic churches for private devotions and for Mass. It is my prayer that Roman Catholics and Protestants will some day be able to share fully in the sacraments. That there should be 'one church' does not seem necessary or even desirable, but there should be intercommunion and a constant dialogue on doctrine, liturgy and service."

From Rochester, New York: "We must unite in Jesus Christ, not in Roman Catholic or Protestant churches. What would we do together—play bingo?"

From Massachusetts: "All of the ecumenical movement will take time but I'm thrilled it's coming. I'm an Episcopalian and two weeks ago a Catholic priest assisted at communion in our church. Of such small things are friendships developed. It can't come fast enough for me."

From Mississippi: "I feel it is the priest and minister who create and dwell on the differences rather than the lay members. It would seem more Christian to concentrate on our similarities and stop all this criticism. Relations here have always been excellent—we do not try to convert each other, which is where trouble begins."

Another comment on leadership came from Illinois: "Our town has an old priest who is not taking kindly ANY changes. One day when he retires and a younger priest comes, the local church may change more. Between the peoples of the churches there have always existed congenial relations."

There is one other comment that did not appear on any ballot and was not reflected appreciably on most. This one originated in an upper room in Jerusalem: "By this shall all men know that ye are my disciples, if ye have love one to another."

48. In Canada the drama of a church destroyed by fire in Moose Jaw, Saskatchewan, brought the faiths together. The 1,600-member St. Andrew's United Church, a 50-year-old gray stone "Cathedral of the Prairies," was destroyed December 15, 1963. The Catholic Women's League held a tea and raised $384 for St. Andrew's; the Ukrainian Orthodox women raised $154. Sixteen choirs combined in a concert on behalf of St. Andrew's and raised $500. Other churches in other locales sent money. The St. Andrew's choir practiced in the Baptist church. A social was held in a local synagogue; the St. Andrew's square dancers practiced in St. John's Anglican Church.

Letters opened many new lines of contact.

a. A group of sisters and their students said:

Please accept this small cheque as an expression of our sympathy for your and Moose Jaw's loss. May we see St. An-

> drew's rise again—a witness to your congregation's faith in
> Christ. With the assurance of our prayers, Sister Anne, the
> staff and students of St. Louis College, Moose Jaw. [This
> note was written on a flowered sympathy card with the
> words, "with sincere sympathy to you."]

And the St. Andrew's pastor, the Rev. Homer R. Lane, answered the sisters:

> Dear Friends . . . Your message touched our people deeply
> and the cheque was the first one received toward the rebuild-
> ing fund. We will always remember your thoughtfulness
> and are so grateful that you remember us in your prayers.
> With God's help we believe a new St. Andrew's building will
> come in time. Meanwhile the congregation continues its
> Christian witness with hope and courage.

    b. The sisters and their superior from Providence Hospi-
tal, Moose Jaw, wrote:

> Reverend and Dear Mr. Lane: . . . Please accept our sincere
> sympathy in the loss of your beautiful church.
>
> When we realized on Sunday evening that the fire was in
> the church, we prayed that no one would be injured or
> suffer a loss of life, and for this particular favour we are
> most grateful to God.
>
> If there is anything we can do to help you, please do not
> hesitate to call on us. Be assured of our prayers for you
> during the strenuous days which are ahead. Sincerely, The
> Sisters of Providence Hospital, Sister Mary Lalemant, Su-
> perior.

    49. Shared giving across denominational and confessional
lines has occurred, planting roots for deeper dialogue, often
spurred on by special occasions. (See collection for the Selma
Good Samaritan Catholic Hospital in a Methodist worship service, in Chapter VI, also some jointly sponsored charitable and
social projects in Chapter VII.) In Detroit the dean of St. Paul's

Episcopal Cathedral, the Very Rev. John J. Weaver, announced a collection to aid the work of the Roman Catholic White Fathers martyrs in the Congo. A Jewish resident of Lafayette, Louisiana, offered the Louisana Baptist Convention $100,000 in cash and a $400,000 site for a new hospital. The Catholic Archdiocese of St. Paul gave 23 stained glass windows valued at $8,000 to the Prince of Glory Lutheran Church in Minneapolis. The windows, from a former Catholic church building sold for an urban renewal site, had not been included in the sale of the church property. The PIME (Pontificium Institutum Missionum Exterarum) Fathers of Maryglade College, Memphis, Michigan, raise $65,000 a year through the aid of an interfaith committee of Protestants, Jews, and Catholics. Our Redeemer Lutheran Church, Minneapolis, whose building was destroyed by fire in 1965, received $1,140 from nearby St. Helena's Roman Catholic Church following a special luncheon and drive for the Lutheran church. St. Mark's Lutheran Church, San Francisco, gave a new pulpit Bible to Catholic Archbishop Joseph T. McGucken, for St. Mary's Cathedral, after the archbishop had spoken at an ecumenical forum at the St. Mark's Church. St. Mark's also gives an annual scholarship to a graduate of Sacred Heart School. The Catholic graduate, selected by the faculty, receives the Lutheran "caritas" award on the basis of his emulation of the virtues outlined in I Corinthians 13.

Cooperation in community united foundation appeals is an example of quasi-ecumenical giving, (a "painless" form as the giver does not know exactly where his precise contribution is going.) More directly, Professor Oscar Cullmann, of the University of Basel and the Sorbonne, created interest with his proposal that the churches achieve a practical bond of unity by having regular reciprocal offerings for one another:

> My proposal is for an offering for one another, by the Catholics for poor and needy Protestants, by Protestants for poor and needy Catholics, which both sides would arrange for the Sunday of the yearly week of prayer. . . . I did not invent this proposal myself. It was suggested to me by the institution in primitive Christianity which provided for the poor in Jerusalem. This had an ecumenical

character, for according to Galatians 2: 9f. it was to bind together the Jewish and Gentile missions, which had peacefully separated. . . . This offering was established in order to be a bond of unity among all Christians, both Jews and Gentiles. . . .

Whatever may be the details of the origin of this offering, it is clear that it was to stress the unity of the church, which was constantly threatened by the question of whether or not a Christian had to be circumcised. . . . Thus the offering was a symbol of unity. Since the unity of the church is no longer possible in the modern situation, an offering can no longer be a symbol of unity. . . .

For this reason the offering which I have suggested for us must have a more modest aim than the offering in primitive Christianity. It would no longer be a symbol of unity, but of *solidarity*, of *brotherhood among all who invoke the name of Christ*. . . .

The offering which I have proposed must be distinguished from the offering in primitive Christianity at still another point: it must be *reciprocal*. When only *one* church existed, it was not reciprocal. . . . In order to be a symbol of Christian solidarity today, the offering must be a reciprocal one. We must keep in mind the fact that the Catholics and Protestants no longer form *one* church, and furthermore, that our separation concerns the concept of the church itself. . . .

In general I can announce that, on the one hand, my proposal was received with enthusiasm by many Catholics and by many Protestants, and that, on the other hand, it met with indifference or scepticism from a certain number of Catholics and a certain number of Protestants. By and large the reception is encouraging. After I had finished lecturing to a large audience in Rome, a Roman Catholic monk who did not make himself known placed a banknote wrapped in paper into my pocket. On my way home I discovered that the following words were scrawled on the paper: "From a Catholic monk for a poor Protestant in Rome as a symbol of Christian solidarity." I delivered the sum to the dean of the small Waldensian seminary in Rome, since he has connections with the Protestant congregation in Rome and the surrounding area. He spoke to his students about this gift, and they, quite spontaneously, took up an offering among themselves from their modest means, and sent the total to the abbot of a large cloister in Rome with the request that this mite go to someone in need. I know of many analogous individual gifts which were contributed by members of one confession for members of the other during the week of prayer last year and this year in Rome, in France, and in Switzerland. Several days after I had given my lecture in the auditorium of the University in Basel, I received a small sum of money which the Roman Catholic students of Basel had contributed during the same week of prayer. They stipulated that it should be for the benefit of a poor Protestant student of theology at our dormitory in Basel, if possible a student from the East Zone.

50. There are "diaries of dialogue"—special articles in magazines—that outline carefully planned encounters on the local scene.

a. A Protestant account of local dialogue appeared in *Christian Advocate* Magazine. The Rev. William K. McElvaney, pastor of the St. Stephen Methodist Church, Mesquite, Texas, tells of the relationship of his parish with the nearby St. Pius Roman Catholic Church, Dallas:*

In October, 1964, we engaged in an event with St. Pius which validated itself in a particularly exciting way. Sixty families from St. Pius came to St. Stephen church on a Sunday evening and were greeted by an equal number of Methodist families.

Preparation for this occasion was begun in early summer. Our planning sessions, including clergy and laity from both congregations, were characterized by honesty, frankness, and good humor.

---

* Reprinted from *Christian Advocate*, January 1965. Copyright © 1964 by The Methodist Publishing House.

The October Sunday evening was designed to evolve around three phases: supper, provided covered-dish style by both groups; explanation of Methodist worship and liturgy for the benefit of Roman Catholics, comparable to their prior explanation to us of their Mass; and a panel composed of clergy and laity from both churches.

At St. Stephen we prepared for this experiment through adult classes, commissions, the weekly church newsletter, and a sermon on that morning. Over 60 adults at St. Stephen were involved in an eight-week study of *An American Dialogue* by Brown and Weigel. I updated this book with lectures on more recent ecumenical happenings. By October 18, we were in a mood of high anticipation.

As Roman Catholic families began to arrive at our church, each Methodist family's task was to introduce themselves to a Catholic family and to serve as their host for the evening. The breaking of bread together symbolized a common need and hope and provided personal relationships at the outset. I would be surprised if some anxieties and doubts did not fade away as separated brothers in Christ shared a common meal at a common table.

After dinner I explained our morning order of worship and other Protestant concepts and practices. Our Sunday morning order of worship was distributed and used as a visual guide. The theological rationale of our architecture and liturgical pieces was also presented. I have discovered that there is a mutual ignorance of Methodists and Catholics about the worship, beliefs, and church practices of the other.

The four-man panel which followed was a rewarding exercise in grass roots ecumenical conversation. St. Pius layman Steve Landregan sketched the changing relationships between Catholics and Protestants since his childhood. St. Stephen layman Bob McGuire traced some of the main features of Catholic-Protestant relations historically.

Father King pointed out that many Catholics are amazed at the rapidity of change brought by the Vatican Council. . . .

I offered the benediction at the conclusion of the evening, Father King having previously given the invocation.

b. A Catholic account of local dialogue appears in the *U.S. Catholic*, by the Rev. Father John A. O'Brien. He describes "An Open House for Unity" sponsored by the Christ Our King Church, Wilmington, Delaware:

Christ Our King has a large and impressive physical plant, stretching two blocks in one direction and a block in the other. Monsignor Roderick B. Dwyer is the pastor as well as the vicar general of the diocese.

Monsignor Dwyer called together a number of leading laymen and explained the project. They responded with enthusiasm and showed their willingness to share with their priest and nuns the responsibility of welcoming their non-Catholic neighbors to their parish home. Later the parish was notified of the plan.

Eventually 150 parishioners were enlisted to plan, usher, guide tours, bake cakes, greet each visitor, and make him feel at home. A girls' choir provided a musical background in the room containing displays and refreshments.

Consisting of a chairman, moderator, program director, treasurer and secretary, the executive committee formulated plans and coordinated activities. Other committees were organized to handle publicity, traffic, refreshments, and training the guides.

When it was made clear that the open house was being launched as a community project to promote understanding and good will, publicity media were made available on a large scale. Local newspapers carried stories and pictures, spot radio announcements were made, and a half-hour program on the Catholic Forum of the Air featured the open house on the Sunday on which the event was held. The cooperation of the National Conference of Christians and Jews, the local branch of the World Council of Churches and various civic groups was secured.

Monsignor Dwyer prepared the following letter of welcome, which was handed to each guest upon his arrival:

My Dear Friend,

It is a pleasure to welcome you to the parish of Christ Our King. I am pleased at the opportunity to have you see our facilities and to explain our worship, and in that way to acquaint you with a Catholic church similar to many you often may have passed.

The people of Christ Our King, and I as their pastor, have a justifiable pride in our parish. A parish is not merely a collection of buildings, but a spirit that animates a community of people.

It is in this spirit that the lay members of the Christ Our King community are most happy to show you some of the workings of our parish. The parish is theirs; they as well as I are your hosts.

I hope you will find your tour enjoyable and informative. I hope also that I shall have the opportunity to meet you personally and extend the warm welcome we sincerely want you to feel in being the guest of the parish of Christ Our King. Sincerely in the Lord, . . .

On the page facing the letter was a plan showing the location of all the buildings of the church plant, along with the following announcement: "The church is the focal point of our parish buildings. In it we worship, praise and glorify God. Hence you will clearly perceive why we begin and end our tour of these buildings with an explanation of the functions of the church. Please enter the church by way of the front doors."

The guide committee recruited all the guides, trained them, and organized them into three groups. Group one was made up of persons who greeted visitors at the church door, gave them a program, seated them in the rear pews until a sizeable group had formed, told them about the church and its history, and made them feel at home.

Group two were stationary guides who had charge of only one area, such as a confessional, side altar, rectory office, and explained this to the group when it arrived. The third group were roving guides, mostly girls, who escorted groups from one viewing area to the next. . . .

With the exception of a priest at the baptismal font and another at the altar, all the explanations were given by the lay guides. By doing this, it enabled the visitors to see that lay people are capable of explaining their religion and answering questions. Three meetings were held to train the guides, plus the rehearsal afforded them at the open house for Catholics on the previous Sunday.

The visitors were taken on a tour of the church, rectory, school, and convent. The Sisters escorted the visitors through their home, showing them the chapel, dining room, recreation room and bedrooms.

Upon completion of the tour, the visitors were escorted to the church hall for refreshments.

Here each parish organization—Youth Activities Council, Boy and Girl Scouts, Holy Name, Sodality, Legion of Mary and Confraternity of Christian Doctrine—had a one table display with two representatives to describe their work. In addition, there was a Bible-Missal display, an exhibit of Mass vestments and a display of pamphlets.

In view of the fact that four inches of snow fell during the preceding night, the turnout of 500 made the January 27 open house all the more gratifying. About 25 ministers and five rabbis came, some with a group of their parishioners, others with their own families. . . .

To deepen and strengthen the bonds of understanding and friendship formed by the open house, Monsignor Dwyer sent the following letter of thanks to every pastor in the Wilmington area:

My dear fellow pastor,

The success of our recent "Open House" at Christ Our King Church exceeded our prayerful hopes, and from comments made to me by many of our visitors, I feel that it has helped to further a genuine spirit of charity, understanding and good will in our community.

The most important single factor in our success was the co-operation and even enthusiasm of so many clergymen of all denominations in the area. Without this response our own efforts would have been in vain.

I wish to thank you, both personally and on behalf of the people of Christ Our King parish for your efforts towards making our "Open House" a success.

May we be blessed by a continued growth in the spirit of genuine charity and understanding that has been exhibited on this occasion. Yours most sincerely, . . .

51. When the local Protestant council of churches meets, or a group of church women get together, or the national conventions of the Presbyterians, Lutheran Church in America, Methodists and others convene, the order of the day is to hear a welcome speech from the local Catholic prelate. From the west coast (James Cardinal McIntyre addressed the annual meeting of Episcopal Church Women) to the East coast (Richard Cardinal Cushing addressed the community church in Westwood and the Sudbury Methodist Church and Jewish synagogues), Catholic prelates, with only a few exceptions, have spoken in Protestant church basements or meeting halls. Archbishop Thomas A. Connolly spoke in a forum meeting at Gethsemane Lutheran Church, Seattle. The Most Rev. Raymond G. Gallagher, Bishop of the Roman Catholic Diocese of Lafayette-in-Indiana, gave the keynote address, February 16, 1966, at the opening of the annual meeting of the Council for Health and Welfare Services of the United Church of Christ in Dallas, Texas. The Most Rev. John J. Wright, bishop of Pittsburgh, addressed Methodist and Lutheran

Church in America conventions in his city in 1964, and was slated
to speak at the assembly of the International Convention of
Christian Churches (Disciples of Christ) in Dallas, Sept. 25,
1966. Archbishop Hallinan, of Atlanta, spoke at the Methodist
Camp in Lake Junaluska. Archbishop John F. Dearden, of Detroit, spoke in Presbyterian and Orthodox meeting halls for a
Detroit Pastors' Union and Detroit Council of Churches Protestant Men banquets respectively.

United Presbyterians meeting in Columbus, Ohio, in May
1965, heard a Catholic bishop from their platform for the first
time. The Most Rev. John J. Carberry, new bishop of Columbus,
who had addressed Protestants previously as bishop of Lafayette,
Indiana, did his job with zest. (In May, 1966, Richard Cardinal
Cushing also greeted the Presbyterian General Assembly meeting in Boston.) Said Bishop Carberry:

> Sentiments of profound joy and gratitude fill my heart as I
> rise this morning, at your gracious invitation, to express to
> you my prayerful good wishes, as well as those of the priests,
> religious and laity of the diocese of Columbus and I join with
> you in your prayer that the blessings of God will be abund-
> antly bestowed upon your deliberations during these mean-
> ingful days of your assembly.
>
> When Pope John XXIII in January of 1959 called for a
> council, little did many of us ever realize what its results
> would be. For me, Vatican Council II has been a deep
> spiritual experience. For our church, it has been a profound
> renewal in many areas, but especially in the field of ecu-
> menism. One of my greatest joys at the Council was the
> realization of the presence of the Protestant and Orthodox
> observers. Daily they joined with us in a spirit of prayer
> and hope.
>
> The Decree on Ecumenism published officially on November
> 21, 1964, will take years for implementation, but little by
> little it is manifesting itself throughout the Christian world.
> It is a realization of Pope John's hope that the prayer of our

Savior at the last Supper may be fulfilled: "Holy Father, keep them in thine name whom thou has given to me that they may be one, as we also are one" (John 17: 11).

We Catholics indeed may be late-comers in the field of ecumenism, but we now come with the joy of ones touched by the spirit of grace, happy to arrive and we regret our delay. Deep gaps of doctrinal differences may stand between Christians, but we need not be discouraged, for there are high grounds of common belief and mutual accord which open ways of deeper understanding, respect and cooperation.

52. Roman Catholic Bishop Leo F. Dworschak, of Fargo, North Dakota, spoke to YMCA executives from six states meeting in Fargo. He said:

So many of the tensions and the points of friction in the past were and still are on the local level. If we had made an honest effort to understand our neighbor's point of view so many of those difficulties could have been avoided. We must approach our brethren . . . in a spirit of repentance. We repent of a fault of which we have been guilty up to now— the fault of a luke-warm, spineless charity whereby we serenely accepted the separation of the churches and did nothing about it. It is our lack of true charity in Christ now that is making the separation continuous.

53. The Most Rev. Alexander Carter, of Sault Ste. Marie, Ontario, Canada, told his friends at the Trinity United Church Club in North Bay, Ontario, the "space ship" toward unity was launched, but realism should govern any immediate hopes for attaining it:

We have more in common than we have separating us. It is so much easier to fear, hate, suspect or despise a person when you've never met him. . . . It will be a long, long road, but we are embarked on that road, gentlemen. It will require patience, honesty, prayer, hope and charity, but the space ship is launched.

54. The Most Rev. Ernest J. Primeau, bishop of Manchester, New Hampshire, spoke to the annual convention of the Protestant Episcopal Diocese of New Hampshire, and there followed this resolution by the Episcopalians:

> This convention expresses gratitude to God for the growth in understanding and Christian concern among the separated Christian bodies marked by the presence of the Most Rev. Ernest J. Primeau, Bishop of the Roman Catholic Diocese of Manchester, and further resolves this convention comment to the congregations of our diocese the forms of action which will continue to foster this spirit in our state:
>
> (1) Through our prayers for continued health and strength of Pope John XXIII, as he seeks to bring to completion the work of the Vatican Council.
>
> (2) Through our efforts in each community to work with the clergy and people of the Roman Catholic Church on matters of social justice and community welfare.
>
> (3) Through initiating wherever possible conversations about our common Christian faith and witness among lay people and clergy of various Christian congregations in each locality.

55. Catholic leaders of religious orders also spoke to Protestants. The Rev. Father Nicholas Maestrini, United States provincial head of the PIME Fathers spoke at a dinner at St. Paul's Episcopal Cathedral, Detroit, May 17, 1964. A former missionary to Hong Kong for 20 years, Father Maestrini is also president of Maryglade College and Seminary, Memphis, Michigan, which trains future PIME priests for work among the destitute areas of the Far East and Latin America. Said Father Maestrini:

> For centuries, we Catholics have called the Protestants our "separated brothers"—and the accent was mostly on "separated." But today, we place the emphasis on "brothers." We now realize that what we have in common as Christians is far more important, much more significant than what

separates us. We have in common: our Faith in Christ, our sacrament of Baptism, our Bible, our membership (through grace) in the Mystical Body of Christ. . . .

Since I have dedicated my life to missionary work, I have a very particular interest in the ecumenical movement. I know from experience that the very limited success of both our Catholic and Protestant missionary efforts during the last three centuries is due largely to the fact that we have presented to the non-Christian world the sad spectacle of a separated Christianity. There is hardly any hope for us to win the non-Christian masses of the world to Christianity . . . and incidentally, they comprise about two-thirds of the world population . . . unless we present a *united* Christian front . . .unless we set them an example of true Christian love and brotherhood.

Recently, I heard Mr. Douglas Hyde, the well-known British communist who converted to the Catholic Faith, recall an enlightening and meaningful episode. He was traveling through a certain country in South East Asia and his native guide pointed out to him that, according to the peculiar customs of the tribe they were visiting, each village of tribesmen lived at the end of a jungle path forking out of the main road. Mr. Hyde asked to visit one of the villages and chose, at random, the first path leading away from the main road. After a short distance, he found that the path divided again into two separate paths.

Surprised, he pointed out this contradiction to the guide. But the guide quickly explained: "This is really the only exception to the rule. There was only one village before. But recently, some of the people were converted to Catholicism and others to Protestantism. Soon after their conversions, they started to fight and finally decided to split the village into two. But I assure you that this is the only exception."

For centuries, our common faith in Christ has kept us at each other's throats. Now, let us greet with joy the dawning of this new era . . . let us speak together, live together and love each other as true brothers in Christ, our Lord and our Savior.

56. In turn, Protestant leaders were often speakers to Catholic groups. The Rev. Wesley C. Baker, minister of the First Presbyterian Church, San Rafael, California, speaking before the Catholic Press Association, San Francisco, October 25, 1963, raised the question of contrasting Protestant-Catholic vocabularies:

I believe that at least half, perhaps more, of the contemporary estrangement between Rome and the "separated brethren" (your term, not mine), is based on the difficulties of transmission, or communication. We receive each other's signals with certain built-in, now outmoded, emotional and traditional colorings that make the final message somewhat distorted from the original broadcast. So, before we can honestly encounter each other eyeball to eyeball, we should make honesty possible by clearing away the semantic underbrush.

To begin at the very simplest level, look at our vocabularies. Catholic life uses a whole lexicon of words, some of which are entirely unknown to the average Protestant, others familiar to us but used in strange context. "Novena," "Monstrance," "Perpetual Help," "Sodality," are samples of words you will have to define, everytime you use them, if we are to know you. Others like "benediction," "congregation," are dear to our hearts, but having quite different meanings; here we'd *both* do well to define. (A benediction is a spoken sentence of blessing, usually quoted directly from Scripture, given at the close of every worship service; a congregation is the assembled group of lay worshipers.) It is quite possible that, thus defined, we might build a more common vocabulary; already many words alien to the Reformation are creeping back into Protestant usage. "Parish," a non-Protestant word, is one of these; most of us use it all the time. In passing, I must take note of a very important word in my particular tradition: "presbytery." To us it is both dio-

cese and bishop, the governing body of episcopal power; to
you it is a room by the altar! How different can you get?

57. Albert C. Outler, delegate-observer to several sessions of
the Second Vatican Council and professor at Perkins School of
Theology at Southern Methodist University, Dallas, Texas,
spurred Catholic laymen on in their responsibilities in a speech
to the 1965 convention of the National Council of Catholic Men,
meeting in Dallas:

> It would seem to me, therefore, that as Catholic laymen, you
> are now committed to a major mutation in your conven-
> tional role, as defined by your familiar traditions of the last
> two hundred years—although I would remind you that it is
> less an innovation than it is a return to an older, more cath-
> olic "catholicism." You are involved in a transition from an
> image sketched in the bromide about "believe, pray, pay and
> obey" to a complex program of cooperation and consulta-
> tion in the life of the church—to the end that the church in
> the world (the laity) may be truly effective. No part of this
> transition will be simple, automatic, perfectly harmonious.

58. Said Methodist Fred Pierce Corson, of the Philadelphia
area, before St. Peter's College, Jersey City, after receiving the
college's Petrean medal:

> Let us remember that the things that divide us are the things
> men have created and the things that unite us are the things
> that have been ordained since the beginning of time.

59. One of the frankest talks before a Catholic audience by a
Protestant was given by the Rev. Dr. Eugene L. Smith, of New
York, at that time general secretary of the Division of World
Missions of the Methodist Board of Missions, and now executive
secretary of the United States office of the WCC. He spoke at the
annual meeting of the Mission-Sending Societies of the National
Catholic Welfare Conference, Washington, D. C., September 24,
1963. He criticized institutionalism and the reluctance of humanity to face the problem of the increasing population explosion:

Mankind is always just one generation away from the eclipse of the Christian faith. This danger is the more acute because the form of godliness so often outlasts its content. Institutions easily survive the death of the spiritual awareness which brought them into being. Baptism by water without baptism by the Spirit is preparation for apostasy, which is more dangerous than paganism. Every generation has to be evangelized anew. The task is timeless. The time is now.

As every age differs from any other, so every time has its own special reasons for urgency in the Christian mission. Our distinctive urgency is the fact that we live in that century which more than any other is marked by social earthquakes. Geological earthquakes occur where "faults" exist in the rock structure. A geological fault is a line where the continuity of the rock is broken. . . . The most alarming phenomena of our age, is the population explosion. It has taken all the vast stretches of time for the world's population to reach three billion. . . .

60. Newspapers helped the getting acquainted process by encouraging the bringing together of Catholics and Protestants in many forms. Starved in the past for any signs of interfaith cooperation to report, newspapers and magazines played up church cooperation. Pope John appeared on the cover of one national news magazine three times. The faces of ecumenical-minded Protestants, such as WCC general secretary Willem Visser 't Hooft and his successor, Presbyterian Eugene Carson Blake also appeared on covers. Pope Paul's meeting with Patriarch Athenagoras ranked in polls for the top ten stories of 1964. Newspapers in an area serving largely one faith began to be interested in the minority. For instance, in Dallas, according to a Catholic diocesan newspaper columnist:

In this great rich sprawling city [Dallas], which is now rising into its second million of population, the Baptists, though only about a sixth of the population, have the major influence. You can see that, for example, by the size of their book stores. Billy Graham is a member of the First Baptist Church. The Baptists' wealth is tremendous, and they are growing. The first building you are apt to see when a community goes up in Northern Texas—and they are mushrooming every day—is a Baptist church.

Second comes the Methodists, then the Presbyterians, and then the Christian Church. All these four leading denominations set the pace for other members of their groups in the United States.

This strong Protestantism, however, did not manifest itself in any coolness to the Church while the CCD [Confraternity of Christian Doctrine] congress was in progress. The arrival of Cardinal Cicognani, the Papal Secretary of State, the Cardinal's response to his welcome, the Mass he celebrated, the procession into Sacred Heart Cathedral received front page publicity.

61. The Catholic bishop of Lausanne, Geneva, and Fribourg—the territory of the World Council headquarters—took it upon himself to bid for better understanding among the faiths through patience and prayer. The Most Rev. Francis Charrière said:

With our separated brethren, we wish to present the Lord with a common supplication, because the grace of baptism has already accorded us a true unity in Jesus Christ.

Together, let us promise Him to put away from our minds and hearts all that oppose His intention to lead us to share the same Eucharistic Bread.

We present ourselves before the Lord such as we are, at once united and separated. Unity permits us to pray together for our mutual sanctification. Separation obliges us to desire that our brethren should see in the Christian message what we ourselves discover there. The source of this suffering resides precisely in this co-existence of unity and division.

Situated on a level of deep faith, common intercession cannot become a cause of confusion, for at one and the same time there increases the joy of saying "Our Father" together and the sadness that we still cannot meet entirely.

It is very certain that the reconciliation which we must ask of God and prepare by our efforts for mutual understanding will come about at the time God so wishes, not by the triumph of one over another, in the temporal manner, nor by abandonment of truth, but by an authentic charity. Let us therefore be fervent in our patience.

62. Iron-Curtain clergymen sought dialogue in various degrees of enthusiasm.

a. In Poland, Witold Benedyktowicz wrote in the Polish (Protestant) *Ecumenical Review:*

We can welcome with deep satisfaction the ecumenical strivings of the Roman-Catholic Church. There have been some changes in the mutual relations of various denominations at least, at certain levels of the hierarchy. It would be much better if some ecumenic moves on the part of the Roman-Catholics had a less tactical character, and were accompanied by an entirely changed attitude towards the "dissident brothers" among the widest masses of the Roman-Catholic community. Unfortunately, it is not so, at least not in our country.

Christian unity is certainly of such significance, that the development and progress of this idea wherever it may occur, could be sincerely welcomed. Therefore, the adherents of ecumenicity do not regret if their idea is spread elsewhere, as it is the case within the Roman-Catholic Church. On the contrary, it will be for them a source of joy and confirmation how great and vital is the ecumenic idea. The adoption and assumption of the ecumenic idea can be considered a plagiarism, but a noble one, enhanced by its very essence.

b. In Hungary, Lutheran Bishop Zoltan Kaldy encouraged the proliferation and multiple nature of dialogue:

While the dialogue of the World Council of Churches with Rome goes on, the world confessional organizations, too, may join in the discussion and—even beyond that—the Churches living in various countries might participate.

We welcome this multilateral nature of the dialogue, for it seems to us that this is the way to insure the independence of the individual Churches, their freedom of decision and criticism, and also to give due consideration to the special viewpoints implicit in their peculiar situations.

For example, the Hungarian Lutheran Church has certain experiences bearing on the "Roman Catholic question"—and these experiences are accumulating even now!—and the ignorance of these would impair the dialogue of the Lutheran World Federation with Rome.

Dialogue between Roman Catholics and other Christians affords a good opportunity to get to know one another more deeply and truly . . . to get rid of the habit of repeating, in monologue fashion, one's own truths and asserting one's own righteousness, and also to learn from one another.

If conducted in the right way, [inter-church dialogue] might indirectly help to bring about a better understanding among the peoples of the world. . . .

Certain Western editors . . . brand some of the views we have expressed on various issues as "attacks," sometimes against the Lutheran World Federation, other times against the World Council of Churches, or against the cause of unity.

Without the intention of attacking anybody or anything, in the course of the dialogue we shall always tell our opinion about the emerging problems; and by doing so, we shall be acting in the interests not of a unity with ulterior motives or of a false unity, but of true unity.

c. In Cuba, Presbyterian leaders in Havana called upon other Cuban churches to engage in conversations to overcome "the sin of our disunity." A statement adopted by the Cuban Presbyterians in 1965 said:

> We are most willing to begin a dialogue which will lead us all to share together in the dynamic life of the Spirit for the sake of the evangelistic action of His church.
>
> The action of the Holy Spirit through this church tells us that no confessional body should exist unless it be for the sake of unity; not merely that unity which the followers of Jesus Christ, in all our various confessions, have already attained, but the visible and effective unity of the mission of one Church of Jesus Christ to the people of Cuba. . . .
>
> We are the fractured church. This state of divisions is sinful, as it obscures the concept of unity and catholicity; it is in effect a denial of our reconciliation one with another. The fact that until today we have been thus able to live with our sin does not mean that we should fortify our scandalous position of division.
>
> We therefore believe that the hour of ecumenical calling of the Church of Jesus Christ in Cuba has come and that it should be expressed in tangible missionary unity.

63. Donald Attwater, of Penzance, England, Catholic author of several books on Eastern Orthodoxy and former contributing editor of *Commonweal* and *Orate Frates,* went so far as to suggest a topsy-turvy dialogue where one group honors the other's saints. He made his proposal in Truro, Cornwall, in January 1965:

> Every country has its own particular problems when it looks at the shocking and disastrous spectacle of Christian disunity. In our own land, 400 years of history have left a heritage of prejudice, fixed ideas and proper loyalties. May I give you an example of the last? Each side, the Reformed and the Catholic, has had its martyrs, and each side is understandably fearful of compromising their memory. Certainly the communion of saints cannot just be shrugged off when the thought of it is found to be inconvenient. But it

can be widened in conception. I venture to suggest it would
be a good thing were Catholics more often to remember the
Reformed martyrs for conscience—the fires of Smithfield;
and were the Reformed to remember the Catholic martyrs
for conscience—the gallows of Tyburn. Surely those French
Catholics who every year make a pilgrimage of reparation
on St. Bartholomew's Eve have got the root of the matter
in them.

A present danger is that many of us are in far too much of
a hurry. There is too much casual talk about "reunion" as
though reconciliations on a large scale were just around
the corner. Only God can bring them about.

64. Too much dialogue, particularly of a bland nature, overlooking the difficult past that Attwater suggests be recalled, can
bring about a numbing experience for the church, rather than
the *aggiornamento* so eagerly talked about.

The Rt. Rev. Stephen Bayne, of Olympia, later to become executive officer of the Anglican Communion (now head of the
Overseas Department of the Protestant Episcopal Church), once
gave vent to his boredom with the parlor variety of ecumenism—
what there was of it. (*The Living Church,* October 2, 1955, p.
14). "Episcopalians give up smoking for an evening," he said,
"the Presbyterians host puts on a clerical collar, the Baptists
consent to read some mimeographed prayers, we accept a budget,
we adopt a resolution against comic books and lo! we have an
ecumenical encounter."

Ten years later, the *Christian Century* was grumbling, and
suggested a way to liven up dialogue:

At times we weary of the overly irenic, super-smooth, oily
ecumenical talk which the gingerly people use to describe
Vatican Council affairs. At such times we like to reintro-
duce a bit of realism into our language. For such realism
there are few better sources than the Nativist era in the
United States a century ago. It was not a lovely era, to be
sure. Men hated their brothers. Convents were burned. The
Irish huddled in ghettos. Protestants in their turn were mis-

trusted. People were killed. Men lived lies in the American
Protective Association, the Nativist movement, the Ku Klux
Klan and the Know-Nothing Party. With the gradual demise
of these forces the language which vivified them began also
to disappear.

You do not need to be an H. L. Mencken or a Bergen Evans
to see what happens to the language when no new salt or
leaven is added. It turns out bland, flat, tasteless. As we
have just remarked, irenic ecumenical talk reflects this
blandness. Pope John, Alexander Schmemann, Albert Outler, Abraham Joshua Heschel—to take top-of-the-mind examples out of hundreds of possibilities—impoverish the language by their failure to think up new epithets or expletives
in reporting on interchurch affairs. Just for fun we thought
we would present a contrast: as a service to readers who
like salty, pithy, epithetical words we shall provide a sample
of the kind of language they used to use in the good old days
—just to show how far we have fallen. Then Roman Catholics
and their leaders were described in language like this—and
we quote phrases exactly: totalitarian rule; the same old
feudal operation; the same old dictator; firm 16th century
mentality, but more tyrannical; his bachelor theologians at
Rome; his hackers (the bishops); his Italian cronies; the
man in the saddle at the Vatican; his perquisites and pro-
motions (used to explain the only reason why anyone anywhere is a Catholic bishop and does not join Luther's
Reformation); these machinations; out of obsequious defer-
ence to a medieval theology of the kind which damned
Galileo; the Roman Church attempts everywhere to fence
off its people from the world about them. . . .

65. The hotter the dialogue, some believe, the better the ecumenism. Noted the Rev. David G. Borden, from Malva, Western
Samoa, in the South Pacific:

One of the important side-effects of the Ecumenical Movement has been the re-discovery of denominational convictions through the turmoil of inter-denominational dia-

logue. Argue with an Anglican and you will appreciate his
position better but you may also believe more ardently in
your own! Now that the Ecumenical Movement has entered
the phase of serious encounter between the Protestant tradition and the Roman Catholic Church, we can expect not only
the beginnings of honest confrontation of one conviction by
another, but also a return by many on both sides to hostile
dogmatic positions, which will bring to mind again the basic
issues of the Reformation. If the Protestant-Roman Catholic dialogue produces a theological crisis for the church,
a wider concern for sound theology and right doctrine, then
its benefits will be immeasurable.

66. Greater sincerity is needed in dialogue, said the Very Rev.
(later elected an Episcopal bishop) James A. Pike of the Cathedral of St. John the Divine in May 1956. He told an interfaith
audience, meeting in connection with the General Assembly of
the Presbyterian Church in the USA, that determination to
hold fast in one's beliefs is necessary in the quest for unity:

> The difficulty is that most of the efforts have been at the
> top level.
>
> Real unity can come only as the rank and file come to take
> a positive view of the special emphases of the various tradi-
> tions, and come to yearn for a unity that is not a lowest
> common denominator but an adding together of all the spe-
> cial insights which the various traditions of Christianity
> have espoused.
>
> Special insights which added together might make up a
> united Christendom are:
>
> The sovereignty of God as emphasized in the Presbyterian-Re-
>     formed tradition.
> The special Lutheran stress on justification by grace through faith.
> Local responsibility as exemplified in Congregationalism.
> Baptist emphasis on separation of Church and State.
> The continuity of the church and the presence, "here and now" of
>     the "communion of saints" in Episcopalianism.
> The Methodist stress on sanctification.

> The "discipline and loyalty" of Roman Catholics.
> The "mystery and awe" of the Eastern Orthodox.
> The "quiet waiting on the Holy Spirit" of Quakers.
>
> We need all these things . . . to grasp them and to appreciate each other we need more inter-relationships on the local level. But, at the same time, it is important that each group hold fast to the emphases which have made it great, not only for its own service, but for its contribution to the coming great church.
>
> We would all be the poorer if any group gives up any of its great insights. The ecumenical effort should bear as its motto the promise of St. Paul, "All things are yours."

67. To Samuel H. Miller, dean of the Harvard Divinity School, getting acquainted should not be just a pleasant experience, but painful, a form of "cross-bearing." He said in an article in *Thought:*

> The ecumenical spirit will have painful responsibilities as well as pleasurable satisfactions. As Christians, we need to be realistic lest we assume too easily that the victory is already ours, when in truth the trumpet call has just been sounded.
>
> It is for such reasons that we must face the reality of what can only be called "the ecumenical cross." If we are faithful to the leading which we see in this new age, we shall know sacrifice and suffering. . . . The cross is not imposed; it is implicit in the situation. . . .
>
> The first (cross) is that we must recover the glad news of God's activity in the world in such a way as to provide all Christians with an exuberant joy and an ineffable peace. We are not doing so at present. The wine skins of the ancient gospel have hardened, the forms in which the gaiety of faith was first communicated have become dull and rigid. The shout of great rejoicing and spontaneity has turned to the yawn of boredom. . . .

There is a second cross to be borne if we are to be responsible as Christians in this ecumenical age. . . . We must learn to speak to a world radically displaced from the cultural traditions of the past, both biblical and classical. . . . We are woefully behind on our homework. Freud and Marx, science and industry, automation and urbanization, atomic energy and space travel stand peering in the windows of our sanctuaries while we act as if they are not there. . . .

Third . . . we must find new resources of compassion. As Christians, our faces have been red with shame ever since Albert Camus administered his well-deserved rebuke of what I can only call our collectivized compassion. For multitudes, compassion is safely vested in the corporate structure of the church, to be handled by the usual machinery of clergy and missionaries. . . .

These, then, are three of the costly responsibilities of the ecumenical age into which Pope John so magnificently and so modestly introduced us, and which Pope Paul now labors to advance and maintain. We shall need to penetrate to a new level of the gospel to sustain the heavy strain of bringing together in meaningful relationship the two estranged traditions of our faith. . . .

There is a fourth responsibility, the heaviest of them all. It is not complicated or abstruse, hard to understand or difficult to imagine. It is ourselves. In a sense this is our hardest cross, our deepest embarrassment, our most aggravating frustration. If the ecumenical gambit fails, it will not be for want of councils, theologians, high ideals, or noble purposes—it will be because you and I will have failed to match the greatness of our day with souls of such stature that the new dream will flow through our deeds and be fashioned in our action.

REFERENCES

*Chapter II*

33. From a 1963 brochure of Foyer Unitas, Rome, S. Maria dell'Anima 30, p. 32.
34. Letter from Sister Alice, Convent of St. Helena, Newburgh, N. Y., Mar. 30, 1965.
35. Sister Mary Luke, "The Council, Ecumenism and Sisters," speech before the American hierarchy and Council observers in Rome, Nov. 4, 1964; text provided by Sister Mary Luke.
36. a. Laurel Elizabeth Keyes, "mother" of the Fransisters, in a pamphlet, *The Fransister Movement* (Denver: Gentle Living Publications, n.d.), pp. 3, 7, 10.
    b. *Ibid.*, p. 4.
37. Letter from the Rev. Konrad Kelley, Jr., rector, St. James' Episcopal Church, Mesilla Park, N.M., Apr. 23, 1965.
38. a. National Catholic Welfare Conference news release, Nov. 3, 1960.
    b. Associated Press, Rome, March 24, 1966.
39. a. *Lutheran World*, IX, No. 4, 332.
    b. *Ibid.*, pp. 332-333.
    c. *Ibid.*, pp. 333-334.
40. Report of the Executive Committee of the World Council of Churches to the WCC Central Committee, in Paris, in *The Ecumenical Review*, XV, No. 1 (Oct., 1962), 71.
41. "Table-Talk With the Russian Observers," as told to Eva-Maria Jung, *The Catholic World*, CXCVI, No. 1, 175, 276-278.
42. From a communique of the Italian News Agency (ANSA), quoted in *The Catholic World*, Feb., 1964, pp. 295-6.
43. "Messaggio del Papa Paolo VI," in *Oriente Cristiano*, anno 4; 4, Oct.-Dec., 1964, p. 13.
44. Eugene Levin, "Pope Makes Historical Gesture," *Associated Press*, in The Miami Herald, Mar. 28, 1964, p. 12-A.
45. National Catholic Welfare Conference translation in *The Pope Speaks*, IX, No. 3, 283.
46. a. World Council of Churches news release, New York office, Nb/14-65. Feb. 18, 1965, p. 2.
    b. "Cardinal Bea and Pastor Boegner Meet at the World Council," The Ecumenical Review, XVII, No. 2 (Apr., 1965), 127-130.
    c. *Ibid.*, pp. 130-134.
47. "What Protestants Think About Catholic Intentions," *Christian Herald*, LXXXVIII, No. 12 (Dec., 1965), 10, 11.
48. a.
    b. —correspondence provided by the St. Andrew's United Church, Moose Jaw, Saskatchewan, Canada.
49. Oscar Cullmann, *Message to Catholics and Protestants* (Grand Rapids: William B. Eerdmans, 1959), tr. by Joseph A. Burgess, pp. 33-42. Used by permission.
50. a. William K. McElvaney, "Ecumenism in Mesquite," *Christian Advocate*, Jan. 14, 1965, p. 11.
    b. John A. O'Brien, "An Open House for Unity," *U.S. Catholic*, Vol. XXIV, No. 8 (Dec., 1963). Used with permission of the author.
51. A speech by the Most Rev. John J. Carberry, Roman Catholic bishop of Columbus, O., May 21, 1965 at a morning session of the 177th General Assembly of the United Presbyterians. Text provided by Bishop Carberry.

52. *The Christian Century*, June 10, 1964, p. 778. Reprinted by permission.
53. *Religious News Service*, Apr. 2, 1963.
54. *Ibid.*, May 14, 1963.
55. The Very Rev. Nicholas Maestrini, PIME, at a dinner at St. Paul's Episcopal Cathedral, Detroit, May 17, 1964. Text provided by Father Maestrini.
56. Rev. Wesley C. Baker, minister, First Presbyterian Church, San Rafael, Calif., before the Catholic Press Association, San Francisco, Oct. 25, 1963. Text provided by Mr. Baker.
57. Dr. Albert C. Outler before the 1965 convention of the National Council of Catholic Men, in Dallas, Text provided by the NCCM.
58. *The Christian Century*, June 2, 1965, p. 718. Reprinted by permission.
59. Dr. Eugene L. Smith, before the Mission-Sending Societies, the National Catholic Welfare Conference, Washington, D. C., Sept. 24, 1963. Text provided by Dr. Smith.
60. Paul H. Hallett, Assoc. Ed., *The Register*, Denver Catholic Weekly, in a column, "Keeping Up With Events," Dec. 10, 1961.
61. *Religious News Service*, John Myers, Geneva, Jan. 11, 1962.
62. a. Witold Benedyktowicz, "Roman-Catholic Ecumenical Movement—a Noble Plagiarism," in the *Polish Ecumenical Review*, Warsaw, No. 2, Apr., May, June, 1964, p. 6.
    b. Lutheran World Federation release, Budapest, Aug 8, 1965, courtesy the National Lutheran Council.
    c. Ecumenical Press Service, Geneva, dateline Havana, No. 27, July 29, 1965, p. 6.
63. Donald Attwater, in a speech at a public interfaith meeting at Truro, Cornwall. Text provided by Mr. Attwater.
64. Pen-ultimate Column, *The Christian Century*, Mar. 3, 1965, p. 287. (In an aside, the writer of "Pen-ultimate" confesses this shocking language is not really forgotten, that its words in fact came from the Jan. 1965 issue of *Church and State* of the Protestants and other Americans United for Separation of Church and State.) Reprinted by permission.
65. A review of H. M. Carson's *Roman Catholicism Today* (London: Inter-Varsity Fellowship) in *The Pacific Journal of Theology*, No. 13, no vol., Dec., 1964, by the Rev. David G. Borden, Malva, Western Samoa, South Pacific, p. 19.
66. *Religious News Service*, May 28, 1956.
67. Samuel H. Miller, "The Ecumenical Cross," *Thought*, XL, No. 156 (Spring, 1965), 8-11.

# three

# Basic Guidelines

The policies of the churches had not kept up with the enthusiasm for dialogue and church unity. The movement of the times, including the spirit of Pope John, was for fresh air and charity in relations with others. Pope John had warned of the "prophets of gloom" in his opening speech to the Second Vatican Council. He was commonly thought of as referring to the Supreme Congregation of the Holy Office (now called the Congregation for the Doctrine of the Faith) and its pessimistic outlook on things (for example, its *monitum* reprimanding biblical scholars in 1961 and its warning a year later against the late Pierre Teilhard de Chardin's writings as dangerous, "especially for the young"). The guideline on inter-Christian relations when John XXIII took office was the "Instruction to Local Ordinaries on the Ecumenical Movement" issued December 20, 1949, signed by no one less than Alfredo Cardinal Ottaviani, the much publicized "conservative," now cardinal secretary but then assessor of the Holy Office, and by the cardinal secretary of the Holy Office, Francis Cardinal Marchetti-Selvaggiani. That document, although it permitted some leeway in ecumenical relations (for example, recitation of some prayers approved by the church at conferences, such as the Lord's Prayer), was nevertheless largely negative; for example, "There is absolutely no *communicatio in sacris* [worship in common and more specifically, participation in regular worship]," discussions are duly "controlled," and "at the end

101

of each year, a report is sent to this Supreme congregation." The
decade 1956-66 saw first the change in the spirit of the law, then
enabling action for updating the law.

68. The important development in Catholic thinking concerning inter-Christian relations came with the approval of the Decree on Ecumenism by 2,054 to 64 prelates of the Second Vatican
Council, November 21, 1964. Promulgated by Pope Paul VI in
the same closing ceremony of the third session of the Council,
the move puts the 550-million Roman Catholics of the world into
the mainstream of the ecumenical movement.

The Decree is divided into an Introduction and three chapters.
The Introduction states that Christ founded only one Church
and division is a scandal. It recognizes, too, that God is inspiring
divided Christians to seek unity and that the unity movement
among non-Roman Catholics is encouraged by the Holy Spirit.
Chapter One deals with general principles for inter-Christian
relations. Originally entitled "Principles of Catholic Ecumenism," it was changed before the final vote to "Catholic Principles
on Ecumenism," recognizing that all Christians are included in
the ecumenical movement and the goal for all is the same. The
principles point out that the main role of Catholics in ecumenism
is renewal of their own faith and that there are valid elements
outside the Roman Catholic Church, although the other churches
(and significantly enough, they are called "churches" here in
this decree) do not have the "fulness" of the means of salvation.

Major excerpts from Chapter II, "The Practice of Ecumenism,"
and Chapter III, "Churches and Ecclesial Communities Separated From the Roman Apostolic See":

> Chapter II: (8.) . . . In certain special circumstances, such
> as in prayer services "for unity" and during ecumenical
> gatherings, it is allowable, indeed desirable that Catholics
> should join in prayer with their separated brethren. Such
> prayers in common are certainly a very effective means of
> petitioning for the grace of unity, and they are a genuine
> expression of the ties which still bind Catholics to their
> separated brethren. "For where two or three are gathered
> together in my name, there am I in the midst of them"
> (Matt. 18: 20).

Yet worship in common (*communicatio in sacris*) is not to be considered as a means to be used indiscriminately for the restoration of unity among Christians. There are two main principles upon which the practice of such common worship depends: first, that of the unity of the Church which ought to be expressed; and second, that of the sharing in means of grace. The expression of unity very generally forbids common worship. Grace to be obtained sometimes commends it. The concrete course to be adopted, when due regard has been given to all the circumstances of time, place and persons, is left to the prudent decision of the local episcopal authority, unless the Bishops' conference according to its own statutes, or the Holy See, has determined otherwise.

(9.) We must get to know the outlook of our separated brethren. Study is absolutely required for this, and it should be pursued in fidelity to truth and with a spirit of good will. . . .

(11.) The manner and order in which Catholic belief is expressed should in no way become an obstacle to dialogue with our brethren. It is, of course, essential that the doctrine be clearly presented in its entirety. Nothing is so foreign to the spirit of ecumenism as a false irenicism which harms the purity of Catholic doctrine and obscures its assured genuine meaning.

At the same time, Catholic belief must be explained more profoundly and precisely, in such a way and in such terms that our separated brethren can also really understand it.

Furthermore, in ecumenical dialogue, Catholic theologians, standing fast by the teaching of the Church yet searching together with separated brethren into the divine mysteries, should do so with love for the truth, with charity, and with humility. When comparing doctrines with one another, they should remember that in Catholic doctrine there exists an order or "hierarchy" of truths, since they vary in their relation to the foundation of the Christian faith. Thus the way will be opened whereby this kind of "fraternal rivalry" will incite all to a deeper realization and a clearer expression of the unfathomable riches of Christ (cf. Eph. 3: 8).

(12.) Before the whole world let all Christians confess their faith in God, one and three, in the incarnate Son of God, our Redeemer and Lord. United in their efforts, and with mutual respect, let them bear witness to our common hope which does not play us false. Since co-operation in social matters is so widespread today, all men without exception are called to work together; with much greater reason are all those who believe in God, but most of all, all Christians in that they bear the seal of Christ's name. Co-operation among Christians vividly expresses that bond which already unites them, and it sets in clearer relief the features of Christ the Servant. Such co-operation, which has already begun in many countries, should be developed more and more, particularly in regions where a social and technical evolution is taking place. It should contribute to a just appreciation of the dignity of the human person, to the promotion of the blessings of peace, the application of gospel principles to social life, and the advancement of the arts and sciences in a truly Christian spirit. It should also be intensified in the use of every possible means to relieve the afflictions of our times, such as famine and natural disasters, illiteracy and poverty, lack of housing, and the unequal distribution of wealth. Through such co-operation, all believers in Christ are able to learn easily how they can understand each other better and esteem each other more, and how the road to the unity of Christians may be made smooth.

Chapter III, Part I (The Special Position of the Eastern Churches): (15.) Everyone knows with what love the Eastern Christians celebrate the Sacred Liturgy, especially the Eucharistic mystery, source of the Church's life and pledge of future glory. In this mystery the faithful, united with their bishop, have access to God the Father through the Son, the Word made flesh who suffered and was glorified, in the out-pouring of the Holy Spirit. And so, made "sharers of the divine nature" (2 Pet. 1: 4), they enter into com-

munion with the most holy Trinity. Hence, through the celebration of the Eucharist of the Lord in each of these
Churches, the Church of God is built up and grows in stature, and through concelebration their communion with one
another is made manifest.

In this liturgical worship, the Christians of the East pay
high tribute, in beautiful hymns of praise, to Mary ever
Virgin, whom the ecumenical Synod of Ephesus solemnly
proclaimed to be the holy Mother of God in order that Christ
might be truly and properly acknowledged as Son of God
and Son of Man, according to the Scriptures. They also give
homage to the saints, among them Fathers of the universal
Church.

These Churches, although separated from us, yet possess
true sacraments, above all—by apostolic succession—the
priesthood and the Eucharist, whereby they are still joined
to us in closest intimacy. Therefore some worship in common (*communicatio in sacris*), given suitable circumstances
and the approval of church authority, is not merely possible
but is encouraged. . . .

Part II (The Separated Churches and Ecclesial Communities in the West) : (19.) The Churches and ecclesial Communities which were separated from the Apostolic See of
Rome during the grave crisis that began in the West at the
end of the Middle Ages, or in later times, are bound to the
Catholic Church by a specially close relationship as a result
of the long span of earlier centuries which the Christian
people had lived in ecclesiastical communion. . . .

At the same time, however, one should recognize that between these Churches and ecclesial Communities on the one
hand, and the Catholic Church on the other, there are very
weighty differences not only of a historical, sociological,
psychological and cultural character, but especially in the
interpretation of revealed truth. To facilitate entering into
the ecumenical dialogue in spite of those differences, we

wish to set down in what follows some considerations which can, and indeed should, serve as a basis and encouragement for such dialogue.

(20.) Our thoughts are concerned first of all with those Christians who openly confess Jesus Christ as God and Lord and as the only mediator between God and man for the glory of the one God, the Father, the Son and the Holy Spirit. We are indeed aware that there exist considerable differences from the doctrine of the Catholic Church even concerning Christ the Word of God made flesh and the work of redemption, and thus concerning the mystery and ministry of the Church and the role of Mary in the work of salvation. But we rejoice that our separated brethren look to Christ as the source and center of ecclesiastical communion. Their longing for union with Christ impels them ever more to seek unity, and also to bear witness to their faith among the peoples of the earth.

(21.) A love and reverence—almost a cult—of Holy Scripture leads our brethren to a constant and diligent study of the sacred text. For the gospel "is the power of God for salvation to everyone who has faith, to the Jew first and then to the Greek" (Rom. 1: 16).

While invoking the Holy Spirit, they seek in these very Scriptures God as He speaks to them in Christ, the One whom the prophets foretold, the Word of God made flesh for us. In the Scriptures they contemplate the life of Christ, as well as the teachings and the actions of the Divine Master for the salvation of men, in particular the mysteries of His death and resurrection.

But when Christians separated from us affirm the divine authority of the Sacred Books, they think differently from us—different ones in different ways—about the relationship between the Scriptures and the Church. For in the Church, according to Catholic belief, its authentic teaching office has a special place in expounding and preaching the written Word of God.

Nevertheless, in the dialogue itself, the Sacred Word is a precious instrument in the mighty hand of God for attaining to that unity which the Saviour holds out to all men.

(22.) By the sacrament of baptism, whenever it is properly conferred in the way the Lord determined and received with the proper dispositions of soul, man becomes truly incorporated into the crucified and glorified Christ and is reborn to a sharing of the divine life, as the apostle says: "For you were buried together with Him in baptism, and in Him also rose again through faith in the working of God who raised Him from the dead" (Col. 2: 12) (cf. Rom. 6: 4).

Baptism, therefore, constitutes the sacramental bond of unity existing among all who through it are reborn. But baptism, of itself, is only a beginning, a point of departure, for it is wholly directed toward the acquiring of fullness of life in Christ. Baptism is thus ordained toward a complete profession of faith, a complete incorporation into the system of salvation such as Christ Himself willed it to be, and finally, toward a complete integration into Eucharistic communion.

Although the ecclesial Communities separated from us lack the fullness of unity with us which flows from baptism, and although we believe they have not preserved the proper reality of the Eucharistic mystery in its fullness, especially because of the absence of the sacrament of orders, nevertheless when they commemorate the Lord's death and resurrection in the Holy Supper, they profess that it signifies life in communion with Christ and await His coming in glory. For these reasons, the doctrine about the Lord's Supper, about the other sacraments, worship, and ministry in the Church, should form subjects of dialogue.

(23.) The Christian way of life of these brethren is nourished by faith in Christ. It is strengthened by the grace of baptism and the hearing of the Word of God. This way of life expresses itself in private prayer, in meditation of the

Scriptures, in the life of a Christian family, and in the worship of the community gathered together to praise God. Furthermore, their worship sometimes displays notable features of a liturgy once shared in common.

The faith by which they believe in Christ bears fruit in praise and thanksgiving for the benefits received from the hands of God. Joined to it is a lively sense of justice and a true charity towards others. This active faith has been responsible for many organizations for the relief of spiritual and material distress, the furtherance of education of youth, the improvement of social conditions of life, and the promotion of peace throughout the world.

And if in moral matters there are many Christians who do not always understand the gospel in the same way as Catholics, and do not admit the same solutions for the more difficult problems of modern society, they nevertheless want to cling to Christ's word as the source of Christian virtue and to obey the command of the apostle: "Whatever you do in word or in work, do all in the name of the Lord Jesus, giving thanks to God the Father through him" (Col. 3: 17). Hence, the ecumenical dialogue could start with the moral application of the gospel.

(24.) Now, after this brief exposition of the conditions under which ecumenical activity may be practiced, and of the principles by which it is to be guided, we confidently look to the future. This sacred Council urges the faithful to abstain from any frivolousness or impudent zeal, for these can cause harm to true progress towards unity. Their ecumenical activity cannot be other than fully and sincerely catholic, that is, loyal to the truth we have received from the apostles and the Fathers, and in harmony with the faith which the Catholic Church has always professed, and at the same time tending towards that fullness in which Our Lord wants His Body to grow in the course of time.

This sacred Council firmly hopes that the initiatives of the sons of the Catholic Church joined with those of the separated brethren will go forward, without obstructing the ways of divine Providence, and without prejudging the future inspirations of the Holy Spirit. Further, this Council declares that it realizes that this holy objective—the reconciliation of all Christians in the unity of the one and only Church of Christ—transcends human powers and gifts. It therefore places its hope entirely in the prayer of Christ for the Church, in the love of the Father for us, and in the power of the Holy Spirit. "And hope does not disappoint, because God's love has been poured forth in our hearts through the Holy Spirit who has been given to us" (Rom. 5: 5).

The entire text and all the individual elements which have been set forth in this Decree have pleased the Fathers. And by the Apostolic power conferred on Us by Christ, We, together with the Venerable Fathers, in the Holy Spirit, approve, decree and enact them; and We order that what has been thus enacted in Council be promulgated, to the glory of God. (Signed by Pope Paul and the Council fathers).

69. Confusion reigned as to how the decree, which now encouraged limited *communicatio in sacris* with the Orthodox and joint prayers (beyond the Lord's Prayer) and Bible services with Protestants, squared with Canon Law 731 and 1258 which said, respectively, no sacraments should be given non-Roman Catholics, and Catholics should not be actively involved in non-Roman Catholic services. The question remained as to whether the spirit of the new decree superseded the letter of canon law or not. (See also Chapter VI). Much was left to one's own interpretation, as Roman Catholics awaited revision of Canon Law by a commission set up by Pope John and continued by Pope Paul.

A negative document arose somewhat surreptitiously. The National Catholic Reporter told of a directive from the apostolic delegate in the United States, Archbishop Egidio Vagnozzi, which asked the United States prelates to put the brakes on ecumenical activities until a future directory was issued.

The apostolic delegate's letter, supposedly "confidential," said:

The Holy See is deeply concerned about some excesses which are taking place in religious services wherein Catholics and non-Catholics participate.

Because these excesses give rise to great wonderment, and indeed bewilderment, among the faithful, the Holy See wishes the bishops to understand that, until the conciliar commission has established specific and definitive norms regarding *communicatio in sacris*, participation in such ceremonies should be avoided.

Undue haste and lack of proper preparation in contacts with our separated brethren could jeopardize the attainment of sound ecumenical results which the council seeks to promote and could, in fact, endanger existing cordial relations with other Christian communities.

70. Within a month of the Vagnozzi incident, the United States bishops on June 15, 1965, released their interim guidelines through the Bishops' Commission for Ecumenical Affairs, as they awaited "a directory for the practice of ecumenism which will be applicable throughout the universal church":

I (*Diocesan Ecumenical Commissions*): In guiding the course of ecumenism within their own dioceses, especially in presenting guidelines for prayer and *communicatio in sacris*, it is highly recommended that local bishops establish diocesan ecumenical commissions. Among the members of these commissions it would be desirable to include priests, religious and members of the laity who, by reason of their expert knowledge, can contribute to the work of the commissions, and who are also representative of the local churches. As the involvement of Catholics in dialogue, in joint action, and in prayer with other Christians increases such commissions could be of inestimable value to the local bishops.

In drawing up directives for *communicatio in sacris* and prayer in common it is also desirable to consult with other diocesan agencies, such as the Diocesan Liturgical Commission, and with leaders of the other churches of the community. The president and executive secretary of the local Council of Churches, for example, might be consulted before issuing regulations for the diocese.

II (*Prayer in Common Between Catholics and Christians of Other Churches*):
In accordance with Section 8 of the Decree on Ecumenism the participation of Catholics with other Christians in services which are not part of the official liturgies of any communion, if these services are devoted to the cause of Christian unity, is highly desirable. Such services could fittingly be called "Ecumenical Services." Participation of Catholics in such services, whether they are held for the sake of promoting Christian unity in accordance with the Decree or, in the spirit of the Decree, for some other purpose, e.g., for peace, in time of public need, mourning, thanksgiving, etc., remains under the guidance of the local bishop.

The place chosen for the conduct of these ecumenical services should provide a worthy setting which is acceptable to all the participants and which, according to the prudent decision of the local bishop, is considered suitable.

With the approval of the local bishop priests are to be encouraged to take an active part in the conduct of services, e.g. by reading Scripture lessons, preaching homilies, offering prayers and giving blessings.

The vesture to be worn at such services is also to be determined by the local bishop. In some circumstances ordinary civil attire may be the only appropriate form of dress for the participating priest. In other circumstances, since it is in accordance with Catholic usage even in the conduct of nonliturgical services, the use of the cassock and surplice may be considered. Another form of dress which is neither liturgical nor merely civil, namely, the use of the ferraiuolo, may be desirable on certain occasions. The value of some kind of "sacred" vesture is not to be underestimated in creating the right atmosphere for prayer in common. In reaching decisions concerning ecclesiastical vesture on these occasions it is highly recommended that there be consultation with the clergy of the other church bodies which are to participate in such services.

On occasion members of the Catholic laity may also be invited to take an active part in Ecumenical Services. They may, for example, be called upon to read the Scripture lessons.

Under the guidance of the local bishop, who may well wish to consult his ecumenical commission regarding the qualifications of the laity invited to take these leading roles, such participation on the part of laymen has much to recommend it. The acceptance of such a policy could become one more manifestation of the Church's doctrine on the laity as found in the Constitution on the Church.

In preparing for and conducting these Ecumenical Services the principle of "reciprocity" should be kept in mind: to accept an invitation may often seem to entail an obligation to extend a similar invitation and to proffer an invitation may imply a readiness to receive one; one should not, therefore, accept an invitation if, according to Catholic norms, one cannot proffer a similar invitation.

All such joint services of prayer should be carefully prepared in accordance with the principle of "collaboration." The leaders of the participating groups should, after careful consideration, agree on the format of the services and on the choice of themes, Scripture reading and hymns. Prayers and hymns and homilies which may be unacceptable either to Catholics or to other Christians are to be avoided.

These ecumenical services, it is hoped, will complement the programs of prayer for unity which continue in our churches.

III (*Communicatio in Sacris*—Principles governing *communicatio in sacris*) :

(1) *Participation of Christians of Other Churches in the Liturgy of the Catholic Church.*

Christians of other communions should be made welcome in attending Catholic liturgical celebrations. It is recommended, however, that great care be taken in issuing general invitations. The sensibilities of other ecclesial communities on proselytizing should also be respected in extending such invitations. It would be well to consult with leaders of other churches in formulating them. It is also worthy of note that general invitations may evoke invitations of a similar nature from other church bodies.

*Baptism and Confirmation:* From the nature of the office of sponsor, Christians of other communions may not be invited to act as sponsors at Baptism and Confirmation. The sponsor does not act only as a friend of the family nor only as one who promises to provide for the Christian education of the person to be baptised or confirmed, but also as a representative of the community of the Catholic faithful. As a representative of the community the sponsor stands as guarantor of the faith of the candidate he presents. A Christian not of our communion cannot be asked to assume this role.

*Holy Eucharist:* The Eucharist is the sign and at the same time is the cause of the unity of the Church. The restoration of Eucharistic Communion is the goal of our ecumenical effort. At the present time, however, except in particular cases of members of the Eastern Orthodox Church intercommunion with Christians of other denominations should not be permitted. . . .

When, however, Christians of other communions are present at the Sacrifice of the Mass in our churches they may be invited to join, if they so desire, in the dialogue, in the recitation of prayers and in the singing of hymns. Christians of other churches may not, however, be invited to assume roles of leadership within the assembly, e.g., that of lector.

One of the great achievements of the Second Vatican Council is the Constitution on the Sacred Liturgy and one of the most important emphases found in this document is that concerning the homily of the Mass (cf. Article 52). The homily is an integral part of the Liturgy and normally will be given by the celebrating priest. In breaking the bread of doctrine the homilist speaks on behalf of the local bishop and, in a sense, on behalf of the entire Episcopal College. A clergyman of another communion cannot be asked to accept such a role.

Following the example of the liturgy of Good Friday it is recommended that public prayers for Christians of other communions be admitted within the liturgical celebrations. It is recommended, for example, that, when the presiding priest judges it appropriate, the names and intentions of Christians of other communions be included within the Prayer of the Faithful.

*Holy Orders:* In the conferral of Holy Orders Christians of other communions must not be invited to take leading roles. For reasons of friendship or courtesy, however, they may be invited to be present.

*Matrimony:* Christians of other churches may be admitted as witnesses and attendants at the celebration of Matrimony within the Catholic Church.

For the celebration of marriage between Catholics and Christians of other communions it is highly recommended that sacred rites be used according to the *Collectio Rituum* of 1964 and that the officiating priest be vested in cassock, surplice and stole.

It is not recommended that clergymen of other communions be invited to take an active role in the ceremony.

*Funerals:* It is recommended that, when requested by the family of the deceased, priests be permitted to conduct funeral services and to lead prayers at wakes for those not of our Church. It is for the local bishop to determine what rites are to be used on these occasions. In such circumstances burial in Catholic cemeteries may be permitted to those not of our communion, especially to spouses and relatives of Catholics. On the occasion of burials in Catholic cemeteries of those who were not Catholics it is also recommended that clergymen of other churches be permitted to conduct graveside services.

*Sacramentals:* The sacramentals of the Church may be given to those not of our communion who desire to receive them.

(2) *Participation of Catholics in the Official Worship of Other Churches.*

The Decree on Ecumenism does envisage *communicatio in sacris,* i.e., the participation of Catholics, under the supervision of the local bishop, in the liturgy of other communions (cf. Chapter II: 8). Catholics may attend official services of other churches which have special civic or social significance especially weddings and funerals. It should be remembered, however, that the Decree on Ecumenism makes repeated commendation for caution and states that "worship in common *(communicatio in sacris)* is not to be considered as a means to be used indiscriminately for the restoration of unity among Christians."

*Baptism and Confirmation:* Catholics may not act as sponsors at the conferral of Baptism or Confirmation in churches not of our communion; for reasons of friendship or courtesy, however, they may be present at these ceremonies.

*Holy Eucharist:* Catholics, accepting Eucharistic separation from their brothers of other churches in a penitential spirit and bearing in mind the principles mentioned above concerning the restoration of Eucharistic Communion, may not participate in the Eucharistic celebrations of other churches. For reasons of friendship or courtesy, however, they may be present at these services.

Catholic priests, remembering the Church's view regarding the homily at Holy Mass, may not accept invitations to preach during the Eucharistic celebrations of other churches.

*Holy Orders:* Catholics may not take an active role in the ordination ceremonies of other churches. Invitations to be present for these ceremonies, with the approval of the local Bishop, may be accepted for reasons of friendship or courtesy.

*Matrimony:* Catholics, under the guidance of the local bishop, may be permitted to serve as witnesses at marriages which are celebrated in churches of other communions.

Catholics should be mindful that attendance at services in other churches is not a substitution for, nor fulfillment of, their obligation to participate in the celebration of Holy Mass on Sundays and days of precept.

IV *(Communicatio in Sacris and Relations With the Eastern Orthodox Church):*

The Decree on the Catholic Churches of the Eastern Rite (cf. articles 26-29) established a new "conciliatory policy with regard to *communicatio in sacris* with the brethren of the separated Eastern Churches." Article 29 places the supervision of this policy in the care and control of local bishops. It encourages combined consultation on the part of these bishops and, if need be, consultation with the bishops of the Orthodox Churches. . . .

A subcommission has been established by the Bishops' Commission under the chairmanship of the Most Reverend Bernard J. Flanagan, bishop of Worcester, and it will be among the tasks of this subcommission to explore, together with representatives appointed by the bishops of the Orthodox Church, this difficult question of *communicatio in sacris.*

> V . . . In offering these recommendations the members of the Bishops' Commission for Ecumenical Affairs are guided by this vision of unity as a "mystery" and consequently share a conviction that Catholic participation in ecumenism must move beyond dialogue, programs of education, and cooperation in social matters to "spiritual ecumenism."

71. Other national hierarchies adopted guidelines to fit their national situation.

    a. In England and Wales, the Catholic bishops were concerned particularly with how much involvement there could be at public functions and worship:

> The hierarchy of England and Wales, gathered together in Rome, decided as follows:

> (1) Elected representatives and public officials may in future attend services in non-Catholic churches in the course of their civic duties. Thus, for example, Catholic councillors may attend the services on Mayor's Sunday in a non-Catholic church or chapel. Similarly, a Catholic Mayor, having celebrated Mayor's Sunday in his own parish church, will be permitted in his official capacity to attend services in other churches. The new regulations apply also to judges, town clerks and other public officials.

> (2) It is permissible for Catholics, for reasons of friendship or courtesy, to attend religious ceremonies in non-Catholic churches on social occasions such as weddings or funerals. In the future a Catholic may be bridesmaid or best man at a wedding between non-Catholics.

> (3) As friendship between Christians grows, invitations are increasingly extended to certain Catholics to attend non-Catholic churches on special occasions such as the induction of a new vicar or minister. These invitations may now be accepted.

> (4) On Remembrance Day Catholics are sometimes asked to

attend services at the local war memorial. This invitation they may now accept. Where combined services are suggested the priest should arrange details with the clergy of the other denominations. It is probably most satisfactory if each group in turn recites the prayers it knows.

(5) The octave of Christian unity has been observed with growing enthusiasm during recent years. It is recommended that, in addition to the fervent observance of the octave in our churches, on one night during the octave all Christians should gather in some suitable hall for joint prayer and talks from Christians of different denominations. It would be appropriate also to read passages from Holy Scripture and to sing hymns that are known to all. If other ways of observance are thought desirable during the octave or on other ecumenical occasions, the priest concerned must consult the bishop.

(6) Suitably qualified priests and laymen may, with the approval of the bishop, accept invitations to speak in non-Catholic churches, provided that the address does not form part of the service.

It is the earnest wish of the bishops that the clergy and laity will wholeheartedly follow the lead given by the Vatican Council. It is hoped that if the norms given above are followed any danger of indifferentism may be avoided. It is clear from the principles enunciated that there can be no sharing in a non-Catholic Eucharist. Nor is it possible for a Catholic to take an official part in a non-Catholic church service. Provided these directions are followed, we need have no fear that true ecumenism will be jeopardized by injudicious action which would easily give a wrong impression on both sides.

b. In Germany, there was an awareness of the many Greek Orthodox workers in Germany from Greece and also an awareness of a recent action of the United Evangelical Lutheran Church in Germany which had told its members on January 7,

1965, not to join in the Eucharist with Roman Catholics and that ecumenism begins with a "loyalty to one's own church." The German Catholic hierarchy responding, ruled:

> The Ecumenical Decree makes a distinction between two kinds of praying together.
>
> (1) The common prayer of Christians of different confessions or denominations [Konfessionen] are due to specific events. An example would be the World Prayer Week from January 18-25. Common prayer is also to be used in cases of general catastrophy and the like.
>
> (2) The common service type celebrations (*communicatio in sacris*). Here the decree distinguishes clearly:
>
> (a) The participation in services of the separated Eastern Churches (Orthodox) about which the decree says in Paragraph 15: . . . "These churches . . . possess true sacraments . . ." We therefore give permission to Orthodox men and women who work in our country in great numbers as guest workers to take part in our celebration of the Lord's Supper or to give them the Sacraments if they wish to do so. We request from the *rectores ecclesiae* also to permit Orthodox priests to have services in their church buildings according to Orthodox rites.
>
> (b) The participation in services of Protestant Churches (preaching service and Lord's Supper). The decree says in Paragraph 22: ". . . they have not preserved the proper reality of the Eucharistic mystery in its fullness . . .", therefore, common services are not possible with them. This fellowship through service is expressively refused through the report of an interdenominational meeting recorded January 7, 1965. This action emphasizes the deep ecclesiological differences between Catholic and Protestant dogmas and they warn against obliterating denominational differences which would lead to indifferent thinking or belief. Even if we do not consider all of their actions as the best solution (in reference to the Jan. 7 report), we have to notice them nevertheless. Our priests and laymen therefore should not embarrass the conscience of our Protestant fellow Christians by inviting them to common service-type

celebrations and *Agapes* [German, "agapen," for the Greek "agapai"—"love-feasts].

(3) Occasionally we have imitations of so-called "Ecumenical Services" mostly coming from foreign countries. They are publicized by the press and TV. These we have to refuse since here the borderline between permissible common prayer and real service is not distinguished. In order to avoid misinterpretations, common hours of prayer should take place only in places other than sanctuaries (prayer rooms, fellowship halls, home of pastor, and other places). If circumstances require another solution permission of the bishop has to be secured. Likewise, liturgical robes are not supposed to be worn at such meetings.

(4) It is self-understood that Catholic Christians can take part in the traditional form in official Protestant activities like baptisms, weddings, consecration of church buildings, and funerals. In turn, it is also possible for Protestants to take part in Catholic activities of the above mentioned type.

(5) If there is a special reason for a common service which requires the participation of a Catholic priest and a Protestant preacher in their official capacity, a special permission of the bishop must be secured. Nothing should happen to pretend there is a common fellowship of churches which does not exist and which could confuse believers.

72. On Catholic Diocesan levels, Lawrence Cardinal Shehan, of Baltimore, who now heads the Bishops' Commission for Ecumenical Affairs, pioneered the starting of Catholic Ecumenical commissions in United States dioceses. Halfway through his first pastoral letter after becoming archbishop in 1962, Cardinal Shehan (then archbishop) announced his plan for the new kind of diocesan commission:

In compliance with the wishes of the Holy See, I propose to establish a Commission on Ecumenism which will pay close attention to everything that concerns the movement toward Christian Unity within this Archdiocese and will thus be able to assist me in my task of prudently promoting and directing this movement as it pertains to the purity of authentic Catholic teaching and to the fostering among Catholics of that spirit of inexhaustible charity so radiantly exemplified by the Vicar of Christ Himself.

While our loyalty to God and to His Divine Son imposes on us an unswerving commitment in essential matters of faith this fullness of truth which Catholic faith confers on our minds should be matched by a fullness of Christian charity in our hearts. Never should it be true of any Catholic that he had enough religion to make him hate, but not enough to make him love.

Since the faith is an altogether unmerited gift, the duty of truth as well as of charity forbids us to find in our beliefs any pretext for arrogance, aloofness, or any sense of personal superiority. This same duty forbids us to presume bad faith in others or to treat our separated brothers with hostility or indifference. . . .

73. Diocesan commissions on ecumenism, waiting for the United States Bishops' guidelines in June 1965, (see section 70) and a forthcoming directory, worked out interim guidelines for interfaith relations on the local level. Their chief concern was offering guidelines and limits for participating in certain interfaith religious services (see Chapter VI for examples).

The Most Rev. John J. Wright, bishop of Pittsburgh, offered this guidance in January 1965, which includes a detailed outline on how to organize a joint service:

Our respective sanctuaries, reserved to liturgical cult, Catholic or Protestant, should not be used for inter-faith prayer gatherings which, excellent in their own right, are quite another kind of service. Most Catholics understand this well; certainly they do who are sensitive to both truth and charity. So do most Protestants, particularly those who, like ourselves in this important respect, see their cult and their liturgy as the outward, sincere expression of inward, deeply felt beliefs, bound up with conscience, rather than any merely arbitrary symbolism or superficial sacred pageantry.

Hence, the not ungenerous caution with which the Council implies how special should be the circumstances of occasion and place where prayer gatherings are held which feature participation of clergy and faithful of different Christian traditions. This caution strongly indicates, especially at the moment, that our respective Catholic, Protestant and Orthodox liturgies and sanctuaries should not be involved in mixed devotional programs which might easily suffer from confusion with respect to those very things which should never be confused and lead to the confusing of people on every side by those who should be the last to contribute to confusion where sacred truths are at issue. Here, too, holy prudence serves both clarity of thought and integrity of action, the two ingredients most necessary (after faith, hope and charity) for accomplishing the Kingdom of God on earth.

Against this background of positive ecumenical purpose and yet prudent concern for conscience (both in ourselves and in our neighbors), we hereby authorize and encourage any pastors of the Diocese of Pittsburgh who wish to do so in accordance with their proper roles and responsibilities, to make common cause with neighbors from among the Protestant and Orthodox clergy in planning neighborhood prayer gatherings for Christian unity wherever such gatherings can be arranged during the Unity Octave, immediately following it or during the Octave of Pentecost and like seasons within the framework of the conditions herein set forth. . . .

The circumstances under which we hereby authorize pastors of the diocese who wish to invite their priests or people to participate in prayer gatherings with other clergy and people who seek the unity for which Christ prayed are the following:

(1) The prayer gathering should be held in a worthy but neutral place other than the church auditorium where are held the proper liturgical or regular religious services of any one of our Christian Churches. Such a suitable place

might be the social hall or library of any one of the local Christian churches, a school hall or any community hall acceptable to the clergy of the various churches who join in planning the event.

(2) The program of the prayer gathering, to be worked out by all the clergy participating, should be characterized by great simplicity in order to provide the broadest base for a sincere coming together of as many Christians as possible and should not involve the wearing of the distinctive liturgical vestments of our several traditions. The basic cassock used in Catholic, Orthodox and some Protestant customs might well be worn or the quasi-academic gown favored by some of the Protestant groups for pulpit wear. Many might decide to limit themselves to the conventional clerical "civil attire" which some Protestants would probably prefer. Christian symbols of agreed general acceptance might well be used to decorate the place where prayer gatherings are held; it is hoped that the Crucifix would, by unanimous agreement, be the focal point of any such decorations.

(3) Any hymns which all present are invited to join in singing should be hymns which, whatever their origin, are presently cherished among all Christians. If it is planned that music special to any Christian tradition be sung, whether for the mutual edification or reciprocal enlightenment of the neighbors and brethren in the Lord who attend, such music should be sung by choirs of the faith which the words of the music proclaims; thus there will be no feigned unity on matters so essential, even for the sake of good feeling and friendship. Catholic Eucharistic motets and Mariological Hymns, in their more celebrated and classical settings, might be heard by non-Catholics with great pleasure, but they should be sung by Catholic choirs or choral societies; it is faintly fraudulent to ask Protestants to join in singing these, except, perhaps, in concerts by glee clubs. Specifically Protestant or Orthodox hymns should be sung by their choirs or choral groups; it is slightly phony for those who do not believe the doctrines expressed in song to

join in the singing of them, however properly one may enjoy the magnificent music.

(4) Any readings and related oral meditations or homilies
should, by agreement of the participating clergy, be prepared in the light of the purpose of the prayer gatherings
i.e. the recollection of God's Will, expressed through His
Incarnate Son, that His creatures become one spiritual
family or flock. The themes of the meditations might best be
from Scripture, but need not be confined to Scripture; passages from the spiritual writings or the eloquence of sensitive Christian souls might often serve well the purpose of
such prayer gatherings for unity. By agreement, the meditations on such occasions should be free from polemic, special pleading and "point-making" of a kind inconsistent
with the purpose of the gatherings and the desire to initiate
or participate in them.

(5) The content of any prayers offered by clergy participating will be, of course, the sacred responsibility of the
individual clergy themselves and will be left to their good
taste and their response to God's grace. However, the
prayers in which persons attending are asked to join actively should be prayers from familiar passages of commonly accepted Scripture or otherwise of universal Christian acceptance as, above all, The Lord's Prayer.

(6) So long as these diocesan requirements, reflecting a
consensus which we have checked with representative Catholic, Protestant and Orthodox neighbors, are acceptable, it
matters little who takes the initiative in sponsoring any
such local prayer gatherings of Christians. If our priests
do, we hope their overtures will be fraternally received; if
the ministers of neighboring parishes do and are prepared
to welcome our participation within the conscientious requirements set forth above, we hope that our pastors will
cooperate or authorize their assistants or other priests of
the diocese to do so.

In any and all cases, we pray that programs devised will
be truly the fruit of a sincere and genuine consensus; that
they will result in increased mutual respect, edification and
charity, rather than any taint of religious indifferentism,
mere natural good fellowship or, above all, the unseemly
rivalry of an effort by any one of us to be esteemed as more
"ecumenical," "progressive" or otherwise praiseworthy than
his neighbors.

I particularly hope that the distinction will be kept crystal
clear between the cult that is of conscience and obligatory,
on the one hand, and this new but wholesome, neighborly
Christian coming together for privileged prayer and meditation on common hopes and purposes. Such crystal clarity
about our sacramental and liturgical duties, as at Mass, and
our Christian privileges, as in these new ecumenical developments, is required for the honor of God and the good of souls.

One final point: Some Protestant clergy and laity may be
loath to take part in programs of this kind. They must not
be accounted for that reason less neighborly, less charitable
or less friendly; indeed, as is often the case with many
Catholics, priests and people, such Protestant Christians in
fact, may be guided by reasons in conscience which make
them the better neighbors and the more trustworthy friends.

If these circumstances are met, some of them grounded in
Church Law, some in reasons of conscience, some in simple
decency, then, please God, prayer gatherings for unity,
whether initiated by Catholic priests or Protestant clergy,
will be implemented by generous neighborhood-wide cooperation of clergy and people alike. The liturgical programs
and requirements of our respective churches will be in no
way denied, neglected, obscured or compromised; truth and
charity will be served, and these are of God. We shall all be
the better for it; so will the community.

74. Taking a wider view of the Decree on Ecumenism, the
Diocese of Bridgeport, Connecticut, actually said Roman Cath-

olics, namely priests, under certain circumstances, could take part (preach) in non-eucharistic portions of regular Sunday morning worship services (see Chapter VI for examples of some attempts across the country in this area). The "Interim Directives for Ecumenical Activities in the Diocese of Bridgeport" reaffirmed a certain measure of reserve as the other guidelines were doing (e.g., limiting explicit approval to participation in the occasional, public or ecumenical, service of worship). But it was clearly more generous in touching on areas, such as the official Protestant service, that other guidelines shunned. The Most Rev. Walter W. Curtis, bishop of Bridgeport, has emphasized, however, that these directives of September, 1965, are "subject to change":

(7) Priests are also encouraged to join ministerial associations or cooperate in the formation of clergy associations.

(8) The World Council of Churches and the National Council of Churches are important factors in contemporary Christianity. To show that they concur with these Councils' sincere search for unity and to be more closely united with them, Catholics may: pray for the success of these Councils and their varied branches, attend their social gatherings such as dinners, etc. and publicly commend their efforts.

(9) The development of the ecumenical spirit depends greatly upon education both at home and in the schools. Catholic parents should try to develop in their children a genuinely ecumenical spirit of Christian love for men of all communions and faiths. Catholic schools should do the same, especially in the lower levels. On the high school and college levels courses of an ecumenical nature or spirit should be presented, and such aids as lectures by and dialogues with experts from other confessions and faiths should be provided. . . .

(14) When Christians gather with their pastors for the specific purpose of praying for the unity willed by Christ, it is permissible, and indeed highly appropriate to conduct

such services in places set aside for the worship of God. Therefore, in addition to making our own churches available for such prayer our clergy and laity may participate in prayer for unity when it is offered in the church of another Christian denomination.

(15) On occasion members of the Catholic laity may also be invited to take an active part in ecumenical services that are not part of any official worship service. They may, for example be called on to read the Scripture lessons.

(16) When an ecumenical prayer service is held in a Catholic Church, the priest who reads from the Scripture should normally make use of an approved Catholic version of the Bible. Participating clergymen of other confessions should be accorded the use of any version they may prefer from among those in use by the major churches. Priests participating in unity services in a church of another confession may use whatever version of Scripture is provided, if a Catholic version is not available.

(17) All such joint services should be carefully prepared in accordance with the principle of "collaboration." The leaders of the participating groups should, after careful consideration, agree on the format of the services and on the choice of themes, Scripture readings and hymns. Prayers and hymns and homilies which might be unacceptable either to Catholics or other Christians are to be avoided.

(18) For the guidance of priests on such occasions it might be noted that: In some circumstances ordinary civil attire may be the only appropriate form of dress for the participating priest. In other circumstances, since it is in accordance with Catholic usage even in the conduct of non-liturgical services, the use of the cassock and surplice may be considered. The value of some kind of "sacred" vesture is not to be underestimated in creating the right atmosphere for prayer in common. In reaching decisions concerning ecclesiastical vesture on these occasions it is highly recom-

mended that there be consultation with the clergy of the
other church bodies which are to participate in such services.

(19) Permission to preach at non-Eucharistic but official
worship services of other communions must be received
from the Ecumenical Commission. Such permission will be
granted only under special circumstances in accordance
with the mind of the [Second Vatican] Council. "Worship
in common *(communicatio in sacris)* is not to be considered
as a means to be used indiscriminately for the restoration
of unity among Christians." (Decree on Ecumenism, Chapter II, 8).

(20) Such speaking appearances must not convey to people
a false sign of unity obtained. They should rather manifest
a longing for the grace of unity. . . .

75. In 1966, the Greek Orthodox in the North and South America Archdiocese found itself besieged with many questions from
local parishes. The Standing Conference of Canonical Orthodox
Bishops in America offered these guidelines:

When the Lord declares, "Where two or three are gathered
in my name, there am I in the midst of them" (Matt. 18:
20), there is no inference of fellowship only within confessional boundaries. So that when we join our otherwise
separated brothers in common supplication, it is an expression of our being bound together by those "ties which God
has not yet willed to reveal to us."

Ecumenical services properly so called are devotional services conducted for special reasons, most commonly for
Christian Unity, especially during the Week of Prayer for
Christian Unity, in January; or for peace, or in time of
public calamity, public mourning, public thanksgiving, etc.

When held in a neutral public place not usually reserved for
formal worship, no special problems arise. But if held in a

church, the service should be publicly recognized as "ecumenical" in character so as to avoid misunderstanding.

There are real difficulties here that ought honestly to be faced. And in facing them and identifying them, we can help make clear a basic Orthodox (and indeed Roman Catholic) position: that unity at the altar (*communicatio in sacris*) must be seen as the ultimate fruit of our labors and of our painful unity efforts, but not the means to that unity.

Permission must be obtained from the Bishop to hold services in Orthodox Churches to which clergy of other communions are to be invited. Such services would follow one of the accepted forms, i.e. Vespers, Matins, Compline, etc. Any accommodation as to the language of such service must have previous sanction.

When participating in a service in a hall or public place, ordinary civil attire will usually be appropriate for an Orthodox priest. In other circumstances he will wear the rason with pectoral cross (if so entitled), or academic dress when indicated. No part of eucharistic vesture, such as stole, is proper.

76. How do you evaluate the interchurch service? The Ecumenical Commission of the Diocese of Kansas City-St. Joseph, not only offered some guidelines, but also prepared some research questions to ask after each ecumenical "event":

It is further suggested: (1) That priests participating in such services wear the cassock and surplice or a house cassock. (2) That such services be held either in a church building or in a place suitable for worship. (3) That such services specifically for unity ought to be characterized by reverent brevity. (4) That such inter-church services be announced specifically for the unity of Christians, and that after they be held, they be evaluated by the priest and the information forwarded to the Diocesan Ecumenical Commission.

The Most Reverend Bishop [Charles H. Helmsing] requests that an intention for the promotion of Christian unity be included in the prayers of the faithful at every scheduled Mass in our parish churches. This intention may be announced in this way: "That all who glory in the name, 'Christian,' may in loyalty to the will of Christ our Lord attain that unity which Christ gave His Church, let us pray to the Lord: Lord have mercy."

*. . . Suggested Evaluation of Inter-Church Prayer Service for Unity:*

(1) When and where held?
(2) How advertised or announced?
(3) a. Participants—Please give names of presiding participants, priests, ministers, and lay leaders.
b. Audience—Please describe size and composition of audience; Catholics, members of other churches, other priests and ministers attending.
(4) Your own appraisal of the service and its apparent fruits.
(5) Your recommendations.
(6) Please indicate any other ecumenical endeavors in which you are engaged, especially in the form of common prayer and dialogues.

77. Few Catholic theologians would predict out loud that the crescendo in Catholic-Protestant relations could result in Catholic membership in the World Council of Churches. Protestants in Geneva also hedged and said they were not structurally set up for such an arrangement. Yet consultants or *periti* at the Vatican Council agreed that there was no theological problem in an eventual alignment of Catholics and Protestants in a reconstituted non-churchly agency which could correlate efforts in international aid and the national poverty war, among other areas.

Then it happened—on the local, and on the state level. A Catholic priest in Birmingham, Michigan, joined a Protestant Pastor's union which functions as a Council of Churches. In Alpena, Michigan, an Inter-Faith Clergy association was formed (the Rev. Allen B. Rice, II, of the First Methodist Church, and the Rev. Father Robert J. Pelletier, pastor of the Nicholson Hill St. Catherine Catholic Church, tied in the voting for the presidency —after casting "lots" in Biblical fashion, Pastor Rice was declared the new president). The Catholic information officer for the Archdiocese of Detroit became a non-voting board member of the Detroit Council of Churches Department of radio and TV. Then in three other parts of the country, Catholic churches actually joined the local Protestant Council of Churches (two Catholic churches in Tulsa, Oklahoma, joined the Tulsa Council of Churches; St. Andrew's Catholic Cathedral, Grand Rapids, joined the Grand Rapids Council of Churches; and the Holy Family Parish, Fort Worth, Texas, joined the Fort Worth Area Council of Churches). (As far away as Maseru, Basutoland, a new area council of churches took in the local Catholic church as "associate member.")

Priests were encouraged to join local ministerial associations in a pamphlet distributed by the Diocese of Winona, Minnesota. And in July, 1966, the National Council of Churches announced that a Jesuit, the Rev. Father David J. Bowman is to be assistant director in the NCC's Faith and Order Department, the first Roman Catholic priest to serve on the NCC staff.

As a guide to local co-operative Council membership, consider the Fort Worth example:

a. To join the Fort Worth Area Council of Churches, as the Holy Family Catholic Parish did on March 25, 1965, an applicant fills out a form that includes this explanation:

> It is our understanding that the Council is a voluntary association of independent churches in Fort Worth and vicinity holding to a common faith in Jesus Christ as divine Lord and Savior, and that its purpose is to provide a channel through which the churches may have fellowship across denominational lines, and through which they may coordinate or undertake jointly any aspects of their programs which they agree may be performed more effectively in a cooperative way.

> We understand also that membership in the Council does not bind or obligate any member church to any commitment or course of action contrary to the beliefs and policies of said church, and that any member church is free to participate in only those phases of the program in which it has an

interest and to refrain from participating in any aspects in which it is not interested. Furthermore, we understand that any church which is a member of the Council may withdraw from membership at any time by official action of the church and written notice to the Council. . . .

With these understandings, our church pledges itself, upon admittance to membership in the Council, to look upon the work of the Council as an important part of the work of this church, performed cooperatively with other churches, to seek to play a strong role in these cooperative endeavors to advance Christ's Kingdom in the Fort Worth area, and to contribute financially to the support of the united endeavors as our church is able. Signed [name of representative and position in church].

b. Past-president Granville Walker, of the Fort Worth Council of Churches, presented the Holy Family Catholic Church's application to the Council with this speech:

It might well be that the application for membership in the Fort Worth Area Council of Churches which I am about to present, could signal the most significant development in the religious life of our community in the memory of any person in this audience. . . .

It may be that this application gives us renewed occasion to consider the real purposes and intent of a Council of Churches. It does not presume to be a church nor aspire to become a "super-church" as is sometimes alleged. Rather the Council is an agency of the churches through which their unity in Christ may be declared, their differences examined, and through which they may act together in a variety of good works, which are grounded in their common faith.

To do this one does not even remotely require that a participating church yield any sovereignty whatever over its own life or its relationship to its own denomination. I think you would require no greater proof of this than that a Roman Catholic Church should request involvement in our local council. For the Roman Catholic Church is justly proud of its uniqueness and its great traditions and is not about to yield them. But so also are the Presbyterians, the Methodists, the Disciples, the Lutherans, and the Episcopal Church proud of theirs and are equally reluctant to surrender them.

But we have reached a point in history when our oneness at those points where we can be one is imperative. We are involved in our times in a complex of scientific, political and social upheavals in which by a few miscalculations the world might find itself in a holocaust which could end in total annihilation. We Christians of all faiths are convinced that the Gospel of Christ holds the key to world redemption and the sole hope for preserving civilization and that only by united action can the churches proclaim that Gospel convincingly. We therefore dare not neglect in such times to seek the fullest understanding both of our mission under Christ and our unity in Him as His agents for the fulfillment of that mission.

This is why there is a Council of Churches. This is why Christian bodies of diverse doctrinal commitments, of divergent forms of ecclesiastical government, of great differences in liturgical traditions are seeking channels by which their oneness in Christ can be manifest and where they can bear a common witness to the world regarding the tremendous problems which beset us on every side.

Mr. President, on behalf of the Membership Committee, it is my privilege to present for membership in this Council the application of the Holy Family Catholic Church of which my beloved friend, Monsignor Vincent J. Wolf is pastor.

78. Then, in the most ambitious arrangement, the entire Roman Catholic Archdiocese of Santa Fe in 1965 joined the New Mexico Council of Churches. The Rt. Rev. Msgr. O. A. Coggiola-Mower, pastor of the Catholic Church of the Annunciation, Al-

buquerque, New Mexico, and representative of the archbishop, the Most Rev. James P. Davis, explained the move and the principles behind it in a speech at the Heights YMCA, Albuquerque. (Later the New Mexico Council of Churches elected to its second highest office, that of vice president, the Rev. Father Robert Schneider, superintendent of schools for the Santa Fe archdiocese.) Msgr. Coggiola-Mower, who spoke extemporaneously, summarizes his speech:

> The membership of the Catholic Archdiocese of Santa Fe in the New Mexico Council of Churches . . . has the same characteristics as the membership of other Christian communities, which retain their beliefs, their form of worship, their independence. There is no specific commitment, no doctrinal concession is either given or expected, nor is there any confusion or unwise fraternizing in the field of dogma and precise theological thinking.
>
> Its purposes, however, could be grouped and presented in the following manner:
>
> (1) To establish a channel of communication which is both dignified and trustworthy.
>
> (2) To make possible the conviction that a general pattern of beliefs unites Christians into a solid entity, which is foolish to ignore and sinful to destroy.
>
> (3) To unite Christians in their efforts of a social, cultural, charitable nature, such as marriage laws, civil rights, obscenity laws.
>
> This membership of the Catholic Church in the New Mexico Council of Churches has been prepared by an atmosphere of cordiality and understanding, which prompted Archbishop James P. Davis to appoint his personal representative [Msgr. Coggiola-Mower] to attend such functions as the installation of the new executive secretary of the New Mexico Council of Churches and the Inter-Faith Festival. . . .

Besides general and personal results of a moral nature, besides common efforts and intelligent participation, the membership will possibly produce other results, like the religious building, a "God's Terminal," presently in the early stages of planning, in which various denominations would have their offices.

Will other dioceses in the United States follow this "first"? Because of the moral and social advantages, because of the spiritual implications, because good things are contagious in the sense that they invite re-thinking and re-evaluating, one feels confident that the example of the Archdiocese of Santa Fe will be followed by other bishops of the country.

79. A "Modus Vivendi" in the form of guidelines for a loosely organized "Christian Council" was drawn up in Nagpur, India, in 1964. Its "constitution" offers a basic form for possible larger inter-Christian structures to follow. The constitution took up these points:

(1) Name: Christian Council of Nagpur.

(2) Objective:
   (a) To promote and engage in such joint religious activities as are decided by common consent.
   (b) To undertake projects of social service.
   (c) To bring about healthy relations with other communities.
   (d) To formulate from the Christian point of view an opinion on matters of public importance.

(3) Membership: Membership in the Council is open to all Christian churches, medical and educational institutions and other Christian organizations listed by the Council and it shall be competent for the executive committee to admit new member bodies and add to the list the names of member bodies so admitted.

Each listed church, institution and organization is entitled to send two representatives to the Council, provided that one of the representatives shall be the head of the institution or the organization and in the case of a church, the priest-in-charge thereof.

(4) Membership fee: Each church, institution and organization co-operating in the Council shall pay an annual fee of 25 rupees. No fees shall be charged from the co-opted members.

(5) Commissions and committees: The Council shall normally function through commissions and committees appointed by the Council or its executive committee to deal with different concerns.

(6) Meetings: The Council shall meet at least twice a year and one half of the number of the members shall constitute the quorum.

(7) Executive Committee: The executive committee shall consist of the office bearers, conveners of commissions and committees and five members appointed by the Council. . . .

80. Official discussion on theological topics were underway in 1965, with full acceleration to come in 1966. Activity was the greatest in the United States where the Most Rev. Ernest L. Unterkoefler, of Charleston, South Carolina, led a United States Catholic bishops' subcommission of the Commission for Ecumenical Affairs which met with Presbyterians on two occasions, November 26-27 in Chestnut Hill, Pennsylvania, and earlier, in Washington, D. C., on July 27. The talks centered around the role and effectiveness of the Holy Spirit. The Most Rev. Thomas A. Murphy, auxiliary bishop of Baltimore, led a Catholic team in talks with Lutherans on July 6-7, 1965 on the Nicene Creed. (see Chapter IV) ; and in Chicago, February 11-13 on Baptism (see Chapters IV and VI) the most Rev. Charles Helmsing, bishop of Kansas City, Missouri led the Catholic team meeting with Episcopalians. And on the exploratory and planning stage were proposed talks with Methodists (the Most Rev. Joseph B. Brunini,

auxiliary bishop of Natchez-Jackson, Mississippi, leading the Catholic team) ; with the Orthodox (the Most Rev. Bernard Flanagan, Roman Catholic bishop of Worcester, Massachusetts; and the National Council of Churches, (the Most Rev. John Carberry, Catholic bishop of Columbus, Ohio). Seven representatives from the Lutheran World Federation and the Roman Catholic Church also held their first consultation, in Strasbourg, France, August 25-27, 1965.

On the wider level, a 14-member joint working group of Roman Catholic and World Council of Churches representatives met at Celigny, Switzerland, and Ariccia, near Rome, in 1965. The wider dialogue was authorized by the Protestants, taking the initiative in response to the new Roman Catholic Decree on Ecumenism, in a meeting of the Central Committee of the WCC in Enugu, Nigeria, in January, 1965. (Earlier, in 1963 at its Rochester, New York meeting, before the United States bishops organized the Commission for Ecumenical Affairs and subsequent chain of talks, the WCC Central Committee had urged new Protestant-Orthodox initiative in dialogue.)

a. At Enugu, the WCC invited official "working groups" of Protestants and Catholics to meet to formulate guidelines for discussing differences and ways to work together:

> The adoption and promulgation of the Decree "De Ecumenismo" by the Roman Catholic Church has created a new situation. The fact that the Roman Catholic Church expresses so definitely its desire to enter into conversation with the other churches and expresses its convictions on the subject is an important new fact in the development of the ecumenical movement. For the Roman Catholic Church thus adopts a number of principles and policies which have guided the churches in the Ecumenical Movement in the past decades. There are points in which the conception of ecumenical relations is the same as that developed in the World Council of Churches and in its member churches. There are other points in which there are considerable differences. The World Council of Churches which has always sought "to draw Churches out of isolation into conference" must surely use this opportunity to do whatever it can do, in the

light of its mandate, to encourage these new contacts and should itself enter into a conversation with the Roman Catholic Church about common concerns and unsolved problems of relationships. . . .

The World Council of Churches and the Roman Catholic Church are not comparable entities. The World Council of Churches is a fellowship of many churches with different confessional backgrounds. The Roman Catholic Church is a single Church. Their cooperation creates therefore special problems. These problems can however best be solved by frank discussion. . . .

A clear distinction must also be made between the subjects which can properly be discussed between the WCC and the Roman Catholic Church and those which can and must be discussed in bilateral conversations between the individual member churches (or confessional bodies) and the Roman Catholic Church.

Among these subjects which belong to the first category we would mention especially: a) practical collaboration in the fields of philanthropy, social and international affairs; (b) theological study programmes which have a specific bearing on ecumenical relations (Faith and Order); (c) problems which cause tension between the churches (e.g. mixed marriages, religious liberty, proselytism); (d) common concerns with regard to the life and mission of the Church (laity, missions, etc.).

It is recognized that these subjects have certain aspects which can best be discussed at the international level, and other aspects which can best be discussed at the national level.

In the light of the above considerations it is proposed that a working group be established composed of eight representatives of the WCC and of six representatives of the

Roman Catholic Church. The task of this group would be to work out the principles which should be observed in further collaboration and in the methods which should be used. When discussing specific fields of work the group could invite persons specially concerned with these fields to sit with them as consultants. The working group would not be able to make any decisions, but elaborate proposals which would be submitted to the bodies they represent, and communicated to the member churches.

The relationships between the WCC staff and the Secretariat for the Promotion of Unity can best be maintained by the regular exchange of visits. . . .

b. In Geneva, in February, 1966, the Central Committee of the WCC reaffirmed its earlier policy at Enugu and issued a joint report with the Vatican outlining a wide field of topics for discussion and implementation between the WCC and Roman Catholics. The report, prepared by the Joint Working Group of 14 (eight Protestants-Orthodox—six Roman Catholics), asked for a continuation of talks on the nature of ecumenism, a joint theological study of the meaning of "catholic" and "apostolic" and an examination of ways of maintaining fruitful contacts in mission work, church and society projects, the laity, the place of Christian women, social service programs, international affairs, Bible translations, and the standardization of texts on the liturgy, and mutual exchange of information.

In regard to practical projects and specific concerns, the Working Group suggested in its report:

The Joint Working Group recommends that consultations should be organized to study present possibilities of collaboration in the sphere of social service activities, emergency and development aid. At these meetings, not only should possibilities of immediate collaboration be studied, but attention should above all be paid to the spiritual inspiration and Christian responsibility that form the basis of all cooperation. . . .

*The International Field.*
This field requires the most urgent collaboration on the part
of all. It would be of the greatest value to Christians engaged in international affairs if they could reach common
convictions concerning the bases for action in this whole
field. The Joint Working Group therefore hopes to be able
to organize in the not too distant future a consultation on
the Christian responsibility in international affairs. This
aspect should be given priority of study.

*Catholic International Organizations.*
The relations between Roman Catholic international organizations and the various departments of the WCC present
particular problems. Which Catholic organization corresponds to which WCC department. The Joint Working
Group has begun to study methods aimed at establishing
contacts which will lead to fruitful cooperation.

*Particular Problems concerning Various*
*Areas of Collaboration.*
*The Bible.*
In several countries joint translations of the Bible are being
undertaken. In certain cases Protestant translations have
been used by the Roman Catholic Church. The Bible Societies and various churches have shown a lively interest
in this joint action. The recent Vatican Council Constitution on Divine Revelation has encouraged such projects. . . .

*Easter.*
The fixing of one date on which all Christians would celebrate Easter is undoubtedly a project worthy of attention.
The Group feels that detailed enquiry and study should be
pursued on this point. Several churches have made their
viewpoints known (see the study undertaken by the "Universal Council for Life and Work"). The Roman Catholic
Church recently stated its position on this matter in the ap-
pendix to the Vatican Council's Constitution on the Sacred
Liturgy.

*Liturgy.*

It is also desirable in the liturgical field that wherever Christians use the same prayers (biblical or other), identical texts should be available. This will greatly facilitate common prayer. We have only to think for example, of the advantages that would accrue from having the same version of the Lord's Prayer in each language. The Group intends to encourage all that can be done along these lines.

*The Continuation of our Work.*

. . . We would mention here, simply as examples, some of the major issues that deserve study in the future:

(a) The training of clergy and laity with an ecumenical outlook. At the same time it might be possible to undertake a study of catechisms and other texts used in religious instruction in which other churches are not always objectively presented.

(b) The doctrine and practice of baptism.

(c) The theology of marriage; and mixed marriages between Christians.

(d) The practical consequences of religious liberty.

(e) Problems presented by proselytism.

(f) Problems of youth.

c. The Joint Working Group set up two special meetings in Rome on October 16 and November 18, 1965, to discuss "joint worship at ecumenical gatherings," and came up with their own general guidelines and points of emphases in the difficult new area of joint special services together. The report of the two meetings said:

1. When Christians meet together they experience a certain unity in a deep fellowship despite their separations

which are still very real. The experience of this fellowship
and an actual growth in it is particularly evident when they
pray together and praise God, when they repent and ask
for God's gift of forgiveness, when they listen to the Word
of God together. What often cannot be grasped and formulated in thoughts and words proves to be a reality in the
common movement to God. Therefore it is decisive for the
ecumenical movement that Christians should meet for common prayer rooted in this common ground.

2. Common prayer, however, should not give the impression that a fellowship exists where this is not so. Nothing,
therefore, should be done which is against the conviction
and the discipline of a church. Any fellowship in worship
which is not confirmed by fellowship in life does not further
the ecumenical cause.

3. Taking into account both these aspects, one must still be
aware of the fact that fellowship must be experienced if it
is to grow. Therefore, rules which may be established should
not be fixed in such a way that exclude further common responsible steps in the direction of more extended
fellowship. . . .

*Prayers and Worship at Ecumenical Gatherings.*
1. If there is to be a further development of the ecumenical movement, it is essential that at ecumenical gatherings
the present situation can find a realistic expression. The
participants must be able to experience both the existing
oneness in Christ and the difficulties still to be overcome.
Solutions which hide the differences must be avoided.

As far as possible the various traditions represented at a
gathering should have the opportunity to participate actively in worship, even if practical considerations seem to
make it difficult.

2. There are various forms of worship which must be distinguished:

(a) Services in which representatives of several traditions participate. It is important that such services are prepared together and are carried out in a representative way. The celebration of the Eucharist is normally excluded at such occasions.

(b) Services composed in a form which can be adopted by the members of any church tradition, e.g. prayers of adoration, Bible readings, prayers of intercession, etc.

(c) Services which are conducted for all those participants in the meeting by one or several members of one church according to the rules of this church. Of course, it is important that as many as possible of the traditions represented should have the opportunity of conducting such prayer. With meetings of short duration, this may prove difficult. However, if a short meeting is one of a projected series, it may be possible for each tradition represented to be responsible for the service in turn at subsequent meetings.

(d) Eucharistic services which are held by one church within the context of a meeting. It should not become the rule that the problem of the Eucharist is bypassed at ecumenical meetings and if eucharistic services are held solutions should not be sought which make visible only one aspect of the problem. Of course, everything must be arranged so that each participant is free to follow his own conscience and the discipline of his Church.

The following considerations may be important:
(1) The meeting itself cannot be responsible for the celebration of a eucharistic service. Only a church can issue an invitation for such a service. It is natural that one of the churches represented at the place where the meeting is held issues the invitation.

(2) If the ecumenical problem is to become visible in all its sharpness, it must be possible to come into contact with varying traditions in the celebration of the Eucharist.

While some churches can invite representatives of other churches to participate in their eucharist, others are not able to do so; and while some are free to accept the invitation, others—for theological and disciplinary reasons—cannot take communion at the altar of another church. Therefore if the gathering lasts long enough it is advisable that there should be at least two eucharistic services—one arranged by a church which, according to its rules may invite other Christians to communicate, the other celebrated by a church which even at ecumenical gatherings is obliged to restrict communion to its own members. If possible, all participants at the gathering should be present at all these different eucharistic services.

(3) The use of the church building for eucharistic services at ecumenical gatherings needs careful consideration, especially in the circumstances where only one church building is available.

(4) A preparatory service for all participants in the gathering has proved to be a significant common act at many occasions. It can contribute to a deeper awareness of the scandal of division. If such a service is held it should be related to all eucharistic services which may be contemplated.

(5) If necessary, the participants in a gathering should have the opportunity to celebrate outside the programme the eucharist according to the tradition of their church without violating their conscience or being unfaithful to their obligations.

It is obvious that when there is a gathering of a certain prolonged duration, all of these forms of worship may find their proper place during the gathering. Thus those under (a) may be most appropriate for the opening and closing services of the gathering; those under (b) and (c) for the regular morning and evening prayer, those under (d) at some time during the gathering according to the time and availability of all that is necessary. It is recognized, however, that particular emphasis on one form of worship may also be proper at prolonged gatherings, in accordance with the particular purposes for which the meetings are being held.

81. The first all-European church organization, the European Conference of Churches, comprising Protestant, Anglican, Orthodox and Old Catholic churches from 21 countries, was formed aboard the liner Bornholm off the coast of Denmark. Its significance, beyond administration and communication, is that it forms a new base, a broader structure for dialogue. The organizing meeting, aboard ship in international waters in order to accommodate East German delegates who could not receive travel permits for Denmark, a NATO country, brought together 250 European churchmen. The Constitution of the Conference of European Churches includes these provisions:

*Article 1:* (a) The Conference of European Churches (hereafter referred to as "The Conference") is an ecumenical fellowship of Churches in Europe which confess the Lord Jesus Christ as God and Saviour according to the Scriptures and therefore seek to fulfill together their common calling to the glory of the one God, Father, Son and Holy Spirit. (b) The aim of their co-operation is, by means of regular meetings, to discuss questions concerning the Churches in Europe and to assist each other in that service which is laid upon the Churches in the contemporary European situation. (c) The Conference is autonomous; it is, however, closely related to the World Council of Churches in the common effort to promote Christian unity and service. (d) Declarations and decisions of the Conference are only binding on any Church participating in its work in so far as they are expressly accepted by that Church.

*Article 2:* (a) The Conference consists of those Churches in Europe which have participated in the meetings of the Conference in Nyborg prior to the acceptance of this constitution and such other Churches in Europe as may later be admitted. (b) Churches which apply for membership shall be accepted if the Assembly so decides by a two-thirds majority of those present with the right to vote. . . .

*Article 8:* The Conference may maintain contact with other ecumenical organizations and confessional bodies. Representatives of such organizations and bodies may be appointed as advisers to the Assembly and to the working groups. . . .

82. The National Council of Churches amended its constitutional preamble, December 1963, in Philadelphia, and continued its commitment toward greater "oneness." A slight change indicated that the quest for oneness is a continuing pursuit that progresses under the providence of God. (In a section on membership, the NCC bylaws approved by the General Board, June 1, 1964, says a church may be considered for membership if "it shall have demonstrated a spirit of cooperation with, and respect for the convictions of other communions.")

a. The new preamble says:

Under the Province of God, communions which confess Jesus Christ as Divine Lord and Savior, in order more fully to manifest oneness in Him, do now create an inclusive cooperative agency of Christian churches of the United States of America to show forth their unity and mission in specific ways and to bring the churches into living contact with one anotner for fellowship, study, and cooperative action.

b. The National Council of Churches also launched its new Division of Christian Unity in January 1964.

The bylaws of the National Council of Churches outline the scope of the new Division:

Division of Christian Unity established to serve as the arm of the Council through which the communions, their boards and agencies, and participating nonmember organizations cooperate to manifest the unity of Christ's church through faith and order studies, through dialogue with nonmember Christian bodies, and through strengthening Christian unity in local communities, states, and regions.

Responsibilities of this Division, in addition to the general responsibilities of each division . . . shall be to:

(a) Encourage and assist the churches to assume and exercise their responsibility for responding to the ecumenical imperative through study, discussion, and action, and in accord with the Constitution, seek to develop closer continuing relations between councils, associations, and movements and agencies of communions working toward common objectives.

(b) Study matters of faith and order bearing on the unity of the churches and promote similar study in the churches, in seminaries, and in conciliar and other organizations in the United States.

(c) Initiate and maintain dialogue with Christian bodies which are not members of the Council, and facilitate contacts with those groups on the part of other major units of the Council.

(d) Promote, extend, and assist the organization and development of councils, associations, and movements and other manifestations of ecumenicity throughout the United States.

(e) Channel the concerns of the conciliar movement in the United States to the churches, to the Council, and to the units of the Council engaged in formulating program.

(f) Extend and promote the program of the Council to and through the conciliar movement in the United States.

(g) Undertake and stimulate study and activity in regard to the cooperation and role of men and women in the total ministry of the church.

c. In June, 1966, in Chicago, the Department of Faith and Order of the NCC's Division of Christian Unity launched a permanent "colloquium" on faith and order, with inter-Christian participation.

1. The colloquium was outlined in the 1965 annual report of the National Council of Churches:

> The Faith and Order Committee voted in June, 1965, to establish a National Faith and Order Colloquium, consisting of up to 100 delegates, to meet annually and to serve as a focal point for Faith and Order study and dialogue in the United States. Although the Colloquium will be sponsored by the Faith and Order Committee, it will have a substantial degree of autonomy from the structures of the National Council in order that persons from communions which are not presently members of the Council can participate in good conscience. There will be full Roman Catholic participation, and there is reason to expect participation from other communions which are not members of the National Council. The first meeting will be held June 12-17, 1966, to consider "The Meanings and Practices of Conversion," a topic which encompasses a series of problems which exist in many areas of Church life. Faith and Order Committees in state and local councils of churches have been asked to study the topic and report their observations to the Faith and Order Department to aid it in planning the Colloquium program so as to include the problems related to conversion as they appear in local communities.

2. Mrs. Theodore O. Wedel, associate general secretary of the NCC in charge of the new Division of Christian Unity, elaborated on the purpose of the Colloquium:

> The purpose of the Colloquium is to make it possible for members of a great many churches, both within and outside the National Council of Churches, to come together once a year to discuss issues of common concern to all Christians . . . The Colloquium will number about 100 persons from most of the member churches of the NCC, and a number of

non-member churches including the Roman Catholic. While
this meeting is sponsored by our Department of Faith and
Order, the Colloquium is considered an independent body
which will have no authority to make decisions but which
will be able, if it wishes, to address issues and questions to
all the churches. We see this as the beginning of a process
similar to the great Faith and Order meetings which have
been held on a worldwide schedule ever since 1927.

83. The National Conference of Christians and Jews broadened
its base in a constitutional change. Instead of being open to
"Protestants, Catholics and Jews," the membership is now for
"Christians and Jews." Christianity was seen in less divisive and
exclusive terms and, said Dr. Lewis Webster Jones, NCCJ president, "since the old bylaw, literally construed, seemed to limit
the kinds of participants to three religious groups, it was deemed
advisable to clarify the wording." The amendment reads:

Believing in a spiritual interpretation of the universe and
deriving its inspiration therefrom, the corporation [NCCJ]
exists to promote justice, amity, understanding and cooperation among Christians and Jews and to analyze, moderate
and strive to eliminate intergroup prejudices which disfig-
ure and distort religious, business, social and political relations, with a view to maintaining at all times a society in
which the religious ideals of brotherhood and justice shall
become the standards of human relationships.

84. Denominations were preparing themselves for dialogue. In
Anglicanism, there was the initiative of the Lambeth Conference
of bishops from 18 far-flung branches of the Anglican Communion which meets every ten years at Lambeth Palace, London.
       a. In 1958, the bishops were cognizant of growing union
plans, interfaith discussions, and increased responsibilities in
regard to church unity. In a resolution, the bishops welcomed
"the permission given by Roman Catholic authority for contacts,
discussions, and co-operation between Roman Catholics and other
Christians, as contained in the document, *Instruction to Local
Ordinaries on the Ecumenical Movement,* issued by the Vatican

Holy Office (see introduction to this chapter). The Anglican bishops expressed "the hope, first, that these permissions [in the *Instruction*] may be more widely and generously used, secondly, that they may be further extended in the interests of Christian understanding and fellowship, and thirdly, that Anglicans will make full use of these and all other available opportunities for promoting charitable understanding."

The bishops' encyclical letter at Lambeth in 1958 to member Anglican churches around the world sought to strengthen their own life for a role of reconciliation in the world:

> We, Archbishops and Bishops of the Holy Catholic and Apostolic Church in communion with the See of Canterbury, three hundred and ten in number, assembled from forty-six countries, under the Presidency of Geoffrey, Archbishop of Canterbury, in the year of our Lord one thousand nine hundred and fifty-eight, send you greeting in the name of our Lord and Savior Jesus Christ. . . .
>
> The Church can be effective as an agent of Christ's reconciling power only in proportion as it is itself reconciled to God and is seeking reconciliation between its members. Every Lambeth Conference since 1878 has recognized this by its concern for the unity of the Body of Christ. We believe that the Anglican Communion has a special opportunity and a corresponding responsibility to help in the healing of the divisions which hinder the Church's ministry of reconciliation. We rejoice in the many signs of closer Christian fellowship, and we thank God for the warmth of friendship between the Churches shown in the World Council of Churches and in other relations between our own and other Communions. . . .
>
> The world is often critical because we seem to move so slowly towards the goal of the visible unity of the whole Church of God. Yet we can thank God that the last ten years have shown so much progress, and we rejoice in the many signs of the strengthening of the fellowship of our Communion with Churches of other and different traditions.

In our last Conference we could not make one unanimous recommendation with regard to the relations between our Churches and Provinces and the newly-united Church of South India. In the ten years that have passed, visits by delegations and individuals have dispelled misunderstandings, and we record with thankfulness that many of our Provinces have been able to establish a limited inter-communion with that Church on which the grace of God has been so abundantly and manifestly bestowed.

The Church of India, Pakistan, Burma, and Ceylon asked that the Lambeth Conference should give advice upon three further schemes for united Churches in Ceylon, North India, and Pakistan. We examined these schemes with the greatest care, and we would express our gratitude to God for the clear evidence of the guidance of his Holy Spirit in the negotiations, which have led to schemes of union which we believe to mark a great and significant step towards the recovery of the visible unity of the Church Universal. We believe that it will be possible for the Church of Lanka [Ceylon] to be from the outset in full communion with Churches and Provinces of the Anglican Communion. With some modification, the Churches of North India and Pakistan could have the same expectation. It is the earnest hope and prayer of all our members that these unions may go forward.

In West Africa and in the Jerusalem Archbishopric plans for reunion are under discussion. In Britain and America conversations are taking place between Churches of our Communion and Churches of the Presbyterian and Methodist traditions. We thank God for drawing us towards a wider and richer Christian unity. Because of our urgent desire to further negotiations and conversations with other Churches we have put forth in penitence and hope a fresh statement of our convictions, believing that we are called to a fresh effort in the cause of the unity of the one Church of God in the love of Christ, in faith and in order, and in fullness of sacramental communion. As we set ourselves afresh to work and pray for such unity, we realize anew that we must seek also so to strengthen the life of our Communion that it may bring the full riches of our traditions and our heritage into the Church that is to be. . . .

b. Arthur Michael Ramsey, Archbishop of Canterbury, in a speech before the Anglican Congress, in Toronto, August 13, 1963, prepared his own church for its "disappearance" someday into a united faith:

Towards other Churches we work for unity in truth and holiness. That work is always one of giving and receiving, and we only give if we are humble to receive. What we may give is not our own, it is a treasure of scriptural and catholic faith and sacrament. As to the goal, it is nothing less than full communion in and of the Catholic Church of Christ. In the process parts of the Anglican family may cease to be precisely Anglican, as united Churches come into being in full communion with us. But whether our Anglican Communion itself will disappear is something which we do not know. We do not know what place particular provinces, or traditions, or patriarchates will have within the unity of God's design, and Canterbury may, like Rome and Constantinople, long have its role in God's service. Meanwhile the work of unity has its time, its *kairoi*, in different parts of the world. For all of us there is in this year the great significance of the Vatican Council. Rome and Canterbury are speaking to one another in a new charity without belittling their respective concerns about truth. And though the road to unity in truth is a long one, the new charity means that already Christendom stands more vividly as a fact before the world. . . .

85. Lutherans were improving their stance for wider and official dialogue by convergence in the United States and around the world. In the United States, the American Lutheran Church was organized in 1960 out of the old American Lutheran Church (German), the Evangelical Lutheran (Norwegian), the United

Evangelical Lutheran (Danish), and Lutheran Free Norwegian. In Detroit, two years later, the Lutheran Church in America was formed out of the Augustana Evangelical Lutheran Church (Swedish), the Suomi Synod (Finnish), the American Evangelical Lutheran Church (Danish), and the United Lutheran Church (a composite of earlier groups). With the older National Lutheran Council, a cooperative agency, now outdated by the new mergers, plans were drawn up for the new more inclusive Luthern Council, in the U.S.A. The 2.6-million member Lutheran Church—Missouri Synod agreed now to join the new agency, and expressed interest in wider talks for the sake of cooperation, but not union. It still stayed outside the pale of the NCC and the LWF.

a. The National Lutheran Council proceeded to endorse formal dialogue with Roman Catholics. The first talks, centering on the Nicene Creed (see Chapter IV), held in Baltimore in July 1965, came after a preliminary meeting in the office of Lawrence Cardinal Shehan of Baltimore, March 16. The Lutheran action followed the formation of the Roman Catholic "Bishops' Commission for Ecumenical Affairs," which would, according to Cardinal Shehan, provide "a point of contact with non-Catholic Christian Churches, ecclesial communities and conferences." Said the National Lutheran Council, in a report by Cyrus Rachie, secretary, and Paul C. Empie, executive, received and endorsed in the annual meeting of the NLC at Los Angeles:

> The establishment by the Roman Catholic bishops of a "Bishops' Commission for Ecumenical Affairs" in recent months makes it possible for Catholic participation to be undertaken on an official basis. This would call for official involvement on the part of the National Lutheran Council itself rather than by an unofficial organization such as the National Lutheran Educational Conference. Therefore, the Executive Committee rescinded its action of Dec. 2-3, 1964 . . . and adopted the following resolutions:
>
> (1) That subject to concurrence by the Lutheran World Federation, the Council as the U.S.A. National Committee of the LWF agree to co-sponsor theological conversations with the Bishops' Commission for Ecumenical Affairs:

(2) That a consultative committee consisting of Dr. George Lindbeck, Dr. Warren Quanbeck, the President and the Executive Director of the NLC be appointed to negotiate the arrangements.

(3) That contact be maintained with the Lutheran Foundation for Inter-Confessional Research and the General Secretary of the Lutheran World Federation during the course of the negotiations and the conversations which would follow.

(4) That the Executive Director work through the Department of Theological Cooperation of the Division of LWF Affairs in providing staff services for the theological conversations.

(5) That the Lutheran Church–Missouri Synod be invited to participate on the same basis as that of its participation in the Lutheran-Reformed conversations.

VOTED: That the costs to the USA National Committee of negotiations for Lutherans–Roman Catholic conversations and for any such conversations in 1965 be met from the USA Committee LWF Reserves.

b. In Africa, Lutheran concepts of unity were evolving rapidly. The third All-Africa Lutheran Conference, meeting in Addis Ababa, in October 1965, asked its 23 participating churches from 13 countries to "examine themselves and the [historic Lutheran] confessions to find whether it is really the essentials of our faith that hinders union with other Churches, or simply our outward customs and organizational problems." It also called on the African Lutheran Churches to "seek to enter into dialogue with other Churches so that we may share [the Christian] faith with them."

The Lutheran Churches in Africa . . . can help to heal the disunity of the Church in several ways:

(1) By careful and prayerful study of the Scriptures and criticism of our church life in their light.

(2) By a friendly understanding attitude toward other Churches and a willingness to learn from them.

(3) By serious dialogue and a common search for theological agreement with other Churches.

(4) By co-operation with other Churches in all matters in which we together can serve God's mission among men. . . .

We do believe that a faithful Christian Church must submit itself to the Scriptures as the only source and norm of Christian teaching and practice, and that church union therefore must be based on agreement in the essentials of the Gospel as the way of salvation and in the sacraments.

86. Presbyterians appeared, among Protestants, to be further in front in setting rules, and generous ones they were, for continuing dialogue.

a. The General Council of the World Alliance of Reformed Churches adopted this report of its standing committee concerning contacts with Roman Catholics in its meeting at Frankfurt-am-Main, Germany, August 1964:

(1) The Alliance can assist our member Churches to understand and share in the dialogue:

(a) by making available more information concerning developments within the Roman Catholic Church and by sharing with the Churches the reports and evaluations of our Observers at the Second Vatican Council;

(b) by stating clearly the issues and questions raised by the Roman Catholic-Protestant dialogue;

(c) by ensuring that as far as possible, different parts

of the world are represented in the choice of official Observers at the Vatican Council.

(2) We recognize the place that the World Council of Churches has taken in giving leadership in this area, and encourage it to continue to take those actions on behalf of all the Churches that may properly be done by it. We are indebted to the World Council for placing the Roman Catholic-Protestant dialogue in the larger context of new understanding between the several branches of the Christian Church, and welcome the increasing contacts with Orthodox, Lutheran, Anglican, and Free Churches.

(3) We recognize that there are certain subjects on which neither the Alliance nor the World Council have been authorized to speak for the Churches—matters of dogma, doctrine and ecclesiological differences—and that here there must be encounter between Church and Church if eventually we are to move toward unity.

(4) As we welcome the new openness of many of our Roman Catholic brethren to new apprehension of truth and new relationship, so we, too, must cultivate minds and hearts that will be hospitable to new convictions and the wider opportunities opening before us.

We must therefore ask ourselves whether we are ready to engage in helpful dialogue with our Roman Catholic brethren. Do we know and can we communicate that for which we stand? Have we the will to engage in fruitful discussion? Have we the skills required to engage in such discussions and to mediate them to our Churches? Have we the firmness to maintain the truth we have already received while being receptive to new understanding?

(5) Likewise, if we ask searching questions of the Roman Catholic Church, and hope for reforms within the life of that Church, we must expect equally searching questions to be asked concerning the Reformed Churches. We must not

fear the dialogue, and must be true successors of the Reformation by making it a continuing process within our own Churches.

(6) We must realize that there is a real element of risk in such encounter with the Roman Catholic Church. Some of our Churches still suffer because of limitations which have been imposed upon them in the past and which continue to be imposed on them in the present. These Churches cannot easily forget the sufferings and injustices which they have known and which some of them continue to know. We therefore run the risk of being misunderstood and of occasioning offense within the Roman Catholic Church as well as within our own family—and therefore we are required to approach these issues with the spirit of forgiveness, patience and understanding.

(7) We must encourage our member Churches to bring the concerns of Roman Catholic-Protestant relations into each local congregation at least in the following ways:

—by encouraging its members to put aside self-complacency, suspicion and prejudice;

—by sharing, when possible, common and mutually acceptable experiences in worship;

—by establishing small study groups with competent members from both Churches;

—by working together in the interest of social betterment;

—by prayer.

(8) Finally, we must always bear in mind that our primary task as Christians, both Protestant and Roman Catholic, is the proclamation of the Gospel of Jesus Christ for the

redemption of the world. In this new day, we seek again the guidance of the Holy Spirit, without whose enabling power all efforts of reconciliation will be in vain.

b. The General Assembly of the Presbyterian Church in New Zealand, meeting in Auckland, in November 1964, presented these procedures:

The Assembly sets before our own church three ways of association with Roman Catholics which should be encouraged and which were commended to its people by the General Assembly of the United Presbyterian Church in the U.S.A., and adds two others.

First—theological dialogues including a common study of the Word of God in Holy Scriptures with Christians of all confessions in order to discern together the meaning of God's will for our common life, to ascertain the form of the Church, and to understand more clearly the issues which separate us.

Second—co-operation in common concerns involving social action at the civic level, such as working toward world peace and racial justice, resettlement of refugees, the problems of juvenile delinquency, the raising of standards of moral conduct.

Third—open discussion of problems arising from differences in theological conceptions, traditions, or church policies and practices; for example, mixed marriages, family planning, religious liberty.

Fourth—sharing in opportunities to worship and pray together. These opportunities may be few but when they arise, as in the desire in this country of Roman Catholics to share in the Week of Prayer for Christian Unity, they should be accepted gladly.

Fifth—personal neighbourliness towards individual Roman Catholics in the general life of society.

> The Assembly encourages such associations with Roman
> Catholics as steps to Christian unity not in the sense of the
> merging of all the churches but to lead separated fellow
> Christians to know honestly where each stands and to cul-
> tivate mutual relationships in the spirit and way to appro-
> priate fellow Christians.

c. Unanimously, United Presbyterians in the U.S.A. approved a report on Relations with the Roman Catholic Church
at the General Assembly meeting in Columbus, Ohio, May 26,
1965. For the first time, a United States Protestant denomination urged its members, on occasions, to attend Mass in the
Roman Catholic churches:

> Ecumenical dialogue will be poorly achieved if unsupported
> by knowledge and study. As preparatory information we
> commend to the attention of Presbyterians two documents
> from the Second Vatican Council, *De Ecclesia* and *De Ecu-
> menismo*. For self-understanding, and for an informed shar-
> ing of experience, the Constitution and doctrinal standards
> of our Church must be familiarly known. The proposal re-
> garding a Brief Statement of our Faith to be considered by
> the 177th and succeeding General Assemblies is a timely
> expression of the same need for the periodic renewal and
> clarification of the creedal heritage of faith that is presently
> transforming the Roman Catholic Church.

> The exploration and sharing of the Christian faith in ecu-
> menical dialogue must be experienced on all levels of the
> church's life. We urge campus pastors, Presbyterian college
> and seminary faculties, and all Presbyterian leaders in the
> academic community, to initiate where possible conversa-
> tions in faith with Roman Catholic leaders in similar
> capacities.

> Local congregations and presbyteries who have meaningful
> encounters in this field of ecumenical relations should be
> encouraged to share them with the Commission on Ecumeni-
> cal Mission and Relations. We urge United Presbyterians

to initiate fraternal relationships in areas such as the following:

(1) Through association: congregations with Roman Catholic parishes; presbyteries and synods, with dioceses and archdioceses.

(2) Through study encounter on particular issues of common concern which involve us all.

(3) In united efforts in the area of human relations, i.e., race, civil rights, urban renewal.

(4) In encouragement and guidance to youth to pioneer in new efforts of understanding and cooperation.

(5) In occasions for common prayer, i.e. the Week of Prayer for Christian Unity, and other ecumenical gatherings.

Let us be particularly aware of the development of Roman Catholic Bible devotions and the opportunities thus afforded for spiritual fellowship. It should be borne in mind that the traditional Roman Catholic and Reformed theological positions on the Holy Communion are radically divergent. Until mutual understanding as to the meaning and intent of this sacrament is achieved through ecumenical discussions, United Presbyterians would be well advised not to receive communion in the Roman Catholic Church, except when on extraordinary occasions an official invitation is given in terms that are able to be accepted in good conscience. Occasional, reverent attendance at Roman Catholic Mass by United Presbyterians is encouraged. . . .

The most enduring and meaningful sharing of insight and experience must take place where people meet people, where Roman Catholics and Protestants bound in mutual citizenship and community concerns have too often been strangers to each other's faith. We urge our congregations to explore new and adventurous ways in which the unity of the Church may be discerned and its full heritage comprehended. No timidity or provincialism of spirit should keep us from ventures in dialogue in the intimacy of community life where theoretical generalization must give way to personal encounter and understanding. This dialogue is not only the domain of the clergy, but one in which laymen participate on all levels of confessional, interdenominational, and ecumenical conversation. . . .

87. Presbyterian Eugene Carson Blake proposed a merger of four Protestant churches in a sermon in Grace Episcopal Cathedral, San Francisco, December 4, 1960, on the eve of the triennial meeting of the National Council of Churches. His move was seconded by the Episcopal bishop of California, the Rt. Rev. James A. Pike, who followed Dr. Blake in the pulpit. The four churches—United Presbyterian, Episcopalian, Methodist and United Church of Christ—formed a Consultation on Church Union to explore merger possibilities and procedures. The four-way consultation was soon joined by two others, the Disciples of Christ and the Evangelical United Brethren churches, and in 1965 opened up to others. The African Methodist Episcopal and the Presbyterian Church in the United States joined the talks. Dr. Blake sought to bring to this continent the successful merger plan of the church of South India of 1947, that brought together the same four initial groups. Blake sought to unite the "catholic," or "continuing" or "sacramental" emphasis, the "Reformed," or Bible emphasis, and the "evangelical" (a term added later to his original wording), an emphasis, characterizing spontaneity and the work of the Holy Spirit. Following prodigious groundwork and careful timing, Blake's proposal arrived on the scene of a Christianity and a world hungry for unity with the effect of a bombshell:

(a.) Such a union as I now propose must have within it the kind of broad and deep agreement which gives promise of much wider union than seems possible at the present moment, looking ultimately to the reunion of the whole of Christ's Church.

First let me list the principles of reunion that are important to all who are of catholic tradition:

(1) The reunited Church must have visible and historical continuity with the Church of all ages before and after the Reformation. This will include a ministry which by its orders and ordination is recognized as widely as possible by all other Christian bodies. To this end, I propose that, without adopting any particular theory of historic succession, the reunited Church shall provide at its inception for the consecration of all its bishops by bishops and presbyters both in the apostolic succession and out of it from all over the world from all Christian churches which would authorize or permit them to take part. . . .

(2) The reunited Church must clearly confess the historic trinitarian faith received from the Apostles and set forth in the Apostles' and Nicene Creeds. . . .

(3) The reunited Church must administer the two sacraments, instituted by Christ, the Lord's Supper (or Holy Communion, or Eucharist) and Baptism. These must be understood truly as Means of Grace by which God's grace and presence are made available to His people. . . .

And now let me list the principles of reunion that are important to all who are of the Reformation tradition.

(1) The reunited Church must accept the principle of continuing reformation under the Word of God by the guidance of the Holy Spirit. . . . The reunited Church must keep Word and Sacrament equally and intimately united in understanding and appreciation.

(2) The reunited Church must be truly democratic in its government, recognizing that the whole people of God are Christ's Church, that all Christians are Christ's ministers even though some in the church are separated and ordained to the ministry of word and sacrament. . . .

(3) The reunited Church must seek in a new way to recapture the brotherhood and sense of fellowship of all its members and ministers. . . . Since it appears to be necessary to have certain inequalities in status in the Church as between members and officers, and as among deacons, presbyters, and bishops, let us make certain that the more status a member or minister has, the more simple be his dress and attitude. Let us seek to make it evident in every possible way that in the Church the greatest is the servant of all. "My brother" is a better form of Christian address than "your grace." A simple cassock is generally a better Christian garb for the highest member of the clergy than cope and miter. And must there be grades of reverends, very, right, most, etc.? . . .

(4) Finally the reunited Church must find the way to include within its catholicity (and because of it) a wide diversity of theological formulation of the faith and a variety of worship and liturgy including worship that is non-liturgical.

The great confessions of the Reformation must have their place in the confession, teaching, and history of the reunited Church. . . . And further, the reunited Church should, as led by the Holy Spirit under the Word, from time to time seek to confess its united faith to the world in new formulations appropriate to its place and time. . . .

Thus the united Church must avoid that kind of legalistic formulation of doctrine which, on the ground of expressing unity of faith, in fact produces a sterile uniformity which breeds alternately neglect and schism. . . .

In conclusion I would remind you that precise ways of formulating such a reunion as I have sketched have been worked out in several ways, particularly in the subcontinent of India in the several plans of union there. One may ask why they have preceded us in this, and alternatively why we should look to their example for light and inspiration toward union here.

The answer to these questions is a simple one. Christians in India recognize themselves to be a small and beleaguered minority in a pagan and secular world. They have realized full well that they could not afford the luxury of their divisions. I submit that even though our numbers and wealth and prestige may be greater than theirs, we too need to recognize that we cannot afford longer the luxury of our historic divisions. . . .

(b.) Four years later Dr. Blake returned to the pulpit at Grace Cathedral and discussed the developments in his proposal. He noted (1) the popularity of the plan enhanced by the interest of mass media, (2) the influence of the Vatican Council and unity minded Popes, John and Paul, on Protestants, (3) counter developments, such as the growing "world-wide confessional relationships"—groupings on the basis of denominations, the Anglican Communion, Baptist World Alliance, etc., and (4) a "lethargy . . . in various quarters an actual hardening of opposition to church union." So in his "second thoughts on Church union," January 24, 1965, at Grace Cathedral, Dr. Blake said:

I cannot emphasize too strongly that no progress whatever may be expected in a church union unless on the one hand we act in the conviction that we are a people chosen by God (set apart and beloved by him) and on the other hand with a humility, a teachableness, a mutual forbearance, a willingness to forgive, and a Christian love which are not natural endowments, but a miraculous gift of grace. . . .

In this spirit, then, let us remind ourselves of three pitfalls that ever threaten to trap those who would unite our Churches.

(1) We must be against any Church union which is established at the expense of truth. It is because I believe we all need each other and can be enriched by the best of each others' faith and life that I press for church union now.

A union produced by compromising convictions is not according to the will of Christ. This is the reason all of us must seek to understand and appreciate each other (and to forgive one another) much more than we usually do. A united church must fully confess the faith received by us all from the ancient fathers and enriched by the insights of the separated fathers and contemporary brothers of our several traditions. The truth of Jesus Christ comprehends and transcends the faith of St. Augustine, St. Ignatius and St. Francis. It includes the insights of Luther, Calvin, Hooker, Newman, Williams and Wesley. It embraces the Christian understanding of William Temple, Nathan Söderblom, Willem Visser 't Hooft and Martin Luther King. The truth of Christ transcends them all and a united church must be built on no less comprehensive a base of Christian truth.

(2) We must be against any church union that is motivated by, or aimed at an outmoded triumphalism. I am indebted to Karl Rahner, the German Jesuit, more than to any other single writer, for making it clear to me in his book entitled, "The Christian Commitment," how important it is for all Christian churches to give up, once and for all, the attitude once almost universally held by them that they ought to try to become powerful enough to dominate any state, society, or culture, in which they are set. Those who still want the church, or churches to dominate American life misread the signs of the times. The churches and their leaders must learn how to serve the world rather than to go on trying, as in the past, to rule it. . . .

There are many Protestants as there are Roman Catholics who look back to the simpler past with a great nostalgia. They want their church, as church, to be dominant again as once it seemed to be. Some would argue for church union in the United States in order to make the church more directly powerful again. This is as wrong as it is dangerous. We dare not conceive or work toward a church union in order to rule or dominate; we must seek church union to become better able to serve. . . .

(3) Finally, we must be against any church union that would in any way threaten the ecumenical movement, or diminish the obligation to continue to cooperate with all Christian Churches in their common witness to the Lordship of Jesus Christ. . . .

I hope my point is clear. Church union must never be thought of as a substitute for, or an alternative to ecumenical cooperation of all Christian Churches. The kind of church union which alone we dare to press for, is one which is recognized clearly as supplementary to all other manifestations of Christian unity, especially those obligations laid upon us all by the new ecumenical insights of the 20th Century. . . .

And so today I say to you:

"Led, I pray by the Holy Spirit, I propose" that we press on in North America to form, with all who will with us, "a united church, truly catholic, truly reformed, and truly evangelical," lest in this revolutionary world we find ourselves so bound to our own past histories that we are unable to be God's instrument for peace and reconciliation across all boundaries of nation, race, or class. And I call upon you to seek this union in the only spirit which Jesus Christ can bless as expressed by the Apostle in my text: "Put on then as God's chosen ones, holy and beloved, compassion, kindness, lowliness, meekness and patience, forebearing one another and, if one has a complaint against another, forgiving each other; as the Lord has forgiven you, so you also must forgive. And above all these, put on love, which binds everything together in perfect harmony." [Col. 3: 12-14].

88. Dr. Blake's merger proposal was well on its way by 1966 as representatives of eight denominations, four added to the original four, agreed to a "set of principles" for merging the eight denominations. Timetable calls for a federation of the churches to be achieved in about 15 years to be followed by a quarter of a century or more of a federation, with a constitution to be worked out for one church after a prolonged period of living together. Meeting in Dallas, Texas, in May 1966, the delegates re-

flected substantial agreement on doctrine, which had been discussed at previous meetings of the Consultation on Church Union (after an organizational meeting in Washington in 1962), in Oberlin, Ohio (1963), Princeton, New Jersey (1964), and Lexington, Kentucky (1965). Essential to the set of principles (originally termed an outline) for union is a mutual recognition and respect of one another's own traditions. Tnere was considerable tension in Dallas over what kind of structure the new church should have, particularly in regard to bishops. The Methodists asserted themselves and insisted on their system of bishops with appointive powers to name pastors to pulpits, maintaining that this insured a free pulpit, with the pastor not responsible to the whims of a congregation. Episcopalians preferred more of a pastoral role for bishops than administrative. Half of the groups in the talks have no bishops at all—United Presbyterians, Presbyterians U.S. (South), Disciples of Christ, and the United Church of Christ. Other churches involved in the talks are Methodist, African Methodist Episcopal, Evangelical United Brethren, and Episcopal. The battle over structure remains, and a section on structure in the original outline was postponed for discussion at Cambridge, Massachusetts, in 1967. The preamble of the 15,000-word "Principles of Church Union" approved in 1966 says:

> We affirm our faith in the one God, Father, Son and Holy Spirit, who has given us our unity in the one holy, catholic, and apostolic church. The people of God exist as one people, and only one, of every nationality and race and tongue. They have been made so in Christ; and he wills that they make this unity evident. There is but one Body; and he into whom we have been baptized wills that this wholeness be clearly seen. There is but one covenant; and he who has sealed it with his own blood wills that this be unmistakably expressed.
>
> We are convinced that the characteristics of the Church which are God's gifts to it, can be fully seen only as the Church becomes visibly one. . . .
>
> We resolve to attempt, under God, a truer expression of the fullness of the Church of Christ than any of the constitut-

ing churches can suppose itself to be. This includes a fidelity
to God's revelation in the Scriptures greater than when
churches merely appeal to the Bible's words to justify their
separate ways, and refuse to allow the same covenant to
yoke them together in common tasks. It includes a more
adequate and credible confession of faith than can be the
case where separate traditions obscure the common inheritance. It includes a public worship and sacramental life
which will manifest more clearly and surely the high priesthood of Christ, and the part of all believers in that priesthood, than is possible behind walls of separation which exclude some of those whom Christ has welcomed. It includes
an ordering of the ministry which will recognize a greater
diversity of the Spirit's gifts, and release those gifts for
wider and more effective service, than is the case where
separated ministries in separated churches are expected to
give priority to the institutional interests of those churches.
Thus we, humbly and penitently, seek to create the conditions for a fuller expression of the faith, the worship, the
ministry, and the mission of the one Church of Christ. . . .

In considering the organization needed to give effect to our
understanding of the Church's true nature, we mean to bear
those objectives particularly in mind, as follows:

(a) *Obedience to mission must be the primary characteristic of the church at every level.* This refers, of course,
to our plain duty to eliminate overlapping and duplication
so that greater energies can be released for the common
task. More, it refers to new structures which will make it
difficult if not impossible for us to avoid being confronted
by God's mission in the world and his command that we
follow. . . .

(b) *Mutual enrichment must be served and guarded.*
Visible unity should take away from us nothing except our
separateness, and add to our common treasury as much
as possible of what is true and good in the tradition of each
of the constituting churches. It should not only permit but

positively encourage the maximum interplay of tradition with tradition, across traditional lines. . . .

(c) *Existing relationships should be maintained and strengthened wherever possible.* The bonds which now exist between the constituting churches and other Christian bodies (confessional, conciliar and the like) should not be severed or modified, except where their continuance would clearly compromise the unity we seek. . . .

(d) *Maximum protection must be given to existing diversities and liberties.* We seek not to diminish freedom under the gospel but to enhance it. The costs of a wider unity will doubtless require sacrifices on the part of all, including the acceptance of new limitations for the common good. . . .

(e) Maximum openness should be provided for continuing renewal and reformation. No visible, earthly body, however idealistically planned, can ever be safe from the corruption of human folly, ignorance and sin. Time and again it has been God's good pleasure to save the church from death, in spite of our failures. . . .

Organization must inescapably reflect our humble awareness of our need for constant reformation, and our determination that such cleansing be unimpeded by pride and prejudice.

Organization equally must be such as not to stifle those who protest. Clearly the church requires norms of ordered life, but we realize that these may sometimes impede rather than assist the work of the Spirit. Therefore we affirm the essential place of the non-conformist in the church as in our society everywhere. We say that any conception of church order or administration which unjustly smothers or minimizes the contribution of such persons may deprive the church of indispensable guides through a time of rapid change and upheaval such as our own.

(f) *It must be a uniting as well as a united church.* This means emphasizing the united church's incomplete and provisional character, its own desire to press steadily forward toward wider unity, both national and international. The separate churches desire not merely to form a new and larger denomination, but to embark on a pilgrimage whose only ultimate goal can be the unity of the whole Body. The act of unification is a sign of trust not in our own dreams or powers but in God's grace, who has given us the "one hope that belongs to your call," so that we may "grow up in every way into him who is the head, into Christ" (Ephesians 4: 4, 15 RSV).

89. Not all denominations, in their statements on church unity, accept the same premises. Differences occur concerning (1) whether visible unity is meant by Christ in his desire for Christians to be one, and (2) whether divisions represent a sin or not. Methodist Bishop Gerald Kennedy, of Southern Californa—Nevada Area of The Methodist Church, and a number of other Methodist bishops disagree with most of the ecumenical leaders on those two points. Bishop Kennedy's view, several times stated in articles, received its widest expression when he wrote and delivered the quadrennium message of the 82-member Council of Bishops of The Methodist Church for the General Conference in Pittsburgh, April 26, 1964. The bishops traditionally review the message before it is presented by its author, and thus the message has the effect of their approval. Bishop Kennedy expressed the bishops' joy over the Vatican Council and ecumenical developments, but also slipped in one of his main objections:

Not all of us are of the opinion that it is profitable for us to spend so much time confessing sins of exclusiveness of which we are not guilty. We hasten to add that we have enough real sins to confess. But we are not sure that God wills the churches of the Reformation to become one organic union. We believe that our pluralism has produced much good fruit, not the least of which has been freedom. We doubt seriously that eliminating our denominations would solve all our problems. We have no intention of apologizing

for our own heritage or slowing down our evangelistic efforts until some proposed merger has been accomplished.
The final goal for any Church is not necessarily merger but
how to use its resources to serve Christ better.

90. The conservative evangelical Protestant position that spiritual unity of all true believers in Christ (and spiritual means
"invisible" here) is the only true unity is summed up by W.
Stanley Mooneyham, former Free Will Baptist chief executive,
evangelical magazine editor (*NAE Action*), and currently a press
officer for Billy Graham in Atlanta. His objection to the idea
that division is a sin parallels that of Bishop Kennedy's, among
the Methodists, and most Baptists, with the possible exception of
the American Baptist Convention. Mooneyham describes a "spiritual unity," but also attempts to go beyond former conservative
limitations and describe an "evangelical" visible unity:

> There are . . . scores of ways in which our spiritual unity
> needs to be—and can be—made visible. . . .
>
> Let me give you a study in contrasts. . . .
>
> For the first scene we have to go to the campus of the Uni-
> versity of Michigan at Ann Arbor. The time is August, 1961.
> Gathered on the campus are nearly 2,000 young people from
> 40 different denominations who are attending the North
> American Ecumenical Youth Assembly.
>
> Here a great to-do was made over the scandal of the division
> of Christendom. One of the speakers—a Burmese Baptist
> layman—declared that "Christians who cannot break bread
> together, or drink the cup of fellowship, renew the scars of
> His (Christ's) body and tear asunder His image." To illus-
> trate his point a veil picturing the face of Christ was cut
> apart publicly and each piece was given to representatives
> of various denominations as a graphic object lesson of their
> divided state.
>
> On the opening night the young people were visibly re-

minded that a joint communion service could not be held by the shining of a spotlight upon an empty chalice around which an interpretive dance was staged.

A news release from one of the sponsoring groups just ahead of the conference asked if it were possible to "awaken the same sense of shame in Christian youth of today" which young ecumenists had in the early days of the movement. I don't know whether or not they succeeded, but I know that at Ann Arbor they made a serious, calculated effort.

For the next scene let us go to the University of Illinois at Urbana just five months later. Gathered here are over 5,000 students coming from every state in the union and 50 foreign countries. They are giving up part of their Christmas holiday to attend the sixth International Student Missionary Convention sponsored by Inter-Varsity Christian Fellowship.

They represent as diverse theological backgrounds as you can possibly imagine. I talked with a young Negro Pentecostal girl from Colorado, a Greek Orthodox engineering student from Lebanon, an Anglican divinity student from Uganda, a Southern Baptist boy from Oklahoma, an Egyptian pastor of the only Protestant church in tiny Kuwait. I lived in a dormitory room with some of them—got up for their early morning Bible study, stayed up for their late night prayer meetings.

I felt their spiritual heartbeat as they wept and asked God to make them strong witnesses on their campuses. I shared in the undiluted Christian love which they lavished on each other. I sensed the deep moving of the Holy Spirit as He pressed the claims of Jesus Christ upon each of them.

And I watched with a tremendous swelling pride as by the scores and hundreds they made the full commitment of life to the Lord who had saved them. Nearly 400 of them definitely committed themselves for missionary service—another 900 pledged to see God's will about it.

As the clock struck midnight to usher in the new year on the last night of the convention, the fieldhouse where they were meeting became a holy sanctuary as they sat down together—some 5,000 of them—and under the leadership of an Anglican bishop from Australia joined in a communion service to share the emblems representing the body and blood of their Lord.

There was no handwringing because they did not all bear the same denominational label. Although they surely were aware of it, it didn't seem to matter—and none of the conference leaders seemed to think that it was important enough at the time to point it out.

I have called this a study in contrasts. At this conference no one mouthed any platitudes about Christian unity; they just went about quietly bearing witness to the oneness which they possessed as disciples of the same Lord.

91. In another vein of dissent, the Canadian Council of Evangelical Protestant Churches strongly contradicted positions of the World Council of Churches, the Second Vatican Council, and the ecumenical movement in general. In the CCEPC statement concerning unity:

The unity sought by the World Council of Churches and by the Roman Catholic Church, however, is a unity that breeds intolerance toward any who disagree with it. This has shown up repeatedly in the attitude of the big denominations toward the religious minority groups of this country. Evangelical Christianity champions religious freedom for everyone—even those with whom they disagree. Religious freedom gives any group the right to propagate its own message, and in the course of so doing, even criticize contrary teaching. This principle applies in every department of Canadian life, and should apply in religion as well.

Men and women being what they are, it is only natural that there will be many differences of opinion on all subjects. Why should we accept this apparent fact in every other

realm but religion? It's all right to differ with others on
politics, on business, on sociology, on penology, on methods
of education, on history, and on international affairs, but
when it comes to religion up goes the hue and cry that "we
must have unity at any price!"

Paul the Apostle once made this observation: "There must
be heresies among you, that they which are approved may be
made manifest among you."

It is too bad that the religious leaders in Canada spend so
much energy and time and money in their wild search for a
phantom unity. Churches could no more get together on a
national or international scale than could newspapers, politicians, or industries. The ecumenical movement was doomed
to fail before it began, because the basis upon which the
modern church leaders want to build church unity is one
of sinking sand. They are trying to unite truth with error.
The Bible says, "Can two walk together except they be
agreed?" The only basis for genuine unity among the
churches is the basis of eternal truth. This truth can be
found in clear, unmistakable terms in the Biblical, fundamental doctrines of true, historic Christianity. This is not
the Christianity of Roman Catholicism, or liberal Modern-
ism. Until men and women learn this simple fact, they will
never find the true unity for which Jesus Christ prayed in
John, chapter 17.

"Holy Father," He prayed, "keep through thine own name
those whom Thou has given Me, that they may be one, as we
are." A little later on in that same prayer, Jesus said,
"Sanctify them through Thy truth: Thy word is truth."
Here it is clearly stated that the truth of the Word of God
(The Bible) is the only acceptable basis for genuine Christianity unity.

92. A more positive statement of evangelicals appeared in an
editorial leading off a special issue on the ecumenical movement
in *Christianity Today*, January 29, 1965. Here again, the unity

or oneness that Jesus talked about is viewed as an invisible achievement only, thus making any need, or realization or hope for unity in this life purely irrelevant. The editorial enumerated these "evangelical principles of Christian unity":

(1) The Church of Jesus Christ is both an actual reality in history and an invisible number of believers known only to God.

(2) The existence of the one Church as churches, extended over time and space, is not per se a contradiction of the Church's essential unity.

(3) The Church is one in Jesus Christ, having one Lord, one faith, one baptism, and one hope. Deeply held differences have given rise to denominationalism. These differences have not destroyed the inner unity of Christians in Jesus Christ but have impaired the reflection of that unity in the visible churches.

(4) By the fragmentary denominational reflection of their unity in Jesus Christ, by their rivalry on mission fields at home and abroad, by sometimes denying to others the liberty of conviction they claim for themselves, churches give imperfect witness to the Gospel and create obstacles to the fulfillment of the mission of the Church.

(5) Churches whose existence derives only from sociological, racial or cultural differences ought not to remain separate and divided. They should seek, wherever possible, union with other churches of like convictions.

(6) Churches whose separate existence is grounded in basic theological differences of faith and order should not ignore these differences, but should seek to resolve them by looking toward a visible manifestation of true unity in Jesus Christ and by recognizing that certain of these differences of faith and order may be as much a part of Christian truth as is the truth concerning the unity of the Church.

(7) In the endeavor to achieve external, visible unity, any ecumenical effort that evades or ignores essential matters of faith and order will lead only to greater confusion and ultimate failure. Any unity not based upon the common theological affirmation of the faith once for all delivered will be an expression in history of something other than what the Church in Jesus Christ is divinely appointed to be.

93. A unique way has been found for churches of conservative bent who want to unite with a cooperative group, namely the National and local Council of Churches, but whose own strength is not sufficient to swing the whole local or state or regional wing of its denomination into the wider alliance. This problem existed in Southern California, where even the more open-minded American Baptists are sometimes conservative on issues. At the 1965 convention of the Southern California (American) Baptist Convention, 500 delegates by a narrow margin voted down a move for membership in the Southern California Council of Churches. The solution for the Baptist churches who wanted to join the Council, as a group with voting rights, but could not do so as a denomination, was to form a special Ecumenical Fellowship of American Baptist Churches in Southern California. (The ABC as a national denomination with offices in the East does belong to the NCC and WCC.) The churches wanting to participate in the regional Council joined this Ecumenical Fellowship, which in turn joined the Southern California Council with the "status" of a denomination, but without splitting from the regional Southern California wing of the American Baptist denomination. The charter statement of The Ecumenical Fellowship of American Baptist Churches in Southern California, January 20, 1965, says:

*Purpose:* In order to express more adequately our oneness in Jesus Christ as Divine Lord and Savior with other believers, we, the undersigned American Baptist churches in Southern California, do hereby voluntarily associate ourselves to seek further fellowship in the Council of Churches in Southern California. We seek this relationship so that we may make our contribution of witness, leadership, and assistance and that we may in return be mutually strengthened by other communions.

*Name:* We express our desire in the name, the Ecumenical Fellowship of American Baptist Churches in Southern California.

*Organization:* We shall be a functioning organization, not designated with ecclesiastical powers, but recognized only as a representative avenue of witness. It shall be understood that we shall automatically disband if the Southern California Baptist Convention becomes a constituent judicatory of the Council of Churches in Southern California.

To assist our fellowship, two officers shall be named as chairman and secretary-treasurer. The chairman shall represent the organization between meetings and shall preside at all meetings. . . .

*Finance:* Funds designated to the Council of Churches in Southern California shall not be channelled through the Ecumenical Fellowship, but shall be designated by the individual churches through the Southern California Baptist Convention.

*Representation:* The Fellowship shall be represented at all proper functions and assemblies of the Council of Churches in Southern California through its officers or elected delegates.

*Meetings:* The Fellowship shall meet at least twice a year to elect officers and delegates, receive reports, discuss current issues, and handle other necessary business.

94. American Baptists nationally have taken an interest in the ecumenical movement and that interest is becoming more theological. In 1964, an endorsement of "cooperative Christianity" was approved by the American Baptist Convention, but in the voting, a strong theological amendment was added and approved:

"in the obedience to the prayer of Jesus that we all be one." The
resolution further said:

> Because the rising power of apostasy and irreligion and the
> resurgence of non-Christian religions present a challenge,
> we would appeal to all American Baptists to take a more vig-
> orous part in the development of a cooperative Christianity:
>
> —By continuing to support whole-heartedly the ecumeni-
> cal movement, as expressed in the World Council of
> Churches, the National Council of Churches, and the state
> and local councils; more specifically, by relating local church
> groups to their counterparts in local cooperative church
> councils . . .
>
> —By cooperation of our American Baptist headquarters
> agencies with the long range programs of other denomina-
> tions, in the hope that the evangelistic, social concerns, edu-
> cational, missionary and stewardship emphases of the var-
> ious denominations might be so timed and coordinated as
> to make a simultaneous Christian impact upon the local
> communities.
>
> —By reaffirming its long-standing policy of comity and
> cooperation with the Southern Baptist Convention concern-
> ing the establishment of churches on the North American
> continent and on overseas mission fields.
>
> —By reaffirming its long-standing policy of cooperative
> church planning and service with all other cooperative de-
> nominations and communions which recognize Jesus Christ
> as Lord and Savior, avoiding the establishment of churches
> in the same immediate areas. . . .
>
> By expressing to the members of the Roman Catholic and
> Eastern Orthodox churches and of the Jewish faith our
> appreciation for the interfaith dialogues presently taking
> place in religious circles everywhere; by working coopera-
> tively with the members of all faiths, and striving earnestly
> to make this a religiously literate nation, whose God is the

Lord, and whose people shall be dedicated to peace and righteousness among all men. We urge American Baptists to clarify for themselves what their contribution should be to this dialogue.

95. Southern Baptists outlined new steps to wider fellowship. "To continue to withdraw from the mainstream of religious life in this country," said Marse Grant, editor of the *Biblical Recorder* of the North Carolina Baptist (Southern) State Convention, in an editorial, Jan. 2, 1965, "will bring further apprehension on the part of those who do not understand the separatist attitude of some Southern Baptists. With the forces of secularism threatening to overrun the church, it would appear that Southern Baptists have many areas of cooperation with other religious groups without any thought of organic union."

The most auspicious step of the Southern Baptists was a move in 1965 to join with other Baptists in forming a North American Baptist Fellowship, a reversal of its refusal to join the Fellowship in 1964. Meeting in Dallas, 1965, the Southern Baptist Convention adopted this report and resolution:

Whereas, we are living in a day when materialism, secularism, and paganism challenge every spiritual ideal for which we stand, and

Whereas, as the continent's largest evangelical denomination, Southern Baptists should exert every initiative and influence to win the North American continent for Christ, and

Whereas, we have a moral obligation to share our strength, our witness and our vision with sister continental Baptist bodies, who in turn will share their strength and insights with us, and

Whereas, Southern Baptists have a genuine desire to conserve the values and continue the gains that grew out of the Baptist Jubilee Advance Program, and

Whereas, Southern Baptists have been an integral part of the Baptist World Alliance since its beginning and have found in it a profitable and useful channel of communication and cooperation with other Baptist bodies that has not hindered or compromised our autonomy or witness as a convention or as individual churches, and

Whereas, the Baptist World Alliance through its executive committee has established a subcommittee to provide a continuing channel of communication and cooperation for the member Baptist bodies of the North American continent, and

Whereas, the bylaws of the Baptist World Alliance specifically limit this subcommittee as follows:

(a) It shall have no authority over any Baptist church or over any Baptist body or undertake any work for which the member bodies are responsible, and

(b) The work of this subcommittee shall be financed within the framework of the Baptist World Alliance budget by funds contributed by the North American member bodies, organizations and individuals, and

Whereas, Southern Baptists are already associated with the Baptist World Alliance, and welcome further opportunities to share mutual concerns with other Baptist bodies, WE THEREFORE RECOMMEND:

(1) That the Southern Baptist Convention accept the invitation of the Baptist World Alliance executive committee to have representation on its "North American Committee." and

(2) That our representation on this committee be elected by the convention, and

(3) That the committee on boards nominate these representatives.

Your (special study) committee respectfully suggests:

(1) To the executive committee of the Baptist World Alli-

ance that the name of this subcommittee be changed from the "North American Fellowship of the Baptist World Alliance," to the "North American Committee of the Baptist World Alliance" in order to describe more accurately its nature and relationship, and

(2) To the convention's committee on boards, that, as far as practical to facilitate meeting and limit expense, representation on the said North American Committee be selected from among the Southern Baptists who represent us on the Baptist World Alliance executive committee.

96. In the expanding dialogue among local parishes and laymen, discussion rules have been suggested. The Most Rev. John Heenan, of Liverpool, now Cardinal archbishop of Westminster, set forth eight preliminary steps for interfaith discussions:

(1) Never accuse non-Catholics of being in bad faith. God judges both them and us. Assume that members of other religions are at least as sincere as ourselves in their beliefs.

(2) Always keep calm when the ignorant attack what they wrongly believe to be Catholic doctrine.

(3) Be ready to answer questions about the Faith, but never argue if you are unable to keep your temper.

(4) In discussions with non-Catholics never, in an effort to please, pretend that differences in doctrine do not matter. That would be insincere and untrue.

(5) Don't deny that the Catholic Church claims to be the one true Church. But don't allege that only Catholics can be real Christians. This is not only false but absurd.

(6) Christian charity does not require us to take part in the worship of other religions, but we should not be more Catholic than the Pope. We may recite publicly the Lord's Prayer and the Apostles' Creed with other Christians. We may also pray with them in private. That is a different matter from

taking part in public worship in which we do not believe.

(7) Join with non-Catholics in working for the good of the whole community. In the social services, trade unions and political parties Catholics should give an example of public spirit.

(8) While fostering Christian unity we must never forget our duty of bringing all men to a knowledge of the truth. Remember that the tragedy of England is not that many Christians are not Catholics but that so many citizens have no religion at all.

97. Becoming more organized, the local dialogue now has a home movement with a discussion guide book, *Living Room Dialogues*, published at the end of 1965 jointly by the National Council of Churches and the Paulist Press. The National Council of Catholic Men also released its program kit on "Grass-Roots Ecumenism" in January 1966. *Living Room Dialogues*, in its introduction, offers these general guidelines "for the benefit of discussion leaders":

(1) You will want to choose a moderator or discussion leader, or you may rotate this responsibility each time. You may want co-leaders, a Roman Catholic and a Protestant, a man and a woman.

(2) How about an observer, a different one each time, not to take part in the discussion, but to observe the process and to give positive suggestions for improving it next time?

(3) In the first session, take time for each person to identify himself or herself—who each is—something of his interests and concerns—his church, etc.

(4) Help to set the stage for learning, growing, sharing, caring, by listening to what is really being said, by accepting each person's contribution and by not judging them. Be open to all ideas and suggestions whether you agree with them or

not. By your own attitude of willingness to learn and change, you will encourage others to do the same.

(5) Take responsibility for helping with the discussion, not having to talk all the time, not having to be right or to prove a point. Help to keep some from monopolizing by encouraging each person to participate. If this is difficult, you might take turns at first to give everyone a chance to participate.

(6) Help to distinguish facts from opinion, but encourage both.

(7) If the group seems to wander, help to recall them to the subject under discussion. Don't try to cover more than one subject in an evening.

(8) Set a firm closing hour and stick to it. Better to go home eager for more than exhausted! Two hours should be the maximum time.

(9) By your own prayer and worship life, help the members of the group to center their interaction, their questioning and seeking in shared and varying kinds of prayer within the group.

(10) Become better acquainted yourself with the wealth of resources of the Churches involved, and of the Christian Faith, and share these with others.

(11) Ask God the Holy Spirit to lead and to change the members of the group, so that individually and corporately they may find new ways of behaving as Christians, in the Church and in the world. Ideas will change but so will lives.

98. Ten Commandment guides for dialogue developed on both sides of the Atlantic.

a. John Cogley, former editor of *Commonweal* and now senior religion editor for *The New York Times*, offered "Ten Commandments for the Age of Ecumenism":

(1) Remember that saints and sinners are to be found in all branches of Christianity.

(2) Do not look to conversion as the proper result of ecumenism.

(3) Do not attempt to achieve charity at the expense of truth.

(4) Do not attempt to serve truth at the expense of charity.

(5) Do not question another's sincerity or lightly impute superstition, ignorance, or fear in order to explain why they believe as they do.

(6) Respect what others deem holy.

(7) Don't defend the indefensible.

(8) Work together for the common good, as citizens equal before the law.

(9) Pray together.

(10) Leave theology to the theologians.

b. In Germany, in 1960, another set of commandments appeared, signed by Dr. Fritz Blanke, professor at the University of Zurich:

(1) We will overcome evil with good.

(2) We will avoid easy generalizations, hurried conclusions and quick judgments.

(3) We will not rejoice in the weaknesses of other churches, but rather in any sign of vitality that we can perceive.

(4) We will do whatever our conscience prescribes, and not

ask all the time whether others have rights on their side or not.

(5) We will not ascribe to adversaries only base motives of special tactics, maneuvers, disguises, and pretentions, but rather we believe that the Holy Spirit moves among others and also gives joy to those that do not have our faith and joy.

(6) Before we tell others of their errors and weaknesses, ask ourselves whether we happen to be affected by similar faults.

(7) We will keep ourselves from self-sufficiency and from denominational [konfessioneller] complacency.

(8) We will beseech God to prevent us from despising others.

(9) We will stay away from all animosities.

(10) As much as we can, we will purify our history and religion books and textbooks of all statements either anti-Catholic or anti-Protestant which could be wrongly polemical.

    c. In Italy, the Rev. Father Battista Mondin, S.X., of Tavernerio, proposed what he called a "Complete Decalogue" that combined both intellectual and emotional dispositions. In an Italian magazine, he gave this decalogue:

(1) Believe in the good faith of the other side and, therefore, do not pretend to convert it.

(2) Have a clear understanding of one's own faith and live up to it fully.

(3) Have a clear knowledge of the faith of the others.

(4) Take up the responsibility for the faults of one's own community.

(5) Face honestly both the problems which cause division and those which help unity.

(6) Avoid any kind of animosity in the discussion.

(7) Do not despise your opponent.

(8) Do not rejoice over the weakness of his Church.

(9) Overcome evil with good.

(10) Believe that God can do even that which seems humanly impossible, that is, re-establish the unity of Christians.

99. Protestants were offering suggestions for "ecumenical etiquette" in preparation for dialogue. Giving an impetus to dialogue through suggestions on how to go about it, the Rev. Dr. Robert McAfee Brown, professor of religion at Stanford University, published in February 1960 six "ground rules" to be observed as "conditions which must prevail if the dialogue is to prove fruitful." His article appeared in both the Protestant *Christian Century* and the Catholic *Commonweal*. He said:

(1) Each partner must believe that the other is speaking in good faith.

(2) Each partner must have a clear understanding of his own faith.

(3) Each partner must strive for a clear understanding of the faith of the other.

(4) Each partner must accept responsibility in humility and penitence for what his group has done, and is doing, to foster and perpetuate division.

(5) Each partner must forthrightly face the issues which cause separation as well as those which create unity.

(6) Each partner must recognize that all that can be done with the dialogue is to offer it up to God.

100.  Attitudes for dialogue were discussed by Arthur C. Piepkorn, of Concordia Seminary, St. Louis, in an article in the *The Lutheran Witness* (Missouri Synod Lutheran) and reprinted in *The National Catholic Reporter*, October 20, 1965. He suggested Lutherans could learn a new set of attitudes and approaches from their Catholic brothers:

*We can learn to watch our language when we talk to and about our fellow Christians of other denominations.*

. . . The Directive on Ecumenism prepared for the guidance of the laity of the Roman Catholic Archdiocese of St. Louis makes some concrete recommendations in this spirit. It calls the term "our separated brethren" well-intentioned but "not a happy usage." It sees the long-used term "non-Catholic" as "unsatisfactory" and "hardly respectful." To use the terms "convert" and "conversion" for baptised members of other denominations who become Roman Catholics it calls offensive since the baptised Christian by the very fact of his baptism pertains to Christ. We could let this praiseworthy concern sensitize us to terms which we habitually use but which are needlessly unpleasant in the ears of others.

*We can learn to take the time to study other denominations thoroughly.*

The Roman Catholic Church in this country is making a serious effort to understand other denominations. The number of Roman Catholic books and articles on Lutheran subjects, to speak only of our own Church, is formidable. . . .

*We can learn to take our agreements and our differences seriously. . . .*

*We can learn from the Roman Catholic Church to think more biblically about the Church. . . .*

*We can learn from the Roman Catholic Church to give more attention to the sacred scriptures.*

This may sound strange because we have habitually thought of the Roman Catholic Church as being a denomination that relegated the sacred scriptures to a secondary position. For a little over 20 years, however, a concern for the written revelation of God and its proclamation to the faithful has been sweeping with ever increasing force through the Roman Catholic Church at every level. . . .

*We can learn from the Roman Catholic Church to take the sacraments more seriously. . . .*

*We can learn from the Roman Catholic Church to think increasingly in terms of the resurrection of our Lord. . . .*

*We can learn from the Roman Catholic Church to give more attention to the blessed Virgin Mary and the saints. . . .*

*We can learn from the Roman Catholic Church to make our worship less clerical. . . .*

*We can learn from the Roman Catholic Church to put our celebrants where they historically belong, facing the worshipping congregation across the altar. . . .*

*We can learn from the Roman Catholic Church to approach the dialogue with meekness, humility, love of the truth, and prayer. . . .*

What this all adds up to is the somewhat paradoxical recognition that we can learn from the Roman Catholic Church to be more Lutheran Lutherans. None of the points mentioned are really alien to our tradition.

101. Reuel L. Howe, a professor and organizer of dialogue, sets some philosophical guidelines for dialogue, with a priority on interpersonal relationships. Dr. Howe is founder and direc-

tor of the interdenominational Institute for Advanced Pastoral
Studies at Bloomfield Hills, Michigan. He says of the person in
dialogue:

> By dialogical person we mean one who, by word or relation-
> ship, is in communication with his environment and open to
> the communication that environment offers, environment in
> this sense including both persons and things. The dialogical
> person is a rare individual, although he need not be. He may
> appear in the guise of any type. He can be a poet, philos-
> opher, scientist, artist, administrator, industrialist, or min-
> ister. Even in the midst of a competitive transaction there
> may pass between two persons a glance in which the eyes are
> instruments of deep personal meeting, and the new creation
> gleams in the midst of the travail of the old. What, then, are
> some of the characteristics of the person in dialogue, the
> qualities by which we may recognize him?

> (1) *The dialogical person is a total, authentic person.* He is
> one who responds to others with his whole being and not
> with just a part of himself, and he is able to listen with his
> heart as well as with his mind. He is *really* present; he does
> not run off on "errands" while he seems to be listening to
> the person before him. . . .

> (2) *The dialogical person is an open person,* one who is
> known first by his willingness and ability to reveal himself
> to others, and, secondly, by his willingness and ability to
> hear and receive their revelation. . . . The dialogical person
> does not talk about himself, but he does offer out of himself
> meaning to which his fellows may make free response. And
> to do this, he has to assume certain risks of communication
> and, therefore, of creativity. . . .

> The dialogical person must also be open to the meaning and
> influence of the dialogue itself. The act of dialogue is one by
> which a person makes himself available to and aware of
> others, and an important part of that relationship is the
> meaning of what each says to the other. . . .

(3) *The dialogical person is a disciplined person.* A disciplined person is one who is able to assume responsibility for himself and others, and accepts the limitations as well as the opportunities the relationship offers. . . .

(4) *The dialogical person is a related person.* By this we mean that he responds to others and is, therefore, responsible. We cannot be individuals going our separate ways. We are tied to each other and dependent on one another. . . .

Therefore, if persons do not accept each other in the structures of relationship, there can be no dialogue. But it is in dialogue that acceptance is given and received. The word spoken in dialogue is an act of faith done in spite of the doubt that it will do any good. The dialogical word is an open word, a word of beginnings, because it is a word of expectation inviting response. In speaking the word of dialogue a person puts himself on the threshold of truth and becomes the servant of God.

102. Three imperatives for "genuine and fruitful" dialogue are suggested by the French Protestant Federation:

It is not our task to create unity, which can only be the gift to us of the Lord himself. Our task is to seek it, to serve it, and to pray for it.

Anyone wishing to take part in this search, this service and this prayer should realize that they involve demands which he cannot evade.

(1) The first requirement is a personal training in the fellowship of his own Church. The ecumenical dialogue is a dialogue between the Churches. The barriers between the Churches doubtless include habits of thought and of religious practice but also, and especially, the articles of belief. Each person engaged in the dialogue represents his Church and should therefore possess a deep and true knowledge of the confession of faith and of the life of his Church. The

Catholic instinctively regards the Protestant as a man of the Bible, and pays particular attention to the place the Bible has in our life. Part of our ecumenical responsibility therefore is to have or acquire a knowledge of the Bible and of theology.

(2) The ecumenical dialogue also requires openness to the other person. We must be ready to listen to him and to understand him, to grasp the depths of the spirituality and faith of his Church, to be able to receive seriously the questions he puts to us, and not to close our eyes to the horizons he shows us. This openness will, of course, always be governed by reference to the truth but the truth will always also be sought and affirmed in charity.

(3) The dialogue will also be conducted within the communion of the Church to which one belongs, for it is a common undertaking. We must look to our pastors and theologians, we must live this search in common prayer, we must have consideration for those who may be disturbed by the prospect of this openness. Finally, it is essential to be on guard against exuberant and spectacular manifestations whose deep significance and implications have not been sufficiently pondered.

If the ecumenical dialogue is to remain genuine and fruitful, this is the price we must pay. Those who do not wish to pay it would do better to keep out of it, but those who wish to engage in it may do so in freedom and they will discover in the course of their search unsuspected treasures from which our Churches and their witness cannot but benefit greatly.

REFERENCES

*Chapter III*

68. *Decree on Ecumenism*, official translation, Typis Polyglottis Vaticanis, 1965, pp. 12-22.
69. "Secret Order to Bishops," *The National Catholic Reporter*, I, No. 18 (Mar. 3, 1965), 1.
70. "Interim Guidelines for Prayer in Common and *Communicatio in Sacris*," mimeographed, Bishops' Commission for Ecumenical Affairs, Washington, D.C., pp. 2-14.
71. a. "Ecumenism in England—The Hierarchy's Statement," *The Tablet*, London, CCXVIII, No. 6499, 1421.
    b. "Die Richtlinien der Plenarkonferenz der Bischöfe der Diözesen Deutschlands für gemeinsame Gottesdienste katholischer und nicht-katholischer Cristen," in *Amtsblatt*, des Bischöflichen ordinariats, Berlin, Vol. XXXVII, No. 5, May 1, 1965.
72. Pastoral Letter, the Most Rev. Lawrence Shehan, archbishop of Baltimore, Jan. 3, 1962.
73. "Official Notice," Jan., 1965, the Most Rev. John J. Wright, Bishop of Pittsburgh.
74. "Interim Directives for Ecumenical Activities in the Diocese of Bridgeport," the Most Rev. Walter W. Curtis, bishop of Bridgeport, Conn., Sept. 13, 1965, pp. 5-7.
75. "Guidelines for the Orthodox in Ecumenical Relations," 1966, from booklet published by the Standing Conference of Canonical Orthodox Bishops in America, written by the Rev. Leonidas Contos, dean, Holy Cross Seminary, Brookline, Mass., pp. 22, 23.
76. "The Practice of Ecumenism," *Clergy Bulletin*, Vol. VIII, No. 49, Diocese of Kansas City-St. Joseph, Office of the Chancellor.
77. a. "Application for Membership, Fort Worth Area Council of Churches," mimeographed, supplied by the Council.
    b. "Remarks," of Dr. Granville Walker, past president, Fort Worth Area Council of Churches, presenting the Holy Family Catholic Church to the Council, Mar. 25, 1965.
78. The Rt. Rev. Msgr. O. A. Coggiola-Mower, pastor, Church of the Annunciation, Albuquerque, N.M., summary of remarks to the Heights YMCA, supplied by Msgr. Coggiola-Mower.
79. "Constitution of the Christian Council of Nagpur," courtesy, the Most Rev. Eugene D'Souza, archbishop of Bhopal, formerly archbishop of Nagpur.
80. a. World Council of Churches, Press Release, Central Committee, No. 49, Enugu, Jan., 1965, "Concerning the Relationship Between the WCC and the Roman Catholic Church."
    b. *The Ecumenical Review*, XVIII, No. 2, April, 1966, 249, 250.
    c. *Ibid.*, pp. 252-255.
81. "Conference of European Churches," Constitution, articles 1, 2, 8, provided by Dr. Glen Garfield Williams, Geneva, executive secretary of the Conference.
82. a. From document distributed and approved at the General Assembly of the National Council of Churches, Philadelphia, Dec. 1-7, 1963, "Recommendations of the General Board Regarding Changes in the Proposed Constitution."

  b. *Bylaws* of the National Council of Churches, Part IV, pph. 2, pp. 10, 11.
  c. 1. Annual report, 1965, NCC
  2. Letter, Feb. 21, 1966, Mrs. Theodore O. Wedel, associate general secretary, NCC, Division of Christian Unity.
83. *Religious News Service*, Mar. 24, 1965.
84. a. "Encyclical Letter to the Faithful in Jesus Christ," *The Lambeth Conference*, 1958 (London and Greenwich, Conn.: SPCK and Seabury Press, 1958), Part I, pp. 17, 23-25.
  b. The Most Rev. Arthur Michael Ramsey, Archbishop of Canterbury, at the Anglican Congress, Toronto, Canada, Aug. 13, 1963, text distributed at the Congress, p. 6.
85. a. "Theological Conversations With Roman Catholics," executive committee report, National Lutheran Council, approved, Feb., 1965, in Los Angeles.
  b. National Lutheran Council release, 65-114, from a report of the LWF from Addis Ababa, Ethiopia, Oct. 25, 1965.
86. a. Bulletin, Department of theology, World Alliance of Reformed Churches and the World Presbyterian Alliance, VI, No. 1 (Autumn, 1965), 10, 11.
  b. General Assembly of the Presbyterian Church in New Zealand, Auckland, Nov., 1964, provided by the Rev. H. S. Scott, general secretary, Presbyterian Church in New Zealand, Wellington, N. Z.
  c. Ecumenical Relations report, approved, May 26, 1965, Columbus, O.
87. a. Eugene Carson Blake, "A Proposal Toward the Reunion of Christ's Church," sermon in Grace Cathedral, San Francisco, Dec. 4, 1960, *Presbyterian Life*, Jan. 1, 1961, pp. 38-40, 42. Used by permission.
  b. Eugene Carson Blake, "Second Thoughts on Church Union," sermon in Grace Cathedral, Jan. 24, 1965, mimeographed text, distributed by the General Assembly's Department of Public Relations, pp. 6-9.
88. *Preamble* to the *Principles* of *Church Union*, Consultation on Church Union, adopted May 4, 1966, in Dallas, Tex., approved redraft, provided by the Rev. George Hunt, executive secretary of the Consultation.
89. Bishop Gerald Kennedy, Bishops' message, General Conference, The Methodist Church, Pittsburgh, Pa., Apr. 26, 1964.
90. W. Stanley Mooneyham, "Evangelicals—Divisive or Dynamic?" *The Dynamics of Christian Unity*, W. Stanley Mooneyham, editor (Grand Rapids, Mich.; Zondervan Pub. House, pp. 104-106.
91. Statement of the Canadian Council of Evangelical Protestant Churches, Toronto, George M. Bowman, chairman, Publications Committee, from files of *Religious News Service*.
92. Editorial, *Christianity Today*, IX, No. 9 (Jan. 29, 1965), 29.
93. Charter Statement, mimeographed, The Ecumenical Fellowship of American Baptist Churches in Southern California, supplied by the Rev. James E. Kilgore, Claremont, Calif., president.
94. Mimeographed, draft resolution on "Christian Unity," approved, May 22, 1964, Atlantic City, N.J.
95. Report on North American Baptist Fellowship, adopted, May 1965, Southern Baptist Convention, supplied by the Executive Committee, SBC.
96. Archbishop John Heenan, of Liverpool, in a pastoral letter, *Religious News Service*, Mar. 8, 1962.
97. William B. Greenspun, C.S.P., national director, Apostolate of Good Will, Confraternity of Christian Doctrine, and William A. Norgren, executive director, Department of Faith and Order of the National

Council of Churches, eds., *Living Room Dialogues* (New York and Glen Rock, N.J.: National Council of Churches and the Paulist Press, 1965), pp. 8-10.

98. a. John Cogley, "Ten Commandments for the Ecumenical Age," *Steps to Christian Unity*, John A. O'Brien, editor (New York: Doubleday, 1964), pp. 249-266.

    b. Fritz Blanke, "Zehn Gebote Oder Gelübde für den Umgang mit Christen Anderen Bekenntnisses," in Oscar Cullmann—Otto Karrer, *Einheit in Christus* (Zurich: Zwingli-Verlag und Benziger Verlag, 1960), p. 57.

    c. Battista Mondin, "Le Regole del Dialogo Ecumenico," in *Fede E Civilta*, Jan., 1962, p. 26.

99. Robert McAfee Brown, "Rules for the Dialogue," published simultaneously in *The Commonweal*, Feb. 19, 1960, and *The Christian Century*, Feb. 17, 1960. Also in John A. O'Brien's Steps to Christian Unity (New York: Doubleday, 1964), p. 60. Copyright in *An American Dialogue*, Gustave Weigel and Robert McAfee Brown (New York: Doubleday, 1960).

100. Arthur C. Piepkorn, "What Lutherans Can Learn From Catholics," in *The National Catholic Reporter*, Oct. 20, 1965, p. 6 (a reprint from *The Lutheran Witness*, Oct., 1965).

101. Reuel L. Howe, *The Miracle of Dialogue* (Greenwich, Conn.: The Seabury Press, 1963) pp. 80-83.

102. Letter to the Protestant Churches in France, from the French Protestant Federation, and the four Unions of French Protestant churches, in a booklet *Recommendations et Conseils en vue du Dialogue avec le Catholicisme Romain* ("Recommendations and Advice for Dialogue with Roman Catholics"), by the Rev. Hebert Roux, director of interchurch relations, Protestant Federation, Centre International Protestant, 8, Villa du Parc Montsouris, Paris.

# four

# Comparing Beliefs

When two people get together to talk, there is comparison of their beliefs and outlook on issues. Even the inflection of two people saying the same word "hello" reflects different attitudes. Conversation invites comparisons. Once there is a desire to get acquainted and a desire to communicate, the words and how they are said are revealing. There is always contrast in conversation. When Catholics and Protestants—so long on different sides of the fence—speak, there is inevitable comparison in words and attitudes.

103. In the course of dialogue, and comparison, Protestants and Catholics have found at least nine areas of agreement, according to one Jesuit, the Rev. Father Bernard Leeming:

> It is worth saying that there is wide agreement, among all Christians, about the following:
>
> (1) The existence of God and his providence over human affairs.
>
> (2) The revelation given to us by God in the Bible. Indeed, it is in the field of biblical scholarship that there is evidence of growing understanding.

(3) The need of faith in God's revelation.

(4) The Fall of man, and man's need for the grace of God; and especially the truth that in all the work of salvation God takes the initiative.

(5) The divinity of Christ, his atonement, and his being the cause of all the grace which we receive.

(6) The divinity of the Holy Spirit, who actively inspires and guides us.

(7) The existence of at least two sacraments, Baptism and the Eucharist, and the use among many non-Catholic bodies of ceremonies not unlike what Catholics call the other five sacraments.

(8) Human responsibility, the resurrection of the dead and the judgment of God to come.

(9) Last, but far from least, a conviction that present divisions of "the Church" are not according to God's will and that we must strive, in a humble and penitent spirit, for unity.

104. In a unique journalistic attempt at dialogue, the *Southwest Louisiana Register* of the Roman Catholic Diocese of Lafayette highlighted similarities and differences by inviting non-Roman Catholics to discuss their beliefs in subsequent issues of the *Register*.

a. A Unitarian, interviewed in the *Register,* talked of truth and oneness:

All Unitarians believe in the brotherhood of man, no matter what race or creed. ... We also believe in the universality of truth; no one single group has a monopoly on truth. All religions have contributed something. One of the most hopeful signs in modern times was when Pope Paul offered a Hindu prayer on his trip to India. The Catholic Church is losing some of its exclusiveness and patronizing approach, so it is now much more possible to share things together.—*Rev. Dr. Robert W. Brockway, professor at the University of Southwestern Louisiana, Lafayette, Louisiana.*

b. A Presbyterian talked of the church as holy and catholic:

Presbyterians believe in the Church of Christ as being one, holy, catholic and universal—just as you do. You preach the Gospel; we preach it. You administer the sacraments. We administer them. The Church of Christ is present. We must recognize each other as genuine, authentic and apostolic churches of Christ. . . . Catholics believe the Church is the Bishops—authoritatively speaking. In our church we believe the Church to be all Christians assembled together. Our governing body is comprised of the courts: the "session" is our local group; the "presbytery" is what you would call diocesan; the "synod" regional, and the "general assembly" national.—*Rev. Frank T. Wallace, minister, First Presbyterian Church, Lafayette.*

c. A Methodist talked of the virtue of a "diversified unity . . . like the earth":

By diversified unity I mean different people, approaches and ways of thinking united by the Bible and the basic truths in life. Like the earth which is unified. There is only one earth. Yet there is diversity on the earth with trees, flowers, hills, water, animals. There is harmony present. . . . Some churches have upheld denominationalism and particular personalities rather than the basic truths. That's prejudice, when a person disagrees with you because you're you, or because you don't belong to the same denomination he does. That's not truth. If you tell me about the Ten Commandments or the Bible, then we can agree because there is truth there. Denominations don't matter.—*Rev. L. D. Jackson, pastor, Trinity Christian Methodist Episcopal Church, Lafayette.*

d. A Baptist talked of similarities of doctrine and "Almighty God" above all:

> Most people are surprised when they hear me say Baptists and Catholics hold much the same beliefs. Baptists believe in the Virgin Birth of Christ—so do Catholics.
>
> Baptists believe Christ led a sinless life, that He actually died for us—a real death, that He arose from the dead from a real grave, ascended into heaven, and that He will come again to judge us. Catholics hold these same beliefs.
>
> Our difference is mainly in "appropriation." In other words, how the graces Christ gives us come to use. . . . The Catholic Church believes Christ's graces come to men through the sacraments. We Baptists believe it requires the "sacrament of personal faith" for a person to receive grace.
>
> The individual must come personally to Christ. There is always the chance for lesser good when a person or institution comes between a person and Christ as an intermediary. . . .
>
> Even in our own Church, there is no superior organization. Each church (congregation) is autonomous, independent.
>
> We do have organization—but from the bottom up; not from the top down. No one can remove me from this church here in Lafayette except this congregation, myself, or, of course, Almighty God.
>
> There is an advantage in having a hierarchy, however, as Catholics do, for example a Bishop can speak out on any issue and every one knows he is speaking for a larger number of people. There is power behind his statement. This can be very good.—*Rev. Perry Sanders, pastor, First Baptist Church, Lafayette.*

105. A Paulist priest compared Protestant evangelical theology with Catholic theology in an article on Billy Graham's "evangel-

ical" theology in the *Catholic World:* Said editor John Sheerin:

> The new evangelicals deserve our admiration and emulation
> for their reverence for the word of God. I want to make clear
> that I am not referring to the old evangelicals, the funda-
> mentalists, nor to the radical evangelicals like the Holy
> Rollers who speak in tongues or handle snakes or go into
> trances. The new evangelicals seem to reject form criticism
> of the Scriptures but they are much closer to Catholics than
> are the fundamentalists in their concept of the inerrancy of
> the Bible. They hold firmly to the divinity of Christ, His
> miracles, the Virgin Birth, the Resurrection, Ascension and
> the Second Coming. . . . The new evangelicals believe
> strongly in regeneration through baptism [Editors note: the
> inadequacy of this statement was acknowledged in a later
> issue of the *Catholic World*], insisting on the absolute need
> for baptismal rebirth and representing the experience of
> being saved through baptism as an emotional and spiritual
> experience that shakes the convert to the roots of his per-
> sonality. We Catholics have a pale and sober concept of the
> work of the Holy Spirit within us in sharp contrast to the
> coming of the Spirit as experienced by the "new evangeli-
> cals"—especially on Pentecost. The new evangelicals frown
> upon "revivals" that are identified with religious intoxica-
> tion, emotional aberrations and the "speaking with tongues."
> Nevertheless they are convinced that a true "revival" genu-
> inely revitalizes the Christian, bringing about a true con-
> trition for sin and filling him with the power of the Holy
> Spirit. Our spiritual writers describe the coming of the
> Spirit in similar terms but would probably frown upon it
> in real life. Psychotherapists may question the permanence
> of conversions experienced at the time of a revival but I do
> not see how any Christian can question the need for every
> Christian to experience a daily change of heart as recom-
> mended by the Council Decree on Ecumenism. As an edi-
> torial in *Christianity Today* has it, a genuine revival means
> a repudiation of complacency, a transformation of careless
> living into vital concern, a practice of self-denial instead of
> self-indulgence, a breaking up of the hardened ground of

cold hearts, a cheerful willingness to obey the Holy Spirit. If that is un-Christian, then the great Catholic saints were un-orthodox.

106. Orthodox share the same seven sacraments with the Roman Catholics (baptism, confirmation, Eucharist, penance, ordination, marriage, anointing of the sick). But the comparison goes beyond these agreements. Many Orthodox scholars, for instance, do not limit sacraments to a precise seven. They recognize that the Bible speaks of many "holy acts," such as foot washing and that sacraments are a part of the "mystery" of the church.

Shortly before the biggest Orthodox group, the 50-million-member Russian Orthodox Church, joined the World Council of Churches, a commission of the Conference of European Churches meeting in Nyborg, Denmark, January 1959, compared Eastern and Western religion and discussed contributions Orthodoxy might make to the Western churches:

What can the Western churches learn from the Eastern Orthodox Church in the present situation, in view of the growth of secularism both in Western and Eastern Europe?

For this purpose the Commission had to ask the speakers and the Orthodox members of the Commission, how (in the Orthodox view) Christians and the Church can exercise a Christian influence on the world in which they live. The answer was absolutely clear and unanimous: individual Christians can exercise this influence through prayer and asceticism (what the Bible describes as "fasting") and the Church exercises it through its liturgy; liturgy, prayer and asceticism are Christianity's weapons against secularism.

It immediately became clear that in the Orthodox Church the concept of the relationship between the life in the spirit (in faith) and life in the world (in the body) is entirely different from the concept which prevails in the Western Churches. This difference gives the impression of a strange "climato" (atmosphere) entirely different from that in the West.

This led to the question (to which the Commission devoted a long discussion) how this difference works out in the practical attitude of Orthodox Christians.

(a) Attention was first drawn to the practical significance of the fellowship of believers (koinonia) in the life of the Orthodox Church. In the West this is not considered so important, the main stress being laid upon the individual Christian personality (Western individualism).

(b) The question of the attitude to suffering revealed a still deeper difference between the Orthodox and Western Churches. Orthodoxy accepts suffering as a cross to be borne; whereas in Western Christianity the general tendency is to release oneself and others from all forms of suffering as quickly as possible. This of course implies an entirely different attitude to the world and its problems.

(c) The fact that the Church in Russia has survived, in spite of the complete lack of any facilities for instructing children in the Christian faith either at school or at Church for four decades since the "separation of Church and State," is due (humanly speaking) to the Christian family. Throughout Orthodox Christendom the family is regarded as a "house-church" (oikos) with its own "altar" where prayers are offered before the ikons. This achievement by the Orthodox Christian family, which maintained the Christian faith in the same way under the domination of the Turks, presents Western Christendom with a very serious question of conscience. The Commission was unanimous in this conviction.

(d) Finally the commission drew attention to a special characteristic in the attitude and behavior of Orthodox Christianity: the readiness to accept martyrdom. Thanks to the character of the Christian family, this attitude is found among all Orthodox Christians, and is not confined to priests or to certain limited circles.

The Christian's influence on the world through prayer and

asceticism was illustrated by the *Zoe* Movement in the Greek Church. This movement has had a perceptible influence in circles which had fallen a prey to luxury and secularism. It was emphasized that the Christian life of prayer and asceticism springs from the liturgy, whereby the life of Christians and the life of the world are transfigured. . . .

107. The vagueness of Orthodox theology and the emphasis on mystery to the extent that there is more openness and less polemics is reflected now in new Protestant and Catholic thinking on the Eucharist, the Lord's Supper. A Catholic ecumenical official notes less rigidity in Roman Catholic thinking on the Eucharist, and invites Protestants to reconsider their views of the Eucharist. Said the Rt. Rev. Msgr. William W. Baum, executive director of the Bishops' Commission for Ecumenical Affairs, to a workshop of 136 Protestants and 92 priests at Kenrick (Catholic) Seminary, St. Louis, discussing the Vatican Council's Decree on Ecumenism:

> We have moved somewhat beyond our classical theology of the validity and invalidity of sacraments; we've ceased to speak in such terms. Nonetheless, there is something wanting for eucharistic fullness, although we recognize the sacredness of these (non-Catholic) actions. . . .
>
> We Roman Catholics are troubled by the attitude of our Protestant brothers toward the Holy Eucharist. We feel that in the communities over which you preside the people are all too little conscious of the Eucharist. For us the Eucharist is not only the sign but the cause. Where the Eucharist is, there is the Church.
>
> You can reproach us, I think, for the fact that our people are not concerned over the significance of the Bible. We are ready to accept your reproach—that we have been neglecting to listen to the Word of God in the Sacred Scriptures.
>
> And we ask you to consider our reproach—that the people over whom you preside have been negligent toward the

> Eucharist. I think Luther and Calvin would be dismayed to see your churches observe the Eucharist only monthly or quarterly.

108. On the other hand, a new emphasis on the "efficacious" reality and presence of Christ at the Eucharist celebration emerged in the Church Union talks among the Episcopalians, Methodists, Presbyterians, Evangelical United Brethren, the Disciples, and the United Church of Christ. The section of the report on "One Table," from the official document of the Consultation on Church Union at Princeton, April 1964, achieved a "Catholic" tone in regard to the presence of the Crucified; it achieved also an Orthodox air of mystery, and a low church tone with "remembrance" in the communion rite, as Baptists, for instance, emphasize. But the consultation document was more than a synthesis—it was a development toward stronger liturgical expression of the Eucharist, with clear "Catholic" overtones:

> *Our Growing Agreement.* We believe it is not necessary in a uniting church that all parties be in complete agreement upon the total range of sacramental theology. Yet there are certain basic affirmations, which responsible study of the New Testament enables us to make, and which seem to represent a growing consensus of interpretation in all our churches.
>
> (1) In the Lord's Supper, symbols and symbolic actions are used. However, the Eucharist is an effective sign; the action of the Church becomes the effective means whereby God in Christ acts and Christ is present with his people. Our affirmation that the Church's Eucharist has effective significance is based upon the promise of Christ as attested in the apostolic Church. "This is my body . . . This is the new covenant in my blood . . . Do this in remembrance of me."
>
> (2) Christ is the minister, the high priest of the Eucharist. It is not our table, but the Lord's Table. It is ours only because it is his. Christ, the living Bread, gives himself to

us, sustaining us and uniting us with himself and to each other. He makes effective for his faithful people all that has been accomplished in his incarnation, atoning death, resurrection, and exaltation. His self-giving is an act of his sovereign freedom. It is the exercise of his gracious Lordship.

(3) Christ is present as the Crucified who died for our sins and who rose again for our justification, as the once-for-all sacrifice for the sins of the world who gives himself to the faithful. His life and death and resurrection are not only remembered by the Church but also become, by God's action in Christ, present and efficacious realities.

The Church corporate and its members are renewed in the covenant of grace and participate in the forgiveness of sin and receive eternal life.

(4) The Holy Communion is the presence of Christ who has come, who comes to his people, and who will come in glory. It is the anticipation and foretaste of the heavenly banquet where the redeemed people of God will eat and drink with their crucified and risen Lord in his Kingdom.

109. While intercommunion—taking communion in one another's churches—seemed the most impossible barrier between the Christian churches, there appeared to be new progress made possible, not so much by developments in the theology of the Eucharist, but of the theology of baptism. There were several new discernible currents of thought, particularly in regard to baptism, but with their implications for the Eucharist. (1) The eight-way Consultation on Church Union, meeting in Dallas in May 1966, to consider an outline of a plan for union, had before it some individual proposals for study prior to its meeting. It was suggested in the preliminary presentations that several forms of baptism could be valid in the united church: there could be infant baptism with a personal and public profession of faith in Christ as Savior later, or a believer's baptism preceded some years before by infant dedication. The idea is that one faith could be expressed in different ways, and in regard to baptism, it would be

one invisible baptism in two visible forms. One form could precede the other in either sequence. (2) The second development
was the general, or at least growing consensus (see following
documents) that all Christians shared the same baptism, that
under basic conditions baptism was as efficacious to salvation for
the one as for the other. Thus, it was reasoned, that instead of
intercommunion being an offense to unity to break the bread of
the Lord's body at the table—when his followers were in reality
divided—there was the fact they were already united in baptism.
Thus, it was asked how could there be an offense to unity, when
the basic conditions of unity already existed—valid baptism into
the body of Christ? Episcopalians and Roman Catholics, and also
the Orthodox and Roman Catholics, faced this issue squarely in
their ongoing talks in the United States. Predictions from the
theologians involved were that intercommunion between Orthodox, Anglicans, and Roman Catholics was possible in a few
years. The Most Rev. Charles Helmsing of Kansas City-St. Joseph
(Missouri) put it more guardedly: "We can't tell how many
years it might take. That's in the hands of God. But sometimes
he works pretty fast." The discussion of the Eucharist continued
into the June 16-18, 1966 talks of the Catholics and the Anglicans.
Essentially, Orthodox, Anglican, and Roman Catholic all believe
in the real presence of Christ in the Eucharist. Anglicans have
considerable latitude within their interpretation, while Orthodox
describe their view of the Eucharist as "more Catholic than
Catholic"; that is, they do not try to separate appearance from
substance but say the whole communion elements are changed
into the body and blood of Christ.

Two Roman Catholic theologians at the Kansas City meeting
with the Episcopalians in February 1966, in papers that represented their personal views, said they found no theological objections to some joint Anglican-Roman Catholic Eucharist services.

a. The Rev. Father Bernard Cooke, S.J., chairman of the
department of theology at Marquette University, Milwaukee,
said:

As we work towards this full Eucharistic communion, we face
the practical and important question: to what extent must

we wait for organizational reunification before we celebrate together Eucharistically, or to what extent will the common Eucharistic celebration itself help to bring about the organizational unity? . . .

Perhaps the most appropriate way is to make a proposal— Why cannot we in the private and controlled situation that is ours in this conference celebrate together the Eucharist? If we can, such common celebration will help immeasurably in establishing the consensus of faith we seek. If we cannot, let us delineate the precise barriers that do exist. These barriers, it would seem to me, would tell us rather definitely the agenda that lies before us in future meetings.

b. The Rev. Father Arthur Vogel, professor of theology at Nashotah House, Episcopal seminary at Nashotah, Wisconsin, said:

Can we believe in the real presence of Christ in the Eucharist and then try to circumscribe his availability by the way we administer the sacrament? Christ comes to expose us, not to have us protect Him.

We must still have norms in the world to judge the acceptance of Christ, for the Christian religion means one thing rather than another; it is not a formless blob of equivocal goodwill. The unity to which we are called in Christ involves the whole man, making explicit demands on his reason and power of judgment.

But the norms themselves must primarily witness to God's gift to us in Christ; they must witness to the total dependence we have on Him in doing His work. Christ's presence in the world is a call to something definite. Our response to it creates a "community of faith." Where such community can be recognized among people who are already members of Christ's Body through baptism, why should such people not be fed together for their common work in the world by Christ's sacramental Body?

If the nature of the Eucharist, the fact of Christ's presence in it, and the means of its production can be essentially agreed upon by members of the Mystical Body, might not their common reception at the Table of the Lord—with the selflessness such participation involves—be the primary means by which God wills to bring about ever-increasing unity among His people?

110. Baptism, as a common denominator among Christians, was underscored at the second round of talks between the Lutherans and Roman Catholics in the United States (between the U.S.A. National Committee of the Lutheran World Federation represented by the National Lutheran Council, and the U.S. Roman Catholic Bishops' Commission for Ecumenical Affairs). Presiding at the meeting in Chicago, February 11-13, 1966, were the Most Rev. T. Austin Murphy, auxiliary bishop of Baltimore, and Dr. Paul C. Empie, of New York, executive director of the National Lutheran Council. In a joint statement, Bishop Murphy and Dr. Empie said:

The series of theological conversations in which we are engaged continue to be exceedingly fruitful. We were reasonably certain that the teachings of our respective traditions regarding baptism are in substantial agreement, and this opinion has been confirmed at this meeting.

At the same time, discussion dealing with several aspects of the subject brought to light the fact that although at times we use the same words with somewhat different meanings, we also upon occasion have quite different ways of saying the same things.

It has been especially interesting to discover that we have common problems related to the development of doctrine in this and other theological areas, and a comparison of approaches to the solution of these problems has been mutually useful. Some points of misunderstanding have been clarified in the process.

We will be examining subjects in future meetings which present greater difficulties, but are encouraged to proceed in the knowledge that the conversations held thus far have deepened mutual understanding and respect while strengthening the bonds of brotherly affection.

111. Even adverse publicity of persons being rebaptized tended to heighten the fact that they really do share a common baptism. Roman Catholics are willing to accept the validity of many Protestant denominational rites of baptism performed in the name of the Trinity. Code of Canon Law (Canon 742, par. 1) says "Baptism without a solemn character . . . can be administered by anyone, so long as the proper matter, form and intention are observed."

The highly publicized exceptions which drew attention to the actual rules were the conditional baptism of Princess Irene, in Holland, and the baptism of Luci Johnson, who was an Episcopalian, both converting to the Roman Catholic faith.

a. The rebaptism of Princess Irene was immediately challenged by the Board of the General Synod of the Dutch Reformed Church. In a letter dated February 7, 1964, to Bernard Cardinal Alfrink, of Utrecht, the board said:

You are doubtless aware that this conversion and particularly the manner in which it was announced to our people has caused widespread dismay.

However much we as a Protestant church may deplore this conversion, we wish to state at the outset that in our opinion Princess Irene has and in a matter like this, which is of such a personal character, needs must have the same undoubted right as any other Dutch citizen to act according to her personal convictions. This does not alter the fact that this conversion to the Roman Catholic Church has deeply disturbed us. We are also very shocked by your failure to make this conversion publicly known as soon as it had taken place. It is our opinion that, since Princess Irene at the time publicly confessed her faith in the Protestant church, the confession of faith which she made in the Roman Catholic Church should accordingly also have been made in public and not been kept quiet with every semblance of ambiguity which it might entail.

We feel justified, therefore, in asking you whether the concealment of this conversion is not contrary to the dignity of the one directly involved and that of the church to which she belonged by virtue of her birth, baptism and confession. This question is all the more urgent since this conversion concerns a member of the House of Orange which is so closely linked with the Protestant Church. Was it not, therefore, we ask ourselves, your imperative duty to ensure that the intended conversion was at least intimated to the church to which Princess Irene could be deemed to belong and that publicity was subsequently given to the decision taken?

Secondly, we would ask you to put an end to the uncertainty which fills us and many others on the question whether and to what extent Princess Irene was administered Holy Baptism on entering into the Roman Catholic Church despite the fact that, as a child, she has already received this baptism in the Protestant church.

Thirdly, we question whether the appreciation of the conversion of Princess Irene as an ecumenical act does not dangerously confuse the real ecumenical relations.

In view of the better understanding which has come about in recent years between the Roman Catholic Church and the Protestant church and of the increased frankness which has flowed from it, we consider it most imporant that perfect clarity be brought in this matter.

In our opinion the ecumenical movement can only be served by an honest recognition of the differences of religious insight dividing the church of Rome and that of the Reformation and by the readiness, despite those differences, to meet each other for Christ's sake and to make a common search for unity in him.—*Signed, P. G. van den Hooff, president, E. Emmen, secretary.*

b. The controversy concerning Princess Irene's rebaptism was somewhat eased when Cardinal Alfrink said that the conditional baptism of Princess Irene would not have taken place had he been consulted with the full information. His answer to the Dutch Reformed officials:

> ... I agree with the Board that an act of conversion is in itself an act before the community and therefore, saving special circumstances, a public one.
>
> Nevertheless I felt I could accede to the wish that this conversion be kept private for the time being, since it was the intention to make a public announcement about it within a short space of time.
>
> I must admit with regret that inter-church relations have been prejudiced by this situation, although I must point out that the practical rules to be observed between us in cases of conversion have not been established with sufficient clarity.
>
> As for my decision, it is my opinion that in these exceptional circumstances there can hardly be any question of a conflict with the dignity of the one directly involved and of the church to which she belonged.
>
> I also regret that I did not pay more heed to the possibility of further consequences, in view of the situation.
>
> In connection with the second question I would state that, due to unfortunate circumstances, i.e., the unexpected absence of witnesses, at the time of the reception (Jan. 2, 1964, in Rome), I was not in possession of the details of the way in which the earlier baptism had been administered, while on the other hand a postponement of the ceremony seemed impracticable. This is the reason why I considered

myself in conscience bound to make the reception into the
church take the form of a positive confession of faith linked
to a conditional baptism. In the liturgical administration
anything likely to wound the other churches is expressly
excluded.

I trust that your board will in its judgment take into account
the delicacy of my position. In-so-far as others, who were
involved, may have failed, allowance should be made for
their lack of experience in these matters and for their assumption that the details were known to me.

For that matter, I am anxious to state that if I had been in
possession of the details of the baptism administered in
1940, with which I have now been supplied, conditional
baptism would have not been required.

It grieves me especially that the ecumenical concept has
also been damaged, as mentioned in your third question.

I share to the full the pastoral concern evidenced in your
query. Accordingly I consider it highly important that every
effort be made to restore the good relations in so far as
they have suffered.

As a basis for this I would, after consultation with the
Dutch bishops, submit the following thoughts:

With a view to clarifying the ecumenical situation and promoting a healthy development of inter-church relations, I
want to state emphatically that the Catholic Church shares
the conviction that the way to Christian unity does not lie
in achieving as many individual conversions as possible.
Only in a common search by all the churches which profess
Christ for one, holy Church designed by Christ, can the lost
unity be regained. However, so long as the division continues, a person's freedom to embrace another church in accordance with his own conscience, must be respected.

The pastoral case surrounding such conversions must always go hand in hand with scrupulous respect for the religious values which are known to exist in other Christian communities and for which these communities must be respected as instruments of God's redemption. Among these religious values, the administration of baptism holds a very special place and therefore the respect for the other Christian churches will be especially reflected in the appreciation of their baptism. . . .

In an individual conversion due respect must also be shown to the pastoral responsibility of the church which is being left. For baptism and confession of faith are also recognized by the Roman Catholic Church as public religious acts, performed amid the local community. In such a public act it would seem a fitting rule that the pastor involved should contact the church which is being left but to which the convert owes his membership of Christ's Church.

Even on the matter of this contact, which has not yet been given a definite practical form, a joint consultation of the churches can lead to a common attitude in which not only the interests of the convert but also the ecumenical interests will be fully guaranteed. . . .

112. About Luci Johnson's rebaptism, objections came from many quarters, particularly among the Episcopalian bishops. The Rt. Rev. Charles E. Bennison, of Western Michigan and the Rt. Rev. James A. Pike, of California, objected out loud. Bishop Pike said Luci Johnson's baptism was an "insult" when the Roman Catholic Church "clearly recognizes as completely valid infant baptism according to the official liturgy of the Episcopal Church." A release from the Vatican Secretariat for Chistian Unity suggested that the requirement for rebaptism was not the official position of the Roman Catholic Church. Catholic baptism must be in the name of the Trinity, include the intent of Christ (rebirth and grafted into his Body), and use water.

A Lutheran executive, the Rev. Dr. Fredrik A. Schiotz, president of The American Lutheran Church, issued this statement, which predicted some positive outcome from the Luci Johnson baptism incident:

> The announcement of the admission of Miss Luci Johnson to membership in the Roman Catholic Church during the 4th of July weekend (1965) accents that our freedom as citizens is also a freedom of religion. It is not uncommon that members of the Roman Catholic Church are admitted to membership in Protestant Churches and likewise that some Protestants seek transfer to the Roman Catholic Church. This wholesome evidence of our freedom of religion is commendable.
>
> The disturbing factor in the announcement of Miss Johnson's transfer was that it was effected through re-baptism. In current ecumenical discussions representatives of the Roman Catholic Church have assured us that the Sacrament of Baptism, held in common by the Roman Catholic Church, the Orthodox Churches and most Protestant Churches, provide a basis for regarding other churches as ecclesial communities. The re-baptism of Miss Johnson seems to say that the validity of the Sacrament of Baptism rests less in the Word of God and more in the church or instrument of administration.
>
> The explanation that the re-baptism occurred by request of Miss Johnson compounds the confusion. It suggests an inadequate pastoral ministry during the period of instruction. The Sacrament's meaning is thus obliterated and it becomes a psychological device to serve the feelings of an individual. ... Perhaps this event will issue in all Christians becoming better informed in the basic teachings of their respective churches.

113. Seeking to avoid further difficulties occurring with the rebaptizing of those whom the church already accepts as validly baptized, Joseph Marie Martin the archbishop of Rouen, France, serving also as president of the French National Secretariat for Christian Unity, sent these recommendations to his priests

charged with local ecumenical contacts. (A similar document for English clergy appeared in the December 1964 *Clergy Review.)*

It is right to doubt sometimes whether a baptism has been administered in conformity with the discipline of a Church. It is not right to doubt *systematically the validity* of all baptisms celebrated in the communions whose ritual has until now been accepted by the Church.

"There should be no rebaptism as a general rule and without discretion, even conditionally" (*Propaganda Fide*, 31 XII 1951). In this matter it is necessary "to act prudently and with the utmost care; the holiness and dignity of the sacrament require this absolutely, as well as the good of the faithful and the tranquility of consciences, which is a prime consideration" (Inst. of the Holy Office, 30 I 1833). If doubts about the validity of the sacrament are too easily and imprudently put forward, the fearful and the scrupulous would never cease doubting about the baptism they had received.

*The need for an inquiry:* Before pronouncing upon the validity, the invalidity or the doubtful character of a baptism conferred outside the Catholic Church, it is necessary to make an inquiry which is "diligent, accurate and prudent," as is said by the replies and instructions of the Roman Congregations, in particular that of the Holy Office of 20 XI 1878 (D.B. No. 1848). . . .

*How to conduct the inquiry:* (1) First of all it is necessary to inquire about the *baptismal discipline* of a particular Church or sect, at a particular time and place. . . .

(2) The inquiry must next establish: *the fact of the baptism* (the rite or ceremony of entry into the community not to be confused with the presentation or blessing of a child): this is relatively easy where there are registers or trustworthy witnesses. *The Validity of the baptism*—here are two questions: (a) Did the ritual used fulfil the required

conditions? (b) Did the minister follow the prescriptions?

*With reference to the discipline today:*

—*in the Lutheran Churches in France,* the ritual and also faithfulness in respecting it can leave no serious doubt as to the validity.

—*in the Reformed Churches in France,* the established ritual is fully satisfactory. It is necessary to inquire, in each particular case, whether it has been observed.

*In practice:* Each case is to be referred to the Ordinary, who will judge, in consultation with the person responsible in the diocese, the attitude to be adopted. Conditional baptism is only legitimate when in the Ordinary's judgment it is impossible to make an inquiry, or where there is the persistence of a prudent doubt after the inquiry has been made (see Canon 732, par. 2). . . . .

The attitude which we recommend towards the baptisms of non-Catholics is no innovation. It is only a question of ceasing to act in a way which crept into practice abusively, and in opposition to the constant practice of the Church. The references made above to the decisions of the Congregations show that in this matter the position of Rome has not changed.

Such an attitude is bound to have important consequences:

—*from the ecumenical point of view:* the fact of taking seriously the baptism conferred in the Protestant Churches is an element in the dialogue. Indeed, a systematic repetition of the sacrament has often appeared as a sign of disdain and intolerance; it has made it more difficult for Protestants to understand the Catholic idea of a sacrament, which is no magic rite acting only in virtue of the material correctness of the words and actions, but is the act of the living Christ in the Church. A change of attitude on the part of Catholics, could not but encourage the Protestant Churches to strengthen their discipline in this matter.

*—from the theological point of view:* baptism, even administered outside the Catholic Church, is an act of Christ. By it, Christ builds up his one and only Church. By it and the other sacraments which remain in the separated communions, he orientates men towards the fullness of his Church.

*—from the point of view of the subject who enters the Church:* he who comes from a Christian communion to the Catholic Church, by an ill-conceived desire for security sometimes asks to be baptized again conditionally. He must be shown that he is not to deny all that was good, true and Christian in the past, but only to purify it and complete it "by communion with a unity which is the fullness of grace and truth" (Congar). The repetition of baptism would signify for him that all that he had lived in the communion from which he came was worthless. To discover that, through his baptism, he had always been united with the Body of Christ and on his way to its fullness in the Church, would be a source of joy and thanksgiving.

114. Presbyterians and Roman Catholics began to consider the possibility of a common baptism rite in December 1965, at the suggestion of the Rev. Richard L. Davies, representing the United Presbyterian Commission on Ecumenical Mission and Relations, in talks with Roman Catholics. A problem in a common baptism rite, as Lutherans particularly point out, is that baptism does not stand alone—into *what* church relationship is one to be baptized?

In the Presbyterian-Catholic talks, the Rt. Rev. Msgr. Henry G. J. Beck, headed the Roman Catholic delegation in the absence of the Most Rev. Ernest L. Unterkoefler, bishop of Charleston, South Carolina, in charge of the contacts with Presbyterians for the U.S. Bishops' Commission for Ecumenical Affairs. Msgr. Beck proposed that an ancient rite, such as that used by St. Hippolytus of Rome in the third century, could be used (only for children of marriages in which one parent was Catholic, the other Presbyterian). "For the moment there is no firm commitment on either the Catholic or the Presbyterian side to authorize such a rule," he said. "We are simply exploring the possibility. Its advantage lies in the fact that it is a product of the Third Century— well before the split between Catholic or Orthodox or Anglican or Protestant." The rite is printed in Gregory Dix's *St. Hippolytus of Rome: The Apostolic Tradition* (London, 1937), pp. 33-38, and *The Apostolic Tradition of Hippolytus*, translated by Burton Scott Easton (London, Cambridge, 1934, 1962), pp. 44-49. The baptism is administered three times, for each member of the trinity in this ancient rite.

An idea for a joint service to renew baptismal vows came up among students of Pax Romana, international Catholic student movement, and the World Student Christian Federation, meeting for a joint consultation October 30-November 2, 1964, at Taizé, France. The report of the conference in *Herder Correspondence*, noted:

> One idea which particularly caught the imagination of the consultation was that of a common service in which Christians of different communions renewed together their baptismal vows, thus stressing the reality of their common baptism. This could take place at the beginning of an academic year, for example, or on a variety of occasions meaningful in the university context. Each should come to know the traditional forms of worship of the others as deeply as possible, but at the same time all should be ready to discover and experiment with new forms of worship particularly meaningful to the university world. While there is a danger of the university parishes being cut off from the general life, of the worshipping Church around them, at the same time it should be remembered that there is an opportunity in the university to train Christians who will be able to serve that Church both in vacations and after they have left the university.

115. For developments in Protestant thinking concerning baptism, consider again the Consultation on Church Union, meeting

at Princeton, in 1964. Its report on baptism represents a growing consensus:

> Concerning the one baptism the following points are affirmed:
>
> (1) *The understanding of baptism as a means of grace.* The primacy of grace must be stressed, whether infant or adult baptism be practiced. The primary significance of baptism lies not in what we do but in what God has already done for us in Jesus Christ, to which faith is our response.
>
> (2) *The understanding of baptism as the decisive work of God leading to the continuing life in God.* The new life on which we enter in baptism must be confirmed in the baptizand and continued in full, glad commitment to Christian discipleship and in joyful anticipation of faith's consummation at the end of the age.
>
> (3) *The meaning of baptism as a corporate act of the Church under the authority of the living Lord.* Baptism is not a private affair. At each baptismal service the faith of all the baptized members is continuously reaffirmed and proclaimed.
>
> (4) *The particular witness of infant baptism.* Infant baptism is the manifestation of our helplessness and of God's grace on our behalf. It is also a witness to the corporateness of the Christian life. In the nurture of the covenant community it always anticipates confirmation or personal confession of faith. Thereby, parental and congregational vows uttered in behalf of the baptizand are fulfilled.
>
> (5) *The teaching emphasized in adult baptism.* Here the stress is on the conscious dedication and commitment of awakened faith. By God's gracious acts the individual is led to make a responsive decision that involves faithful obedience to the call of God in Jesus Christ. Since in actual practice adult baptism often follows upon the dedication

of the individual in infancy, the witness of the Christian community is used to prepare and nourish the baptizand in the faith in which he is baptized.

(6) *The common search for fulness of spiritual life.* In spite of tensions within our communions, and weaknesses of practice, infant baptism and adult baptism both seek to express and fulfill the same spiritual life. Both seek to include infants within the one fold of Christ's Church, and both seek to nurture these little ones in the one faith which thereby can reach mature, responsible expression.

The New Testament does not lay great stress on the particular manner in which baptism is administered. It seems clear, however, from the Biblical record that immersion was usually practiced in New Testament times. We acknowledge that as early as the first part of the second century effusion (i.e. baptism by pouring water) was practiced by the Church, and since that time there has been variety in baptismal practices. In a united church it would be possible to baptize by immersion, pouring, or sprinkling.

In summary, baptism will include the following:

(1) The use of water in the name of the Father, the Son, and the Holy Spirit.

(2) A confession of sin and repentance, an affirmation of faith, and a promise of a life of obedience to Christ on the part of the baptizand or his sponsors.

(3) The administration normally by an ordained minister in the presence of the sponsoring congregation, except in unusual circumstances.

The one baptism which is the visible basis of our unity requires that we affirm the following:

(1) Baptism is essential for full obedience to our risen Lord.

(2)  Careful instruction should precede or accompany every instance of baptism.

(3)  Since baptism incorporates us into the body of Christ, it is to be administered once.

(4)  Neither infant baptism nor adult baptism should be imposed contrary to conscience.

116. Concerning authority in the church, Protestants are re-thinking the role of bishops, and Roman Catholics have reviewed the role of the pope in terms of shared authority, or reigning in cooperation with a "college" of bishops. (For documents on the papacy, a prime point of conflict, see next chapter.) The 1965 session on the Consultation on Church Union, then involving six denominations, in Lexington, Kentucky, accepted a bishop-centered report on "The Ordained Ministry in a United Church." The report commits the architects of a future union plan to include bishops in the proposed new church that would unite 23-million Methodists, Episcopalians, Evangelical United Brethren, United Church of Christ, Disciples, and Presbyterians (the AME and Presbyterian Church in the United States were added in 1966):

Since, under normal conditions, office and authority in the church should be conveyed through the action of those officers who have been duly chosen to convey it, the historic episcopate commends itself as personifying the continuity of churchly authority. In a united church the historic episcopate, to be constitutionally defined, will be honored as God's given and acceptable channel for authorizing the ministry of Word and Sacrament, although not as the exclusive channel for such authorization.

Authority as given and exercised in the church is both limited and derived. It is limited not only by the fact that the ordained minister is always under God and so a servant of God's people, but also by the defined scope of that authority and by the freedom and responsibility which belong to all those within the ministering community. Moreover such au-

thority is derived; we possess authority only when we stand
under it. Hence, true authority, in the united church we are
proposing, should serve as a God-given means through
which the gospel of Christ becomes effective in the upbuild-
ing and mission of the church. . . .

117. The Vatican Council approved the principle of collegiality,
first, in a series of test votes, October 30, 1963, then in an official
endorsement of the total schema on the church, promulgated November 21, 1964, by Pope Paul.

To the Protestant, "collegiality" seems to mean a distribution
of power; to some Catholic observers, such as Cardinal Siri of
Genoa, collegiality, emphasizing the bishops as a group "under
the pope," strengthens the papacy. Nevertheless, there appeared
the broadening of the base of authority, and a growing dialogue
not only among the bishops but between bishops, priests and laymen, a spirit of the mentality of collegiality spreading through
the church.

a. Four "propositions" concerning collegiality and a fifth
dealing with spreading some responsibilities in the liturgy in
lower ranks by reconstituting the order of deacons after 1,000
years, approved in the test vote of October 30, 1963, are:

(1) Whether the Fathers accepted the episcopal consecration as the supreme degree of the sacrament of order.

(2) Whether the Fathers thought that every legitimately
consecrated bishop in communion with the Roman Pontiff
was a member of the *corporis episcoporum* ["episcopal
body"] of which the pope is head and principal unity.

(3) Whether the Fathers accepted the body or college of
bishops as the successor to the College of the Apostles in the
office of evangelizing, sanctifying and ruling the flock;
whether they together through this college, together with its
head, the Roman Pontiff (and never without this head),
possesses full and supreme power over the whole church.

(4) Whether the aforesaid power of the college of bishops

united to its head is something of divine law.

(5) Whether the Fathers favor the restoration of the active diaconate according to the needs of the Church in different regions.

b. The new Constitution on the Church said concerning collegiality:

> Just as in the Gospel, the Lord so disposing, St. Peter and the other apostles constitute one apostolic college, so in a similar way the Roman Pontiff, the successor of Peter, and the bishops, the successors of the apostles, are joined together. . . .
>
> Bishops, as successors of the apostles, receive from the Lord, to whom was given all power in heaven and on earth, the mission to reach all nations and to preach the Gospel to every creature, so that all men may attain to salvation by faith, baptism and the fulfilment of the commandments (cf. Matt. 28: 18; Mark 16: 15-16; Acts 26: 17).
>
> To fulfill this mission, Christ the Lord promised the Holy Spirit to the Apostles, and on Pentecost day sent the Spirit from heaven, by whose power they would be witnesses to Him before the nations and peoples and kings even to the ends of the earth (Acts 1: 8; 2: 1 ff; 9: 15). . . .
>
> The infallibility promised to the Church resides also in the body of Bishops, when that body exercises the supreme magisterium with the successor of Peter. . . .

c. Pope Paul talked of reforming and internationalizing the Roman Curia, September 21, 1963, then a year later discussed directly the wider concept of collegiality in his speech, September 14, 1964, opening the third session of the Council:

> The Fathers of the First Vatican Council proclaimed and defined the truly unique, supreme powers which Christ granted

to Peter and transmitted to his successors. Some saw in this pronouncement a diminution of the authority belonging to bishops, the successors of the Apostles. They felt it made ecumenical councils superfluous and that it would prevent the calling of any future councils, even though canon law recognizes their supreme authority over the Universal Church.

To be sure, the present Ecumenical Council will confirm the doctrine of the last Council regarding the prerogatives of the Supreme Pontiff. But it is also particularly concerned to describe the prerogatives of the bishops and accord them full honor. . . .

As for Us, We are delighted to acknowledge the bishops as Our brothers, to call them "elders," as St. Peter did, and to regard Ourself as their "fellow-elder." Like St. Paul We are happy to regard them as "partakers of our sufferings and our comforts." Now Our concern is to demonstrate to them Our respect, Our esteem, Our love, and Our sense of solidarity. . . .

As the successor of Peter, We, in spite of Our unworthiness, exercise full power in the Church and are therefore your head. But this does not mean that We seek to diminish your authority. On the contrary, We are the first to show it due respect. And if Our Apostolic Office requires Us to put certain limits on the exercise of episcopal authority, to reserve certain things to Ourself, to set down guidelines and proper modes of action, you know full well that the welfare and unity of the universal Church, is the motivating factor. Her need for a supreme leader becomes more acute as she spreads out farther over the earth, as the dangers and problems of her people in various circumstances become more urgent and more serious, and We might add, as the means of travel and communication become more accessible.

This concentration of the Church's power on one central co-ordinating point will always be exercised with due moderation; and it will always take into consideration the useful faculties and functions granted to local Ordinaries. It should not be regarded as a setup prompted by the will to dominate. In all truth, Venerable Brothers, it represents a form of service. It fits in with the unitary, hierarchial nature of the Church. It provides the strength, the beauty, and the luster which Christ promised to His Church and continues to lavish on her throughout the ages. . . .

118. Concerning the Church, both Protestants and Catholics can talk of "The People of God," and as a special community or fellowship (*koinonia*) guided and coalesced by the Holy Spirit.

a. In the Constitution on the Church of the Second Vatican Council, the Church is inclusive and parallels to a degree Protestant emphasis on the invisibility of the true Church:

Christ instituted this new covenant, the New Testament, that is to say, in His Blood (cf. 1 Cor. 11: 25), calling together a people made up of Jew and Gentile, making them one, not according to the flesh but in the Spirit. This was to be the new People of God.

For those who believe in Christ, who are reborn not from a perishable seed but from an imperishable through the word of the living God (cf. 1 Pet. 1: 23), not from the flesh but from water and the Holy Spirit (cf. John 3: 5, 6), are finally established as "a chosen race, a royal priesthood, a holy nation, a purchased people . . . you who in times past were not a people, but are now the people of God." (1 Pet. 2: 9, 10).

That messianic people has Christ for its head, "Who was delivered up for our sins, and rose again for our justification" (Rom. 4: 25), and now, having won a name which is above all names, reigns in glory in heaven. The state of this people is that of the dignity and freedom of the sons of God, in whose hearts the Holy Spirit dwells as in His temple. . . .

All men are called to belong to the new people of God. Wherefore this people, while remaining one and only one, is to be spread throughout the whole world and must exist in all ages, so that the decree of God's will may be fulfilled. . . .

It follows that though there are many nations there is but one people of God, which takes its citizens from every race, making them citizens of a kingdom which is of a heavenly rather than of an earthly nature. . . .

The Church recognizes that in many ways she is linked with those who, being baptized, are honored with the name of Christian, though they do not profess the faith in its entirety or do not preserve unity of communion with the successor of Peter. For there are many who honor Sacred Scripture, taking it as a norm of belief and a pattern of life, and who show a true apostolic zeal.

They lovingly believe in God the Father Almighty and in Christ, the Son of God and Saviour. They are consecrated by baptism, in which they are united with Christ. They also recognize and accept other sacraments within their own Churches or ecclesiastical communities.

Many of them rejoice in the episcopate, celebrate the Holy Eucharist and cultivate devotion toward the Virgin Mother of God. They also share with us in prayer and other spiritual benefits. Likewise we can say that in some real way they are joined with us in the Holy Spirit, for to them too He gives His gifts and graces whereby He is operative among them with His sanctifying power. . . .

   b. The "Protestant appeal" in the "People of God" concept is noted by the French Dominican ecumenist, the Rev. Father Yves Congar (who additionally believes the term "people of God" is not fully adequate for Catholic theology) :

The ecumenical interest of the idea of the People of God is obvious, especially in the dialogue with Protestants. Let us speak of this dialogue. This idea provides many points of agreement and encounter. What Protestants like about the category of People of God is first, the idea of election and of call, everything depends on God's initiative. Then it is the historicity that it involves in the sense of incompletion and of movement toward eschatology. It suggests less sharply defined frontiers, because it is composed of a multitude assembled by God himself. On the one hand, Protestants are happy to find in the frank use of People of God, a way of avoiding institutionalism with its intemperate use of ideas of "power" and infallibility, and on the other hand, the romanticism of a biological concept of the Mystical Body whose favorite expression is that of "continued incarnation . . . "

c. Away from the scholars, "What is the church?" is discussed in student bull sessions as it is discussed by the sages in the sacred aula of the church. In one Protestant bull session, transcribed at the Church of England Youth Camp in Ryde, England, a Rev. Mr. Bean proposed this definition of the church, which parallels a Catholic view:

Mr. Bean: "There are all sorts of answers that one could give: the Church is the community of the baptized, isn't it? —those who are brought into the fellowship of Christ's Church through the sacrament of baptism, if you want a straightforward answer. And that includes everybody who has been baptised by water and in the name of the Father, and of the Son, and of the Holy Ghost. But that is obviously a very wide definition and it obviously doesn't count for very much in the way in which, perhaps, you want to think of it. The Church is a company of people who are in fellowship with one another and in fellowship with Our Lord. It's a sort of friendship really, isn't it? Those are the sort of words that you begin to want to use when you think of the Church. It's a community of people, a company of people, a fellowship, a family. It's those who were brought into fellowship with each other through their sense of love for their loved one, Jesus, or God, or Our Lord."

119. The visibility of the church,—a term at one time more

consistent with Roman Catholic exposition—gained new consideration among Protestants.

Discussing the church as a "golden candlestick" (Rev. 1: 12-16), a Protestant weekly, the independent Baptist *Watchman-Examiner* deduced a visibility of the church from the candlesticks (seven) as visible parallels of the church:

> The church, as the seven golden candlesticks (Rev. 1: 12-16) indicate, is visible. There is far too much talk about the "invisible church." Since the church is a witness and a light, how can it be invisible? Since it consists of heaven born souls commissioned to be missionaries to the entire world, how can they be invisible? A witness is never invisible. A church consisting of witnesses of Jesus could never be invisible. The church is to be seen, heard, and heeded. Salvation is not a hidden thing done in the dark. The Saviour was crucified on a hill on the highest cross of three that all the world might see him. Even Pilate drew the attention of the Roman Empire to the Son of man when he cried out, "Behold the man!"
>
> There are far too many people hiding in the delusion that they may be secret Christians. How can a candlestick, bearing an eternal light, be secret? We are an open book, read of all men, seen of all men, and in the mercy of God used by him to bring to all men the knowledge of the saving grace of our Lord Jesus Christ. . . .

120. The Nicene Creed, of A.D. 325, common to both Catholics and Lutherans was the topic of conversation in the first United States dialogue session of Lutherans and Catholics meeting at the chancery of the Archdiocese of Baltimore, July 6, 7, 1965. Luther had continued the use of the Nicene Creed originally written to combat the heresy of Arius who had maintained that Christ was created, that there was a time when he "was not." However, Luther had allowed a substitution of a hymn in its place. It was because of Luther, some scholars say, that "Catholic" was dropped in the creed in some Protestant use, and "Christian" substituted. In the new Service Book and Hymnal, used in most United States Lutheran churches, which have always re-

tained the Creed, "catholic" for "Christian" is allowed. Scanda-
navian and French and Spanish Lutheran ritual books use the
word "catholic" in the Creed.

The U.S. (NLC) Lutherans issued jointly with the Catholic
representatives this statement summarizing the discussion on the
Nicene Creed:

> In praise to God, and in gratitude for those gifts of His
> Spirit whereby he steadily draws His people to unity in
> Christ, we rejoice in this first official theological conversa-
> tion in the United States between Roman Catholic and Lu-
> theran believers.
>
> Those regularly appointed to arrange for and summon this
> meeting selected the topic for discussion: The Status of the
> Nicene Creed as Dogma of the Church.
>
> The main points of the conversation are summarized in the
> following paragraphs:
>
> (1) We confess in common the Nicene Faith and therefore
> hold that the Son, Our Lord Jesus Christ, who was made
> man, suffered, died, and rose again for our salvation, is true
> God; that He is from God the Father as Son, and therefore
> other than the Father; that the Godhead is one and undi-
> vided; and that the Holy Spirit, together with the Father
> and the Son, is to be worshipped and glorified.
>
> (2) The Nicene Faith gathers up and articulates the biblical
> testimony concerning the Son and His relationship to the
> Father.
>
> (3) The Nicene Faith, formulated by the Council at Nicaea
> in 325 and developed in the Nicene-Constantinopolitan
> Creed, was a response to contemporary errors. The Church
> was obliged to state her faith in the Son in non-biblical
> terms to answer the Arian Question.
>
> (4) The confession that Our Lord Jesus Christ is the Son,

God of God, continues to assure us that we are in fact redeemed, for only He who is God can redeem us.

(5) The Nicene Faith, grounded in the biblical proclamation about Christ and the trinitarian baptismal formulas used in the Church, is both doxology to God the Father and dogma about God the Son.

(6) As we reflect upon the role of dogma in our separated communities, we are aware of the following:

(a) The Nicene Faith possesses a unique status in the hierarchy of dogmas by reason of its testimony to and celebration of the mystery of the Trinity as revealed in Christ Our Savior, and by reason of its definitive reply to an ever-recurring question. This does not imply that the Nicene Faith exhausted the richness of Scripture regarding the person of Christ. For example, the Council of Chalcedon in 451 confessed that He was "in every respect like us, except without sin."

(b) We are agreed that authoritative teaching in the Church serves the people of God by protecting and nurturing the Faith. Dogma has a positive and a negative function. It authoritatively repudiates erroneous teaching, and asserts the truth as revealed in the saving deeds of God and in His gifts to His Church and to His world.

(c) The way in which doctrine is certified as dogma is not identical in the two communities, for there is a difference in the way in which mutually acknowledged doctrine receives ecclesiastical sanction.

(d) Different understandings of the movement from Kerygma (primitive proclamation of the Gospel) to dogma obtain in the two communities. Full inquiry must therefore be made into two topics: first, the nature and structure of the teaching authority of the Church; and, secondly, the role of Scripture in relation to the teaching office of the Church.

(7) We together acknowledge that the problem of the development of doctrine is crucial today and is in the forefront of our common concern.

121. Confession came in for new discussion. On the Catholic side, the Rev. Father Arthur F. LeBlanc, Newman Center chaplain at Ohio State University, suggested that the traditional means of confession be replaced by a group absolution as a "liturgical act" before the Mass. To him the current means of confession were "egocentric." He proposed that the penitent, if he had doubts about the nature and extent of his sins, could consult the priest before the liturgical rite, although, he realized that his proposal was "hemmed in" by the Council of Trent which called for all sins to be confessed audibly. Nevertheless, he pointed out the reasonableness of group confession in a special rite. "Consider that the Eucharistic meal is preceded by a liturgical act, that the reception of Matrimony is preceded by a liturgical act and that ordination is incorporated in a liturgical act," he pointed out.

On the Protestant side, the "confessional" has been rediscovered. The idea of private confession had formerly been considered strictly Roman Catholic, but a few Lutheran, Anglican, and even Reformed churchmen began to have new ideas about the confessional. One was the Rev. Earl Jabay, chaplain at the New Jersey Neuro-Psychiatric Institute, Princeton, New Jersey:

I invite those who wish to confess to God in my presence to sit before . . . a small table against the wall. This table is the size of a small desk and is covered with white linen. The Bible lies open on it, and behind it is a bronze cross about nine inches high. On either side of the cross are two candles . . .

One doing this faces a blank wall except for the Christian symbols on the table. The whole idea of the confessional is that one turns away from man and addresses God. For this reason, I am seated behind the parishioner and slightly to the right. By this arrangement we are both reminded that the dialogue is with God, while I as a pastor am only a confidential witness. It is necessary, however, to first give the parishioner an explanation of how to proceed.

When the person is seated before the table and I am out of his line of vision, I say something like this:

"You and I are now in the presence of God. Let your body relax completely for a few minutes and open your spirit to experience God's presence. (Pause.) What we talk about here will always be a secret with us. I assure you that you are completely safe in my presence to reveal anything to God. (Pause.) I encourage you to speak of anything which has been hidden, anything for which you feel regret, anything for which you feel guilty. This is a time to be completely open with God. (Pause.) You may begin when you wish, or wait for a time. We have plenty of time. There is no hurry."

Then I am silent and while we are waiting, I pray for this person who, by the mercy of God, is now displaying such magnificent courage—a courage combined with an exquisite humility. And slowly, each burdened word is lifted to God. No pastor would ever divulge what he hears, but I can say this. The depth of revelation is far greater in the confessional than I have ever experienced in face-to-face counseling.

122. It used to be that every chapter of the Bible, all 1189 not counting the Apocrypha, differed in the Catholic and Protestant versions. Now Catholics and Protestants have discovered they can share the same Bible, the same wording. The new Roman Catholic edition of the Revised Standard Version changes 67 textual readings or footnotes on the text (example of footnote change: "The denarius was worth about twenty cents" in the RSV, and "The denarius was a day's wage for a laborer" in the RSV-CE—John 12: 5). Most frequent change is the substitution of "brethren" for "brothers," a change made 17 times in the Catholic Edition. No changes were necessitated on strictly theological grounds, although perhaps "brethren" gets across the Roman

Catholic view that the "brethren" were not blood brothers of Jesus in Matt. 12: 46-50, for instance.

But within a year, the Protestant version of the RSV won approval for Catholic use, without the textual changes that appeared in the Catholic edition of the RSV. Nevertheless, footnotes accompanied the text to explain Catholic interpretation in several instances, particularly the regarding of Christ's "brothers" as "relatives," an interpretation permitted in the Aramaic thought patterns of Jesus' time. Approved—with an official imprimatur by Richard Cardinal Cushing, of Boston—was the *Oxford Annotated Bible with the Apocrypha,* containing strictly the Protestant RSV Scriptures.

A host of joint Bible translations are underway, among them a joint translation in preparation by the French Bible Societies and the French Catholic publishing house, Editions du Cerf. The Anchor Bible (Doubleday) is already coming off the press, in 38 volumes, each volume the work of a Catholic, or Protestant, or Jewish scholar. Permission has been granted for a Catholic translation by Joseph Cardinal Frings aided by Protestants in Cologne; Protestants aided Unité Chrétienne, in Lyon, in a translation of the Gospel of Luke; in Holland, a Protestant Bible society helped in a translation of the New Testament by the Catholic Bible Society of St. Willibrord that won praise from Bernard Cardinal Alfrink. Cardinal Alfrink of Utrecht also put his imprimatur on a Protestant translation of the Book of Psalms in the native tongue of the people of Friesland. In Wales, Archbishop John Murphy gave permission for a joint translation of the Bible under Protestant W. R. Williams, principal of the Protestant Theological College at Aberystwyth. Bishop Peter W. Bartholome, of St. Cloud, Minnesota, put his imprimatur on the first book (Father Vincent A. Yzermans, *Death and Resurrection)* in which texts from the Protestant RSV had been included for Scripture readings; and also his imprimatur is on the new Catholic RSV mentioned above. The abridged *Children's Bible* of the Golden Press, New York, has a Catholic, Protestant, and Jewish panel of editors. A new Citizens Bible edited by Catholic, Protestant, and Jewish scholars, with excerpts from various Bibles, mostly the RSV, will provide a common manual for nonsectarian, cultural Bible courses in public schools. (Presbyterians and Roman Catholics in the United States agreed in 1965 to prepare a joint Bible study booklet.)

The new Catholic edition of the RSV, making its debut in 1965, was considered a milestone in inter-Christian relations by Catholics:

a. Said the late Albert Cardinal Meyer, of Chicago, in the preface:

> We welcome with keen satisfaction the Catholic edition of the New Testament according to the Revised Standard Version. It comes near to fulfilling one of the deepest aspirations of the ecumenical movement, since it provides all Christians with a translation of the Word of God which they can share. . . .
>
> The love and veneration of the Sacred Scriptures is a common bond. It moves both ourselves and our separated brethren to a constant and diligent study of the Holy Pages. . . .
>
> With our separated brethren, we also affirm the divine authority of the Sacred Books. For us Catholics, however, there is importantly also a special relationship between the Scriptures and the Church, in which, according to the Catholic Faith, the Church's authentic magisterium has a special place in expounding and proposing the written Word of God. Nevertheless, in the dialogue itself, the Sacred Word is an extraordinary instrument in the powerful hand of God for attaining to that unity, which the Savior holds out for all men.
>
> The present edition of the New Testament should help usher in a happier age when Christian men will no longer use the Word of God as a weapon, but rather, like our forefathers before the time of the Reformation, will find God and Father of Our Lord Jesus Christ speaking to them within the covers of a single book. This edition, then, is one of the first results of the modern ecumenical movement among Christian people to emphasize our common veneration for the written Word of God.

b. Richard Cardinal Cushing, of Boston, says on the flyleaf of the new edition:

> With great joy do I give my approval to this Catholic Edition of the Revised Standard Version of the New Testament.
>
> Those responsible for its preparation state in the introduction that they have had constantly in mind an ecumenical purpose. I wholeheartedly endorse their aims and believe that this edition will do much to promote a greater bond of unity and a more fraternal climate between Protestants and Catholics.
>
> The very fact that we have adopted their text is a high tribute to Protestant scholarship; their willing consent is a tribute to their Christian concern. The adoption of this text is also a sign of the advance of biblical science and of the improved relations of Catholic and Protestant scholars.
>
> I pray that this edition will do much good for the advancement of the spirit of Christian charity and mutual understanding between the Churches.

c. A Catholic *Commonweal* editorial said:

> The publication of a "Catholic edition" of the Protestant Revised Standard Version (RSV) of the New Testament is a major ecumenical triumph. The very lineage of the RSV suggests a measure of the victory. As the introduction to the Catholic edition notes, the RSV is "an authorized version of the American Standard Version, published in 1901, which was a revision of the King James Version, published in 1611." In a roundabout way, then, Catholics today can buy and read a version of the Bible which is a direct descendant of that version which, above all others, they scorned and condemned for centuries. In the middle of the nineteenth century American Catholics went to court to keep the King James Version from being read to their children in public schools. That their great-great-grandchildren will now be

free to buy and read an offspring of that Version is a measure of the distance both the churches and exegesis have
travelled in recent years.

123. Here is a comparison of the Catholic RSV with the Protestant RSV at two points:
    a. In Matthew 1: 18-19 of the Catholic RSV, "send her
away" is substituted for "divorce." The Catholic edition reads:

Now the birth of Jesus Christ took place in this way. When
his mother Mary had been betrothed to Joseph, before they
came together she was found to be with child of the Holy
Spirit; and her husband Joseph, being a just man and un-
willing to put her to shame, resolved to send her away
quietly.

    b. "Full of grace" for "O favored one" is the Catholic RSV
substitution in Luke 1: 26-28:

In the sixth month the angel Gabriel was sent from God to
a city of Galilee named Nazareth, to a virgin betrothed to
a man whose name was Joseph, of the house of David; and
the virgin's name was Mary. And he came to her and said,
"Hail, full of grace, the Lord is with you!"

124. In Tanganyika (now Tanzania) Catholics and Protestants
mapped a common Bible. The Swahili Bible will follow a Protestant text, but also add the 14-book inter-Testament Apocrypha
carried by Catholics. The new Swahili Bible will also have footnotes and a commentary by Catholic theologians, subject to approval by both Catholic and Protestant panels.
    In an announcement of the joint effort in Tanganyika, the
Catholic secretariat of the Tanganyika Episcopal Conference
said:

The Tanganyika Episcopal Conference has reached agree-
ment with the British and Foreign Bible Society through the
Bible Society in East Africa and in co-operation with the
Christian Council of Tanganyika for the use of the text of

the complete Union Swahili Bible. As an immediate aim, the intention is to publish a Catholic edition of the Swahili Bible, using the text accepted by the non-Roman Churches affiliated with the Christian Council of Tanganyika, which is used in East Africa since 1953. The Deutero-canonical books and selected notes and commentary from the "Bible of Jerusalem" will be incorporated under the conditions set down by the Holy See in giving approval for this project. The Christian Council of Tanganyika will arrange for making this new edition available to non-Roman Catholic readers. As a long-range aim, it is the intention of the Tanganyika Episcopal Conference and the Christian Council of Tanganyika to set up a joint committee to:—

(1) begin a revision of the Bible text itself to improve it in the light of recent scholarship and with the hope of arriving at one text that would be equally acceptable to both Roman and non-Roman Christians alike; and

(2) begin a revision of the notes and commentary to adapt them to the African environment and with the hope that they would become equally acceptable to both Roman and non-Roman Christians alike.

125. The former general secretary of the World Council of Churches, the Rev. Dr. Willem A. Visser 't Hooft, made this observation on what Protestants and Catholics can learn from one another in Bible study:

The Bible belongs far more to all the confessions than any one confession realizes. In the old days it was thought in most confessions, and to a certain extent this is true even today: the Bible is "our" book. The Bible belongs to "us," and if others talk about the Bible and try to quote it, they are really doing so without any right, and are not really serious about it, for "we" are the people of the Bible. That is what I meant when I said that the Bible was divisive. But today it is more generally realized, even if not all are willing to admit it openly, that the Bible belongs to other confessions too. . . . The Bible is more Catholic than most Protestants have realized, and is more Protestant than most Catholics have realized. This is precisely what makes the present situation so interesting. Take, for example, the whole new approach of *Formgeschichte,* the study of the specific oral traditions out of which the New Testament has grown. Curiously enough, this new approach has been developed by Protestants. Catholics have been quick to conclude that, if it is true that the Bible has grown out of certain traditions, Protestants should accept the full Roman Catholic concept of tradition. . . .

This new situation must not lead us to the purely relativistic conclusion that, since there are . . . various aspects of the biblical message, it is everyone's book, and everyone can draw his own conclusions. That would be very unecumenical. It means rather that we have to take our ecumenical encounter on this particular meeting-ground of the Bible very seriously. . . . There is, in the ecumenical encounter, the possibility of mutual correction. If we stand in great open-mindedness before one another, we may succeed in curing one another's blind spots.

126. The old stereotypes—that Protestants followed the Bible, and Catholics followed tradition—were obviously gone. Catholics enthroned a 500-year-old copy of the Bible each day at the Second Vatican Council. The prelates quoted Scripture texts at the Council with such profusion that one would be hard put to tell whether it was not Billy Graham speaking rather than a Cardinal.

Protestants had been engaged in the critical study of the sources of the Bible particularly for the last one hundred years, and Roman Catholics, latecomers to the scene of higher criticism had showed increased interest since Pius XII's *Divino Afflante Spiritu* of 1943 telling Catholic scholars they could proceed in their critical Scriptural studies. The Dead Sea Scrolls did much to throw together scholars (e.g. Protestants Wright, Albright, Cross, Freedman; Catholics de Vaux, Skehan, Milik); as they studied the oral and community sources, the "traditions" behind the Scriptures, both sides discovered the link between Scripture and tradition.

The Divine Revelation Constitution promulgated on November 18, 1965, at the Second Vatican Council, committed Roman Catholic scholars to critical studies of Scripture and the sources or traditions behind the Scriptures. Secondly, it linked Scripture and tradition, avoiding any theory that would make a clear distinction between Scripture and tradition as two independent sources. The document also links Word and Sacrament, important for Protestants, and encourages both Bible study and joint Catholic-Protestant translations of Scriptures:

> (9) . . . There exists a close connection and communication between sacred tradition and sacred scripture. For both of them, flowing from the same divine well-spring, in a certain way merge into a unity and tend toward the same end. For sacred scripture is the word of God inasmuch as it is consigned to writing under the inspiration of the divine Spirit, while sacred tradition takes the Word of God entrusted by Christ the Lord and the Holy Spirit to the Apostles, and hands it on to their successors in its full purity, so that led by the light of the Spirit of truth, they may in proclaiming it preserve this Word of God faithfully; explain it, and make it more widely known. Consequently it is not from Sacred Scripture alone that the Church draws her certainty about everything which has been revealed. Therefore both sacred tradition and Sacred Scripture are to be accepted and venerated with the same sense of loyalty and reverence.

> (10) Sacred tradition and Sacred Scripture form one sacred deposit of the word of God, committed to the Church. Holding fast to this deposit the entire holy people united with their shepherds remain always steadfast in the teaching of the Apostles, in the common life, in the breaking of the bread and in prayers (see Acts 2: 42 Greek text), so that holding to, practicing and professing the heritage of the faith, it becomes on the part of the bishops and faithful a single common effort.

> But the task of authentically interpreting the word of God,

whether written or handed on, has been entrusted exclusively to the living teaching office of the Church, whose
authority is exercised in the name of Jesus Christ. This
teaching office is not above the word of God, but serves it,
teaching only what has been handed on, listening to it devoutly, guarding it scrupulously and explaining it faithfully in accord with a divine commission and with the help
of the Holy Spirit, it draws from this one deposit of faith
everything which it presents for belief as divinely revealed.

It is clear, therefore, that sacred tradition, Sacred Scripture and the teaching authority of the Church, in accord
with God's most wise design, are so linked and joined together that one cannot stand without the others, and that all
together and each in its own way under the action of the one
Holy Spirit contribute effectively to the salvation of
souls. . . .

(11) . . . In composing the sacred books, God chose men
and while employed by him they made use of their powers
and abilities, so that with Him acting in them and through
them, they, as true authors, consigned to writing everything
and only those things which he wanted.

Therefore, since everything asserted by the inspired authors or sacred writers must be held to be asserted by the
Holy Spirit, it follows that the books of Scripture must be
acknowledged as teaching solidly, faithfully and without
error that truth which God wanted put into sacred writings
for the sake of our salvation.

Therefore "all Scripture is divinely inspired and has its use
for teaching the truth and refuting error, for reformation
of manners and discipline in right living, so that the man
who belongs to God may be efficient and equipped for good
work of every kind" (2 Tim. 3: 16-17, Greek text).

(12) However, since God speaks in Sacred Scripture
through men in human fashion, the interpreter of Sacred

Scripture, in order to see clearly what God wanted to communicate to us, should carefully investigate what meaning the sacred writers really intended, and what God wanted to manifest by means of their words.

To search out the intention of the sacred writers, attention should be given, among other things, to "literary forms." For truth is set forth and expressed differently in texts which are variously historical, prophetic, poetic, or of other forms of discourse. The interpreter must investigate what meaning the sacred writer intended. . . .

But, since Holy Scripture must be read and interpreted in the same spirit in which it was written, no less serious attention must be given to the content and unity of the whole of Scripture. . . .

For all of what has been said about the way of interpreting Scripture is subject finally to the judgment of the Church, which carries out the divine commission and ministry of guarding and interpreting the word of God. . . .

(18) It is common knowledge that among all the Scriptures, even those of the New Testament, the Gospels have a special preeminence, and rightly so, for they are the principal witness for the life and teaching of the incarnate Word, our Saviour. . . .

(21) The Church has always venerated the divine Scriptures just as she venerates the body of the Lord, since especially in the sacred liturgy, she unceasingly receives and offers to the faithful the bread of life from the table both of God's word and of Christ's body. She has always maintained them, and continues to do so, together with sacred tradition, as the supreme rule of faith, since, as inspired by God and committed once and for all to writing, they impart the word of God Himself without change, and make the voice of the Holy Spirit resound in the words of the prophets and Apostles. Therefore, like the Christian religion itself,

all the preaching of the Church must be nourished and reg-
ulated by Sacred Scripture. For in the sacred books, the
Father who is in heaven meets His children with great love
and speaks with them; and the force and power in the word
of God is so great that it stands as the support and energy
of the Church, the strength of faith for her sons, the food of
the soul, the pure and everlasting source of spiritual life. . . .

(22) Easy access to Sacred Scripture should be provided
for all the Christian faithful. That is why the Church from
the very beginning accepted as her own that very ancient
Greek translation of the old testament which is called the
Septuagint; and she has always given a place of honor to
other Eastern translations and Latin ones, especially the
Latin translation known as the Vulgate. But since the word
of God should be accessible at all times, the Church by her
authority and with material concern sees to it that suitable
and correct translations are made into different languages,
especially from the original texts of the sacred books. And
should the opportunity arise and the Church authorities approve, if these translations are produced in cooperation with
the separated brethren as well, all Christians will be able
to use them. . . .

127. All major Protestant conferences dealing with the question of Scripture in terms of church unity have since asserted the
role of tradition in the church. At the Fourth World Conference
on Faith and Order in Montreal in 1963, "tradition" was dissected, outlined in chalk, diagrammed with great complexity by
German scholars, and even debated in the seminars by Catholic
and conservative Protestant observer guests as well as by the
main-line Protestant and Orthodox accredited delegates. The
term was so well dissected that every Protestant could admit, if
he wished, that he accepted one or several kinds of tradition:

We find ourselves together in Montreal, delegates of churches
with many different backgrounds and many different histories. And yet despite these differences we find that we
are able to meet one another in faith and hope in the one

Father, who by his Son Jesus Christ has sent the Holy Spirit
to draw all men into unity with one another and with him.
It is on the basis of this faith and hope, and in the context of
a common prayer to the one God, Father, Son and Holy
Spirit, that we have studied together anew the problem of
the one Tradition and the many traditions, and despite the
fact of our separations have found that we can talk with one
another and grow in mutual understanding. . . .

In our report we have distinguished between a number of
different meanings of the word *tradition*. We speak of the
*Tradition* (with a Capital T), *tradition* (with a small *t*) and
*traditions*. By *the Tradition* is meant the Gospel itself,
transmitted from generation to generation in and by the
Church. By *tradition* is meant the traditionary process. The
term *traditions* is used in two senses, to indicate both the
diversity of forms of expression and also what we call confessional traditions, for instance the Lutheran tradition or
the Reformed tradition. In the latter part of our report the
word appears in a further sense, when we speak of cultural
traditions. . . .

As Christians we all acknowledge with thankfulness that
God has revealed himself in the history of the people of God
in the Old Testament and in Christ Jesus, his Son, the mediator between God and man. God's mercy and God's glory
are the beginning and end of our own history. The testimony
of prophets and apostles inaugurated the Tradition of his
revelation. The once-for-all disclosure of God in Jesus Christ
inspired the apostles and disciples to give witness to the
revelation given in the person and work of Christ. No one
could, and none can, "say that Jesus is Lord, save by the
Holy Spirit" (I Cor. 12: 3). The oral and written tradition
of the prophets and apostles under the guidance of the Holy
Spirit led to the formation of Scriptures and to the canonization of the Old and New Testaments as the Bible of the
Church. The very fact that Tradition precedes the Scriptures points to the significance of tradition, but also to the
Bible as the treasure of the Word of God.

128. Dr. Kirsten E. Skydsgaard, a professor of theology at the University of Copenhagen and a delegate of the Lutheran World Federation, at the Second Vatican Council, noted in a German language quarterly, *Reformatio*, published in Zurich, the growing consensus of Catholics and Protestant concerning tradition as "living tradition":

> It can no longer be a matter of: Scripture and Tradition in the sense of the general customary interpretation of the formula. Scripture and Tradition cannot be conceived of as two coordinated quantities. The interpretation of the Council of Trent, which moreover was the interpretation of that whole period, that two such sources of revelation exist independently of one another cannot be maintained. But neither can we accept the modern Roman Catholic conception of Scripture *in* Tradition as an organ—even though a fundamental one—of the stream of Tradition flowing alive through time. This view purports to mean "Scripture extended into a Tradition." Tradition as an unfolding of the embryo contained in Scripture . . . These thoughts stem most deeply from a different concept of revelation, and we must ask the Roman-Catholic theologians to seriously consider whether this concept: Living Tradition, *so* explained, really corresponds to the Biblical thinking of Revelation. In an evangelical concept of Tradition it is primarily a question of an *Event*, namely the transmission of the salvific word of God which seeks to be heard and believed, of a constantly deeper penetration into the Biblical perceptions connected with this salvific event. Here, in fact, it is also a question of a living tradition, but how different from the same word in modern Roman Catholic theology! We are both approaching the same concept but are far removed from one another in this encounter.
>
> And yet perhaps this very word "living traditions," even though it is conceived of fundamentally differently on both sides, can provide a basis for a dialogue between Roman and evangelical theologians who are willing to listen to one another.

129. Protestants also rediscovered the 14-book Apocrypha, which appears in the Latin Vulgate and subsequent Catholic Bibles, but not in the Hebrew Bible from which the Protestant canon comes. However, Luther's Bible contained it, as did the Sixth American translation of the 20's. The Rev. Donald D. Donihue, a Methodist pastor in California, writing in the *Christian Advocate*, found the Apocrypha relevant and useful for the Protestant minister:

There are great values to be realized by the inclusion in any minister's preaching schedule of sermons based on books of the Apocrypha. . . .

In these . . . books of intertestamental literature we have much material which may be used to undergird and demonstrate the efficacy of the Gospel of Jesus Christ. . . .

Here we have a body of literature which represents a transition of Old Testament concepts to New. In various ways our New Testament presupposes not only the thought categories and understandings of the Apocrypha, but of the Pseudepigrapha as well.

Ecclesiasticus 5:11 is to be found in James 1: 19. The similarities between Hebrews 11: 32ff. and 2 Maccabees 6-7 are too strong to be coincidental. . . .

Finally, we would do well to make a place for the Apocrypha because the men and women who came to life on its pages had experiences related to our time. Within these pages we possess a fertile field for homiletics.

Consider The Prayer of Manasseh. Here is a good place to begin preaching on the Apocrypha, for Manasseh is mentioned in 2 Chronicles 33: 6 where we read, "He did much evil in the sight of the Lord." Manasseh's prayer is liturgical in form. How eloquently it expresses man's deepest longing to be reconciled to God.

> In Tobit we encounter a strong, personal, religious devotion
> on the part of one man. We see warm family ties not often
> found in our time but greatly needed. We see the role of
> charity in religious life. Are these themes unrelated to
> Jesus Christ?

## REFERENCES

### Chapter IV

103. Bernard Leeming, S. J., "General Problems of Ecumenism," in R. J. W.
     Bevan's, *The Church and Christian Unity* (New York: Oxford University Press, 1963), p. 11.
104. a. *Southwest Louisiana Register*, Diocese of Lafayette, Louisiana,
        interview with the Rev. Dr. Robert Brockway, by Peggy Siegmund,
        Feb. 18, 1965, p. 3.
     b. *Ibid.*, interview with the Rev. Dr. Frank T. Wallace, by Henry Libersat, Feb. 4, 1965, p. 2.
     c. *Ibid.*, interview with the Rev. L. D. Jackson, by Peggy Siegmund,
        Mar. 11, 1965, p. 3.
     d. *Ibid.*, interview with the Rev. Perry Sanders by Henry Libersat,
        Mar. 18, 1965, p. 2.
105. John B. Sheerin, C.S.P., "Dialogue With Evangelicals Like Billy
     Graham," *The Catholic World*, CCI, No. 1203 (June 1965), 160.
106. "Ecumenical Chronicle," *The Ecumenical Review*, XI, No. 3 (Apr.,
     1959), 321, 322.
107. *The Catholic Weekly*, Dec. 25, 1964.
108. *Consultation on Church Union*, annual summary booklet, Princeton,
     N.J., Apr., 1964, Vol. 3 (distributed by the Rev. George Hunt, executive secretary, Box 69, Fanwood, N. J.), pp. 31, 32.
109. a., b. Release, Executive Council, The Episcopal Church, New York,
     dateline Kansas City, Feb. 9, 1966.
110. Joint statement given to the press by Bishop Murphy, and Dr. Empie,
     February 13, 1966.
111. a. Letter from the Board of the General Synod of the Dutch Reformed
        Church, Feb. 7, 1964, to Bernard Cardinal Alfrink, *Documentation
        Hollandaise du Concile*, L. G. M. Alting von Geusau, "The Ecumenical Situation in Holland," No. 132a, p. 7.
     b. Reply from Bernard Cardinal Alfrink, Apr. 25, 1964 to the letter
        of the Board of the General Synod of the Dutch Reformed Church,
        *Ibid.*, p. 8.
112. Fredrik A. Schiotz, statement distributed by the Office of Public
     Relations, The American Lutheran Church, Minneapolis, July 7, 1965.
113. Joseph Marie Martin, archbishop of Rouen, in "Ecumenical Notes and
     Documentation," in *One in Christ*, a "Catholic Ecumenical Review,"
     Sheffield, England, I, No. 1 (1965), 69-71.
114. "Ecumenism in the University," *Herder Correspondence*, II, No. 1
     (Jan., 1965), 10.
115. *Consultation on Church Union*, op. cit., pp. 27, 28.
116. Approved report of commission I, "The Ordained Ministry in a United
     Church," Consultation on Church Union, mimeographed report, pp. 2-4.
117. a. cf. "Vatican II: Collegiality and Diaconate," Rev. Father John J.
        King, *Homiletic and Pastoral Review*, LXIV, Apr., 1964, 572, 580.

b. *Constitution on the Church*, National Catholic Welfare Conference translation, St. Paul Editions, pp. 31-37 (III: 22-25).

c. Pope Paul, The Bishop's Role, *The Pope Speaks*, X, No. 2 (1965), 111.

118. a. *Constitution on the Church, op. cit.*, pp. 15-24 (II: 9-15).

b. Yves Congar, "The Church: The People of God" in *The Church and Mankind*—Dogma, Vol. 1, *Concilium*, Edward Schillebeeck, editorial director (Glen Rock, N.J.: Paulist Press, 1964), 28.

c. From "group B's report on the training week" at the Diocese of London Youth Camp in Ryde, Bishop Lovett's School, Aug. 1-8, 1964, p. 2.

119. Editorial, "The Nature of the Church," *Watchman-Examiner*, Lawrence Slaght, ed., LI, No. 46 (Nov. 14, 1963), 835.

120. "Summary Statement," *The Status of the Nicene Creed as Dogma of the Church*, published jointly by representatives of the U.S.A. National Committee of the Lutheran World Federation and the Bishops' Commission for Ecumenical Affairs, pp. 31, 32.

121. Earl Jabay, "The Healing of the Soul: How to Conduct a Confessional," fifth in a series. *The Church Herald*, weekly of the Reformed Church in America, Jan. 22, 1965, p. 9.

122. a. Albert Cardinal Meyer, Preface, in *The New Testament, Revised Standard Version, Catholic Edition* (New York: Thomas Nelson and Sons, 1965), p. vii.

b. Richard Cardinal Cushing, *ibid.*, p. vi.

c. Editorial, *Commonweal*, (LXXXII), No. 13 (Aug. 6, 1965), 549.

123. a. *The New Testament, RSV, Catholic Edition, op. cit.*, p. 1.

b. *Ibid.*, p. 51.

124. Bulletin of the Catholic Secretariat, Tanganyika Episcopal Conference, NB 7/64: FvD/sa, Mar. 26, 1964.

125. Willem Visser 't Hooft, "The Bible in an Ecumenical Setting," *The Student World* (Geneva: World Student Christian Federation), XLIX, No. 1, (first quarter), 1956, 47-49.

126. *The Constitution on Divine Revelation*, NCWC translation, St. Paul Edition.

127. Section II, "Scripture, Tradition and Traditions," *The Fourth World Conference on Faith and Order* (New York: Association Press, 1964), P. C. Rodger, Lukas Visher, eds., pp. 50, 51.

128. Kristen E. Skydsgaard, "Schrift und Tradition," "Bemerkungen zum Traditionsproblem in der neuren Theologie," *Reformatio*, Evangelische Zeitschrift fur kultur und politik, 14 Jahrgang, Heft 3, Mar., 1965, pp. 178, 179.

129. Donald D. Dunihue, "Why Preach on Books of the Apocrypha?" *Christian Advocate*, Sept. 24, 1964, pp. 13, 14, and the Methodist Publishing House.

# five

# Progress in Trouble Areas

The layman knows little about the natural law or crisis theology, Thomas Aquinas or Karl Barth. But mention the Pope, or Mary or censorship or Church and State to the Protestant and you've named some fighting words. Or mention Luther, or sects, or birth control to the Catholic and you are likely to have another ruffled response. When books were written on dialogue one hundred years ago, the books weren't called such things as *An American Dialogue* by a priest and Protestant clergyman together (such as Gustave Weigel and Robert McAfee Brown's effort in 1960). The books were written individually and polemically. Matthew Poole called his book in 1843 *Dialogue between a Popish Priest and an English Protestant* (Presbyterian Board of Publication, Philadelphia). And the subtitles were loaded, exaggerated words: "The danger of Popery," "of the merit of good works," "the Romish Church declines all judgment but her own." As for style: "The several discourses, arguments, and answers which I have put into the Papists' mouth, are such as were first taken out of their mouth; and so it is but a piece of justice and restitution to return them thither." That was a long time ago, but the antagonism against certain words still exists. A Baptist church official in Rome told the story of a Baptist pastor's daughter, who was hearing very much about Mary in the Christmas season in Rome. She knew that her Baptist parents, however, regarded Mary in somewhat less esteem than Mother of God. So one day the little girl heard something at school that made her eyes twinkle. The six-year-old rushed home. She announced that Mary had been put in a stable by a manger. "At least they have put her in her place!" she said.

Catholic youngsters, just as the little Protestant girl in Rome, have had inbred in them a response to certain words. And an extolling of the Reformation and the reformers, namely Luther, surely was cause enough to punch a Protestant boy in the nose! Catholic parochial children were taught: "The doctrines of Wycliff and Hus appealed to the worst passions, exciting directly to rebellion against authority. The same was true in a worse degree of Luther's doctrines, exciting not only to rebellion against authority, but appealing to the worst form of intellectual pride" (Section on church history, in *Bible History*, by the Most Rev. Richard Gilmour, Roman Catholic bishop of Cleveland, Benziger Brothers, Inc., New York, 1924, p. 292). Even the 1952 Confraternity Edition of the Baltimore Catechism says: "The founders of Christian sects were not saints and generally were not holy or edifying men. The sects have not given saints to the world. Their truths are but fragments of the doctrines of the Catholic Church. The holiness of their members is due to the means that the sects have salvaged from Catholic worship. Moreover, these sects cannot point to miracles wrought in their favor" (no. 160, Baltimore Catechism No. 3, Benziger Brothers, Inc., New York, 1952, p. 90)

The ominous reference to all non-Roman Catholic groups as "sects" is fading. Newspapers, informed by their religious advisers, seldom use the word anymore. Vatican documents have even taken to speaking of "churches and ecclesial communities separated from the Roman Apostolic See" instead of "sects" or they say, "separated brethren," or "brothers in Christ." And there has been progress in all of the trouble areas, as well as language.

130. The Eastern Orthodox can accept the Pope as first among equals, and so can the Anglicans. (Said the Most Rev. Arthur Michael Ramsey, archbishop of Canterbury, in a Chicago visit in October 1959: "I am willing to accept the Pope as a presiding

bishop among the bishops of Christendom, but not as infallible.")
A letter writer (B.J.K., Berwick, Pennsylvania) asked columnist
Vladimir Borichevsky, of Philadelphia, if the Orthodox ever recognized the Pope, and Borichevsky answered in *The Russian Orthodox Journal:*

> Yes she [Orthodox Church] did and still does recognize the
> Pope. She recognizes him as the Pope of Rome, that is, the
> Bishop of Rome. For the first ten centuries the Bishop of
> Rome was one of the patriarchs of the Church. The title
> "Pope" was first used not by the Bishop of Rome but by the
> Patriarch of Alexandria who is still referred to as the Pope
> (Father) of Alexandria.
>
> When the city of Rome was the capital of the Roman Em-
> pire, the Bishop of Rome was considered the first patriarch
> or "The first among equals." His primacy was a primacy of
> honor and dignity because he was the Bishop of Rome, the
> first city of the Roman Empire. When Constantine trans-
> ferred the capital to Constantinople, Rome remained for a
> while the capital of the Western Empire, but the real capi-
> tal of the Empire became Constantinople which was also
> called "The New Rome."
>
> To this day, as a matter of courtesy and respect, the Bishop
> of Rome is called the "Pope of Rome" but in doing this the
> Orthodox Catholic Church does not accept or acknowledge
> as valid for the One True Catholic and Apostolic the claims
> of the Pope of Rome to be the Vicar of Christ on earth, and
> the infallible head of the Church. . . .

131. Speaking to an interfaith convocation at the Roman
Catholic St. Mary-of-the-Woods College, Terre Haute, Indiana,
April 15, 1965, the late Metropolitan Antony Bashir, head of the
Syrian Orthodox Church in the United States and a vice president of the National Council of Churches, proposed a series of
approaches to unity including what he called a "restatement" of
the papacy to "synthesize" traditions of both East and West:

In my opinion maximum effectiveness of any negotiations will ultimately depend on the methods employed, among which I consider the following to be of primary importance.

(a) The initial meetings and discussions must be restricted to Orthodox Catholics and Roman Catholics. . . .

(b) If the Roman Pope was, or is, sincerely interested in more than diplomatic overtures, His Holiness must begin by addressing Orthodoxy through the Oecumenical Patriarch, as Primate of the Church, calling for a joint commission of theologians and canonists with a large Orthodox membership to prepare an appropriate agenda for inclusion in a letter carrying the signature of His Holiness the Pope as Primate of the West and His All Holiness the Oecumenical Patriarch as Primate of the East, and addressed to both Churches.

(c) The meeting which would follow, although it might not arrive at immediate union, would provide an opportunity for the Holy Spirit to act and might well lead to eventual unity.

(d) The major difficulty between Orthodoxy and Rome is the question of the basis for the Papal Primacy and the concomitant dogma of Papal Infallibility. One cannot minimize the differences, evident and implied, in these dogmas, nor forget the discouraging history of the attempts at solution, but is it not possible that the time has arrived when the two mutually exclusive but closely related teachings, an infallible Church Primate, may be so restated as to synthesize both traditions on a new and higher level? This is a daring, perhaps rash, conception, but Our Lord will not hold us guiltless if we choose lesser problems for easy solution while we neglect the divisions among those who call upon His name.

132. For a quarter of a century, Lutheran Oscar Cullmann has lectured off and on in Rome, where he takes his annual Easter vacation. His views on Peter in his book *Peter: Disciple, Apostle,*

*Martyr,* have created a sensation. Protestant Cullmann maintains that (1) Peter indeed went to Rome (a point not conceded by many Protestants) and (2) Christ meant to build His church on Peter as a person. However, Cullmann, always makes clear, this does not mean the establishing of a perpetual papacy based on Peter. Nevertheless, Cullmann's efforts have done much to bridge one of the difficult disagreements between Protestants and Catholics:

> "You are rock (Jesus said), and upon this rock I will build my Church." In Greek Simon's title reads *Petros,* with the masculine ending. We have seen that the name *Kepha* was reproduced in Greek by Petros. But Jesus says that he will build his Church upon this *Petra.* The words that should correspond do not really correspond here. In the Aramaic, however, we have both times the same word *Kepha:* "You are *Kepha* and upon this *Kepha* I will build my Church." Thus here the name and the thing are exactly identical. Therefore we must assume that the saying was originally coined in Aramaic.
>
> The Semitic character is confirmed by various other observations: The designation of the father of Peter in *bar-yona,* the expression "flesh and blood" for "men," the word pair "bind and loose," then also the strophic rhythm—three strophes of three lines each—which is found similarly in other sayings of Jesus, for example, Matthew 11: 7-9 and 11: 25-30; and further the illustration of the rock as foundation, to which there is an exact parallel in the rabbinical literature, where Abraham is mentioned as the rock of the world.
>
> The fact that only Matthew gives the saying also points to the Palestinian origin of the tradition. Still another consideration can be cited to show that the tradition is very early. The story would scarcely have been handed on at a time when Peter no longer stood at the head of the Jerusalem church and James was already the leader there. The saying must thus have been transmitted at a time when Peter was still in

Jerusalem. The very early character of the tradition, which is vouched for by the Palestinian character of the verses, naturally does not prove beyond question that the utterance must come from Jesus, but it nevertheless is an important *presupposition* for that conclusion. . . .

All Protestant interpretations that seek in one way or another to explain away the reference to Peter seem to me unsatisfactory. No, the fact remains that when Jesus says that he will build his *ekklesia* upon this rock, he really means the person of Simon. Upon this disciple, who in the lifetime of Jesus possessed the specific advantages and the specific weaknesses of which the Gospels speak, upon him who was then their spokesman, their representative in good as well as in bad, and in this sense was the rock of the group of the disciples—upon him is to be founded the Church, which after the death of Jesus will continue his work upon earth.

The Roman Catholic exegesis must be regarded as correct when it rejects those other attempts at explanation. On its part, however, it proceeds in an even more arbitrary way when it tries to find in this text a reference to "successors."

133. Pope Paul was asked by an Anglican bishop in Canada to reconsider the validity of Anglican rites of ordination and consecration of bishops. The Rt. Rev. George N. Luxton, bishop of Huron, with residence in London, Ontario, Canada, brought the subject up, first in an audience with Pope Paul in 1965, then in a letter. The matter had been considered closed from a Roman Catholic viewpoint since Pope Leo XIII, advised by a special commission, declared on September 13, 1894 (*Apostolicae curae*) "that ordinations performed according to the Anglican rite are utterly invalid and altogether void." Leo had objected to wording changes and differences in "intent," that is, not sharing the same view of the Sacrifice of the Mass at the rite. To Bishop Luxton, the discovery of common ground shared by Anglicans and Roman Catholics in ancient rites, with new interpretations in theology, were sufficient cause for a new look at Anglican orders by the Vatican. Bishop Luxton summarized his request,

which includes an interesting proposal for "intermingling" Roman Catholic, Orthodox and Anglican Orders:

My request to Your Holiness is appropriately a triple one:

(1) That you ask one of your Commissions to review the matter of Anglican Orders, to compare afresh the Anglican Ordinal with the Early Ordinals, with the Roman one described by Hippolytus (known to the Commission [of Pope Leo XIII] only in the Ethiopic Version and not consulted by them in texts which subsequently have been better authenticated); the Eastern Rite of St. Sarapion (not known to the Commission); the later Byzantine Rite, the Gregorian and the Gelasian Sacramentaries, as well as the Spanish Mozarabic rite. *In all these the matter and form are very close to that of the English Reformation Ordinal.* . . .

To Anglican scholars studying the whole field it seems as if the assessors who advised Pope Leo XIII against the recognition of Anglican Orders, were declaring at the same time that the Orders of the Eastern Church and indeed the Orders of the early Roman Church were likewise invalid, *for all these primitive Ordinals were similar in form, matter and intent to the English Ordinal.* When this new study, which I am requesting, is set in our present climate of theological dialogue, we believe that your Commission would arrive at different conclusions. Our conviction in this matter is strengtnened by the fact that in recent years new interpretations of the doctrine of Eucharistic Sacrifice have been proposed by distinguished scholars in the Roman Catholic Church (reference to Eugene Masure, Maurice de la Taille, and Abbot Anscar Vonier). Since the heart of the argument in "Apostolicae Curae" turns on the understanding of Eucharistic Sacrifice by the English Reformers, these new interpretations by your own theologians seem to call for a reconsideration of the earlier verdict of seventy years ago.

(2) A second request is that Your Holiness should consider at some point in the years ahead, an action towards the

Anglican Communion similar to that which your Holiness and the Patriarch Athenagoras completed at the end of the Vatican Council, *and revoke the sentence of excommunication and anathema as passed by Pope Pius V in 1570 on Queen Elizabeth I and "all those that cleave to her,"* and set forth in the Bull "Regnans in Excelsis," which released all subjects of the Queen from obedience to "her and her orders, mandates and laws." It would be a gracious act on your part if this excommunication, so heavily freighted with secular and political concerns, could be lifted from our people and Church, and if our two Churches might again, after four hundred years, resume normal Christian relationships of mutual respect and affection. Such action on your part would be the recognition and confirmation of a relationship that is already being established between us, and would be the preface to new co-operation and unity. Perhaps this might be an appropriate way to celebrate in 1970 the quadricentennial of the earlier Bull of 1570.

(3) My final request is that you also consider, as a further step of Christian brotherhood, *the intermingling of the Orders of the Roman Catholic Church with our own Orders and with the Orders of other communions which are in full inter-communion with us*; e.g. the Old Catholic Church and the Church of Sweden. Already three lines met in the consecration of William Laud, Archbishop of Canterbury (1633-1645), the English line through Mathew Parker, a second through the Archbishop of Dublin, Hugh Curwen, and a third line through Marco Antonio de Dominis, Archbishop of Spalato (Split) who joined the English Church in 1616. Presently in our Communion other Churches are blending their Orders with ours in many services for the consecration of Bishops, and we anticipate an increase in this experience as the Churches in the various regions of our Communion enter into union with their Christian neighbours.

In our November discussion you indicated your familiarity with our Anglican relationship with the Old Catholics of

Europe; and you noted that the intermingling of Anglican Orders with theirs (in 1931 and 1932 and subsequently) is relevant to any modern review of Anglican Orders. I am suggesting to Your Holiness a method by which an initial step of unity could be taken between our two Churches, *one that would render unnecessary all future debate regarding the validity or non-validity of Anglican Orders* (i.e., the presence of Roman Catholic Bishops at Anglican Consecrations of Bishops, and their participation as co-consecrators). This would move our churches towards a similar relationship to that existing between the Roman See and the Oriental Rites. I recall also that this possibility came to your mind at the close of my November [1965] audience with you, and that you mentioned having heard it under discussion. Perhaps here, in an ultimate Federation of the three Churches, the Roman Catholic, and the Anglican Communion, *and in the fusion of our Holy Orders,* there may be found a next great step towards Christian Unity.

134. A historical point of tension centering around the Papacy was corrected December 7, 1965, during the final decree ceremony of the Second Vatican Council concurrently with another meeting in Istanbul. In the simultaneous ceremonies Pope Paul VI and Ecumenical Patriarch Athenagoras I withdrew the mutual excommunication of each group that dates back to 1054. In that year, the quarrel between Pope and Patriarch, which had been going on for centuries, came to a head. Pope Leo IX interfered with churches in Sicily loyal to the Patriarch, who in turn, with the acquiescence of the metropolitan of Bulgaria, closed Latin churches. The patriarch, Michael Cerularius, also pressed the quarrel theologically, following earlier charges of the controversial Photius, a ninth century patriarch, condemning the use of unleavened bread in the Latin-rite churches in the West. Leo sent his legate, Cardinal Humbert, with an excommunication of Michael Cerularius and all his followers, a document laid on the high altar of St. Sofia in Constantinople (Istanbul) in 1054. Theologians in Rome in 1965 reviewing history questioned the validity of the excommunication which was actually carried out after Leo IX's death; they noted also that it excommunicated a people, whereas it should have been individual and personal (the

excommunication against Luther, for example, is considered valid, directed toward an individual; and because it did deal with an individual, Lutherans at the Council expressed little interest in any possible removal of Luther's excommunication).

At the close of the Second Vatican Council in 1965, a representative of the Ecumenical Patriarch exchanged a kiss of peace with Pope Paul VI and accepted for the patriarch the common declaration annulling the earlier anathema. Dressed in somber black robes and head piece, the Orthodox representative, Metropolitan Melition of Heliopolis and Theira, circled the central Bernini altar in St. Peter's after the annulment and drew applause from the white mitred bishops comparable to that of applause for Pope Paul. In Istanbul, the same declaration was read in St. George's Cathedral, with Lawrence Cardinal Shehan, of Baltimore, heading a Vatican delegation.

Pope Paul VI and Patriarch Athenagoras I, recalling their previous rapport in their Jerusalem confrontation, removed the "psychological" stigma of the years with this declaration:

> (1) Grateful to God who mercifully favored them with a fraternal meeting at those holy places where the mystery of salvation was accomplished through the death and resurrection of the Lord Jesus, and where the church was born through the outpouring of the Holy Spirit, Pope Paul VI and Patriarch Athenagoras I have not lost sight of the determination each then felt to omit nothing thereafter which charity might inspire and which could facilitate the development of the fraternal relations thus taken up between the Roman Catholic Church and the Orthodox Church of Constantinople.
>
> They are persuaded that in acting this way, they are responding to the call of that divine grace which today is leading the Roman Catholic Church and the Orthodox Church, as well as all Christians, to overcome their differences in order to be again "one as the Lord Jesus asked of His Father for them."
>
> (2) Among the obstacles along the road of the develop-

ment of these fraternal relations of confidence and esteem, there is the memory of the decisions, actions and painful incidents which in 1054 resulted in the sentence of excommunication leveled against the Patriarch Michael Cerularius and two other persons by the Legate of the Roman See under the leadership of Cardinal Humbertus, legates who then became the object of a similar sentence pronounced by the Patriarch and the Synod of Constantinople.

(3) One cannot pretend that these events were not what they were during this very troubled period of history. Today, however, they have been judged more fairly and serenely. Thus it is important to recognize the excesses which accompanied them and later led to consequences which, in so far as we can judge, went much further than their authors had intended and foreseen. They had directed their censures against the persons concerned and not the churches; these censures were not intended to break ecclesiastical communion between the sees of Rome and Constantinople.

(4) Since they are certain that they express the common desire for justice and the unanimous sentiment of charity which moves the faithful, and since they recall the command of the Lord: "If you are offering your gift at the altar, and there remember that your brother has something against you, leave your gift before the altar and go, first be reconciled to your brother" (Matthew v. 23-24), Pope Paul VI and Patriarch Athenagoras I with his synod, in common agreement, declare that:

(a) They regret the offensive words, the reproaches without foundation, and the reprehensive gestures which, on both sides, have marked or accompanied the sad events of this period [A.D. 1054 and events leading to it.]

(b) They likewise regret and remove from memory and from the midst of the Church the sentences of excommunication which followed these events, the memory of which has influenced actions up to our day and has hindered closer relations in charity; and they commit these excommunications to oblivion.

(c) Finally, they deplore the preceding and later vexing events which, under the influence of various factors—among which, lack of understanding and mutual trust—eventually led to the effective rupture of ecclesiastical communion.

(5) Pope Paul VI and Patriarch Athenagoras I with his synod realize that this gesture of justice and mutual pardon is not sufficient to end both old and more recent differences between the Roman Catholic Church and the Orthodox Church. Through the action of the Holy Spirit, those differences will be overcome through cleansing of hearts, through regret for historical wrongs, and through an efficacious determination to arrive at a common understanding and expression of the faith of the Apostles and its demands.

They hope, nevertheless, that this act will be pleasing to God, who is prompt to pardon us when we pardon each other. They hope that the whole Christian world, especially the entire Roman Catholic Church and the Orthodox Church will appreciate this gesture as an expression of a sincere desire, shared in common, for reconciliation, and as an invitation to follow out, in a spirit of trust, esteem and mutual charity, the dialogue which, with God's help, will lead to living together again, for the greater good of souls and the coming of the kingdom of God, in that full communion of faith, fraternal accord and sacramenal life which existed among them during the first thousand years of the life of the Church.

135. Concerning Protestants, the things that bothers them the most, says an Augustinian priest scholar, the Rev. Father Gregory Baum, of St. Michael's College and St. Basil's Seminary, Toronto, besides the authority of the church centered in the papacy, is the role of Mary in the Church. There are develop-

ments on both sides. Roman Catholics themselves are showing a widening concern about an overemphasis on Mary, despite some extension of devotion and titles of Mary such as Pope Paul's ruling "that from now on the whole of the Christian people should use this sweetest of names (Mother of the Church) to pay more homage to the Mother of God," on November 21, 1964, with a similar plea on February 2, 1966—The veneration of Mary "is essentially linked with that of Christ, deriving from and leading to it." However, Pope Paul as Cardinal Montini, before he became pope, in a speech to a Liturgical Study week at Vicenza, sought clearly to limit devotion to Mary to "its pure goal":

> The liturgy is not only a means of teaching us dogmatic truth; it is also a school of holiness and one of the principal means of uniting our souls with Christ. Hence it is to be hoped that the work of this Congress will be devoted especially to this aspect of Marian liturgy. This will, where necessary, bring devotion to the most blessed Virgin back to its pure goal, so that it recovers its real function of bringing souls to Jesus by the speediest, most total and most loving transformation possible of the old man into the new man of righteousness and Christian holiness. Any other form of Marian piety, insufficiently orientated in this direction, would thereby necessarily show itself as deficient and as displeasing to the heavenly Mother.

136. A formula for better understanding between Catholic and Protestant concerning Mary is suggested by the Rev. Father Walter J. Burghardt, S.J., of Woodstock College:

> The Catholic vision of Mary—theology—and the Catholic veneration of Mary—devotion—*is* an obstacle to the union of the churches; but the obstacle is *not* insuperable. What is imperative here is understanding—on four levels. . . .
>
> First, Catholics must understand why Protestants reject the Catholic vision and veneration of Mary. Second, Protestants must understand why Catholics see Mary and honor her as they do. Third, Catholics must re-examine their pres-

ent position on Mary—mind and heart, theology and devotion—to discover if, and to what extent, they have given
Protestants cause for legitimate concern. Fourth, Protestants must re-examine their present position on Mary—mind
and heart, theology and devotion—to discover if, and to what
extent, that position does injustice to God and to His Christ.

137. On the Protestant side there is occasional new interest
in Mary. An example is that of the Rev. Father Colin Stephenson, an Anglican administrator of the 40-year-old Shrine to Mary
at Walsingham (the scene of a 1,200-year-old English Catholic
shrine to Mary). "Walsingham has great value ecumenically, because Catholics find it hard to understand the apparent Protestant coolness toward Mary, and because Protestants need to engage in dialogue about her," said Father Stephenson. He argues
that Anglicans are committed to Marian devotion because the
Council of Ephesus A.D. 431 called Mary "Mother of God" and
the Church of England is committed by its 39 Articles to the
conclusions of that Council. He suggests these ways of honoring
Mary in his little 11-page pamphlet, "Our Solitary Boast":

> The classic prayer to our Lady is the "Hail Mary": "Hail
> Mary, full of grace, the Lord is with thee: blessed art thou
> among women and blessed is the fruit of thy womb, Jesus.
> Holy Mary, Mother of God, pray for us sinners, now and in
> the hour of our death."

> Although this prayer is addressed to our Lady, it is pri-
> marily in honour of our Lord's Incarnation, of which she
> is the symbol. . . .

> There are many other prayers and devotions for the use
> of those who wish to foster in their spiritual life a devotion
> to our Lord's mother. . . .

> We should do well to observe devoutly the feasts in our
> Lady's honour, and to remember that these are like the
> birthdays of the mother of a human family; and we can

show no greater piety towards her than in going to the "family table" and attending Mass and receiving Holy Communion.

There are many other Marian devotions such as visiting her Shrines and going on pilgrimage, joining in processions in her honour and lighting candles, and putting flowers around her image in church or in our own home. There are some people who object to these practices and to some of the expressions used about our Lady, which they find offensive or sentimental; but in a family, different members have different ways of expressing themselves, and perhaps if outsiders could hear us talking to our human mothers at moments of affection, they would say the same things. . . .

When one becomes conscious of the family nature of the Church, an easy familiarity with our Lady and the saints will be found to give our prayer life a balance which is lacking when this is absent. . . .

Devotion to our Lady as the mother of Christians is essentially a family devotion. Mary herself said "all generations shall call me blessed," but all generations have done better than this, and they have called her every "pet name" imaginable. She is Our Lady of Good Counsel, the Mystic Rose, the Star of the Sea, Our Lady of Walsingham, Our Lady of Lourdes and of a thousand places where she is particularly honoured. Those who do not understand the family, personal nature of these titles sometimes accuse us of thinking of her as different people when we invoke her by different names. If they did but know, the truth is even more astonishing than they suspect, for each of us has our own "Our Lady," because she is your mother and my mother, and it is to you that Jesus is saying now "behold your Mother."

138. The difficulties engendered by proselytizing, or recruiting, from the ranks of other faiths were largely solved. On the Protestant side, a 1960 statement of the Central Committee of the World Council of Churches faced the issue squarely:

Proselytism is not something absolutely different from witness: it is the corruption of witness. Witness is corrupted when cajolery, bribery, undue pressure or intimidation is used—subtly or openly—to bring about seeming conversion; when we put the success of our church before the honour of Christ; when we commit the dishonesty of comparing the ideal of our own church with the actual achievement of another; when we seek to advance our own cause by bearing false witness against another church; when personal or corporate self-seeking replaces love for every individual soul with whom we are concerned. Such corruption of the Christian witness indicates lack of confidence in the power of the Holy Spirit, lack of respect for the nature of man and lack of recognition of the true character of the Gospel. It is very easy to recognize these faults and sins in others; it is necessary to acknowledge that we are all liable to fall into one or the other of them ourselves. . . .

Having due regard for the nature of the ecumenical fellowship represented by the World Council of Churches, we at the same time recognize certain principles which we believe should guide churches in their mutual relationships and which, if followed, might provide objective and generally applicable standards of practice. . . .

(1) that we in our churches respect the convictions of other churches whose conception and practice of church membership differ from our own, and consider it our Christian duty to pray for one another and to help each other rise above our respective shortcomings. . . .

(2) that we recognize it as the primary duty of every awakened Christian to strive prayerfully for the renewal of that church in which he is a member:

(3) that we recognize the right of the mature individual to change his church allegiance if he becomes convinced that such change of allegiance is God's will for him;

(4) that since grave obstacles to brotherly relationships between churches are created when some churches are denied the religious liberty which is accorded to others, all Christians should work towards the establishing and maintenance of religious liberty from all churches and all their members in every land;

(5) that we disavow any church action by which material or social advantages are offered to influence a person's church affiliation, or undue pressures are brought to bear on persons in times of helplessness or stress;

(6) that while it is proper for churches to make clear their position with regard to marriages between persons belonging to different communions, the conscientious decision of marriage partners as to their future church allegiance should be respected;

(7) that before a young child is received into the membership of a church other than that of the present affiliation of the parents or guardian, a due pastoral concern for the unity of the family should be exercised. . . .

(8) that due pastoral care should be exercised before receiving anyone into the membership of a church if he is already, as the member of another church, under discipline by that church, or if there is evidence that his reasons for seeking membership in a different church are worldly or unworthy;

(9) that whenever a member of one church desires to be received into the membership of another church, direct consultation should be sought between the churches concerned; but if conscientious motives and sound reasons are apparent, no obstacle should be placed in the way of such change of membership before or after its accomplishment;

(10) that while there may be situations where a church al

ready present in a given area seems to be so inadequate in
its witness to Christ as to call for more faithful witness and
proclamation of the Gospel to its members, the first effort
of other churches should be patiently to help that church
towards its renewal and the strengthening of its own witness and ministry. . . .

139. Proselytism received a blow in the Second Vatican Council's Decree on the Mission Activity of the Church, which called
for joining in cooperative efforts, rather than dividing forces on
the church frontiers:

(6) . . . By the very necessity of mission, all the baptized
are called to gather into one flock, and thus they will be able
to bear unanimous witness before the nations to Christ their
Lord. And if they are not yet capable of bearing witness
to the same faith, they should at least be animated by mutual love and esteem. . . .

(12) . . . Let Christians labor and collaborate with others
in rightly regulating the affairs of social and economic life.

With special care, let them devote themselves to the education of children and young people by means of different
kinds of schools, which should be considered not only as the
most excellent means of forming and developing Christian
youth, but also as a valuable public service, especially in the
developing nations, working toward the uplifting of human
dignity, and toward better living conditions.

Furthermore, let them take part in the striving of those
peoples who, waging war on famine, ignorance, and disease,
are struggling to better their way of life and to secure peace
in the world. In this activity, the faithful should be eager
to offer prudent aid to projects sponsored by public and
private organizations, by governments, by various Christian
communities, and even by non-Christian religions.

140. Moving beyond anti-proselytism and mere practical tolerance to the innate rights and dignity of all men, the question of religious liberty, raised constantly by Protestants, engendered the greatest amount of concern and interest for the longest period of time in the Second Vatican Council. Moved out of the Schema on Ecumenism in the first session, the document on religious liberty was made a separate item in the second session; expected to be approved, the special declaration was delayed, amidst protests until the third session. Controversy followed it in October 1964 during the third session when an attempt was made to move the religious liberty declaration to a mixed commission from the more "open-minded" Secretariat for the Promoting of Christian Unity.

a. However, the document stayed with the Secretariat, with only a committee named for making "suggestions," after 17 cardinals wrote Pope Paul:

> Your Holiness:
> It is not without great distress that we have learnt that the declaration on religious liberty in spite of the fact that it is in complete accordance with the will of the majority of the Fathers, is to be sent to a mixed commission for which, it is said, four members have already been chosen, three of whom appear to be out of sympathy with the general trend of the Council in this matter. For us this news is a source of extreme concern and of the greater misgivings. Countless numbers of people all over the world know very well that the declaration has already been drafted and they well know in what sense.
>
> On a subject of such importance, every appearance of a violation of Council rules and of its liberty will bring with it an immense prejudice against the Church in public opinion. Impelled by our anxiety, we ask Your Holiness with the greatest urgency that the above-mentioned declaration should be returned to the normal procedure of the Council and be dealt with according to the accepted rules lest great evil result for all the people of God.

Meanwhile, if Your Holiness believed that a mixed commission was necessary, such a commission, according to our humble opinions, should be formed from the conciliar commissions as is laid down in article 58, paragraph 2, of the rules.

b. At the end of the third session, when a vote on the religious document was scheduled, 200 "conservative" bishops suddenly asked for a postponement, and won approval from Council President Eugene Cardinal Tisserant. Caught by surprise and "stunned," the majority secured 441 signatures, later augmented the number to 1,000 and sent an appeal to the Pope, who nevertheless sustained the ruling. The bishops implored him:

To the most Holy Father:
Reverently but urgently, very urgently, most urgently [*instanter, instantius, instantissime*], we ask that a vote on the declaration on religious liberty be called before the end of this session of the Council lest the confidence of the world, both Christian and non-Christian, be lost.

141. The final session of the Second Vatican Council opened with the assurance that the Council would at last act decisively on religious liberty. Action came swiftly, within a week of the reconvening of the final session, but not without the Pope having to intervene and overrule the Council's Central Co-ordinating Commission which had sought another delay (on grounds there might be too many negative votes). The vote for the religious liberty declaration was 1,997 to 224. Two months later when it was voted on in a final form the vote was 1,954 to 249. In the formal endorsement in the final decree ceremony on December 7, the vote was 2,308 to 70 votes. Although the declaration clearly stated that there was one true church (". . . one true religion subsists in the Catholic and Apostolic Church")—a statement which some observers felt was out of place in this document—it nevertheless was hailed by Protestants and Catholics alike for replacing the negative concept of toleration with the positive concept of religious liberty as a matter of church doctrine and as an inherent characteristic of man's natural dignity. Going beyond

Pope Leo XIII's encyclical of 1888 which assured only toleration, the new Declaration on Religious Liberty said:

> (2) This Vatican Council declares that the human person has a right to religious freedom. This freedom means that all men are to be immune from coercion on the part of individuals or of social groups and of any human power, in such wise that no one is to be forced to act in a manner contrary to his own beliefs, whether privately or publicly, whether alone or in association with others, within due limits.
>
> The council further declares that the right to religious freedom has its foundation in the very dignity of the human person as this dignity is known through the revealed word of God and by reason itself.
>
> This right of the human person to religious freedom is to be recognized in the constitutional law whereby society is governed and thus it is to become a civil right.
>
> It is in accordance with their dignity as persons—that is, beings endowed with reason and free will and therefore privileged to bear personal responsibility—that all men should be at once impelled by nature and also bound by a moral obligation to seek the truth, especially religious truth.
>
> They are also bound to adhere to the truth, once it is known, and to order their whole lives in accord with the demands of truth. However, men cannot discharge these obligations in a manner in keeping with their own nature unless they enjoy immunity from external coercion as well as psychological freedom.
>
> Therefore the right to religious freedom has its foundation not in the subjective disposition of the person, but in his very nature.
>
> In consequence, the right to this immunity continues to

exist even in those who do not live up to their obligation of seeking the truth and adhering to it and the exercise of this right is not to be impeded, provided that just public order be observed. . . .

(10) It is one of the major tenets of Catholic doctrine that man's response to God in faith must be free: no one therefore is to be forced to embrace the Christian faith against his own will. . . .

It is therefore completely in accord with the nature of faith that in matters religious every manner of coercion on the part of men should be excluded. . . .

(11) God calls men to serve Him in spirit and in truth, hence they are bound in conscience but they stand under no compulsion. God has regard for the dignity of the human person whom He Himself created and man is to be guided by his own judgment and he is to enjoy freedom. . . .

(12) . . . In the life of the People of God, as it has made its pilgrim way through the vicissitudes of human history, there has at times appeared a way of acting that was hardly in accord with the spirit of the Gospel or even opposed to it.

Nevertheless, the doctrine of the Church that no one is to be coerced into faith has always stood firm.

Thus the leaven of the Gospel has long been about its quiet work in the minds of men, and to it is due in great measure the fact that in the course of time men have come more widely to recognize their dignity as persons, and the conviction has grown stronger that the person in society is to be kept free from all manner of coercion in matters religious. . . .

142. In the spotlight was Spain which, by a tradition that goes back to Bonaparte in 1808 and more recently to a concordat with

the Vatican in August 1953, does not guarantee the same rights
of worship to minority groups as it does to Roman Catholics.
The religious liberty statement by the Second Vatican Council
was expected to change the climate in Spain, and in certain areas
of Latin America. The Spanish Constitution says: "The profession and the practice of the Catholic religion, which is that of the
Spanish State, shall enjoy official protection. None shall be mo-
lested for his beliefs or private practices. No other ceremonies
or external demonstrations than those of the Catholic religion
shall be permitted." (Constitutional Charter of the Spanish People of 1946 Article 6 of the Bill of Rights).

Emilio Garrigues, minister counselor, of the Spanish embassy,
Washington, offered this interpretation of the constitution in
September 1962 in a letter just before the start of the Second
Vatican Council:

> In spite of what you may read to the contrary in the Ameri-
> can press, a Protestant problem cannot properly be said to
> exist in Spain. The number of Protestants in the country
> varies between twenty and thirty thousand, a minute per-
> centage in a population of thirty millions. Furthermore, of
> this number only approximately one-half are Spaniards. The
> Spanish Constitution guarantees religious freedom and
> states that no one shall be molested on account of his be-
> liefs, or prevented from the private exercise of his particu-
> lar cult. This legal limitation to "private exercise," and the
> prohibition on proselytizing are a consequence of Spain's
> centuries old religious unity. Spain is essentially and tradi-
> tionally a Catholic country. Ninety-nine per cent of the in-
> habitants of Spain are Catholics.
>
> Although there is no actual problem with regard to the
> Protestant and Jewish religions in Spain, the Government
> is at the present time making a study of the matter of mi-
> nority groups in general. As the Ambassador replied dur-
> ing a question and answer period following his recent ad-
> dress to the National Press Club in Washington, ". . . we
> are in the process of establishing a status for the Protes

tants which will avoid in the future such misunderstandings and we will give to the Protestants the position that they have the right to have in Spain under Spanish Law."

143. Despite general guarantees, specific legislation in Spain to support non-Catholics has been lacking. Most Spanish Protestants and Orthodox services are in private homes; no signs can be posted. Printing and distribution of non-Catholic Bibles and posters and literature have been banned. Protestant seminaries are curbed; military chaplains are Catholic, and Protestant clergy are not draft exempt. The head of state must be Catholic.

But now Spain began to follow the mood of the Second Vatican Council. The most dramatic examples: the Most Rev. Narciso Jubany Arnau, of Gerona, permitted non-Roman Catholic services to be held in the churches of his diocese during the peak of the tourist season. Three Protestant groups in the Canary Islands, a Spanish possession, received permission to advertise an eight-day crusade in the local newspaper. A new Spanish law was proposed to guarantee public worship rights but postponed for consideration until the Council acted on religious liberty, and for other reasons in 1966 (further negotiations, possible referendum). Nevertheless, the talk was of fuller freedom. In March 1966, for instance, a bishop, the Most Rev. Hauro Rubio Repulles, of Salamanca, Spain, and the Rev. Father Amadeo de Fuenmayer, of the Pontifical University of Pamplona, called for amending of the Concordat and other regulations, to insure religious freedom.

a. The ABC newspaper, published by conservative monarchists in Madrid, said in an editorial during the Council in March 1963:

Our brothers of the separated Churches have received the grace of baptism and many of them enjoy, as we do, other sacramental graces. Their Sacred Book is ours and a considerable part of their Creed is identical with that of Nicaea.

It is necessary to abandon all old resentments and enmities, without abandoning one jot of our irreproachable religious orthodoxy. Relations with the separated Churches must not

be placed on a level of ancient historical rivalries or on dia-
lectic disputes.

b. Gen. Francisco Franco in a 1965 New Year message
said he favored "religious freedom"; and in a similar message,
in 1966, he pledged his country to the "teachings" of the Church
(which would include its declaration on religious liberty). He
said more specifically in the 1965 New Year's message:

Our tradition, which has so often been the object of inten-
tional detraction, is that of a tolerant nation respectful of
the rights of the human person.

In our country, history has caused men of different races
and beliefs to live together for centuries. In our monuments,
literature and history, one finds their contributions gathered with respect and embodied in our national personality.

Spaniards must nourish no doubt or suspicion concerning
the exercise of freedom of conscience that we have been
practicing and which we only want to carry to perfection
following the inspiration given by our mother the Church.
We have nothing to fear on this road, since truth has nothing to fear from error. . . .

We are confident, because we shall faithfully follow the
Church on the better way toward the supernatural good of
each one of us. We shall attain here a way of living together
in consonance with the principles of Christian charity.

If Spain goes with her head down, we shall remain back-
ward, without the crusade of brotherhood and love the
Church is initiating.

144. In Latin America, dialogue came to most of the countries
in some form or another. In Bolivia, where only two percent of the
population is Protestant, the Catholic newspaper in La Paz,
*Presencia*, praised a Protestant crusade that had the Gospel as
a backdrop. In Chile, a Maryknoll father in Santiago called for

Catholics to cooperate with Pentecostals in a literary program. Prelates talked readily of amiable contacts with Protestant clergy, often no more than a get-acquainted talk in the chancery or at a public gathering. The Fourth Latin American Lutheran Congress in July 1965, in Lima, gave the world a chance to mirror developments in Latin America.

a. The president of the Lutheran World Federation, the Rev. Dr. Fredrik A. Schiotz, of Minneapolis, paid a courtesy call on Juan Cardinal Landazuri Rickets at the Cardinal's Palace in Armas Square in the center of Lima. Dr. Schiotz reported that Cardinal Rickets said "I will pray for your work." Earlier a representative of the Cardinal, Professor Gerardo Alarco of the Catholic University in Lima, addressed the opening ceremonies of the Latin American Lutheran Congress. On behalf of the cardinal, Professor Alarco said:

> The disciples of Christ have entered a new stage of our mutual relationships. They are no longer relationships of rivalry which see in the community or in the church across the street a rival or perhaps enemy institution.
>
> We have all found a new road which certainly follows more faithfully the will of the Lord for all of us. Not that all our grave differences have disappeared. We all know that there are, for example, very different conceptions of the nature of the church. But the Lord of the church is showing us the way we must follow.
>
> We hope that if we follow it faithfully, the Lord will some day repair the breach that has been produced among His disciples and will lead us to the unity which He has in store for us.

b. At the end of that Latin American Lutheran Congress delegates adopted this statement which they called the "Lima Message":

> Delegates of the Fourth Latin American Lutheran Congress, meeting together in the Peruvian capital from July 10-15,

1965, send a warm Christian greeting to all the Lutheran churches and congregations in the hemisphere and to all Christians in general. During these meetings we have been edified and strengthened, and in accord with the general theme of our congress: "Responsible Presence of the Lutheran Church in Latin America," we have received a new vision of our common task.

We have been made to feel anew our responsibility before God for all our other brothers in Christ at whose side we live and work in Latin America. We give thanks to God for the new atmosphere of fellowship and mutual drawing together among the different Christian denominations, which we understand to be the fruit of the action of the Holy Spirit in our modern world. Love for the whole church of Jesus Christ which is inherent in the Lutheran creed, as well as the needs of the present era, oblige us to seek a frank and responsible encounter with other Christian churches, for the purpose of examining anew our convictions in the light of the Word of God. We seek this encounter with the joyful confidence that the central message of the Reformation of the 16th century is a gift which God has given us to share with all other Christians. This message proclaims the mighty presence of Jesus Christ in His Word and in the Sacraments to make us children of God, free to serve our neighbor in love. . . .

We are responsible for a Christian witness directed to the whole society of the Latin American countries. We recognize that our churches should not exist as an end in themselves, but that they are sent to live in and for the world. This responsibility falls not only on pastors but concerns every member of our churches. The message of the love of God in Jesus Christ should be transmitted by all of us to a world in which God apparently has no place. In such a world we are not sent to pursue denominational interests, but to give witness to the drawing near of God in Jesus Christ. This task demands that we come out of the traditional isolation and fragmentation in which our churches have lived, and it may be that this involves new forms and ways of witnessing. We invite all our churches and congregations to employ with open minds and hearts such new forms as the Lord of the Church may provide us.

145. There was progress in the trouble spot, Colombia. (News of violence from Colombia in early 1966 centered on the death of a priest, Camilo Torres, who led a band of guerrillas against government forces.) In a five year period before the 1956-66 decade, G. Elson Ruff, editor of *The Lutheran*, reported 42 Colombian Protestant churches were destroyed by fire or dynamite. Fifty-one Protestants in Colombia were murdered because of their religion (cf. *The Dilemma of Church and State*, Muhlenberg, Philadelphia, 1954, p. 23). Protestants have in recent years reported violence, particularly in the "Mission Territories" which make up three-fourths of the country. There a 1953 missions treaty is still in vogue, although the treaty had never been ratified by Congress. "Government officers are in effect subordinated to the Roman Catholic Mission Chiefs" (*The Ecumenical Review* reported in July 1961, p. 484.) "So, in spite of the general improvement of the situation, in these territories the Roman Catholic Church goes on claiming spiritual monopoly, Protestant services are forbidden and even Protestant Indians are violently attacked." Two years later, by 1963, dialogue had apparently come to Colombia, to the extent that reports of violence had faded almost entirely. In the capital, Bogota, Roman Catholic priests and Lutheran clergy, for instance, sat down together to discuss "Christ Today in Latin America." There were complaints from the Moody Bible Institute that its Literature Mission division had been refused an import license to bring 25,000 religious books into Colombia. But that appeared to be the exception. The conservative Protestant magazine, *Christian Life*, reported in June 1965, that Catholic leaders were even sponsoring showings of Billy Graham's film, "Lucia," in Catholic schools and parishes. It reported that Archbishop Lopez Umana and 75 clergy and nuns attended one screening. The article also cited the Pocket Testament League which was invited by Catholics to show their film in a Catholic high school, then, "after the showing, priests assisted PTL workers in handing out Gospels of St. John." Epis-

copal Bishop David B. Reed, of Bogota, gives a picture of the changes in once-troubled Colombia:

I was gone from Colombia for six years and was immediately struck, upon my return, by the openness of everyone in the area. So far, I have only presented myself officially to representatives of the Roman hierarchy in Quito and Guayaquil, Ecuador, Bogota and Barranquilla, Colombia, but in every case I was cordially received by the bishop upon whom I called. Encouraged by this I proceeded to ask the bishop coadjutor of Bogota for assistance at the time of our clergy retreat in Bogota. He not only made a conference center available for our use but also arranged for a Benedictine priest to lead the meditations on our retreat. This Benedictine, an American, participated with us in everything except the sacramental Holy Communion.

I think that the contact that we had with this priest did a great deal to help us understand the barriers within their own Church that make it difficult for Roman Catholic clergy to relate themselves to us as we are. Certain legalistic barriers which may have existed in the past have been dropped but there is an emotional, intellectual, and cultural barrier that still exists.

Although it did not involve any of the hierarchy we were very excited by the participation of top level Roman Catholic lay people in the memorial service held for Sir Winston Churchill. The President of Colombia, his entire cabinet, their wives and a major portion of the diplomatic corps in Bogota attended the service which was held at St. Alban's Episcopal Church and the Union Church of Bogota (an interdenominational congregation). I know of no other instance in this traditionally Roman Catholic country where a President has officially attended a service in a Protestant Church.

146. Christian democracy parties in Latin America exemplified ecumenism. Rafael Caldera, labor expert and head of the

Christian Democratic party of Venezuela, spoke at a conference of the Catholic Inter-American Cooperation Program in Chicago, January 27, 1965:

> Christian Democracy has had to overcome many misconceptions. One that is still prevalent is its supposed confessionalism. Christian democracy is not in any way a religious movement; nor does it have a confessional character. Christian Democratic parties include among their members Catholics, Protestants, Jews, agnostics, professing the widest variety of conceptions and creeds. The name Christian does not represent a religious position but the conviction that Christian values and the spirit of Christianity can best fulfill successfully the requirements of social justice and defeat Marxism in the struggle to conquer the soul of the people. We believe that the Social Christian inspiration overflows the boundaries of a given creed. And it is pleasant for us to observe how the ecumenical spirit developed in the Second Vatican Council has come to reinforce the attempts at rapprochement among all men who understand and support democracy, who share the principle of social solidarity and defend the imperative demands of social justice.

147. Roman Catholic African prelates, focusing on the rights of individuals, were early pacesetters in a renewed Roman Catholic Church interested in the freedom of the individual and of societies. Seven members of the hierarchy of Northern Rhodesia, headed by Francis Mazzieri, OFM, apostolic vicar and bishop of Ndola, signed this joint pastoral letter "addressed to the Catholics of all races," January 6, 1958, in Lusaka, six years before Northern Rhodesia left the Federation of Rhodesia and Nyasaland to become the Republic of Zambia:

> Since the human race is essentially one, all men possess the same basic human rights. The Church declares that God gave every man certain rights when He gave him a soul. Among these rights the following are relevant:

> The right to life and bodily integrity.
> The right to the necessities of life and to a decent living.
> The right to worship.
> The right to the normal development of his faculties.
> The right to private property and ownership.
> The right to sojourn and movement.
> The right to marriage and to family life.
> The right to give his children the education of his choice.
> The right to associate with his fellowmen.
> Man cannot live in society or freely enjoy his rights unless
> he does his duty towards society and respect the rights of
> his fellowmen. . . .

We warn all Catholics against falling into the snares of the apostles of hatred "who come to you in sheep's clothing, but are ravenous wolves within" (Matt. 7: 15), and who under the cloak of love for one group preach hatred or contempt of another. Those who have attained a higher standard of culture are not only forbidden by Jesus Christ to despise their less cultured brethren or to deny them the right and means to attain to a higher culture, but they are obliged to help them to attain to that position even if this demands sacrifices on their part. . . .

148. Stirred by a concern for freedom and individual responsibility in a new society, the Most Rev. W. T. Porter, archbishop of the Cape Coast, and four others, issued this pastoral letter of the Hierarchy of the Gold Coast and British Togoland, June 5, 1956:

> Soon the country will be experiencing again the turmoil of a general election and We desire to urge upon you understanding and a calm sense of your responsibility as citizens. It is well known that every sincere practicing Catholic is of necessity a good citizen for he who strives to observe the laws of God and the Church in every aspect of his life is at the same time discharging faithfully his duty to his neighbors and his country. That indeed represents the ideal of citizenship.

> Good citizens try to understand the problems and needs of

their country and will not be carried away by mere slogans
and electioneering catch-words. They estimate such things
at their true value, but the real issues which elections involve, they scrutinize at the bar of reason and according
to the Ten Commandments of God.

There will be different parties, each with a political programme which it honestly believes to be the best for the
country. An honest difference of opinion is always worthy
of the highest respect and in a politically healthy community will never be allowed to generate intolerance, hatred
and violence, which so frequently happens. . . .

149. In Tanzania, the Catholic bishops in their Christmas
letter of 1960 went beyond guaranteeing rights of non-Roman
Catholics to ask for compassion and "charity":

We do not deny the fact of the sincerity of the majority
of non-Catholics. . . . They are following their conscience
. . . And once his conscience has spoken he must follow it,
he must do what for him is the will of God. Whether his conscience speaks to him truly or falsely, he must follow it.
. . . And if he is obliged to follow his conscience, he must be
free to follow it, he has a right to follow it, and others must
respect his right to follow it. . . . This right will apply to
every field, especially to the religious field, where a person
is free to choose his religion and to worship God in the way
his conscience commands him. . . .

We should never forget the immediate purpose of social action: the betterment of temporal order and the alleviation
of temporal ills. . . . They have an end in themselves. We do
not teach a child mathematics merely to convert him. . . .
In fact, on the natural level, each social service has its own
end, and our carrying it out is motivated by our duty of
collaborating with our fellow citizens, also those not of our
religion, in an effort towards the common good; then, on a
higher level, we Christians should be motivated by supernatural charity, love and compassion for our fellowmen in
need.

150. In the United States political arena, John F. Kennedy insisted on strict separation between church and state, thus alleviating old non-Roman Catholic fears of a Catholic President. As a candidate, he asserted on Sept. 12, 1960, in Houston, before 500 members of the Greater Houston Ministerial Association:

I believe in an America where the separation of church and state is absolute—where no Catholic prelate would tell the President (should he be a Catholic) how to vote—where no church or church school is granted any public funds or political preference—and where no man is denied public office merely because his religion differs from the President who might appoint him or the people who might elect him.

I believe in an America that is officially neither Catholic, Protestant nor Jewish—where no public official either requests or accepts instructions on public money from the Pope, the National Council of Churches or any other ecclesiastical source—where no religious body seeks to impose its will directly or indirectly upon the general populace or the public acts of its officials—and where religious liberty is so indivisible that an act against one church is treated as an act against all.

For while this year it may be a Catholic against whom the finger of suspicion is pointed, in other years it has been, and may someday be again, a Jew—or a Quaker—or a Unitarian —or a Baptist. It was Virginia's harassment of Baptist preachers, for example, that led to Jefferson's statute of religious freedom. Today, I may be the victim—but tomorrow it may be you—until the whole fabric of our harmonious society is ripped apart at a time of great national peril.

Finally, I believe in an America where religious intolerance will someday end—where all men and all churches are treated as equal—where every man has the same right to attend or not to attend the church of his choice—where there is no Catholic vote, no anti-Catholic vote, no bloc voting of any kind—and where Catholics, Protestants and Jews, both the lay and the pastoral level, will refrain from those attitudes of disdain and division which have so often marred their works in the past, and promote instead the American idea of brotherhood.

This is the kind of America in which I believe. And it represents the kind of Presidency in which I believe—a great office that must be neither humbled by making it the instrument of any religious groups, nor tarnished by arbitrarily withholding it, its occupancy, from the members of any religious group. I believe in a President whose views on religion are his own private affair, neither imposed upon him by the nation or imposed by the nation upon him as a condition to holding that office.

I would not look with favor upon a President working to subvert the First Amendment's guarantee of religious liberty. . . . And neither do I look with favor upon those who would work to subvert Article VI of the Constitution by requiring a religious test—even by indirection—for if they disagree with that safeguard, they should be openly working to repeal it.

I want a Chief Executive whose public acts are responsible to all groups and obligated to none—who can attend any ceremony, service or dinner his office may appropriately require of him—and whose fulfillment of his Presidential oath is not limited or conditioned by any religious oath, ritual or obligation.

This is the kind of America I believe in. . . .

151. American Baptist Stanley Stuber, caught in the spirit of understanding, scratched out altogether a paragraph in an earlier edition of his *Primer on Roman Catholicism for Protestants* which dealt with the fears of the Protestants about "what would happen to democracy in the United States if the Roman Catholic Church got, through a majority of numbers or by White House influence, dominant power?" The reference was written before the election of President Kennedy. In a thorough

topsy-turvy gesture, Stuber, a New York book editor, changed the dedication in the new edition from a Baptist leader to the Pope himself:

> [1953 edition] Dedicated to Mrs. Leslie E. Swain, former President of the American Baptist Convention and member of the Central Committee, World Council of Churches.

> [1960, revised edition] Dedicated to the living memory and continuing influence of Pope John XXIII and to his *aggiornamento*.

152. With Lyndon B. Johnson, Protestant fears concerning Catholics had largely subsided. The new president moved to introduce a Federal Aid to Education bill that permitted aid to parochial schools on behalf of the culturally and economically deprived, but administered under local public offices. The bill encourages public schools under Title I to open up their facilities for part-time use by private schools including parochial schools, in order to qualify for their share of $1 billion channelled into school districts to aid children whose parents make less than $2,000 per year. This is the "shared-time" procedure (see Section 176). Under title II, $100 million would go to provide library and textbook aid administered by public agencies. Title III provides $100 million for "supplementary educational centers and services" administered through local "consortia" or representative councils.

Title II concerning "school library resources, textbooks, and other instructional materials, says:

> (Sec. 201.) (a) The Commissioner shall carry out during the fiscal year ending June 30, 1966, and each of the four succeeding fiscal years, a program for making grants for the acquisition of school library resources, textbooks, and other printed and published instructional materials for the use of children and teachers in public and private elementary and secondary schools.

> (b) For the purpose of making grants under this title, there

is hereby authorized to be appropriated the sum of $100,-
000,000 for the fiscal year ending June 30, 1966; but for the
fiscal year ending June 30, 1967, and the three succeeding
fiscal years, only such sums may be appropriated as the
Congress may hereafter authorize by law.

(Sec. 202.) (a) From the sums appropriated for carrying
out this title for any fiscal year, the Commissioner shall
reserve such amount, but not in excess of 2 per centum thereof, as he may determine and shall allot such amount among
the Commonwealth of Puerto Rico, Guam, American Samoa,
the Virgin Islands, and the Trust Territory of the Pacific
Islands according to their respective needs for assistance
under this title. From the remainder of such sums, the
Commissioner shall allot to each State an amount which
bears the same ratio to such remainder as the number of
children enrolled in the public and private elementary and
secondary schools of that State bears to the total number of
children enrolled in such schools in all of the States. . . .

(b) The amount of any State's allotment under subsection
(a) for any fiscal year which the Commissioner determines
will not be required for such fiscal year shall be available
for reallotment from time to time. . . .

(Sec. 203.) (a) Any State which desires to receive grants
under this title shall submit to the Commissioner a State
plan, in such detail as the Commissioner deems necessary,
which—

(1) designates a State agency which shall, either directly or through arrangements with other State or local
public agencies, act as the sole agency for administration of
the State plan;

(2) sets forth a program under which funds paid to the
State from its allotment under section 202 will be expended
solely for (A) acquisition of library resources (which for
the purposes of this title means books, periodicals, docu-

ments, audio-visual materials, and other related library materials), textbooks, and other printed and published instructional materials for the use of children and teachers in public and private elementary and secondary schools in the State, and (B) administration of the State plan, including the development and revision of standards relating to library resources, textbooks, and other printed and published instructional materials furnished for the use of children and teachers in the public elementary and secondary schools of the State. . . .

(3) sets forth the criteria to be used in allocating library resources, textbooks, and other printed and published instructional materials provided under this title among the children and teachers of the State, which criteria shall—

(A) take into consideration the relative need of the children and teachers of the State for such library resources, textbooks, or other instructional materials, and

(B) provide assurance that to the extent consistent with law such library resources, textbooks, and other instructional materials will be provided on an equitable basis for the use of children and teachers in private elementary and secondary schools in the State which comply with the compulsory attendance laws of the State or are otherwise recognized by it through some procedure customarily used in the State;

(4) sets forth the criteria to be used in selecting the library resources, textbooks, and other instructional materials. . . .

(5) sets forth policies and procedures designed to assure that Federal funds made available under this title for any fiscal year will be so used as to supplement and, to the extent practical, increase the level of State, local, and private school funds that would in the absence of such Federal funds be made available for library resources, textbooks,

and other printed and published instructional materials, and in no case supplant such State, local, and private school funds;

(6) sets forth such fiscal control and fund accounting procedures as may be necessary to assure proper disbursement of, and accounting for, Federal funds paid to the State. . . .

(7) provides for making such reports, in such form and containing such information, as the Commissioner may reasonably require to carry out his functions under this title, and for keeping such records and for affording such access thereto as the Commissioner may find necessary to assure the correctness and verification of such reports.

(b) The Commissioner shall approve any State plan and any modification thereof which complies with the provisions of subsection (a). . . .

(Sec. 205.) (a) Title to library resources, textbooks, and other printed and published instructional materials furnished pursuant to this title, and control and administration of their use, shall vest only in a public agency.

(b) The library resources, textbooks, and other printed and published instructional materials made available pursuant to this title for use of children and teachers in any school in any State shall be limited to those which have been approved by an appropriate State or local educational authority or agency for use, or are used, in a public elementary or secondary school of that State. . . .

153. Shared-time, or dual-time arrangements that bring parochial school children into the public school for general courses, began to win acceptance across the United States after thirty years of unheralded effort in scattered places across the country, such as Hartford, Connecticut, and Oconto, Wisconsin. Cath-

olics permitted a small percentage of their schools to experiment with using dual facilities. In Michigan alone, fifty public school districts across five dioceses entered the dual arrangement. An estimated 400 school districts in 40 states were involved in shared-time plans in 1966.

The National Council of Churches' General Board issued this policy statement on June, 1964, concerning "dual school enrollment" (the vote was 103 for, 0 against, 2 abstentions) :

> Protestants and Orthodox are conscious of the financial difficulties under which their Roman Catholic brethren and others labor in supporting two systems. While this predicament is not accurately described as "double taxation" it does involve additional costs. We are concerned, as Christians, to explore dual school enrollment, as one possible solution to this problem.
>
> Dual school enrollment is here defined as an administrative arrangement in which the school time of children is shared between public school and church day school. Students who are enrolled in a church day school are also enrolled in a nearby public school for part of their general education.
>
> In dual school enrollment each school system remains in control of its own facilities, curriculum, schedules, and other administrative functions. Decisions to provide for dual school enrollment must be made and detailed arrangements worked out community by community by the responsible boards or administrators involved.
>
> We know of no legal opinion holding that dual school enrollment violates the federal constitution. Most states' constitutions or educational legislation appear either to permit or not to forbid dual school enrollment.
>
> We therefore approve further experimentation with, and continuing evaluation of, dual school enrollment for classroom instruction as a viable provision for those who, for conscience sake, maintain separate schools.

We believe that boys and girls now limited by the resources of some religious day schools will be benefited by the equipment and program offerings for the portion of the time they attend the public school. We believe that benefits will ensue for all children if those now enrolled in separate systems have the opportunity to associate with each other through dual school enrollment. We believe that this association and intermingling of the children in the school will result in a broadened support for public education and will serve to unify our now partially divided communities. At the same time, "We reaffirm our support of the system of public education in the United States of America. It provides a context in which all individuals may share in an education which contributes to the full development of their capacities. It serves as a major cohesive force in our pluralistic society." It is our hope that dual school enrollment may prove to be a means of helping our nation to maintain the values of a general system of public education, yet at the same time meeting the needs of those who desire a system of church-related education, while upholding the historic American principle of the separation and interaction of church and state.

154. The Rt. Rev. Frederick J. Warnecke, Episcopal bishop of Bethlehem, Pennsylvania, suggested an entirely new and radical proposal of aid to parochial schools that avoids the controversies over church-state relations in regard to parochial school aid. He suggested that Protestants donate money to the Catholic school system. In turn, he proposes greater openness in parochial school enrollment:

In Christian charity, why should there not be gifts and support for Roman Catholic parochial schools by other Christian Churches and by individuals of those Churches? Why should we not help our Roman brethren in solving this problem?

We have all given to Roman Catholic hospitals gladly. We have all given to Lutheran hospitals equally happily. We have all given to Moravian schools whole-heartedly. We give to colleges quite without regard to their religious affiliations. Why should we then not give to help Roman Catholic parochial schools?

Could there be a concerted effort of Christian Churches to help one another in this area of education across ecclesiastical boundaries in our concern that all children in America should receive a good education?

This may seem to be a radical proposal, but is it not in keeping with Christian charity for one another? Why should it seem strange that whatever our differences we help those who are ultimately and basically our brothers in Christian faith?

And would it not be magnificent if such a concept could come freely from Anglican, Orthodox and Protestant Churches to the Roman Catholic Church! We will help you bear this burden! We will do it gladly as your Christian brothers!

And then I would think that a second step might well be to consider ways by which children of various Christian communions might attend Roman Catholic parochial schools if they desire to do so. I would readily grant that at this very moment there is not any direct barrier to this. I am sure that Episcopal people would be welcome in Bethlehem Catholic High School. . . .

What a magnificent step toward Christian charity would be taken if the Roman Church would share its great parochial school system with other Christians on the simple basis of common acceptance as disciples of the Lord Jesus Christ.

All Christian Churches presently do this on the college level. Church institutions and social agencies are open to all in need whatever their allegiance.

Has not the time come for equal charity in the primary and secondary schools which care for so many American children in their formative years?

155. The new cooperation of the churches in education on the elementary level and in other areas of welfare (see Chapter VII) received encouragement from the "General Findings" of the First National Study Conference on Church and State in Columbus, Ohio. Sponsored by the National Council of Churches Department of Religious Liberty, a year before the hearings and action on the President's Federal Aid bill, the 400 delegates from 24 Protestant and Orthodox churches had said:

While the functions of church and state are distinct, they often overlap. At times they lead in a separate direction and at other times they clash. In this country there has been both separation and interaction, harmony and tension. The nation which adopted the First Amendment at the same time considered itself both Christian and Protestant and saw no contradiction in passing laws which required Sunday observance, prayer and Bible reading in the public schools. Its actions attested to historical interaction as well as to separation of church and state.

In recent decades, in part through the enrichment of immigration, a predominantly Protestant society developed into a pluralistic society. This has raised crucial questions concerning both separation and interaction between church and state. In this country the relationships between church and state are now many and varied. Between and around these institutions is a rich and rapidly changing culture composed of many traditions, interests and aspirations. Separation and interaction within this voluntaristic and pluralistic culture result in change in the form and relationships of institutions and social structures. . . .

In recent decades a development has occurred which is expressed in the ambiguous term "welfare state." More and more, the programs of social welfare—church-related, non-

sectarian and governmental—have been employed by government to meet human needs. Church-related, as well as
voluntary agencies generally, are making use of public funds
made available in a variety of ways to assist in this task.
This has raised new and practical questions for church-
state relations.

The necessity for new attention to the problems of church-
state relations arises not only from the expansion of governmental programs into areas where churches and other
voluntary agencies have served and continue to serve, but
also from the transition of this country from a predominantly Protestant to a religiously pluralistic society.

To find their place in our pluralism the society requires that
Protestant churches redefine their position. . . .

Under some well-defined circumstances, government may
legitimately support specific programs of church-affiliated
health and welfare agencies. The sole purpose of any governmental policy in this respect must be the promotion of a
clearly identifiable public interest as against a private interest of an individual or religious group. The important
considerations here are:

(1) that the government program must not be aimed primarily at the support of religious institutions or objectives;

(2) that any support of church-affiliated agencies must be
an incidental part of a large program directed to appropriate public interests;

(3) that the agency does not discriminate on the basis of
race, color, creed [18 delegates registered their dissent to
the insertion of the word "creed" in this series] or national
origin; and

(4) that reversionary clauses, limited to a fixed and reasonable period, be written into all contractual arrangements to

insure that funds, buildings, and equipment are not diverted from the purposes for which they were originally acquired. . . .

156. A Lutheran executive, Dr. Robert E. Van Deusen, suggested not only a re-examination of church-state attitudes but a dropping of the term "church-state." Dr. Van Deusen, secretary of the Washington office of the National Lutheran Council, made his proposal before the annual meeting of the Christian Action Council, Columbia, South Carolina, December 2, 1965. Referring to the First Amendment to the U.S. Constitution, ("Congress shall make no law respecting an establishment of religion or prohibiting the free exercise thereof") he noted:

Two basic principles are stated here: (1) that all religious faiths shall have equal status, that none shall be a favored or "established" religion; and (2) that religious groups shall have freedom to function without interference from the state.

These are important principles. The right to equal treatment by the government and the right to exist and function as a church—these are not negotiable. They are written into the U.S. Constitution and form one of the cornerstones of American democracy. When they are violated, we have a legal right and a moral obligation to defend them.

It is these rights that concern us when we talk about the separation of church and state. I wonder if we would not be able to think more clearly if we would drop the phrase (which is negative in concept and fuzzy in application) and put ourselves through the semantic discipline of finding other words to say exactly what we mean.

The *autonomy* of the church, for example—its right to make its own decisions without government interference. Or the *integrity* of the church—the necessity for the church to be what it is, the body of Christ, rather than a channel for carrying out government policy. Or its *freedom to witness*—

the moral necessity of expressing its inner convictions, even when they run counter to political expediency.

These principles have a very important bearing on the search for a positive and constructive relationship between the church and the government. They leave room for co-operation between church and state in areas of common concern. But they also set certain limits beyond which the church can not go in its selective partnership with the government.

157. In the area of censorship and the regulation of morals, there were less negative approaches, and rather, a drawing together, and some common projects (see Chapter VII). There still remained the *Index of Forbidden Books*, first drawn up in 1559 and supported in canon law (1384-1405, 2318). The last edition was in 1948, but additions have been made in the *Acta Apostolicae Sedis*, official publication of the Vatican. And a revision of the Curia in December 1965, abolished the position of "commissario" and the assistant in charge of censuring books for the Holy Office (renamed to be the Congregation for the Doctrine of the Faith). In 1966, the Congregation's secretary Alfredo Cardinal Ottavani, said the *Index* would never again be updated. The *Syllabus of Errors* of Pius IX which listed in 1864, eighty condemned propositions, remained largely forgotten, with the church in dialogue with all people, even atheists and Communists, rather than conducting forthright condemnation.

Pope John XXIII had set the pace for greater charity regarding censorship:

The Ecclesiastical Censor must not be carried away by that spirit of intransigence which destroys without rebuilding, discourages instead of comforting . . .

In a varied and flexible field like that of cultural and literary production, where one is confronted by the most varied and unpredictable facts of human behavior, adorned with the polish of artistic form, it is very important for the censor to be able to steer his course with ease, and to be able not only to identify positive aspects and to point out negative ones, but also to provide adequate orientation in delicate border-line cases, whose doctrinal and moral aspects are not susceptible to clear-cut distinctions.

Last, but not least, the censor needs charity, the sovereign virtue, which fulfills the teaching and the practice of the Law; charity guards our judgment against coldness and feelings of contempt, while softening possible harshness through the sweet delicacy which it imparts to the soul. . . .

158. Leading church-state scholar, John Courtney Murray, S.J., of Woodstock (Maryland) College, further elaborated on the matter of censorship and criticized the role of unilateral censors in literature and art:

People in general have a fairly clear notion of what obscenity is. And people in general can make, for themselves, a pretty good judgment on whether a particular work is obscene. Certainly the Code of Canon Law seems to suppose that the ordinary Catholic can make this concrete judgment for himself. I repeat, for himself. The question is, who can make it for others, i.e., as a censor?

Here a distinction is in order. Certainly the ordinary father and mother ought to be qualified to act as censors within the family and to decide what their children may or may not be prudently exposed to, in the way of reading, movies, etc. But I should not think that the ordinary father or mother, *qua* such, is qualified to act as censor within society at large, or to decide what literature and movies may be displayed before the general public. Society has an interest in the artist's freedom of expression which is not necessarily shared by the family. If adult standards of literature would be dangerous for children, a child's standard of literature is rather appalling to an adult. If therefore any censorship is to be administered in the interest of society, the professional competence of the literary critic must play a role in the process.

159. In the decade, 1956-1966, Roman Catholic thinking concerning films changed considerably. The National Legion of Decency, organized in 1934 as a film rating body, responsible to the Bishops' Committee on Motion Pictures and Television, evolved from a largely watchdog, negative committee to a more positive, discriminatory and creative body, in line with a wider mainline Protestant ethic. Catholics and Protestants were still at odds as to the rating of some debatable films in 1965. For example, the "Pawnbroker," an account of the struggles of a New York survivor of German concentration camps received a "C" or condemned rating from the Legion of Decency, while some Protestants were praising the movie strongly. (Example: Bishop James A. Pike, Episcopal bishop of California in a letter to the producer said: "I have just seen the 'Pawnbroker,' a motion picture which must be one of the truly significant religious (because it deals with ultimate matters) films of our time . . . I do not hesitate to include the two brief scenes of relevant nudity in my recommendation. I find this motion picture important not despite its realism, but because of it." The Legion, in spite of its rating of the "Pawnbroker," showed much more flexibility and an affinity to more discriminating cultural consensus. At the outset of the past decade, the Legion developed, in 1957, an A-3 rating class —"morally unobjectionable for adults." (Before, there had been only two classes, "morally unobjectionable for all"—A-1, and "morally unobjectionable for adults and adolescents"—A-2. In 1963, the Legion moved its "Separate Classification" (for "morally unobjectionable for adults, with reservations") to an A-4 status, which put such films as "Lolita," "La Dolce Vita," "The Collector," and "The L-Shaped Room" into the A Category.

In 1964, an "educational affiliate" was added to the Legion (or Office) to help in education for better film appreciation. In 1965, the Legion changed its name to the more neutral sounding National Catholic Office for Motion Pictures.

The more positive approach was in evidence on February 2, 1966, when the National Catholic Office for Motion Pictures (the former Legion of Decency) started giving awards to films of "outstanding" merit, a new category. In the first award list, along with "Sound of Music" were two very frank films depicting the seamy side of life—"Darling" and "Juliet of the Spirits," in the A-3 and A-4 ratings. Said the Most Rev. John J. Krol, archbishop of Philadelphia, who made the presentations: "The purpose of the awards is to give public recognition to films of outstanding merit and to assure makers of such films that their efforts are genuinely appreciated by the national Catholic community."

A major development that predated the change of the Legion's name, was the adoption of a new pledge in 1959. A former pledge, basically negative, said: "I condemn indecent and immoral motion pictures and those which glorify crime or criminals. I promise to do all that I can to strengthen public opinion against the production of indecent and immoral films, and to unite with all those who protest against them. I acknowledge my obligation to form a right conscience about pictures that are dangerous to my moral life. As a Member of the Legion of Decency, I pledge myself to remain away from them. I promise, further, to stay away altogether from places of amusement which show them as a matter of policy."

The new pledge, following the mood of Pius XII's 1957 encyclical, *Miranda Prorsus,* in which Catholics were asked to promote the good in movies as well as to discourage what was considered immoral and indecent, said:

> I promise to promote by word and deed what is morally and artistically good in motion picture entertainment. I promise to discourage indecent, immoral, and unwholesome motion pictures, especially by my good example and always in a responsible and civic-minded manner. I promise to guide those under my care and influence in their choice of motion pictures that are morally and culturally inspiring.
>
> I promise not to cooperate by my patronage with theatres which regularly show objectionable films. I promise as a member of the Legion of Decency to acquaint myself with its aims, to consult its classifications, and to unite with all men of good will in promoting high and noble standards in motion picture entertainment.

160. The question of birth control by artificial means continued to be a source of conflict between Catholics and Protes-

tants. The matter was further complicated by the discovery of a
hormone pill that duplicates the natural secretion of progesterone
from the ovary and prevents and controls ovulation without directly prohibiting conception. Controversy centered on Dr. John
Rock, one of the developers of the pill, a Boston Catholic who is
clinical professor emeritus of gynecology at Harvard Medical
School. His book, *The Time Has Come,* though it lacked an imprimatur, was commended by Richard Cardinal Cushing for its
"eloquent and much-needed plea for Federal grants to perfect
the so-called rhythm system so that it might become a means of
controlling births, [a means] which is not only morally acceptable but also scientifically accurate." Belgian theologian Louis
Janssens came out in favor of the oral contraceptive pill regarding it as licit as rhythm when a married couple's intentions are
moral. One priest, the Rev. Father Arnold A. McMahon, was recalled to Rome by his order, The Society of the Divine Word, for
an outspoken statement in a Birmingham, England, newspaper
favoring artificial means of birth control and calling the present
church teaching "a disastrous mistake."

Pope Paul expanded plans for a commission set up by Pope
John to study birth control and the pill. Three churchmen and
three laymen met as a nucleus in September 1963, and 12 in January 1964. Pope Paul enlarged the commission further to some
70 experts, then in 1966 named 16 prelates and 20 experts from
the previous larger commission to prepare a definitive statement on birth control. Pope Paul told the larger commission in
1965:

> The problem . . . may be summarized as follows: In what
> form and according to what norms must married couples
> fulfill, in the exercise of their mutual love, this service of
> life to which they are called by their vocation? The Christian
> answer will always be inspired by a consciousness of the
> duties and the dignity of the conjugal state, in which the love
> of Christian married couples is enabled by the grace of the
> sacrament of matrimony and by the greatness of the gift
> which is called life given to the child.
>
> As the custodian of God's law, natural and positive, the
> Church will not permit that the price be minimized nor the

sublime originality of love, which is capable of surpassing itself in the reciprocal gift of the married couple, and therefore in the even more disinterested gift of each of them to a new being. . . .

We wanted the bases of your research to be wide so that various trends of ideological thought would thus be better represented, so that countries which experience grave difficulties on the sociological plane would by virtue of your meeting, make their voices heard, so that laymen and particularly married couples would have their qualified representatives in such a great undertaking.

Here you are now engaged in a new and decisive stage of your labors. We trust you will continue to pursue them to the end with courage. We were saying a short time ago: The question is too important, the uncertainties of some persons are too painful for you not to feel driven by a sense of urgency, which is that of charity, toward all those to whom we owe an answer. Your labors, we hope, very much will use these elements.

161. Catholics and Protestants found themselves agreeing on the general role of responsibility in conceiving children, if not on theology, methods, or details.

Pius XII on the Feast of the Epiphany in 1957 wrote:

Our thoughts go out to the great number of children who are deprived by poverty, sickness, war, and other unfortunate circumstances, of the normal means of formation; especially to orphaned children, practically or completely abandoned, whom life has so soon drawn into its violent whirlpools and immersed in bitter suffering. There are already so very many of these, who have been harmed in body and spirit by inexplicable mishaps. But how many more are innocent victims of the failures of others, and of the material and moral miseries of the social environment in which they live.

The question is how these deplorable conditions can best be remedied. Whose duty is it, in the first place, to prevent a renewal of the bitter lamentations of bereaved mothers, which clouded the infancy of Jesus in the very mystery of the Epiphany?

There can be no doubt that this duty rests primarily with the parents. It is saddening to consider how many young couples, at the time of conducting marriage, have an extremely inadequate idea of the duties that will later devolve upon them as the educators of their children, or of the demands that this office will impose.

When the infant comes into the world, he must have a home to receive him—a home capable of providing him with everything necessary to keep him in good health, and to assist him in acquiring and developing those faculties of mind and heart that will enable him to take his proper place in society when the time comes.

162. The National Council of Churches General Board, with Orthodox delegates abstaining, in 1961 said the responsibility of parenthood must be evaluated in terms of the family's situation in society:

Responsible parenthood . . . means to weigh the claims of procreation in relation to the total purposes of the marriage and the situation of the family in society. For most couples, the new knowledge of human reproduction and of means to avert conception affects ethical decisions regarding parenthood. But the responsibility, to be exercised in prayer and trust, has deeper roots.

Within the purposes of marriage ordained by God, there are a number of considerations concerning parenthood which need to be taken into account in trying to determine the number and frequency of pregnancies. These include:

(1) The right of the child to be wanted, loved, cared for, educated, and trained in the "discipline and instruction of the Lord" (Eph. 6: 4). The rights of existing children to parental care have a proper claim.

(2) The prospects for health of a future child, if medical and eugenic evidence seem negatively conclusive.

(3) The health and welfare of the mother-wife, and the need for the spacing of children to safeguard them.

(4) The social situation, when rapid population growth places dangerous pressures on the means of livelihood and endangers the social order.

Reasons such as these enter into the calculations of responsible parenthood. At the same time, parents need to remember that having children is a venture in faith, requiring a measure of courage and confidence in God's goodness. Too cautious a reckoning of the costs may be as great an error as failure to lift the God-given power of procreation to the level of ethical decision. . . .

Periodic continence (the rhythm method) is suitable for some couples, but is not inherently superior from a moral point of view. The general Protestant conviction is that motives, rather than methods, form the primary moral issue, provided the methods are limited to the prevention of conception.

163. That familiar sounding term, "responsible parenthood" appeared in a draft of the Second Vatican Council's Schema 13 on "The Church in the Modern World" and found an increasing emphasis among Catholic theologians. The population explosion was a legitimate concern, said the Rev. Father John A. O'Brien, professor of theology at the University of Notre Dame. Writing in the Protestant *Christian Century*, August 28, 1963, he noted the NCC statement and similar Jewish statements "are much the same as those which Catholic theologians and sociolo-

gists are stressing in their statements on responsible parenthood." The NCC concern for other factors in marriage beside
procreation found an echo in the aula of the Second Vatican
Council among Leo Cardinal Suenens, of Mechelen-Brussels, and
others. In the initial debate on the famous Schema 13 on "The
Church in the Modern World," three prelates were particularly
vocal in outlining the wider dimensions of Catholic thought on
birth control. Joseph Reuss, of Mainz, Germany, said that sexuality in humans is not the same biologically as among the animals; man's relationships in a family-centered society is also
dependent on his sexuality, which exists not just for a means of
propagation, he said. Paul-Emile Cardinal Leger, of Montreal,
said each individual act did not have to be viewed as a means of
propagation and that marriage in general, not each act, should be
viewed in terms of propagation. Cardinal Leger, along with
Patriarch Maximos IV Saigh, Melchite patriarch of Antioch, rejected the idea that procreation and married love have respectively first and second rank in marriage. The two goals of marriage, they said, are intimately related. Cardinal Leger put it
this way:

> A certain pessimistic and negative attitude towards human
> love has prevailed which can be attributed neither to Scrip-
> ture nor to tradition but to philosophies of the past cen-
> turies, and which has obscured the importance and the
> legitimacy of conjugal love in marriage. . . .
>
> It is absolutely imperative to propose human conjugal love—
> and I mean human love, where both body and soul are in-
> volved—as an end in itself of marriage, as something which
> is good in itself and which has its needs and laws of its
> own. The Schema [Church in the Modern World] re-
> mains too hesitant on this point. It is not much use if the
> Schema avoids the term "secondary end" but can only pre-
> sent love as being at the service of fecundity. In such an im-
> portant matter, the clear principles should be stated. Other-
> wise, this fear with regard to conjugal love which has
> paralyzed our theology for such a long time might persist.
> Conjugal love is good and holy in itself and should be ac-

cepted by Christians, without any false fear, together with
its needs and the laws proper to it. Isn't this mutual help
and love the very things which husband and wife solemnly
swear they will give each other at the time of their marriage? And unless love is declared as an end of marriage, the
tie which binds husband and wife together cannot be cor-
rectly understood. The partners of a marriage consider each
other not as simple procreators, but as people loved for their
own sakes.

It is not enough, however, firmly to establish the doctrine
which looks at marriage as a *state*. Unless the end of the
actions themselves are touched upon, in their most general
principles, the difficulties which worry married couples and
parish priests cannot be solved. . . .

It must be affirmed that the intimate union of husband and
wife has an end in love as well. And this end is the *finis
operis*, legitimate in itself, even if it is not directed towards
procreation.

164. In the Constitution of the Church and the Modern World
(formerly Schema 13), the bishops at the Second Vatican Council
moved toward a liberalization of absolute positions on birth control, (at least so the document is interpreted by Dr. John Noonan,
head of the Natural Law Institute at Notre Dame University and
a consultant to the papal commission on birth control). The
Church in the Modern World document leaves it to the parents
to determine the size of their families, recognizes other purposes
in marriage than merely bearing of children, and for the first
time disassociates contraception from abortion. There is also an
awareness of population problems. While there is no clear change
of earlier positions, there was no longer a ranking of the goals of
marriage; and conjugal love and the happiness of the couple was
no longer second to responsibilities of procreation:

(49) Part II, Chapt. I. The Biblical Word of God several
times urges the betrothed and the married to nourish and

develop their wedlock by pure conjugal love and undivided affection. Many men of our own age also highly regard true love between husband and wife as it manifests itself in a variety of ways depending on the worthy customs of various peoples and times.

This love is an eminently human one since it is directed from one person to another through an affection of the will; it involves the good of the whole person, and therefore can enrich the expressions of body and mind with a unique dignity, ennobling these expressions as special ingredients and signs of the friendship distinctive of marriage. This love God has judged worthy of special gifts, healing, perfecting and exalting gifts of grace and of charity. Such love, merging the human with the divine, leads the spouses to a free and mutual gift of themselves, a gift proving itself by gentle affection and by deed; such love pervades the whole of their lives: indeed by its busy generosity it grows better and grows greater. Therefore it far excels mere erotic inclination, which selfishly pursued, soon enough fades wretchedly away. . . .

(50) Marriage and conjugal love are by their nature ordained toward the begetting and educating of children. Children are really the supreme gift of marriage and contribute very substantially to the welfare of their parents. The God Himself Who said, "it is not good for man to be alone" (Gen. 2: 18) and "Who made man from the beginning male and female" (Matt. 19: 4), wishing to share with man a certain special participation in His own creative work, blessed male and female, saying: "Increase and multiply" (Gen. 1: 28).

Hence, while not making the other purposes of matrimony of less account, the true practice of conjugal love, and the whole meaning of the family life which results from it, have this aim: that the couple be ready with stout hearts to co-

operate with the love of the Creator and the Savior, Who
through them will enlarge and enrich His own family day
by day.

Parents should regard as their proper mission the task of
transmitting human life and educating those to whom it has
been transmitted. They should realize that they are thereby
cooperators with the love of God the Creator, and are, so to
speak, the interpreters of that love. Thus they will fulfill
their task with human and Christian responsibility, and,
with docile reverence towards God, will make decisions by
common counsel and effort. Let them thoughtfully take into
account both their own welfare and that of their children,
those already born and those which the future may bring.
For this accounting they need to reckon with both the material and the spiritual conditions of the times as well as of
their state in life. Finally, they should consult the interests
of the family group, of temporal society, and of the Church
herself. The parents themselves and no one else should ultimately make this judgment in the sight of God. But in their
manner of acting, spouses should be aware that they cannot
proceed arbitrarily, but must always be governed according to a conscience dutifully conformed to the divine law
itself, and should be submissive toward the Church's teaching office, which authentically interprets that law in the light
of the Gospel. . . .

Marriage to be sure is not instituted solely for procreation;
rather, its very nature as an unbreakable compact between
persons, and the welfare of the children, both demand that
the mutual love of the spouses be embodied in a rightly ordered manner, that it grow and ripen. Therefore, marriage
persists as a whole manner and communion of life, and
maintains its value and indissolubility, even when despite
the often intense desire of the couple, offspring are lacking.

(51) This Council realizes that certain modern conditions
often keep couples from arranging their married lives har-
moniously, and that they find themselves in circumstances

where at least temporarily the size of their families should not be increased. As a result, the faithful exercise of love and the full intimacy of their lives is hard to maintain. But where the intimacy of married life is broken off, its faithfulness can sometimes be imperiled and its quality of fruitfulness ruined, for then the upbringing of the children and the courage to accept new ones are both endangered.

To these problems there are those who presume to offer dishonorable solutions indeed; they do not recoil even from the taking of life. But the Church issues the reminder that a true contradiction cannot exist between the divine laws pertaining to the transmission of life and those pertaining to authentic conjugal love. . . .

165. Across the country, by 1965, civic and welfare agencies were beginning to permit the distribution of birth control information, especially when the welfare agent was asked by the client to do so. Illinois, Michigan, West Virginia, Ohio faced this new attitude in decisions on the local and state levels. The controversy reigned all over again, but there was an absence of hostility and a measured desire to reason together. Archbishop Karl J. Alter, of Cincinnati, suggested these eight rules that "might well be considered in helping to minimize the controversy" over birth control proposals:

(1) Neither party to the controversy ought to impose its view on the other in the formation of the public conscience.

(2) Both should respect the religious liberty and rights of conscience of the individual; every form of coercion or penalty for lack of conformity should be avoided.

(3) Overpopulation is relative and is a highly complex phenomena; its solution should not be oversimplified.

(4) Scientific studies of fertility and sterility are to be highly recommended. Much research is now being conducted.

(5) Rash interference with the natural functions of human organisms can be dangerous, as was discovered tragically in the use of thalidomide.

(6) The poor and underprivileged should not be made the victims of social experimentation; nor should they be made to forfeit relief if found to be conscientious objectors.

(7) There are no unmarried mothers without there being at the same time an equal number of derelict fathers. Both constitute a social problem of controlling illegitimate births. Easy access to the use of contraceptives, and their positive recommendation, are dangerous to the youth of our country. To furnish contraceptives in cases of illegitimacy is more than a subtle encouragement to engage in extra-marital relations.

(8) The Catholic Church has never retreated from the teaching that the use of artificial contraceptives is immoral. It does not, however, condemn any and every form of regulating the period of fertility. At the present time research studies are being conducted, and when medical science reaches firm and definite conclusions on the effects of various forms of regulation, the Church will be in a position to apply moral principles to the facts. The Church has no desire to impose its own teaching on others, but acts only as an authorized teacher for its own members.

166. Showing growing consensus in the public area of the birth control controversy concerning toleration of minority rights the United States Supreme Court ruled as unconstitutional a 1789 Connecticut statute (originally drawn up by Protestants, but championed by Catholics) that said: "Any person who uses any drug, medicinal article or instrument for the purpose of preventing conception shall be fined not less than fifty dollars or imprisoned not less than sixty days nor more than one year or be both fined and imprisoned." Protestants and Catholics generally concurred by 1965 that the law should be repealed and little commotion followed the ruling that said the law was not a moral question but an invasion of privacy. However, commotion was to

come again when the Most Rev. Patrick A. O'Boyle, archbishop
of Washington, and William B. Ball, legal representative of the
National Catholic Welfare Conference, issued statements opposing a pending Senate bill that would provide Federal funds for
the dissemination of information and materials dealing with
birth prevention. It was one thing to tolerate birth control by
artificial means, another thing to actively promote it, they said.
Nevertheless, in an area in which controversy was sure to continue for many years, the Supreme Court decision acquiesced in
by the faiths was a milestone of a sort in consensus. Justice
Douglas delivered the opinion of the Court in the case of *Estelle
T. Griswold* [who heads the Planned Parenthood League of
Connecticut] *et al.*, appellants, versus *State of Connecticut:*

> Coming to the merits, we are met with a wide range of ques-
> tions that implicate the Due Process Clause of the Four-
> teenth Amendment. . . . We do not sit as a super-legislature
> to determine the wisdom, need, and propriety of laws that
> touch economic problems, business affairs, or social condi-
> tions. This law, however, operates directly on an intimate
> relation of husband and wife and their physician's role in
> one aspect of that relation.
>
> The association of people is not mentioned in the Constitu-
> tion nor in the Bill of Rights. The right to educate a child
> in a school of the parents' choice—whether public or private
> or parochial—is also not mentioned. Nor is the right to study
> any particular subject or any foreign language. Yet the
> First Amendment has been construed to include certain of
> those rights. . . .
>
> The right of "association," like the right of belief (*Board of
> Education* v. *Barnette*, 319 U.S. 624), is more than the right
> to attend a meeting; it includes the right to express one's
> attitudes or philosophies by membership in a group or by
> affiliation with it or by other lawful means. Association in
> that context is a form of expression of opinion; and while
> it is not expressly included in the First Amendment its exist-
> ence is necessary in making the express guarantees fully
> meaningful. . . .

Specific guarantees in the Bill of Rights have penumbras, formed by emanations from those guarantees that help give them life and substance. See *Poe* v. *Ullman*, 367 U.S. 497, 516-522 (dissenting opinion). Various guarantees create zones of privacy. The right of association contained in the penumbra of the First Amendment is one, as we have seen. The Third Amendment in its prohibition against the quartering of soldiers "in any house" in time of peace without the consent of the owner is another facet of that privacy. The Fourth Amendment explicitly affirms the "right of the people to be secure in their persons, houses, papers, and effects against unreasonable searches and seizures." The Fifth Amendment in its Self-Incrimination Clause enables the citizen to create a zone of privacy which government may not force him to surrender to his detriment. The Ninth Amendment provides: "The enumeration in the Constitution, of certain rights, shall not be construed to deny or disparage others retained by the people." . . .

The present case, then, concerns a relationship lying within the zone of privacy created by several fundamental constitutional guarantees. And it concerns a law which, in forbidding the *use* of contraceptives rather than regulating their manufacture or sale, seeks to achieve its goals by means having a maximum destructive impact upon that relationship. Such a law cannot stand in light of the familiar principle, so often applied by this Court, that a "governmental purpose to control or prevent activities constitutionally subject to state regulation may not be achieved by means which sweep unnecessarily broadly and thereby invade the area of protected freedom." *NAACP* v. *Alabama*, 377 U.S. 288, 307. Would we allow the police to search the sacred precincts of marital bedrooms for telltale signs of the use of contraceptives? The very idea is repulsive to the notions of privacy surrounding the marriage relationship.

We deal with a right of privacy older than the Bill of Rights —older than our political parties, older than our school system. Marriage is a coming together for better or for worse,

hopefully enduring, and intimate to the degree of being
sacred. It is an association that promotes a way of life, not
causes; a harmony in living, not political faiths; a bilateral
loyalty, not commercial or social projects. Yet it is an association for as noble a purpose as any involved in our prior
decisions.

167. Concerning celibacy, Pope Paul withdrew celibacy as a
topic from the Second Vatican Council in the discussions on the
priestly life. However, discussions around the Council reiterated
the fact that celibacy is not a matter of divine law but of the
legislation of the church. Among the Eastern-rite Roman Catholics, there are married priests, when the marriage occurs before
ordination. The practice, however, has been discontinued in the
United States. Also Eastern-rite prelates are not allowed to be
married. The Council permitted the restored role of married
deacons, a practice that has not been ordered for the United
States.

Several Protestant ministers, who had families, among them a
former Lutheran minister from Detroit, Ernest Adam Beck,
were dispensed from celibacy vows and were ordained priests.

Protestants, in the meantime, occasionally began to cite value
in celibacy. A case in point was the Protestant monastery community at Taizé, France, which finds its vocation in celibacy.
Said Max Thurian, assistant prior:

> Christian marriage and Christian celibacy are equal states
> and for that reason we must speak of them together. Both
> have the nature of a vocation, and, as such, both involve
> renunciations and also special joys. This is learnt by every
> minister in his pastoral work among married and single
> people—it cannot be said that one way of life has more dif-
> ficulties than the other. What is important in every case is
> that there should be an unrestricted choice of the Lord's will
> for us.
>
> Nowadays contemporary Protestantism is working out a
> theology of marriage which is more stable and in accord-
> ance with the New Testament, but there is scarcely any sign

of a corresponding theology of celibacy. The theological revival, by a return to the scriptural texts and to patristic
sources, is not adequate to enable Protestants to overcome
their strong reactions—sometimes uncontrolled and uncon-
trollable—against celibacy. They revolt against the renun-
ciation of love between men and women. It seems to us that
tension on this level comes from the refusal to consider
Christian celibacy as a vocation as genuinely grounded as
Christian marriage.

Marriage and celibacy are two Christian absolutes which
concern the whole of one's being. In a world disorganized
by sin, their aim is to show forth visibly the new order established by the coming of Christ. . . .

168. A consensus on the general principles of marriage and
family life was reached by Protestant, Roman Catholic, Jewish
and Orthodox leaders in the United States. The agreement was
made public as it was adopted by the General Board of the National Council of Churches, June 2, 1966, meeting in New York.
"A Joint Statement on Marriage and Family Life in the United
States" agreed that "sexuality is a wondrous gift from God" and
that "parenthood called for the responsible use of all God-given
talents in the raising of children." The statement was prepared
by leaders of the National Catholic Welfare Conference, the
Synagogue Council of America, and the National Council of
Churches.

To help families develop foundations for personally meaningful and socially responsible behavior, we offer the following affirmations on which our historic faiths unite.

We believe, and unite in affirming, that God, the Creator
of the Universe and the Father of all mankind, did create
us male and female and did establish families as part of his
Divine Plan. Because of our understanding of this Plan,
we believe and unite in affirming that our sexuality is a
wondrous gift from God to be accepted with thanksgiving
and used within marriage with reverence and joy.

We believe and unite in affirming that our understanding of God's plan for marriage ideally calls for lifelong commitment in fidelity to a continuing, supportive relationship in which each partner helps the other to develop to fullest capacity. We are united in our belief that God is an active partner in sustaining and enriching the husband-wife relationship in marriage.

We believe and unite in affirming that children are a trust from God and that parenthood is a joyous, though strenuous, adventure in partnership with God for the procreation and nurturing of each child. Parenthood calls for the responsible use of all of our God–given talents and abilities in this adventure.

We believe and unite in affirming that family life is the cradle of personality and character for each child and creates an environment for the societal values of each succeeding generation as well as the principal source of meaningful personal relations for each adult member of our society. All children need a father and a mother firmly united in love to guide their growth into manhood or womanhood and to provide the emotional security that fosters development toward mature and responsible relationships between men and women.

We believe that the family is the cornerstone of our society. It shapes the attitudes, the hopes, the ambitions, the values of every citizen. The child is usually damaged when family living collapses. When this happens on a massive scale, the community itself is crippled.

There are no easy answers to all the complex problems facing marriage and family living in the world today, and we are aware that there are many fronts on which we must work. We can never finish the task; neither are we free to ignore it.

Therefore, we the major religious groups in the U.S., join

forces in exploring all ways and means available to preserve and strengthen family life in America to the end that
each person may enjoy fulfillment in dignity, justice and
peace.

169. A key problem in Catholic-Protestant relations is the
mixed marriage. Protestants throughout the Second Vatican
Council, as the spirit of ecumenism developed, constantly suggested that a place to begin to demonstrate ecumenism was in
mixed-marriage regulations. Protestants, such as Max Thurian,
of the Taizé community, who, like others, called the problem
"grave" in an article in *Ecumenical Experiences* (edited by Luis
V. Romeu: Westminster, Maryland: The Newman Press, 1965, *cf.*
pp. 153, 154), wanted Roman Catholics to go further than Catholic sacramental theology would permit. He suggested children be
brought up in the church "chosen by the couple before the marriage." Catholic Canon Law has had the four-fold requirement
that the non-Catholic spouse is not to interfere with the Catholic's spouse's practice of religion; secondly, he or she must promise to raise the children Catholic; third, the non-Catholic must respect the marriage as a sacrament; fourth, the ceremony must
not be repeated in a non-Catholic Church. Catholics marrying
before another besides a priest was no longer excommunicated,
—a Protestant minister could add a blessing in the home afterwards. The nuptial mass could be celebrated at the Catholic rite
in a mixed marriage, thanks to a slight change from the Holy
Office in 1965. Yet the Baltimore Catechism, for instance, was
still asking for active efforts by the Catholic spouse to convert the
non-Catholic partner. The bishops at the Second Vatican Council
voted 1,592 to 427 in the Council's third session to put the matter
in the hands of Pope Paul.

Then, suddenly, on March 18, 1966, just as the Archbishop of
Canterbury, Arthur Michael Ramsey was about to embark for
Rome to visit Pope Paul VI with the promise that he would raise
the question of mixed-marriage restrictions to the Pope, Pope
Paul in a new document, *Matrimonii Sacramentum,* signed by
Alfred Cardinal Ottaviani, pro-prefect of the Congregation for
the Doctrine of the Faith, but "by authority of His Holiness Pope

Paul VI" lifted some of the more negative aspects of Catholic
mixed-marriage practices. A Catholic, for instance, marrying
before another besides a priest was no longer excommunicated,
although still denied the sacraments (which in effect is still about
the same thing, minus the legal term of excommunication and
some paper work, as one chancery canon law expert put it). But
now also the promises did not have to be written, guaranteeing
the rearing of the children as Catholic, although such promises
were expected from the Catholic spouse, with assurances that the
non-Catholic spouse would still assist in rearing the child Catholic, but if this was against one's conscience, the matter was to be
appealed to Rome. Catholic officials said they would still seek the
signatures on the old forms of the promises, unless one objected.
Ramsey, meeting with Pope Paul, reportedly objected to continuing the unilateral promises and to the fact that the vows had to
be said in a rite before a priest, although a minister could stand
beside the priest in the sanctuary and now add a blessing. But
the changes did not go unappreciated. While wanting more basic
changes, Protestants were nevertheless enthusiastic, especially
concerning the spirit in which the changes were made. Said the
Rev. Dr. Robert C. Dodds, ecumenical affairs director of the
National Council of Churches, "The relaxation of the regulation
which used to require the non-Catholic member to sign a pledge
before marrying . . . reduces tension between our communities
and encourages the development of sensitive consciousness
among all who participate in mixed marriages. Other aspects of
the papal document . . . show the compassion of Pope Paul VI as
well as his concern to maintain the integrity of the faith. We
look forward to studying with our Roman Catholic brothers the
full implication of this document." Pope Paul took cognizance of
the changing times, the views of Protestants, and of his own
bishops in the new document which he regarded as somewhat
tentative, subject to approval by acceptance and workability in
practice:

> . . . . One cannot deny that the characteristic conditions
> of our time have rapidly brought about radical transforma-
> tions in social and family life, making it more difficult than

in the past to observe the canonical discipline regarding mixed marriages.

In truth, as circumstances now are, contacts between Catholics and non-Catholics are much more frequent, the ways of life and the similarity of habits are closer, thus there is more easily born a friendship between them from which, as experience teaches, there come more frequent occasions of mixed marriages.

Accordingly the pastoral concern of the Church, today more than ever, is that the sanctity of marriage, in conformity with Catholic teaching, and that the faith of the Catholic spouse, even in mixed marriages be safeguarded and that the Catholic education of the children be assured with the greatest possible diligence and efficaciousness. . . .

The new discipline suggests that the rigor of the present legislation be mitigated regarding mixed marriages, certainly not as regards divine law, but in regard to certain norms, of ecclesiastical law by which the separated brethren often feel offended. . . .

By the authority of His Holiness Pope Paul VI there are issued the following norms which, should they gain positive approval from practice, will definitely be introduced into the Code of Canon Law which is currently being revised.

I. (1) Let there be always borne in mind that it is always necessary to keep away from the Catholic spouse the danger to his faith and that one must diligently provide for the Catholic education (cf. Canon 1060).

(2) Let the local Ordinary or the pastor of the Catholic party take care to inculcate in grave terms the obligation to provide for the Catholic baptism and Catholic education of the offspring. For the fulfillment of this obligation a guarantee will be asked for by means of an explicit promise on the part of the Catholic spouse, that is to say, by means of the cautions.

(3) The non-Catholic party, with due delicacy, but in clear terms must be informed of the Catholic teaching regarding the dignity of Matrimony and especially regarding its principal qualities, which are unity and indissolubility.

He or she must also be informed of the Catholic party's grave obligations to safeguard, preserve and profess his faith and to have the offspring which will be born, baptized and educated in the faith.

And so that this obligation may be guaranteed, the non-Catholic spouse should also be invited to promise openly and sincerely that he will not create any obstacles in the fulfillment of that duty.

If then the non-Catholic party thinks he may not formulate this promise without violating his conscience the Ordinary must refer the case with all its particulars to the Holy See.

(4) Although under ordinary conditions these promises must be made in writing, it is however within the power of the Ordinary—either by means of rules of a general character or in each individual case—to establish that these promises of the Catholic party and of the non-Catholic party or of both be given in writing or not, as well as to determine how mention of it is to be inserted into the matrimonial documents.

II. If it is ever the case, as sometimes happens in certain regions, that the Catholic education of the child is rendered impossible, not so much by the deliberate will of the spouses but rather because of the law and customs of peoples, from which the parties cannot separate themselves, the local Ordinary, after considering everything carefully, can dispense from this impediment, so long as the Catholic party is disposed, in so far as he knows and is able to do it, to take every possible step that all the offspring to be born are baptized and educated in a Catholic manner and that at the same time this be guaranteed by the good will of the non-Catholic party. . . .

III. In the celebration of mixed mariages, the canonical
form must be observed according to the norm of Canon
1,094. This is required for the very validity of the marriage.
If, however, difficulties arise, the Ordinary must refer the
case with all its particulars to the Holy See.

IV. In regard to the liturgical form, as an exception to
Canon 1,102, numbers 3 and 4, and Canon 1,109, number 3,
there is conceded to local Ordinaries the faculty of permit-
ting the celebration of mixed marriages using the sacred
rites with the usual blessing and discourse.

V. There must be avoided absolutely any celebration in the
presence of a Catholic priest and a non-Catholic minister
in the simultaneous exercise of their respective rites.

However it is not prohibited that, the religious ceremony
having ended, the non-Catholic minister addresses some
words of good wishes and exhortation, and that prayers may
be recited in common with non-Catholics.

What is referred to above may be done with the consent of
the local Ordinary and with due precautions to avoid the
danger of scandal.

VI. Local ordinaries and pastors should be attentively vig-
ilant that families resulting from mixed marriages lead a
holy life in conformity with the promises made, especially
as regards the Catholic instruction and education of the
offspring.

VII. The excommunication provided for by Canon 2,319,
paragraph 1, number 1, for those who celebrate a marriage
before a non-Catholic minister is abrogated. The effects of
this abrogation are retroactive.

In establishing these new norms it is the mind and intention of the Church, as has been said above, to provide for
the actual needs of the faithful so as to favor with a warmer

sense of charity the reciprocal relations between Catholics and non-Catholics. . . .

170. A basic trouble area in Protestant-Catholic relationships is the nature of faith. Does one earn his salvation or does it come by free grace? The question of "merit"—the granting of a spiritual reward for an act done for God— has troubled Protestants. Merit, and the companion practice of granting indulgences (a remission of punishment on the basis of intention and acts performed) was a chief concern of Luther in his 95 theses or topics of debate at the start of the Protestant Reformation. Luther's motto was "justification by faith" as trust over against faith as an intellectual assent and objective action. Modern-day Lutherans, however, find it hard to agree on faith and its relation to good works which accompanies faith as a by-product if not as an initial ingredient. In the Lutheran World Federation meeting in Helsinki in 1962, delegates were unable to restate the idea of "justification" in agreeable terms for the modern age, and thus postponed action on that report. Theologian Hans Küng has sought to delineate some points of convergence in his volume, *Justification*. Catholic and Protestant theologians discussed "justification" in the 1965 biennial educational meeting of the Dominican Fathers, Province of St. Joseph, at La Salle College, Philadelphia.

A Detroit Catholic priest and a Grosse Pointe Protestant minister debated faith and "merit" on their weekly dialogue program over Detroit's WXYZ-TV. Participants were the Rev. Father Raymond Ellis, assistant director of the Archdiocesan Confraternity of Christian Doctrine (recently transferred to St. Cecelia Parish), and the Rev. Dr. Bertram deHeus Atwood, pastor of the Grosse Pointe Memorial (Presbyterian) Church. They sat back in a booklined study, and took on all the difficult issues: Authority, Mary, Purgatory, birth control, etc. On Merit:

DR. ATWOOD: "By grace ye are saved through faith—that not of yourself, it is a gift." But then what about this merit— we don't understand. . . .

FATHER ELLIS: Well, we feel that all merit is actually, when we talk about merit, what Jesus Christ earned. Fundamentally it is what Jesus earned. When Jesus was humbled and obedient unto death, his Father exalted him and raised him up and gave him a name that we must all honor and kneel before. . . . He earned a reward from his Father in his humanity to be Son of God, raised and placed at the right hand of the Father. Now I am united to Jesus Christ. I can do nothing unless I am one with him, in union with him. So once I am in union with Jesus, then everything I do is actually as though Jesus were doing it. So all of my actions from thenceforth are Jesus' actions.

ATWOOD: So it is Jesus' merit and not your merit.

ELLIS: It is actually our merit—it's Jesus and I together. I could not merit without Jesus with me. Now nothing I do is any value if I do it only alone. But with Jesus Christ I merit before the Father, it means that my merit and Christ's merit are the same. So his cross and my cross are the same. I don't know if that's very clear—it's very heavy theology.

ATWOOD: I'm sure it's heavy but the point that I'd like to make is that certainly Christ didn't do certain things in order to win a reward. He did it out of love. He didn't say I'm going to humble myself in order that God will like me. And this is what I think we Protestants worry about in the use of the word "merit"—that I'm doing this in order to win God's approval. What you're really saying is that Christ so forgot himself that he was one with the Father. It's when I forget about myself and forget about rewards that I find God's merit for me, or a reward. Is that what you're saying?

ELLIS: Yes, I am. And when I say that—we're talking about reward, we're talking about merit—Jesus talked about reward many times. He says that "do this and your reward will be great in Heaven." That your Father will see you in secret and reward you. He didn't mean for us to be ostentatious and to do things primarily for reward. We know that isn't the most perfect way to act. But that if we were simply to be in union with Christ and do these things, Jesus tells us that with himself we will be glorified. That we will share in his glory, we will share in his reward. . . . Ultimately it is Jesus Christ who is praised above all and it's his reward that we participate in.

ATWOOD: That's very good. One thing that sometimes I think Protestants talk about, and maybe Roman Catholics, is . . . they sort of act sometimes as if we must do certain things now so that our reward will be great in Heaven, namely, so I'd better take on this suffering, I'd better do this sacrifice—it may not show up in this life but in the world to come I'm going to have a bigger house, and I'm going to be sure of my salvation. We even talk about "getting stars in our crowns" as if Heaven itself is something I can achieve.

ELLIS: . . . Paul in the epistles talked . . . I do believe it was to the Romans or to the Corinthians—he called them, "You're my crown." So he did know, and he says, "Now there is a waiting for me, a reward which the just Judge will give me."

ATWOOD: Right. But it isn't as if the reward that comes— that you're looking for the reward. You know that somehow you're right with God and that God has accepted you and therefore it's nothing of your own doing.

ELLIS: Right. We do teach that . . . to concentrate on Jesus Christ, love Jesus Christ. . . .

ATWOOD: Forget about yourself.

ELLIS: Yes, and the very love of Jesus Christ will be our reward. That he himself will communicate himself to us.

ATWOOD: All right. If this is what merit means, I think, first thing I think it's a bad word because it misleads me.

ELLIS: Well, Jesus used. . . .

ATWOOD: He used the word "reward". . . .

ELLIS: But he's kind of luring us off to our own level when he talks about reward because we understand it.

ATWOOD: Right, but he also said to the Pharisee, Go ahead and pray on the street corner and you'll get your reward. And what he meant was, the reward they were going to get was that they'd be seen of men. And sometimes we do say our prayers, or are pious, because we want public approval and not worry about God's approval.

ELLIS: I think we can pretty well agree on that.

ATWOOD: O.K.

171. The Catholic attitude toward indulgences (introduced at the second Vatican Council for opinions only and withdrawn) is changing, or at least is being seen from a different viewpoint, according to the Rev. Father Gregory Baum, a member of the Secretariat for Promoting of Christian Unity, and editor of *The Ecumenist*, Toronto. He says:

> None of the promulgated documents of Vatican II have made any reference to the Church's power to grant indulgences. What does this silence mean? At the time of the Reformation the controversy about indulgences was much in the foreground. In a special Decree on Indulgences the Council of Trent confirmed the late medieval doctrine on indulgences as expressed in the bull *Unigenitus Dei Filius* of Pope Clement VI, and the *Professio Fidei Tridentina* specifically acknowledges "the power to grant indulgences left by Christ to the Church and their most salutary use by the Christian people." Yet the dogmatic Constitution on the Church of Vatican II, while dealing with the hierarchical powers in the Church (ch. 3), with man's transformation in holiness (ch. 5) and his final destiny (ch. 7) does not make a single reference to indulgences. . . .

What is an indulgence? It is a remission of temporal punishment due to sins for which pardon has already been received. Thanks to "the treasury of merits" received from Christ and the saints, the Church has "the power" to remit the temporal punishment that remains a Christian's due after he has received divine forgiveness, and to do this in acts of varying intensities, effecting partial or total remission, reaching the living by way of absolution and the dead by way of intercession. . . .

When the documents of the magisterium describe the granting of indulgences as "a power to remit" temporal punishments, they use the word "power" in an improper sense. It seems to refer to the power of the Church's intercession. A prayer of the Church as the community of the redeemed offered in the name of the Redeemer will always be heard, especially if it pleads for the perfect reconciliation of a contrite brother. This is the Church's "power" with which she assists her members in their liberation from temporal punishment. Indulgences are a special kind of prayer offered by the Church.

The official documents of the magisterium dealing with indulgences often speak of "the treasury of merits" that the Church has received from Christ and the saints. What is meant by this treasury of merits? Is it permissible to think of this treasury as some kind of spiritual bank or ledger in which are kept the benefits merited by Christ, and his saints for the salvation of mankind? Or is this simply a figurative way of saying that Christ, the One Mediator, remains in the midst of his people and that his offering of himself, accompanied by the surrender to God in his brothers in whom he, the one source of grace, is active, remains always available to the Christian community? The Constitution on the Church does not use the term "treasury of merits"; it places into the foreground the presence of the One Mediator in the community, and the trust the Church has in the prayer of her Savior. . . .

The Catholic will always acknowledge the right of the

Church to institute the kind of prayer called indulgences and appreciate what this sacramental has done for the Christians of an age; but if he believes that the gaining of indulgences does not help Christians of our own day to enter more intelligently, actively and easily into the process of complete reconciliation with their Lord, then he may legitimately hope that the granting of indulgences will be discontinued in the Church. The silence of Vatican II on indulgences may indeed be the first step in this direction.

172. And Luther, who opposed the sale of indulgences, came in for some rethinking, too, on both sides. The question now was no longer would he change today, but rather would he have started the Reformation today at all? (Lutheran Bishop Otto Dibelius of Berlin said in a 1965 Reformation Sunday service, if the Roman Catholic Church was the same 450 years ago as it is today Luther would have stayed a Catholic.) The Rev. Dr. Carl E. Braaten, professor of systematic theology and ethics at the Lutheran School of Theology, Maywood, Illinois, said in an address at Clarke College, a Catholic girls' school, in Dubuque, Iowa:

First, we must realize in all honesty that the Roman Catholic Church is not the same unreformed church she was in Luther's time.

Nor can we be so sure that were Luther living within the conditions of present-day Catholicism he would sound his call to reform in the same uncompromising fashion, especially . . . if he knew that his Reformation would in the long run turn out so many illegitimate and idiotic Protestant offspring. . . .

The farthest thing from Luther's mind was to make his reform movement into an independent church named after him that would exist permanently outside of and in competition with the Roman Catholic Church. . . .

The tragedy is great enough that the split was necessary for the sake of the truth of the Gospel. A still greater tragedy is that what was intended to be a temporary situation, an interim period, for the sake of reforming the one church, has become a permanent arrangement with no end in sight.

The Reformation was not intended to bring about a Protestant Church, much less a collection of Protestant churches. The Reformation was a movement of protest for the sake of the one church.

The Reformation was a necessity, but we Protestants have made a virtue out of a necessity—a picnic out of a tragedy—thereby deluding ourselves.

173. A Lutheran pastor, the Rev. John C. McCollister, of the Bethlehem Lutheran Church, Lansing, Michigan, a guest speaker at St. Paul Catholic Seminary in Saginaw, attempted to clarify the position of Martin Luther: Here are sample questions which he fielded, and how he answered the future priests:

QUESTION: What right did one man, Martin Luther, have in rebelling against the Church?

ANSWER: If it were just one man, then we would not have had a Reformation. What Martin Luther was doing was a reflection of the thoughts of a great number of people. And, this was not just a one-shot affair. You will remember what happened to John Hus when he attempted to make some of the same criticisms. . . . He was burned at the stake. Let me again remind you that Luther did not want to start another branch of the Christian Church; his attempts were aimed at reforming the then present Church. Again, the feeling of a great number of the Christians demanded that something be done. This was not a one man campaign.

QUESTION: Does the Lutheran Church still regard the Pope as being the Anti-Christ?

ANSWER: No. To be sure, many of the 16th century reformers regarded the Pope in this regard, but let us remember

that a lot of what was said during this time on both sides
was said in the heat of passion. Therefore, we must consider the times and the circumstances in which these comments were made.

174. A German priest discounts Luther's nailing of his 95
theses on the door of the Castle church in Wittenberg in 1517 as
"legend." The priest's conclusion has Luther, apart from legend
of him as a boisterous schizmatic, standing as a towering symbol
of a devoted monk opposed to evil. The Rev. Father Klemens
Honselmann, a theological professor in Paderborn, Germany,
gives his views in a German quarterly, *Theologie und Glaube*
(his views were shared by Erwin Iserloh, Catholic historian at
Münster University in West Germany, in 1966). Said Father
Klemens:

> Luther himself never spoke of affixing his theses [to the
> door]. Not until after Luther's death did Melanchthon de-
> clare that Luther had attached his theses to the castle church
> door in Wittenberg on October 31. Since Melanchthon did
> not come to Wittenberg until 1518, however, he cannot have
> spoken as an eye witness. Where he got his knowledge is
> unknown. . . .
>
> It was those friends to whom Luther had sent his hand-
> written theses who caused the printing of the theses. . . .
> Luther emphasizes that he was not seeking wide publicity,
> but rather that he was concerned about the clarification of
> the question of indulgences through discussion or a written
> dialogue with scholars. He is surprised by the rapid and
> wide distribution of the printed versions. . . . The approval
> of the educated world, of many princes and also of the
> simple people made the arrangement of a disputation sense-
> less. . . . The pictures of the monk puffed up with power
> are unhistorical. . . .
>
> Luther's significance is not thereby called into question.
> Indeed, I should like to say that after the collapse of this
> legend he stands even more imposing: Not the revolutionary
> who by nailing his theses on the castle church in Wittenberg

wished to alert the Christian world to its shortcomings, but rather the monk who was still striving in the interests of the Church, who through his private distribution of his theses sought to overcome an evil in the Church, drew the masses, without actually wishing to do so, to himself.

Only the approval of the masses transformed the monk enthusiastic for reform, Martin Luther, into the reformer.

175. Martin Luther was regarded as somewhat of a forgotten saint by some Catholics (however, Father Godfrey Diekmann, editor of *Worship,* said he could use articles for his magazine from four Lutheran liturgical periodicals *if* they would stop calling Luther "Blessed Martin").

Luther's "canonization" was insisted on by the "lesser" theologians. When thirty Sisters of Notre Dame who teach in Rosary High School, St. Louis, visited Grace Lutheran Church in that city, they were willing to concede Luther's presence in Heaven with Pope John. In their thank-you note to the pastor, the Rev. Gerhardt Nitz, they said:

May the Christ whom we both follow lead us up that rather dangerous path, as portrayed in your last window, to His eternal Kingdom where, perhaps right now, Martin Luther and Pope John XXIII are discussing the prayer we Catholics will soon say.

176. Reflecting the change in Catholic-Protestant relations in troubled areas, even concerning Luther himself, was the glowing tribute of Luther from a young American priest, the Rev. Father James J. Kavanaugh, writing in his former weekly "Heart to Heart" column in diocesan papers:

I couldn't help thinking, as he [the liberal Catholic German theologian Hans Küng] spoke, of another young Catholic priest and theologian from Germany who was rather badly received some 400 years ago.

He wasn't interested in touring America at that time, since the Indians actually weren't too high on theology. But he did send up a few skyrockets in Germany, which, unfortunately, weren't too well understood in Rome.

He saw the 16th Century greed of bishops, the ignorance of priests and the superstition of people who thought more of honoring the bottled blood and relics of saints than they did of God's Own Word.

He spoke violently, with the brutality of speech the German genius provides. He divided Christendom with the fire of his oratory and the courage of his biting convictions.

The Catholic Church wasn't ready to hear him and ordered him to crawl back into his cocoon. But he wasn't about to. Finally he was excommunicated, dragging thousands of Christian soldiers with him.

This man and priest, Martin Luther, had a lot of sensible things to say. And if we read his writings today, we discover that much of what he wanted has found its place in the Catholic Church.

He was young and rash, extreme and troubled, but a rare genius who might have taken his place side by side with Thomas Aquinas and Bernard and Charles Borromeo. For all we know, he may have been God's instrument to wake up a Christianity grown soft and worldly.

REFERENCES

*Chapter V*

130. The Very Rev. Vladimir Borichevsky, Philadelphia, "Father Vladimir Answers Your Questions," in *The Russian Orthodox Journal*, Dec., 1961, p. 13.
131. Metropolitan Antony Bashir, U. S. Archdiocese, Syrian Antiochian Orthodox Church, speech delivered Apr. 15, 1964, at the St. Mary-of-the Woods (Catholic) College, Terre Haute, Ind., in the St. Mary-of-the-Woods *Alumnae News*, Spring-Summer, XXXIX, No. 2, 4, 5.
132. Oscar Cullmann, translated by Floyd Filson, *Peter: Disciple, Apostle, Martyr* (Philadelphia: The Westminster Press, 1962) pp. 192, 193, 213. Copyright, 1962, SCM Press Ltd., London.
133. From English translation of Latin letter addressed to Pope Paul VI by the Rt. Rev. George N. Luxton, bishop of Huron (Canada), Decem-

ber, 1965, and published by Bishop Luxton, in 1966, under the title "A Local Item in the Roman Catholic-Anglican Dialogue—1965-1966," pp. 3, 4.

134. "Joint Declaration: Rome-Istanbul," Dec. 7, 1965, mimeograph copy, distributed at Vatican Council press office.

135. Quote from H. Schütte, *Um die Wiedervereinigung im Glauben* (Essen: 1959), p. 148; translated in Hans Küng, *The Council, Reform and Reunion*, translator Cecily Hastings (New York: Sheed and Ward, 1961), p. 127.

136. Walter J. Burghardt, S.J., "Mary: Obstacle to Reunion?" *Ecumenism and Vatican II*, Charles O'Neill, S.J., ed. (Milwaukee: The Bruce Publishing Company, 1964), p. 64.

137. Colin Stephenson, *Our Solitary Boast* (London: Church Literature Association, n.d.), pp. 9-11.

138. "Revised Report of the Commission on 'Christian Witness, Proselytism and Religious Liberty,'" Central Committee, World Council of Churches, St. Andrews, Scotland, 1960, *The Ecumenical Review* (October, 1960), No. 1, pp. 82, 87, 88.

139. "Decree on The Missionary Activity of the Church," promulgated by the Second Vatican Council, Dec. 7, 1965, NCWC translation.

140. a. Tablet, CCXVIII, No. 6492, Oct. 24, 1964; translated from *Le Monde*.
    b. New York Times, Nov. 20, 1964; cf. also La Civilta Cattolica, anno 116, I, No. 4, Feb. 20, 1965, p. 329.

141. "Declaration on Religious Freedom, on the Right of the Person and of Communities to Social and Civil Freedom in Matters Religious," promulgated Dec. 7, 1965, by the Second Vatican Council, NCWC translation, St. Paul editions.

142. Letter from Emilio Garrigues, Minister Counselor, Spanish Embassy, Washington, Sept. 13, 1962.

143. a. *Religious News Service*, Mar. 26, 1963, Madrid.
    b. *National Catholic Welfare Conference* release, Jan., 1965.

144. a. Prof. Gerardo Alarco, Catholic University, Lima, Peru, *National Lutheran Council* news release, 65-80, July 19, 1965, p. 5.
    b. Text, *NLC* release, 65-81, July 20, 1965, p. 3.

145. Letter from the Rt. Rev. David B. Reed, Episcopal Bishop of Colombia with Ecuador, Feb. 16, 1965.

146. Text of speech distributed at the Catholic Inter-American Cooperation Program, Chicago, Jan. 27, 1965, p. 14.

147. Joint Pastoral Letter of the Catholic bishops of Northern Rhodesia, Jan. 6. 1958, in Lusaka, in *The Church to Africa*, Pastoral Letters of the African Hierarchies (London: The Sword of the Spirit, 1959), pp. 18-21.

148. Pastoral Letter of the Hierarchy of the Gold Coast, *Ibid.*, pp. 128, 129.

149. News Release, Catholic Secretariat, Tanganyika Episcopal Conference, Dar es Saldam, Tanzania, FvD/CWDS, NB. 19/63, Nov. 2, 1963, p. 2.

150. Editorial, "The Church-State Legacy of John F. Kennedy," *Journal of Church and State*, VI, No. 1 (Winter, 1964), 10-11, and Associated Press, Sept. 13, 1960.

151. Stanley Stuber, *Primer on Roman Catholicism* (New York: Association Press, 1953, 1960), dedication page.

152. Public Law 89-10, 89th Congress, H.R. 2362, Apr. 11, 1965, government printing, pp. 10-12.

153. "A Protestant and Orthodox Statement Regarding Dual School Enrollment," adopted by the General Board, National Council of Churches, NCC code 13.6-1, June 4, 1964.

326

154. The Rt. Rev. Frederick J. Warnecke, Episcopal Bishop of Bethlehem, Cathedral Church of the Nativity, Bethlehem, Pa., sermon, Feb. 28, 1965.
155. "General Findings," First National Study Conference on Church and State, Department of Religious Liberty, NCC, Columbus, O., Feb. 7, 1964, official text, mimeographed, pp. 1-5.
156. Robert E. Van Deusen, "Changing Patterns in Church-State Relations," a speech at the annual meeting of the Christian Social Council, Columbia, S.C., Dec. 2, 1965.
157. Pope John XXIII, "Siamo Lieti," an address to a group of visiting Ecclesiastical Censors, Nov. 18, 1959, in *The Pope Speaks*, translated by Louciana G. M. Rose, VI, No. 1 (1959), 78-80.
158. John Courtney Murray, S. J., *We Hold These Truths* (New York: Sheed and Ward, 1960), p. 72.
159. NCWC release, Nov. 30, 1960.
160. Pope Paul VI, translation of a French language address delivered Mar. 27, 1965, *National Catholic Reporter*, I, No. 23 (Apr. 7, 1965), 10.
161. Pope Pius XII, "Di Gran Cuore," a radio address translated from Italian text by Charles E. Spence, in *The Pope Speaks*, IV, No. 1 (Summer, 1957), 10.
162. "Responsible Parenthood," a pronouncement adopted by the General Board of the NCC, Feb. 23, 1961, code 31.1-2.
163. *The Tablet*, CCXVIII, No. 1,494, Nov. 7, 1964, pp. 1255, 1256.
164. "Decree of the Pastoral Constitution on the Church in the Modern World," NCWC translation.
165. The Most Rev. Karl J. Alter, archbishop of Cincinnati, *NCWC* release, in the Southwest Louisiana Register, Mar. 11, 1965, p. 1.
166. U.S. Supreme Court, No. 496, Oct. Term, 1964, Estelle T. Griswold et al, Appellants, v. State of Connecticut, June 7, 1965, government printing, pp. 1, 3, 5-7.
167. Max Thurian, *Marriage and Celibacy* (London: SCM Press Ltd., 1959), p. 15.
168. National Council of Churches, mimeographed text, "A Joint Statement on Marriage and Family Life in the United States," by the National Council of Churches, Synagogue Council of America, approved by the NCC General Board, June 2, 1966.
169. National Catholic Welfare Conference translation.
170. Transcript of station WXYZ-TV program, "Dialogue," the Metropolitan Detroit Council of Churches in cooperation with the Archdiocese of Detroit.
171. Gregory Baum, "Silence on Indulgences," *The Ecumenist*, III, No. 3 (Mar.-Apr., 1965), 37-39.
172. Carl E. Braaten, Lutheran School of Theology, Maywood, Ill., address at the Clarke College (Catholic girls' school), Dubuque, Ia., Chicago Daily News Service, Nov., 1964, report by David Meade, Chicago Daily News.
173. John C. McCollister, Bethlehem Lutheran Church, Lansing, Mich., speech at St. Paul Catholic Seminary, Saginaw, text provided by Pastor McCollister, p. 6.
174. Klemens Honselmann, "Die Veröffentlichung der Ablassthesen Martin Luthers 1517," *Theologie und Glaube*, Paderborn, I (1965), 1, 18, 22, 23.
175. Quoted in *Lutheran Layman*, Apr. 1, 1965, p. 12.
176. James J. Kavanaugh, "Heart to Heart" column, syndicated, *Michigan Catholic*, Aug. 27, 1964.

# six

# Worship Trends--Together

It is now possible for Roman Catholics and Protestants to meet together in prayer and praise to God with greater ease. Just how far they can or cannot go "together" is still a matter of debate, since overall guidelines tend to be fairly general, and specifics are left up to the local hierarchies, still feeling their way in inter-Christian relations. Participation in the regular services of a Protestant church by a Catholic is treated with caution, and according to some, is implicitly, if not explicitly prohibited (see Chapter III, including contrast between Pittsburgh and Bridgeport). Nevertheless, dialogue has shifted the emphasis of Protestant-Catholic relations from a purely negative attitude of "Stay away from Protestants" to "how far can we really go in contacts with Protestants," sometimes determined by reading between the lines. The emphasis has come to the spirit of the law, and not the letter. There is now the element of love and charity, such as was evident when Evangelist Billy Graham visited Houston in October 1965. Catholics were permitted under certain circumstances to attend the Graham rallies. The attendance, said the Galveston-Houston diocesan ecumenical commission, "can be permissible for Catholics acting with ecumenical charity and with a penitential awareness of their inability to participate actively in the service." The commission said further that those who attended the rallies "should first of all bear in mind that talks by Dr. Graham show a wholesome fidelity to God's word." They should, therefore, although they were not encouraged to attend, "avoid any kind of negative attitude or antagonism toward him. Such an attitude would be a violation of charity."

The Code of Canon Law of 1918, though superseded in ecumenical matters by the Second Vatican Council's Decree on Ecumenism, nevertheless, until another code is formulated, is still appealed to on occasion. But even that code, once considered quite clear in a negative way, is now seen to be vague in areas, such as in regard to the question of "participation" in non-Roman Catholic services. The interpretation of the code has been compounded by the recognition of the "two principles," a negative principle: avoid scandal and a semblance of union when union does not exist, and a positive principle, when "participation" in joint services could be a means of grace.

According to Canon 1258:

> (1) It is unlawful for Catholics to assist actively in any way at, or to take part in, the religious [or "worship"] services of non-Catholics [. . . "partem habere in sacris acatholicorum"].
>
> (2) A passive or merely material presence at funerals and weddings and similar solemnities of non-Catholics may be tolerated for the sake of civil duty or honor, because of a grave reason, to be approved by the Bishop in a doubtful case, provided there is no danger of perversion or scandal present.

177. Even before the Decree on Ecumenism was promulgated this whole question of "communication" or "participation" (*communicatio*) in "worship" (*sacris*) with non-Catholics for Roman Catholics and the possibility of participation with Protestants for greater positive purposes were seen by the Rev. Father Gregory Baum, in his bi-monthly *The Ecumenist*, as evolving to wider limits:

> *Communicatio in sacris* is a technical term referring to the participation of Christians in the worship of Churches which are not their own. *Communicatio in sacris* in the strict sense signifies a participation in the sacramental life

of other Churches, especially in the eucharist, but *communicatio in sacris* in a wider sense signifies a sharing in any form of prayer offered by members of other Churches. The assistance of a Christian at the worship of another Church is called *active* if he exercises a special function in this worship as minister, godparent, or someone in similar capacity or, in a wider sense, if he shares in it as part of the worshipping people.

Present canon law forbids *communicatio in sacris*. In Canon 731, pph. 2, it is forbidden to administer the sacraments to non-Catholic Christians, even when they ask for it. In Canon 1258 it is declared illicit for Catholics to take any active part, or assist actively, in the sacred actions of non-Catholic Christians. The canon specifies that a purely passive assistance may be tolerated, for a grave reason, at non-Catholic funerals, weddings, similar solemnities. Since Canon 1258 belongs to the section of the Code entitled "De Cultu Divino," the sacred actions in which Catholics are forbidden to share are undoubtedly the various forms of public worship of other religious bodies. Canon 1258 cannot be understood as prohibiting Catholics from praying with other Christians in meetings of a private character.

Since the directives of the Code are uniformly negative in regard to *communicatio in sacris* and do not make allowances for the difference between Orthodox liturgies and Protestant worship, many commentators on canon law have thought that the participation of a Catholic in the liturgy of another Church is an intrinsically illicit action (Vermeersch/Creusen, *Epitome Juris Canonici*, ed. 1954, vol. III, p. 11). In the English-speaking world Catholic authors have even tended to regard as illicit any sharing in the prayer of non-Catholic Christians. This attitude arose during the history of Catholics in England. To attend the service at the parish church of the Establishment and to pray with members of that Church was, in the century of the Reformation, regarded as a sign of abandoning the Catholic position in favor of the Anglican Church. Even in their last moments the Catholic martyrs refused the consolation of common prayer with priests of the Established Church.

The negative legislation of the Code, however, does not give a complete picture of Catholic practice in regard to *communicatio in sacris*. While canon 731 forbids giving the sacraments to other Christians, several decisions of the Roman Congregations have permitted giving the sacraments of penance and anointing to baptized non-Catholic Christians who are dying. Some canon lawyers extend these permissions to include the giving of the viaticum (cf. Vermeersch/Creusen, *op. cit.*, p. 12). It is also legitimate for Catholics in danger of death, in the absence of their own priest, to ask for the sacraments from an ordained priest belonging to a separated Church. These practices show that *communicatio in sacris* may not be regarded as intrinsically illicit.

178. Meanwhile, more and more the Protestant service comes to resemble the Mass. So noted Professor Cyril C. Richardson, of Union Theological Seminary, at the Roman Catholic-Protestant Colloquium at Harvard in March 1963. The outward characteristics of Protestant worship was really the first part of the Mass:

The modes of worship that characterize the Protestant denominations today are beginning to betray an increasing uniformity. There is a general Sunday morning service in the Presbyterian, Methodist, Lutheran, and Congregationalist traditions which, while there are differences in detail, nonetheless has assumed a basic pattern. It opens with a choral procession and with a sentence from Scripture, which is followed by a confession of sins and absolution. Then there is a responsive reading from the Psalter followed by hymnody or a chant. After this there comes the morning lesson and then the pastoral prayer, which may be a single long prayer or divided into shorter collects. The service tends to reach its climax in the sermon, which is followed or preceded by an anthem, the collection of alms, and a hymn. The service concludes with a benediction and a recessional.

This structure in essence is, of course, the first part of the Mass. There have been many changes but tne main outline of intercessory prayer, psalmody, and sermon goes back to the Synagogue service that the early Christians inherited from Judaism.

179. The proposed new denominational church services of Protestants reflect elements of the Roman Catholic Mass, not only in order, but in words and content, as Protestants as well as Catholics seek to get back to the earliest of liturgical forms.

For the United Presbyterians, more Latin words and actions paralleling the Mass appear in the rubrics of a new proposed order of worship. While Roman Catholics are getting away from the Latin, Protestants are holding on to it and adding some Latin terms. The new proposed Presbyterian service presents such words as *Kyrie Eleison* (Greek), *Agnus Dei, Gloria Patri, Gloria in Excelsis, Pax . . ., Sursum Corda, Sanctus, Benedictus qui venit.* . . . Recent Catholic trends to involve the people more in the Eucharistic celebration, e.g., by processions of the faithful with the offerings of the bread to the altar, are reflected, in "an interpretation of the Service for the Lord's Day." ("Among the new provisions in the service is the suggestion that when the Sacrament is observed, the elements, or a portion of them, may be brought forward at the time of the offering and placed upon the Lord's Table in accord with a quite early Christian practice" —*Service for the Lord's Day*, an interpretation, Westminster, 1964, pp. 45,46.) And in 1965 Roman Catholics and United Presbyterians agreed to publish together a common book of Bible study and worship, "in view of the common bond in the Lordship of Jesus Christ that already exists between members of the two communions." The book, to be used for the Week of Prayer for Christian Unity and other joint services, was decided on at a meeting of the U.S. Bishops' Commission for Ecumenical Affairs and the United Presbyterian Commission of Ecumenical Mission and Relations in November 1965, at the Krisheim Study

Center, Philadelphia. Co-authors are to be the Rev. Father
Maurice Schepers, O.P., professor of fundamental theology, St.
Stephen's College, Dover, Massachusetts, and the Rev. Dr. John
T. Middaugh, pastor of the Brown Memorial Presbyterian
Church, Baltimore.

In the Lutheran Church in America, attempts have been made
to dramatize the worship, particularly during Holy Week. Like
the Presbyterians, the Lutherans reflect the interest in the procession as a part of the Sunday morning worship rite. The Lutheran
"proposed Order for Holy Week and Easter" calls for a procession on Palm Sunday, "if possible to be made outdoors." There
are also services for Tenebrae ("shadows") representing the
darkness that covered the earth on the ninth hour, to be celebrated three nights a week—Wednesdays, Good Friday and an
Easter Vigil on Saturday. (Roman Catholics rarely use the rite,
primarily a monastery office. It is permitted, however, in the
Cathedral on Wednesday night of Holy Week.) "None of these
services has been taken verbatim from the current Roman Cath-
olice use," said the Rev. Dr. Edgar S. Brown, Jr., director of the
LCA Commission on Worship, "though the entire Western
Church is indebted to Rome for the preservation through the centuries of their form and structure. The fact is that we have conceded the Roman title to much that is the proper inheritance
of the ecumenical church, of which the Lutheran church is an
important part." Here is the Lutheran Tenebrae service (first
day) with explanation:

> *All present shall repeat the Lord's Prayer and the Apostles'
> Creed silently.*
> ANTIPHON: Hide not thy face from thy servant, for I am
> in trouble: hear me speedily.
>
> PSALM 69.
>
> ANTIPHON: (repeated) The first candle is extinguished.
>
> ANTIPHON: Thou shalt quicken me again: and shalt bring
> me up again from the depths of the earth.
>
> PSALM 71.
>
> ANTIPHON: (repeated) The second candle is extinguished.

ANTIPHON: Arise, O God, plead thine own cause: forget not the voice of thine enemies.

PSALM 74.

ANTIPHON: (repeated) The third candle is extinguished.

THE LESSON: Lamentations 1: 1-6, 12.

THE RESPONSORY FOR LENT.

ANTIPHON: Hide thy face from my sins: and blot out all mine iniquities.

PSALM 51.

ANTIPHON: (repeated) The fourth candle is extinguished.

ANTIPHON: With thee is the fountain of life: in thy light shall we see light.

PSALM 36.

ANTIPHON: (repeated) The fifth candle is extinguished.

ANTIPHON: Thou in thy mercy hast led forth thy people: which thou hast redeemed.

The Canticle *Cantemus Domino*

ANTIPHON: (repeated)

ANTIPHON: The Lord doth build up Jerusalem: he gathereth together the outcasts of Israel.

PSALM 147.

ANTIPHON: (repeated) The sixth candle is extinguished.

ANTIPHON: He was oppressed, and he was afflicted, yet he opened not his mouth: and the Lord hath laid on him the iniquity of us all.

The *Benedictus*

ANTIPHON (repeated)

During the Benedictus, the candles on the Altar are extinguished and, at its conclusion, all other lights in the Church are extinguished except the central candle which remains lighted on the hearse or seven-branched candlestick. This candle is removed from the hearse or candlestick and held at the Epistle corner of the Altar while the Antiphon is repeated. The candle is then placed behind the Altar or so screened that its light is not seen.

*The congregation may kneel: The minister shall say:*
For our sakes Christ became obedient unto death:
   *(Response)* Even the death of the Cross.
By the obedience of One:
   *(Response)* Shall many be made righteous.

Then shall follow a moment of silence, during which all shall say silently the Lord's prayer.

*Then shall the minister say:*
Almighty God, we beseech thee graciously to behold this thy family, for which our Lord Jesus Christ was contented to be betrayed and given up into the hands of wicked men, and to suffer death upon the Cross. *Amen.*
*After a space of silence, the Minister shall make a loud noise by striking a bench or book, and all present shall do likewise. The candle shall be taken from behind the Altar and held aloft before it. All rise and leave the Church in silence.*

180. An independent movement, called Western Orthodoxy, has come to the fore in the last few years, with an adapted rite of its own. Attention has been called to the century-old movement by the secession of the Rev. Edwin West, formerly rector of St. Mark's Episcopal Church, Palo Alto, California. West crossed paths with California bishop James A. Pike, quit his parish and went off to be an assistant rector in Houston. But a group, favoring West in the St. Mark's congregation, seceded, founded a new congregation and called West back as pastor. West renounced his orders and adopted the Western Orthodox Liturgy.

The movement, which numbers fifty churches in the United States, was developed by Dr. Joseph J. Overbeck, a Catholic professor in the theological faculty at Bonn. A liberal, he reacted against growing Catholic conservatism that came to a head at the First Vatican Council over the definition of Papal infallibility in 1870. While others quit the church to found the Old Catholic Churches, Overbeck left the priesthood; first to become a Lu-

theran, then to try to revive a Western church as he believed it
must have been before Medieval additions. He felt the Orthodox
church was the closest to Christ, containing some of the oldest
sees and having been sealed off from the West for centuries. He
was not ready to abandon Western religion, however—only to
adapt it to modes shared by East and West before the schism of
1054. In so doing, he felt he had restored a religion palatable
to a wide number of Catholics—to "Anglicans" who wanted to
get back to the old English church of St. Alban, the Venerable
Bede, and St. Edmund, and Orthodox and Catholics who wanted
only to recover the religion of the ecumenical councils before the
schism. The quasi-ecumenical Western Orthodox, who at least
were interested in common origins, rejected the papacy, the
dogma of the Immaculate Conception, Purgatory, and enforced
celibacy. The Eastern Orthodox confirmation, or Chrismation,
which follows baptism would be used; leavened bread would also
be used, and communion would be given under two species:
bread and wine. And there is an inclusion of the Orthodox "epiklesis," a special prayer invoking the power of the Holy Spirit
after the Consecration. Here is the Canon of the Mass for the
Western Orthodox and the Epiklesis:

> The Canon said by the celebrant in a low voice is the most
> solemn part of the Liturgy.
>
> Therefore Most Merciful Father, we humbly pray and be-
> seech thee through Jesus Christ thy Son our Lord, that thou
> wouldst be pleased to accept and bless these gifts, these offer-
> ings, these holy, spotless sacrifices, which we offer thee in the
> first place for thy holy Catholic Church, that thou wouldst
> vouchsafe to keep her in peace under thy protection, to bring
> her to unity and to guide her throughout the world: like-
> wise for N our Patriarch, for N our Metropolitan, for the
> Holy Synod of Antioch, for the President of these United
> States, and for all Orthodox believers who hold the Catholic
> and apostolic faith.
>
> Remember, O Lord, thy servants and all here present whose
> faith and devotion are known unto thee, for whom we offer,

or who offer to thee this sacrifice of praise for themselves and those belonging to them, for the salvation of their souls, for their health and welfare, and who pay their vows to thee, the eternal, living and true God. (Remember those for whom special intention is to be made.)

In communion with, and venerating first the memory of the glorious and ever-virgin Mary, Mother of our Lord and God Jesus Christ; and also of thy blessed apostles and martyrs (here individual saints may be named) and of all thy saints, through whose prayers grant that in all things we may be guarded by the help of thy protection. Through the same Christ our Lord. Amen.

We therefore pray thee, O Lord, mercifully to accept this offering of our service and that of all thy family; to order our days in thy peace, to deliver us from eternal damnation, and to number us in the flock of thine elect. Through Christ our Lord. Amen.

Which offering, we beseech thee, O God, to bless, consecrate, approve, make worthy and acceptable in every way, that it may become for us the Body and Blood of thy most beloved Son, Jesus Christ, our Lord.

Who, the day before he suffered, took bread into his holy and venerable hands and, with his eyes lifted up to heaven unto thee, God his almighty Father, giving thanks unto thee, he blessed, brake and gave it to his disciples, saying:

Take and eat ye all of this, for

THIS IS MY BODY

In like manner after he had supped, taking also this excellent chalice into his holy and venerable hands, again giving thanks unto thee, he blessed it, and gave it to his disciples saying: Take and drink ye all of this, for

THIS IS THE CUP OF MY BLOOD OF THE NEW AND
ETERNAL TESTAMENT, THE MYSTERY OF FAITH,

WHICH SHALL BE SHED FOR YOU AND FOR MANY
UNTO THE REMISSION OF SINS.

As oft as ye shall do these things, ye shall do them in remembrance of me.

Wherefore, O Lord, we thy servants, as also thy holy people,
calling to mind the blessed Passion of the same Christ thy
Son our Lord, his resurrection from the dead and glorious
Ascension into heaven, offer unto thy most excellent majesty
of thy gifts bestowed upon us a pure host, a holy host, a
spotless host, the holy bread of eternal life, and the chalice
of everlasting salvation.

Upon which vouchsafe to look with a favorable and serene
countenance, and to accept them as thou wert graciously
pleased to accept the gifts of thy just servant Abel, and the
sacrifice of our patriarch Abraham, and that which thy
high priest Melchisedec offered unto thee, a holy sacrifice, a
spotless victim.

### THE EPIKLESIS

And we beseech thee, O Lord, to send down thy Holy Spirit
upon these offerings, that he would make this bread the
precious Body of thy Christ, and that which is in this cup
the precious Blood of thy Son our Lord Jesus Christ, trans-
muting them by thy Holy Spirit.

Amen. Amen. Amen. . . .

181. Lutheran Max Lackmann, of Soest, Germany, hopes Lu-
theranism will someday become a German Catholic rite within
the Roman Catholic Church. (The Most Rev. Andreas Rohracher,
Catholic archbishop of Salzburg, has made a similar proposal that
the Lutheran Church be accepted as a separate branch in the
Roman Catholic Church with its own "Evangelical [Lutheran]-
Catholic" patriarchate.) Lackmann is a co-founder of the League
for Evangelical-Catholic Reunion, which has developed an
"Evangelical Mass."

a. The "Evangelical Mass" has these parts:

Preparatory Prayers
Entrance (Introit)
Song of Praise (Gloria)
Collect
Epistle
Alleluia—Hymn for the Week—(Gradual)
Gospel
Sermon
The Great Church Prayer
The Confession of Faith (Credo)
The Lord's Banquet—
Offertory Procession and Preparation of Gifts
Mixing of Wine With Water
Prayer Over the Offerings
The Preface and Thanksgiving Prayer
Words of Institution
The Our Father
The Greetings of Peace
The Sacred Meal—Priest's Communion
Communion—Admonition
Communion Hymn
Thanksgiving Prayer
The Dismissal
The Blessing

b. The Canon of the Evangelical Mass permits greater latitude in the nature of the Sacrifice (it is a presentation among other gifts, rather than a clear re-enactment—offering an "unblemished sacrifice" rather than the "victim" as the Roman wording has it) and there is wider latitude in the concept of the communion of saints. From the Evangelical Mass:

PRIEST: Be praised, Holy and Almighty God, Lord of heaven and earth. We glorify thee in the community of all thy saints. Thou hast been merciful upon your creatures, and, thou nast sent into our flesh the Savior, Jesus Christ, thy Son. In his name and in his remembrance we are gathered together, and we pray thee: Send down upon us thy Holy Spirit, and fill the household of thy entire Church with Him; through Him sanctify and renew us in body and soul; through Him sanctify these gifts, that they may become for us the body and blood of thy praiseworthy Son, our Lord Jesus Christ.

*(At the Words of Institution over the bread the priest takes
the ciborium—as at the words over the wine he takes the
chalice—in his left hand. . . .)*

Who in the night in which he was betrayed, took bread;
and, when he had given thanks, he brake it and gave it to his
disciples saying, TAKE, EAT; FOR THIS IS (sign of cross) MY
BODY WHICH IS GIVEN FOR YOU; THIS DO IN REMEMBRANCE
OF ME. After the same manner also, he took the cup, when
he had supped, and, when he had given thanks, he gave it
to them, saying, DRINK YE ALL OF IT; THIS CUP IS THE NEW
TESTAMENT IN (sign of cross) MY BLOOD, WHICH IS SHED
FOR YOU, AND FOR MANY, FOR THE REMISSION OF SINS; THIS
DO, AS OFT AS YE DRINK IT, IN REMEMBRANCE OF ME.

Therefore remembering, O Lord, heavenly Father, thy Son,
our Lord Jesus Christ, his saving passion and death, his
resurrection from the dead, and also his glorious ascension
into thy heavenly kingdom, where as our high priest he
represents us forever before thee, we offer to thy divine
majesty, from among thy gifts to us, this perfect, holy, and
unblemished sacrifice, the sacred bread of everlasting life
and the chalice of eternal salvation.

Let us all, who will partake at this altar of the sacred body
and precious blood of thy Son, be filled with all the blessings
of heaven! And since we all are, through the fellowship of
his body and blood, one body in Christ, gather thy people
together from all the ends of the earth, so that we, with all
the saints, may celebrate the wedding feast of the Lamb in
his kingdom.

*At the following words the Priest raises the ciborium with
his left hand and the chalice with his right to the level of
his eyes.*

PRIEST: Through him, and with him, and in him be all
honor and glory to thee, God, almighty Father, in the unity
of the Holy Spirit, forever and ever.

CONGREGATION: Amen.

*(All continue for a while in silent adoration.)*

182. A growing uniformity in worship is expressed in the new church buildings, especially in the pace-setting designs from Europe. Over the last forty or so years since World War I, the liturgical movement linking the congregation and the priesthood, coupled with a new openness in design techniques and materials, freed the European churches, Catholic and Protestant alike, from imitations of bygone centuries. Architect Arland A. Dirlam, of Boston, former president of the Church Architectural Guild of America and a three-time winner of citations at the Guild's annual conventions, noted in 1962 that "the new post-war churches of Europe, both Protestant and Catholic are remarkably similar in architecture."

"Importance of the preaching of the word is exemplified in every post-war continental church," he said. "The pulpit has a positive, permanent, elevated position. The priest or pastor, while assuming a new or rather a more obvious presentation of his role as a fellow worshipper, is continuing to assume and fulfill his assigned responsibility as a spiritual leader. . . . "European churches have returned to the basic fundamentals and quest for corporate worship."

In 1966, a fund-raising effort conducted in the United States by Consolata Missionary, John Garbolino, and others, sought to revive old St. Stephen Rotondo, built in A.D. 470 on the Caelian, highest of Rome's hills, as an ecumenical church to be used for ecumenical rites. In Kansas City, the first new ecumenical parish, St. Mark's was launched. Roman Catholics, Presbyterians, Episcopalians and the United Church of Christ will each contribute $100,000 a year to support the new parish. Although there is to be a common sanctuary, each group will conduct its own rites separately; much like the pattern in the armed forces. St. Mark's will provide special social projects for its inner city parish.

Catholics and Anglicans in Kompala, Uganda, sought to raise $22,400 in 1966 to jointly build a chapel for 200 at the local Mulago Hospital. A common chapel for all Christians was built by three architects—Protestant, Catholic and Orthodox—at Mt.

Serein on a slope of Mt. Ventoux in southern France. Catholic Bishop James Navagh of Paterson, New Jersey has organized an interfaith advisory building committee for his Diocese.

On the National scene a tri-faith Center for Interfaith Research on Religious Architecture was established officially after three years of consultations on September 13, 1965. Sponsors were the American Institute of Architects, the Commission on Synagogue Administration of the Union of American Hebrew Congregations and Central Conference of American Rabbis, the Department of Church Building and Architecture of the National Council of Churches of Christ in the USA, and the National Catholic Liturgical Conference. The center, to have a minimum staff of six, is to have a budget of $1,615,000 for its first five years.

a. The philosophy of the new center was outlined in a 1962 statement of the Interfaith Research Steering Committee on Religious Buildings which later gave birth to the proposal for a center.

> PREAMBLE: When we build religious buildings, we do not begin with what we believe about God and our reasonable response to building in our time and place. We must realize that we do not worship *in* our religious buildings but that we also worship *with* them. If we do not know what we believe or if we do not believe earnestly or deeply . . . or, if we are unable to give a reason for the faith that is in us, we cannot inform the architect or open him to inspiration. In view of the rapidly changing nature of our society and the ever increasing investment of funds in religious buildings, it is deemed advisable that a thorough study of the situation be undertaken.
>
> PURPOSE: The promotion of a religious architecture and art, through the materials and techniques presently available, expressing a meaningful and spiritual affirmation and manifesting a living tradition in forms that speak in a positive way to our contemporary society.

b. Some of the projects to be undertaken by the new Center for Interfaith Research on Religious Architecture:

(1) The collection, examination and systematization of materials and relevant writings from all of the disciplines related to the Center's concerns.

(2) Study of the rise and varied development of church and synagogue architecture, particularly in America and within the context of changing American culture.

(3) Particular studies of the historical, theological and liturgical development of each of the religious communities as that development affected patterns of religious buildings.

(4) Contemporary inclusive and particular studies of religious building trends and of related trends in redefinition of the mission of the various religious bodies in America.

(5) Systematic data collection from all religious bodies on particulars of building activity, trends, problems. . . .

183. There is one week of the year, when Catholics and Protestants make a point of praying together in special services. It is the Week of Prayer for Christian Unity, from January 18 to January 25. The week in its current form owes much to Abbé Paul Couturier, of Lyon (see Chapter II), who proposed an interfaith week of prayer in an article in the *Revue Apologetique* in December 1935. The Week got underway in Lyon in January the next year. Couturier brought the emphasis of prayer for unity, rather than conversions.

There had been a week of prayer for unity among Roman Catholics in connection with the Festival of St. Peter's Chair that traces back to the seventh century. Called "chair" of St. Peter, it marks the day when St. Peter traditionally first sat in his episcopal chair and became the first pope. Since 1908, the feast day had been widened into an octave which includes the day plus the seven following. This development, curiously, was spurred by two Anglican priests, Spencer Jones and Paul Wattson, who had attempted to launch the Church Unity Octave among Anglicans. When Wattson was converted nine months later to Catholicism, the observance of a unity octave passed into the hands of Catholics. Only, with Wattson it was a prayer for return.

Meanwhile the Faith and Order movement of the Protestants and Orthodox called for prayers for unity at Pentecost. But in 1940 it recommended the January week of prayer to the churches. When the World Council of Churches was organized in 1948, the Faith and Order movement, now an official WCC commission, took on active sponsorship of a January Week of Unity. Now the Faith and Order Commission of the WCC and the Roman Catholic Association for Christian Unity, which continues the work of Abbé Couturier, in Lyon, sponsor the week on the international level. In the United States, the week of prayer for unity is promoted by the National Council of Churches and the Friars of the Atonement, Graymoor, Garrison, New York, which Father Paul Wattson founded and to which he brought the "octave" (a word disliked and discarded later by Couturier).

Among United States Roman Catholics the Week of Prayer for Christian Unity which influenced dialogue, itself became influenced by the growing dialogue, and in 1960 the intentions for prayer were modified to tone down the call for "return" of non-Roman Catholics. The Rev. Father Angelus F. Delahunt, superior general of the Franciscan Friars of the Atonement, center for the Octave started by Father Paul Watson, announced these new intentions, with the original ones in parenthesis:

> Jan. 18—The union of all Christians in the one true Faith and in the Church. (Return of the "other sheep" to the fold of St. Peter, the One Shepherd.)
>
> Jan. 19—Return of separated Eastern Christians to communion with the Holy See. (Return of all Oriental separatists to communion with the Apostolic See.)
>
> Jan. 20—Reconciliation of Anglicans with the Holy See. (Submission of Anglicans to the authority of the Vicar of Christ.)
>
> Jan. 21—Reconciliation of European Protestants with the Holy See. (That the Lutherans and Protestants of Continental Europe may find their way back to the Holy Church.)

Jan. 22—That American Christians become one in union with the Chair of Peter. (That Christians in America may become One in communion with the Chair of Peter.)

Jan. 23—Restoration of lapsed Catholics to the sacramental life of the Church. (Return to the Sacraments of lapsed Catholics.)

Jan. 24—That the Jewish people come into their inheritance in Jesus Christ. (Conversion of the Jews.)

Jan. 25—The Missionary extension of Christ's kingdom throughout the world. (Missionary conquest of the world for Christ.)

184. In the United States, three leading clergymen of the three major Christian faiths in January 1965, jointly asked their constituency to join in the Week of Prayer for Christian Unity. The three were the Rev. Dr. Eugene Carson Blake, stated clerk of the United Presbyterians; Joseph Cardinal Ritter, of St. Louis; and Archbishop Iakovos, primate of the Greek Orthodox Archdiocese of North and South America. On the local level, the Week of Prayer for Christian Unity was heralded with equal interest. In Massachusetts, for example, Richard Cardinal Cushing and the Rev. Albert J. Penner, president of the Massachusetts Council of Churches, together sent out this letter, which they signed, to Massachusetts Protestants and Catholics:

Dear Brothers in Christ:

We enter this new year of our Lord 1965 with great expectation and profound humility. The work of the Holy Spirit in our time fills us with great hope: all Christians throughout the world are becoming more and more aware of the tragedy of our divisions, the sinfulness of our separations, and the imperative of our being one in our common Lord. This is a most encouraging sign of the Spirit's work in gathering all believers in Christ into the unity he wills.

Yet at the same time we cannot but realize that the work of unity is a divine activity and that mere human efforts avail nothing if the Lord does not build up his household. For these reasons and in this same spirit of hope and humility we send this joint letter to you, our Christian brothers. . . .

During this week, it is also urgent that clergy and laity find ways of meeting with separated brothers, joining with them in Christian conversation and praying with them for the unity the Lord wills. There are many ways of doing this; we suggest the following few possibilities: a deepening of the bond of friendship among the clergy of each community; meetings of clergy for the purpose of dialogue and to examine common civic and social responsibilities; public meetings and discussions in which separated brothers come to know one another and understand more deeply the seriousness of our division; joint services consisting of scripture readings, homilies and prayer.

As has been frequently observed, the most fruitful efforts for unity are those which are born and grow not in great church councils but in the hearts and lives and churches of the local community. For this reason, we urge all Christians not only to observe the coming Week of Unity, but also to make unity a constant concern during the entire year.

With humility and hope in our reconciling Lord,
    Albert J. Penner, president, Massachusetts
    Council of Churches
    Richard Cardinal Cushing, Archbishop of Boston

185. Around the world, reports of the cooperation of the churches of both faiths in the observance of the Week of Prayer for Christian Unity were many in 1964 and 1965. Nearly 2,000 Roman Catholics and Protestants took part in unity week services at Protestant and Catholic churches in Haarlem, The Netherlands; in the Town Hall of Oxford, England, the Rev. Father Paul Verghese, of the Syrian Orthodox Church in India and mem-

ber of the WCC staff in Geneva, paid tribute to Pope John XXIII; in Chicago, the late Albert Cardinal Meyer joined with Protestants in a service of prayer at the Chicago Theological Seminary; in Pueblo, Colorado, 50 Episcopalians and 35 Roman Catholics held a three-hour discussion; in Ottawa, Canada, 1,000 gathered for an interfaith service—a minister led the prayers, a priest gave the sermon; in Buenos Aires Lutheran Orthodox and Roman Catholic churches held joint prayers for unity; in Cairo, Egypt, services alternated among Protestant, Coptic, and Orthodox each night; in Munster, Germany, 400 met in a Catholic Student Hostel for an interfaith service; in Copenhagen, there was an interfaith procession to various churches for services; in Newburyport, Massachusetts, 150 persons of the Roman Catholic Immaculate Conception Parish visited churches of other faiths to hear pastors explain their beliefs; in New Orleans 5,000 of all faiths visited the Greek Orthodox Cathedral of the Holy Trinity.

On January 21, 1964, eighty persons joined in an Anglican oriented Evening Prayer service during the Week of Prayer for Christian Unity at Margaret Hall School for Girls, Versailles, Kentucky:

> The school Chaplain, the Rev. William H. Dunphey, officiated at the service, which is one of the two daily Offices of Prayer in the Book of Common Prayer of the Episcopal Church. Intended for worship by clergy and lay people in parishes, the Office combines elements drawn from the Monastic Breviary Hours of Vespers and Compline with lessons from the Old and New Testaments and ancient collects of the season.

> The first lesson, from Jeremiah 31: 1-14, was read by the Rev. John E. Cleek, pastor of the Baptist Church in Milville, Kentucky. The second lesson, from Ephesians 4: 1-16, was read by the Presbyterian minister of Versailles, the Rev. W. B. Eyster. The congregation participated in the singing of three hymns, the responsive reading of Pss. 122 and 133, the Magnificat and Nunc dimittis, and in the recitation in unison of the Lord's Prayer and the Apostle's Creed. The Rev. Father Carroll Stuhlmueller, C.P., Professor of Scrip-

tural Studies at the Passionist Seminary in Louisville, Kentucky, preached the sermon, taking as his text the words of Jesus Christ, "The Kingdom of God is in the midst of you," from St. Luke 17: 20, 21.

The service was held in the school gymnasium where a temporary altar was erected and adorned with two lighted candles. A crucifix was hung behind the altar. Only the officiant was vested, in a surplice. Father Stuhlmueller wore the habit of the order. . . .

The service of Evening Prayer was the climax of a Vigil of Prayer which was offered in the school chapel, where the Blessed Sacrament is reserved. During the period of the Vigil from noon until the service began at 7:30 p.m. one or more students, faculty members, or local lay persons was praying for Christian Unity. An informal gathering and animated conversation followed the service. . . .

186. In 1966, the situations of joint prayer services during the Week of Prayer for Christian Unity again circled the globe. An estimated 1,000 unity meetings were held in Britain including the Trafalgar Square rally with a procession down Whitehall ending in Westminster Abbey with a service of evensong. Over all, the participation of the Orthodox was more notable. In Paris, the president of the Protestant Federation of France, Pastor Charles Westphal, spoke in an inter-Christian service held at the Russian Orthodox Cathedral; the Orthodox Basilica of St. Victor in Marseilles hosted a jointly sponsored service with Joseph Cardinal Martin of Rouen, Protestant Marc Boegner, and Russian Orthodox Archbishop Bloom, as speakers. In Geneva, a representative of the Moscow Patriarchate, Msgr. Antoine, exarch for Western Europe of the Moscow Patriarchate of the Russian Orthodox, gave the sermon in a joint service at the Cathedral of St. Pierre. In Vienna, an Ecumenical Youth Council held a jointly sponsored service in a Greek Orthodox Church; in New York, the Holy Trinity Greek Orthodox Cathedral joined eight Catholic parishes and 18 Protestant churches in a service at St. Ignatius Loyola Roman Catholic Church; in San Francisco's Grace Epis-

copal Cathedral, the Rev. Father Theodore Mackin, S.J., of the University of Santa Clara's theology department, and Southern Baptist, John McGlendon, of Golden Gate Seminary, San Francisco, took part in a service in which Lutheran Joseph Sittler of the University of Chicago Divinity School was the preacher; in Seattle, Orthodox, Protestants, and Roman Catholics took part in a service in the Seattle Center arena—among the speakers were the Most Rev. Thomas A. Connolly, Catholic archbishop of Seattle, and the Rev. Robert A. Thomas, president of the Greater Seattle Council of Churches; in Taipei, Taiwan, Catholic Auxiliary Bishop Paul Cheng, Episcopal Bishop C. L. Wong, and the Rev. H. C. Cheng, acting moderator of the Presbyterian Church of Formosa, joined in a service.

For the first time, in 1966, a common leaflet for the Week of Prayer for Christian Unity in the United States was prepared under the sponsorship of the World Council of Churches' Commission of Faith and Order, the NCC's Department of Faith and Order, and with the recommendation of the United States Bishops' Commission for Ecumenical Affairs. "We look upon this joint effort as an important step in the development of our working relationship with National and World Councils of Churches," said the Very Rev. Msgr. William W. Baum, executive director of the Bishops' Commission for Ecumenical Affairs.

Here is the order of service for the first day (January 18) in the common leaflet of 1966 for the Week of Prayer for Christian Unity:

*Introduction:* Save us, O Lord our God,
*and gather us from among the nations*
that we may give thanks to thy holy name
*and glory in thy praise.* (Psalm 106: 47).

*Hymn or Psalm 100.*

*Prayer* [various prayers of the faiths are included in the booklet]

*First Lesson:* Genesis 12: 1-5.

*Second Lesson:* Romans 15: 7-13.

*Confession of Faith:* The Apostles' Creed

*Homily or Meditation:*

When God calls Abraham, solitary and powerless as he is, he anticipates his gathering together of the multitudes of mankind. By the coming of Christ, son of Abraham and Savior of the world, the blessing conferred upon the people of the Covenant is extended to all nations. The hope of Israel becomes the hope of many peoples; new voices, new languages can now give praise to the God of mercy and lovingkindness.

Thus it is with the Church of God: a little flock amidst the thronging nations of the earth, yet promised to be "a great multitude which no man could number, out of every nation, and of all tribes, peoples, and languages" (Rev. 7: 9). Are we then aware of this universal vocation of ours, for transcending our national and racial limits and our narrow denominationalism? Do we live as those who "receive one another, as Christ also received us, to the glory of God (Rom. 15: 7) ?"

> *Litany* [selections from the Liturgy of the Reformed Church of France and from the interdenominational service in Montreal, July 21, 1963, during the Fourth World Conference on Faith and Order].

*Intercession:*
For the unity of all Christian people for their renewal and sanctification in truth and love—for the World Council of Churches and other councils of churches—for the World Evangelical Fellowship—for all movements and organizations serving Christian unity—for responsible teaching within the churches—for faithful perseverance in common and private prayer. [On other days of the eight-day Octave, other churches, and groups, including the Roman Catholic Church are remembered in this final intercession.]

> *The Lord's Prayer.*

> *The Blessing:*
> Let us bless the Lord. *Thanks be to God.*

May the God of steadfastness and encouragement grant you to live in such harmony with one another, in accord with

Christ Jesus, that together you may with one voice glorify
the God and Father of our Lord Jesus Christ. Amen. (Romans 15: 5, 6).

187. By 1966, not only had the half-century old week of joint
prayers in January developed to a wider context, but other periods of the church year were being adapted to joint prayer and
Bible programs also. Pentecost was natural for this (Germany
and Latin American countries observe the Week of Prayer for
Christian Unity then), but surprisingly enough, so was the traditional Protestant Reformation Sunday. Across the United
States, the annual Reformation rallies, often anti-Catholic in
tone because of the long-time emphasis on Martin Luther's break
with Rome accompanied by his alleged hammering of a list of
challenges to the Church of Rome on a university church door in
Wittenberg, around October 31, 1517, were revised as Festivals
of Unity. In several cases, Catholic priests were heard. The Rev.
Father Bruce Vawter, of Kenrick Seminary, St. Louis, spoke to
a Reformation rally in Fulton, Missouri. He reviewed some of
the causes leading to the Reformation, and answered questions.
He had been invited to be the speaker by the United Campus
Christian Fellowship of Westmister College, a Presbyterian-
related school, and William Woods College (Disciples of Christ).
In Chicago, the Rev. Father John L. McKenzie, S.J., spoke, along
with Lutheran (Missouri-Synod) clergymen at a Reformation
observance at the University of Chicago's Rockefeller Chapel, in
1965. In Santa Cruz, New Mexico, the Santa Cruz Area Council
of Churches sponsored an interfaith forum on "Re-examining
the Reformation" held in the First Congregational Church with
cooperation of the Messiah Lutheran Church which had previously held an interfaith forum of its own; Reformation Sunday, Oct. 31, 1965, was marked in Dubuque by a joint Catholic-
Protestant Ecumenical Assembly at the Dubuque Senior High
School. The program was planned by a six-member committee,
made up of Catholic and Protestant representatives. The 90-
minute program included a combined choir concert representing
churches and convents of the city and several sermonettes by the
various clergy. The 450th celebration of the nailing of the 95
theses on the door of the cathedral church in Wittenberg will be

observed with repentance and renewal rather than polemics, said the Rev. Dr. Malvin H. Lundeen, in charge of an Inter-Lutheran committee for the event in 1967.

In Kansas City, Missouri, the Council of Churches in 1964 and 1965 changed the name of the annual Reformation rally to Festival of Faith and proceeded to invite area Roman Catholic clergy.

a. Catholics in Kansas City received this invitation in 1964 for the new kind of Reformation Day service from Shrum Burton, president of the Council, addressed to the Most Rev. Charles H. Helmsing, Bishop of Kansas City-St. Joseph:

> As president of the Council of Churches of Greater Kansas City, it is my happy privilege to forward an invitation extended by our administrative committee, in observance of the renewal and the reform that comes in a traditional observance of the Martin Luther emphasis. We have been seeing a change in our attitudes that we hope is positive. Instead of talking of a Reformation day service we now designate this as a festival of faith observance. Our invitation is a most cordial one to members of the Roman Catholic community to share in the importance of inner renewal. In our service on Nov. 1, 1964, we would be happy if members of the clergy could participate in the clergy processional. We would be happy for any degree of participation, that might enable us to venture further ways of ecumenicity.

b. The reply to Mr. Burton, who is also pastor of the Country Club Methodist Church, Kansas City, came the next day, October 23, written in absence of the bishop, by the chancellor, the Rt. Rev. Msgr. Joseph V. Sullivan:

> In the absence of his excellency Bishop Helmsing, I am pleased to acknowledge receipt of your kind letter to the Bishop of October 22, forwarding an invitation to share in the observance of the festival of faith. I have discussed your suggestion with our Vicar General and with some of the members of the Diocesan Ecumenical Commission. The priests of the commission as well as some of the lay mem-

bers of the Catholic Councils of Men and Women will be present for the observance and the other clergy will be advised that they are welcome to attend. Perhaps from this will grow greater response annually to this observance. The Diocese is happy to cooperate with the Council of Churches of Greater Kansas City in every way to promote love, fellowship and understanding among all the people of God and to promote renewal.

188. In Cincinnati, the Reformation Sunday was dropped altogether with a recommendation that World Wide Communion Sunday, the first Sunday in October, be observed instead. Cincinnati Council of Churches Executive Director Richard D. Isler wrote the local pastors in June 1964:

Dear Fellow Clergymen:

The purpose of this letter is to inform you that the annual Festival of Faith, traditionally held for the past 17 years on Reformation Sunday, will not be held in October of 1964. The Board of Directors of the Council of Churches has come to this decision for basically two reasons.

The first is the declining interest displayed in Cincinnati and in other cities across the country in this type of an event. The second reason for the cancellation of the 1964 Festival is the continuing financial difficulty being experienced by the Council. As you know, the Festival has constituted an "out-of-pocket" loss of between $1500 and $2000 each year.

In light of the cancellation of the Festival, it is suggested that area and neighborhood ministerial groups and federations of churches may wish to hold their own Reformation Day services.

Another suggestion which we would heartily commend to you is the holding of neighborhood services of ecumenical worship on the evening of World Wide Communion Sunday, the first Sunday in October. There are few days in the Chris-

tian year which more vividly illustrate our basic oneness in
Jesus Christ and the tragic division of His Church. All who
bear the name of Christ gather around His table on that day.
Even at such a gathering for the Sacrament, we are reminded that there are barriers which prevent us from par-
taking together of His Body and Blood.

A worship service on the evening of World Wide Communion Sunday on a neighborhood basis would remind us
that despite our separations we are One in Him. If such
services are undertaken, it would be entirely appropriate
to make overtures to the Roman Catholic priests and
churches in our neighborhoods, soliciting their prayers and
cooperation. We live in a time when new approaches and
experimentation of an ecumenical nature are demanded.
With best wishes, I remain

> Sincerely,
> Richard D. Isler
> Executive Director

189. Catholics and Protestants continued to find many ways to
get together for worship, despite the fact that they avoided the
regular periods of worship, such as the Mass, or the Protestant
Sunday morning worship services. In Leeds, England, in 1964,
more than 700 Catholics and Anglicans formed a living torch-
light cross at a Christmas carol service held in the open air.
Catholics formed the upright beam with their torches and the
Anglicans formed the arms of the cross. At Westminster Abbey,
London, a Catholic priest, the Rev. Father Edmund Jones, a
Benedictine, led the prayers from the pulpit in a three-hour
prayer service for Christian Unity on the Feast of the Transfiguration with Protestant, Anglican, and Orthodox leaders also
participating. Two hundred Anglican clergy and laymen put a
petition for Christian unity on the altar of the Catholic shrine at
Aylesford, England; the petition said: "We make an act of reparation for all the evils that were done by our forefathers at the
Reformation in destroying this holy shrine. We have prayed this
day for the reunion of Christendom and the healing of the six-
teenth-century breach between Rome and the Anglican Com-

munion." In Kobe, Japan, successive ecumenical services were held in the Anglican Cathedral, a Roman Catholic church, and a Union (Protestant) church. Sponsor was the Kobe Ecumenical Study Group, representing clergy and laymen of the three faiths. In the Union Church, the Rev. Father Pietro Peretti, S.J., gave the sermon and said that "unity is not uniformity" but that there was room for many kinds of liturgies. A pilgrimage of English Roman Catholics and Anglicans went to Russia to conduct an all night prayer for unity, August 28, 1965, in the Trinity-Sergius Monastery at Zagorsk. A service of intercession for "Christians suffering persecution in Russia" was held in the Eglise des Etrangers in Paris in May, 1964, with Catholic Jean Danielou, Orthodox Boris Bobrinskoi, and Pastor André Dumas standing beside each other at the altar—an Orthodox choir chanted a liturgy remembering all the persecuted, with the congregation responding "kyrie eleison." Marking the World Day of Prayer, March 5, 1965, Orthodox, Catholic, and Protestant women held prayer services together in Tokyo, Hong Kong, Lagos, Nigeria, Nuku'alofa, Tonga. In Albuquerque, New Mexico, on January 3, 1965, 2,000 persons met for an interfaith service in the civic auditorium. The service included a prayer by the Rev. Harry Summers, executive secretary of the New Mexico State Council of Churches, and talks on "The common dignity of all men" by a local rabbi, a priest, and a minister. In a Thanksgiving eve service in a Roman Catholic church in Park Ridge, Illinois, a Southern Baptist minister gave the sermon. In San Antonio, Texas, on Pentecost Sunday, June 2, 1963, an "Evening of Ecumenical Witness" (it was repeated in 1965 and 1966) drew 5,000 Protestants and Catholics. The program was arranged under the auspices of the Most Rev. Stephen A. Leven, Catholic auxiliary bishop of San Antonio; Methodist Bishop Paul V. Galloway, of San Antonio; Episcopal bishops Everett H. Jones and R. Earl Dicus (suffragan), of the Diocese of West Texas. Bishop Leven and Methodist Bishop Fred Pierce Corson, of Philadelphia, were speakers. Here is the Order of Service:

*Presiding:* Bishop Everett H. Jones, Episcopal Diocese of West Texas.

*Call to Worship and Witness:* Bishop Jones.

*Hymn,* "Holy, Holy, Holy": To be sung by all (Congregation standing).

*Invocation:* Dr. Samuel Terry, Pastor, Madison Square Presbyterian Church, San Antonio.

*Hymn,* "We Gather Together": To be sung by choir (Congregation seated)—Choir represents 18 churches, directed by Gerald Ingraham, associate professor of music, Our Lady of Lake College.

*Introduction of Speaker:* James M. Gaines, former president, San Antonio Chamber of Commerce.

*Address:* Bishop Stephen A. Leven, auxiliary bishop, Archdiocese of San Antonio.

*Hymn,* "Love Divine, All Love Excelling": To be sung by choir. (Congregation seated.)

*Introduction of Speaker:* Bishop Paul V. Galloway, Methodist Bishop of San Antonio-Northwest Texas Conferences.

*Address:* Bishop Fred Pierce Corson, bishop of The Methodist Church, Philadelphia, Pa.

*Hymn,* "Faith of Our Fathers": To be sung by all (Congregation standing.)

*Benediction:* Dr. S. H. James, pastor, Second Baptist Church, San Antonio.

190. Roman Catholics and Protestants joined together in an ecumenical thanksgiving service for the passage of the Civil Rights Bill. Sponsored by the Grand Rapids Council of Churches, the service was held in St. Paul's Methodist Church, Grand

Rapids, with the Rt. Rev. Msgr. Charles W. Popell, pastor of St.
Andrew's Catholic Cathedral, as speaker.

"A Christian Memorial Service for Civil Rights Workers"
was held in Tokyo, October 25, 1964, at the Union Church.
Participants included the Rev. Father John Clarkston, S.J.; the
Rev. Samuel Cox, Methodist; James Dator, Episcopal layman;
Sam H. Franklin and Emery Fleming, Presbyterian laymen; the
Rev. Thomas Harris, Reformed Church in America missionary;
the Rev. Lloyd Neve, Lutheran seminary professor; the Rev.
Hallam Sorrock, vice president of the International Christian
University, and the Rev. Donald Wheeler, American Baptist.

> The order of worship:
>
> *Call and Invocation*—James Dator.
>
> *Hymn*—"Once to Every Man and Nation"
>
> *Thanksgiving Litany*
>
> *Speech*—"The Cause and the Victims," Sam Franklin
>
> *Litany of Confession*
>
> Reader: Let us confess our sins to Almighty God.
>
> We confess our collective guilt before Thee for the murders
> of many persons who have been killed because of their race
> and in the struggle for civil rights.
>
> Congregation: Forgive us and help us, we humbly beseech
> Thee, O Lord. . . .
>
> *Speech*—"Expression of Sympathy and Support," John
> Clarkson, S.J.
>
> *Prayer of Intercession:*
>
> Reader: O Lord, hear our prayer.

Congregation: And let our cry come unto **Thee**.

Reader: Let us pray: That all perpetrators of wrong may be turned from evil ways and given new hearts to serve Thee and their fellowmen.

Congregation: Hear our prayer, O God.

Reader: That members of Citizens' Councils, the Ku Klux Klan, and like organizations may cease to desecrate the image of man as revealed in the Lord Jesus Christ . . . [There followed special intercession for civil rights martyrs James Chaney, Andrew Goodman, and Michael Schwerner, and their families and others.]

*Speech*—"The Tragedy as a Call to Dedication," Donald Wheeler.

*Speech*—"Significance of This Event for Japanese Christians," Masao Takenaka, professor of Christian Ethics, School of Theology, Doshisha University, Kyoto.

*Prayer of Dedication.*

*Hymn*—"In Christ There is No East or West."

*Benediction.*

191. A cooperative Christmas pageant has been put on by Oklahoma City Catholics and Protestants during the Christmas season, since 1963, at the Oklahoma City Municipal Auditorium. The Christmas program, "The Prince of Peace," intersperses music with a chronological acting out of God's redemption of man, beginning with the first encounter of God with man at the Garden of Eden. Sponsored by the Roman Catholic Churches of Oklahoma City and the Greater Oklahoma City Council of Churches, the pageant which is subtitled "The Story of the Advent—the coming of Christ—from the promise first given by God at Eden to the humble manger in Judea," begins with an in-

troduction by the Rev. Father Edward Jeep, of St. Patrick's
Catholic Church: "As Man is turned out of Paradise for suc-
cumbing to Satan's temptations, God promises later redemption. But sin spreads, and the Flood is sent to wash away the
sinners. Through Noah, God makes certain Man will have another chance. But even then Man continues his sinful ways. . . ."

In Christ Church, Cambridge, Massachusetts, Sunday, November 29, 1964, at 4:30 P.M. the congregations, choirs, clergy of
Christ Church and St. Paul's Roman Catholic Church, all took
part in an Advent ecumenical service. Nearly 1,000 heard the
service in the church or in the overflow space in the parish house,
hall and library, while about 200 had to be turned away. Participating clergy included the Rt. Rev. Anson Phelps Stokes,
Episcopal bishop of Massachusetts, the Most Rev. Thomas J.
Riley, auxiliary bishop of Boston, the Rt. Rev. Augustine F.
Hickey, vicar general of the Archdiocese of Boston, the Rev.
Gardiner M. Day, rector, Christ Episcopal Church, Cambridge,
and the Catholic and Protestant chaplains at Harvard. "This was
not a regular Advent service such as one would have found normally on that particular Sunday in Advent in either of the two
Churches," said the Rev. Gardiner Day. "It was, indeed, a very
special Advent service worked out with great care by the Roman
Catholic chaplain, Father [Joseph] Collins and our Episcopal
chaplain, the Rev. William J. Schneider. I composed the opening
bidding prayer in litany form and the two chaplains chose the
lessons and other prayers, etc., all of which had to be approved
by the proper authorities in each church. The combined choirs
of the two churches numbered about 80 people and occupied a
considerable portion of the front pews of the church as well as
the choir stalls in the chancel. In the sanctuary near the altar
were Roman Catholic Bishop Riley, Episcopal Bishop Stokes,
Msgr. Hickey, rector of St. Paul's Church, myself as rector of
Christ Church and the two chaplains." The service followed this
order:

*Processional Hymn:* "O Come, O Come Emmanuel"

*Bidding Prayer:* The Rev. Gardiner M. Day

Dearly Beloved in the Lord, we are gathered together to

dedicate ourselves to God that our hearts and minds being cleansed and purified by His Holy Spirit, we may on this first day of Advent observe our growing unity of spirit by preparing for the celebration of God's revelation of Himself in the birth of His Son, Jesus Christ, our Lord, on Christmas.

Let us first in a moment of silence confess our own unworthiness and our own sinfulness. . . . (There follow nine prayers in unison, each preceded by a period of silence, and then a concluding period of silence and prayer.)

*Silence*

*Closing Prayer* of litany to be said in unison by the congregation:

Almighty God, give us grace that we may cast away the works of darkness, and put upon us the armour of light, now in the time of this mortal life, in which thy Son Jesus Christ came to visit us in great humility; that in the last day, when he shall come again in his glorious majesty to judge both the quick and the dead, we may rise to the life immortal, through him who liveth and reigneth with thee and the Holy Ghost, now and ever. Amen.

*Scripture:* Isaiah 7: 10-15: The Rev. Joseph I. Collins. (Revised Standard Version.)

*Homily:* The Rt. Rev. Anson Phelps Stokes.

*Hymn:* (kneeling) "Creator of the Stars of Night" (Six stanzas alternating between the Men's Choir, congregation, and St. Paul's Choir School Boys.)

*Collect* (New Roman Missal) : The Rt. Rev. Msgr. Augustine F. Hickey.
Hasten, we beseech Thee, O Lord, and delay not; and bestow upon us the help of Thy heavenly power, that they who trust in Thy goodness may be helped by the consolations of

Thy coming. Who livest and reignest, with God the Father, in the unity of the Holy Ghost, God, world without end. Amen.

*Hymn:* "Of the Father's Love Begotten"

*Scripture:* Romans 13: 11-14a: The Rev. William J. Schneider. (Revised Standard Version.)

*Homily:* The Most Rev. Thomas J. Riley.

*Choral Response* from Advent Cantata No. 61, Johann Bach: Combined choirs and instrumental ensemble.

*Collect* (New Roman Missal) : The Rt. Rev. Augustine F. Hickey.

O God, Who settest straight what has gone astray, and gatherest together what is scattered, and keepest what Thou hast gathered together, we beseech Thee in Thy mercy to pour down on Christian people the grace of union with Thee, that putting aside disunion and attaching themselves to the true shepherd of Thy Church, we may be able to render Thee due service. Through our Lord Jesus Christ, Thy Son, Who liveth and reigneth with Thee in the unity of the Holy Ghost, God, world without end. Amen.

*Offertory Sentence:* The Rev. William J. Schneider.

*Chorale:* "Zion hears her watchmen's voices," from Cantata No. 140, Johann Bach: Men's Choir and Instrumental Ensemble.

*Hymn:* (Stanzas 1 and 2 Congregation standing) : "Wake, Awake for Night is Flying" (sung in parts by all).

*A Prayer of St. Chrysostom:* The Rt. Rev. Augustine F. Hickey.

Almighty God, who hast given us grace at this time with one accord to make our common supplications unto thee;

and dost promise that when two or three are gathered together in thy Name thou wilt grant their requests; Fulfill
now, O Lord, the desires and petitions of thy servants, as
may be most expedient for them; granting us in this world
knowledge of thy truth, and in the world to come life everlasting. Amen

*Blessing:* The Rt. Rev. Anson Phelps Stokes.

*Recessional Hymn:* "Now Thank We All Our God."

192. The Roman Catholic parish of St. James in Schwechat,
Austria, near Vienna, held a joint Catholic-Protestant service
February 1, 1965, reportedly the first combined service in Aus-
trian history. The Catholic pastor read the prayers, a Protestant
minister gave the sermon based on John 1: 35-42. "The point
was: Go to Jesus and take your brother with you," a spokesman for the parish said. Here is the outline of that service:

*Hymn:* "Praise the Lord, the Mighty King of Honors!"

*Psalm 121* (122—King James)

*Hymn:* "Praise the Lord Who Rules Everything so
Splendidly"

*First Scripture:* Ezekiel 34: 11-16.

*Response:*
Leader: I am the good shepherd.

All: I know my sheep, and my sheep know me, and I give
my life for my sheep. (John 10: 14,15.)

*Litany:* Psalm 22 (23)

*Response:* (same)

*Hymn:* "Praise to the Lord Who Prepares You Artfully
and Finely"

*Second Scripture:* Ephesians 4: 1-6

*Leader in Prayer:* Let us pray. O God, Father of Our Lord Jesus Christ, let us recognize the great dangers of our inner conflict. Take from us all hatred and all prejudice and whatever may hinder us in attaining true harmony, so that we may henceforth be but one heart and one soul, as there is also only *one* body and *one* spirit, *one* hope for our calling and *one* Lord, *one* faith and *one* baptism, *one* God and *one* Father of us all.

*All:* Let us be united through the holy bond of truth and of peace of faith and of love so that we may praise and glorify you with the Holy Spirit through Jesus Christ, our Lord. Amen.

*Confession of Faith: (Stand—all pray in common, each his own text, the Catholics the Catholic text, the Evangelicals the Evangelical text).* I believe in God. . . .

*Hymn:* "Praise the Lord and His Lofty Holy Name!"

*Third Scripture:* John 1: 35-42

*Sermon*

*Hymn:* "Speak Christ, our Shield, to Me"

*Litany of Thanksgiving*
   *Leader:* We thank you, Father, for life and wisdom, which you gave us through Jesus, Your Son.
   *All:* Glory to You in Eternity! . . .

*Litany of Confession*
   *Leader:* Let us repent in the presence of our Lord, Jesus Christ, and let us confess humbly our sins against unity: For our fights which are quite often full of irony, stubbornness, and exaggerations toward our Christian brothers, for

our unforgiving spirit and our judgment.
*All:* Have mercy on us, Lord! . . .

*Litany Invoking the Holy Spirit*
*Leader:* Let us ask the Holy Spirit for unity in truth and in love,
That we might be led through love out of our ignorance, our prejudices and unconscious animosities.
*All:* Hear us, God Holy Spirit! . . .

*The Lord's Prayer* [The closing words used by Protestants appeared as optional in parenthesis: "Dein ist das Reich" etc.]

*Hymn:* "Praise and Glory to God"

*Prayer:*
*Leader:* Remember, Oh Lord, Your Church.
*All:* Release or redeem it from all evil, and complete it in your love. Bring them from all directions into your church together, which you have prepared for them. For yours is the power and the glory in all eternity.

*Prayer of Blessing:*
*Leader:* Let us praise the Lord!
*All:* Thanks to the Lord in Eternity!

*Apostolic Blessing:* The Lord bless you and keep you. . . .

193. A pattern for joint services was set by Pope Paul VI himself December 4, 1965, in a parting liturgy celebrated jointly with Protestant observers in the presence of the bishops and cardinals of the Second Vatican Council at St. Paul's Outside-the-Walls, traditional place of the burial of St. Paul, a great cavernous church, with a high oblong ceiling ringed by paintings of the popes. Seated at the main altar, facing the Council fathers in the nave of the church, Pope Paul had at his left the Protestant and Orthodox observers, at his right some seventy cardinals. In

his brief homily, Pope Paul reviewed his pleasure of having the observers at the Council, and in a voice almost trembling bid them a fond farewell. "Your departure with the end of the Council leaves in us a loneliness which before the Council we did not know, and which now makes us feel sad," he said. "We would like to have you with us always! The great problem of the re-establishment of unity in the visible Church which pertains to all those who have the good fortune and responsibility to call themselves Christians must be studied in its depth. If not today, then tomorrow it will be possible to find its solution—slowly, gradually, generously."

The ecumenical rite, held in the same church where Pope John XXIII had announced his plans for a Council, "seems to be a go-ahead for Christians everywhere in the world," was the way a Protestant participant, the Rev. Dr. Albert C. Outler, of Perkins School of Theology (SMU), Dallas, put it. "Anything less would fall short of the Pope's and the observers' example."

The rite demonstrated not only a tacit recommendation of joint ecumenical rites but involved the Pope himself, setting a precedent, and a format:

(I) *Entrance Chant*

During the entrance of the Holy Father, who will be accompanied by the monks of St. Paul's Abbey, Psalm 26 (Protestant number 27) is sung in Latin. The choir of monks chant the verses of the psalm. After each verse, the entire congregation sings the refrain.

> *Choir:* The Lord is my light and my salvation.
> *All* repeat: The Lord is my light and my salvation.
> *Choir:* The Lord is my light and my salvation;
> whom should I fear?
> The Lord is my life's refuge;
> of whom should I be afraid? *Response*
> etc.

(II) *Introductory Prayer*

*The Abbot of St. Paul's:* Let us beseech God, the almighty

Father, not to take into account our sins but to renew in us true zeal for repentance so that in his kindness he may pour into our hearts the Holy Spirit, who will bestow on us the joys of eternal salvation.

*All pray in silence.*

*The Holy Father:* O Lord, come to the assistance of your servants and be merciful to those who implore your mercy. Restore your creation in those who glory in you as their creator and ruler, and preserve it when once restored. Through Christ Our Lord.

*All:* Amen.

(III) *Scripture Readings*
*All are seated.*

*The first reading is read by Rev. Albert C. Outler* (1 Chron. 29: 10-18).

*All rise and sing the following hymn* (in English)
> Now thank we all our God
> With hearts and hands and voices,
> Who wondrous things hath done,
> In Whom His world rejoices. . . .

*The second reading is read by the Rev. Pierre Michalson S.S.* (Rom. 15: 1-6).

*All rise. The choir of monks intones* Alleluia *three times.*

*All repeat:* Alleluia, Alleluia, Alleluia.

*Choir* (in Latin) : To you I lift up my eyes, who are enthroned in heaven; behold, as the eyes of servants are in the hands of their masters.

*All:* Alleluia, Alleluia, Alleluia.

*Choir:* As the eyes of a maid are on the hands of her mistress, so are our eyes on the Lord, our God, till he have pity on us.

*All:* Alleluia, Alleluia, Alleluia.

*The third reading, from the Gospel of St. Matthew, is read in Greek by Archimandrite Maximos (*Matthew 5: 1-12*)*

*Homily by the Holy Father.*

(IV) *Litany*

The invitation to prayer and the invocations, which will be said alternately in English and French, are recited by the Very Rev. Canon Peter John Maan and the Very Rev. Msgr. H. Francis Davis.

My dear brethren, let us pray to the God of our fathers, that he may be pleased to preserve the wonders of his power and of his mercy in his Church.

(1) For peace from on high and for the salvation of our souls, let us pray to the Lord. Response: Kyrie eleison.

(2) That his holy Church may be preserved from every evil and be made perfect in his love, let us pray to the Lord. Response: Kyrie eleison.

(3) That the pastors of every Christian communion may be faithful servants of the gospel of Christ, let us pray to the Lord. Response: Kyrie eleison.

(4) For all who are gathered here, for those from all over the world who pray with us that we may devote ourselves to the works of peace, of love and of justice, let us pray to the Lord. Response: Kyrie eleison.

(5) For all who bear the name of Christ, that the word of the Lord may be fulfilled and their unity may be perfect, let us pray to the Lord. Response: Kyrie eleison.

(6) For all Christians suffering trials and afflictions, for all who have need of the mercy and assistance of God,

and for all who are seeking the light of Christ, let us pray to the Lord. Response: Kyrie eleison.

*Prayer:* May our prayer rise to your glorious throne, O Lord, and may our request not return to us unheeded. Unite our lips and our hearts in praise and repentance, so that one day, in the fullness of the communion of your Church we may advance together towards your kingdom, which has no end. Through Christ Our Lord.

*All:* Amen.

(V) *The Lord's Prayer*

*The Holy Father* (in Latin) : Instructed and commanded by the prayer of the Savior himself, let us humbly pray to the Almighty Father.

*All recite the Lord's Prayer, each one in his own language.*

(VI) *Final Invocation*

*The Holy Father:* The grace of the Lord Jesus Christ and the love of God the Father and the communion of the Holy Spirit be with you all.

*All:* Amen.

*All sing the canticle Magnificat (Luke 1: 46-55) in Latin.*

194. Students at the University of Tulsa are receptive to novelty and cooperation to a considerable degree, perhaps more than their peers. They entered into a variety of worship experiences among Catholics and Protestants and even dared to attempt to trod on sacramental ground. Chaplain C. Robert Kelly (Presbyterian) at the Presbyterian-related University of Tulsa describes the frontiers of ecumenical worship among students in the *Federation News* of the World Student Christian Federation and in a letter amplifying the article in the *Federation News:*

The first structured worship together took place at evening prayer in 1963-64. The groups joined in the sponsorship of this daily service. Each communion accepted responsibility for two weeks, with the understanding that the service would be according to the form of the presiding group, but that all would use a common lectionary and intercessory prayer list. There were some humorous as well as some deeply moving moments. One evening a Catholic layman, who was leading the service, brought rosaries for everyone; some of the Protestants were a bit concerned over the resultant "Hail Marys"! Some weeks later the shoe was on the other foot when a Baptist student leader asked all present to take turns leading in sentence prayers. There was an exchange of glances among some from higher church traditions, but all rose to the occasion! Among the moving events was the service held at the time of the assassination of President Kennedy, which was during the week when the Roman Catholics were in charge. Several hundred students and faculty came to a service usually attended by ten or fifteen, and the Roman Catholic chaplain and I shared in leading prayers for our country and for the Kennedy family.

The activities of Holy Week were planned together, with all groups uniting in the Good Friday service. We used the traditional form of service with the "Seven Words from the Cross," each campus pastor and the university chaplain giving one of the meditations. Two years ago the Roman Catholics and Episcopalians were hosts to the other groups for a Paschal Meal in which was incorporated the gospel account of the Lord's Supper. We broke bread together, and took the cup, and heard the words of institution even though the occasion was regarded as being non-sacramental. Last year we repeated the experience with the Lutherans added as co-hosts. . . .

[Another] step to ecumenical understanding is the sharing of the sacraments. This year we have taken some small steps towards trying to understand the sacramental nature of our relationship. The setting for this has been the university's Thursday morning (11 A.M.) chapel service. This service is voluntary, and comes at an hour when many other activities are being carried on—including intramural sports played almost on the chapel lawn! However, it is the one announced worship service for the university.

Within this setting, we have turned to a very ancient practice—the division of the service into the Mass of the Catechumens and the Mass of the Faithful. Many of our services today still reflect the time when there was a service of instruction, ending with the proclamation of the word, and followed by a sacramental service for the faithful.

According to our plan, each of the six communions—Presbyterian (arranged by the UCCF), Episcopal, Methodist, Roman Catholic, Southern Baptist, and Lutheran—conducts four weeks of chapel services. For the first three weeks, the service is in the form of instruction for the communion, and includes praise, prayer, the proclamation of the word, and sometimes a credal affirmation. Leadership from other traditions is used. The fourth week, the sacrament of the Lord's Supper is observed. For example, the Presbyterians used the new "Service for the Lord's Day" each week, ending with the full service the fourth week. Episcopalians used the service of Ante-Communion (not Morning Prayer), and the sacrament the fourth week.

There have been problems. Chief among them has been the closed nature of some of our communion services. For example, the Southern Baptists, in conscience, can only have communion within the established congregation, and will not have a sacramental observance. However, they have invited all those present to join them for lunch at the Baptist Student Union following the service! We have left the response to the invitation to the table to the conscience of the worshipper. The Episcopal priest stated that in special services of an ecumenical nature in a college situation the administration of the Holy Communion is permitted in the Episcopal tradition. Some who were not Episcopalians responded.

At no point in our search for ecumenical understanding have we become more aware of our real separateness than in the sacramental observance. During the weeks when we worship as catechumens, there is a real sharing of worship. Those in the low church tradition enter into such things as the singing of the Nicene Creed, and those of another heritage accept the leadership of free prayer or gospel song. However, as the sacrament is observed, an invisible barrier is reared and some become "observers" and others "participants." We try to touch each other through this barrier, but become keenly aware that we are not yet one in Christ. . . .

[From his letter Chaplain Kelly explains further] Both Catholics and Protestants participated together in *all* the services. At least both attended all services, and the leadership was drawn from both groups. The choir had both Catholics and Protestants. . . .

We followed the order of worship which would lead to the sacrament including Bible reading and preaching for three weeks, and then on the fourth week had the sacrament. In the case of the Catholics we used the Mass (or the foremass) up to the point of the sacrament for three weeks. The fourth week we had a full Mass (even a Solemn High Mass). I (Presbyterian) read one of the lessons in that service.

We had similar services with Presbyterians, Episcopal, Methodist, and Lutherans. The Catholics and the Lutherans did not have "open" communion, and those who had had a part in the liturgy to that point then became spectators.

195. The Rt. Rev. Angus Dun, retired Episcopal bishop of Washington, received communion in January 1965, at a Roman Catholic church, perhaps the first Protestant Episcopal bishop to do so. The occasion was a Mass at Holy Trinity Roman Catholic Church, Georgetown, concluding "A Week of Christian Conversations in Georgetown." The Rev. Father Thomas T. Gavigan, pastor, celebrated the Mass; the Rev. William Sharp, rector of St. John's Episcopal Church, said a prayer of intercession; the Rev. John D. Wing, curate of Christ Episcopal Church, read the Epistle, and Bishop Dun joined Roman Catholics who took communion. A professor of Scripture at Catholic University, Washington, the Rev. Father Geoffrey F. Wood, was quoted later in the year in the Washington *Post* as suggesting some further discussion in the area of intercommunion, but he added "how this

can come about I don't know, and there are some niceties here
that are difficult."

A communion service, following the order of the Disciples of
Christ, with considerable ecumenical overtones, was held in the
little Cane Ridge Meeting House, about thirty miles out in the
blue-grass country from Lexington, near Paris, Kentucky, for
the Consultation on Church Union meeting in Lexington to discuss a six-way merger plan of Protestants. The service was an
anachronism in every way. Church executives in their business
suits walked among the moss-covered tombstones in the morning
light where coonskin and deerskin pioneers had walked and worshipped a century and a half ago. The Cane Ridge log cabin,
birthplace of the Disciples, was built in 1791. Barton Stone, one
of the founders whose tall obelisk tombstone towers with a slight
lean in the cabin's graveyard, had described in his lifetime a day
at the site in 1801: "The roads were literally crowded with
wagons, carriages, horsemen and footmen moving to the solemn
camp. The sight was affecting. It was judged, by military men
on the ground, that there were between twenty and thirty thousand collected. Four or five preachers were frequently speaking
at the same time. . . ." Here, then, the modern men in modern
suits, filed on April 7, 1965. Most of the group, representing the
six negotiating denominations and as many outside observing
denominations, sitting on the old planks, received and partook of
the bits of crackers and the juice during communion administered
by Disciple George Beazley, president of the Disciples Council
on Christian Unity, with the aid of lay Disciple elders from
nearby Kentucky churches. A Catholic priest, the Rev. Father
George H. Tavard, of Mount Mercy College, Pittsburgh, sat in
the middle of the "pot-pourri" of Protestants. The elements
passed him by as he observed—a humble Catholic priest sitting
through a communion service in a log cabin that gave birth to
a Protestant denomination! The service, one of four held in connection with the Consultation, followed this pattern:

*The Call to Worship*
The cup of blessing which we bless, is it not a participation in the blood of Christ? The bread which we break, is it
not a participation in the body of Christ?

Because there is one loaf, we who are many are one body, for we all partake of the same loaf. (1 Cor. 10: 16-17.)

*The Invocation*
Almighty Father, Whose dear Son, on the night before He suffered, did institute the Sacrament of His Body and Blood; Mercifully grant that we may thankfully receive the same in remembrance of Him, Who in these holy mysteries giveth us a pledge of life eternal; the same Thy Son Jesus Christ our Lord, Who now liveth and reigneth with Thee and the Holy Spirit ever, one God, world without end. Amen.

*Hymn:* "Beneath the Cross of Jesus"

*Bible Lecture:* Dr. Paul Minear

*Call to the Lord's Table:* Dr. Beazley

"I am the bread of life; he who comes to Me shall not hunger, and he who believes on Me shall never thirst" (John 6: 35).

*Reading of the Scripture:* Mark 14: 17-25

*Prayer of Confession*

*Hymn:* "Bread of the World"

*Words of Institution:* 1 Cor. 11: 23-34

*Breaking and Blessing of the Bread*

*Words of Institution:* 1 Cor. 11: 25-26

*Pouring and the Blessing of the Fruit of the Vine*

*Participation in the Bread and Wine*

*The Benediction*

Now may God of peace Who brought again from the dead our Lord Jesus, the great shepherd of the sheep, by the blood of the eternal covenant, equip you with everything good that you may do His will, working in you that which is pleasing in His sight, through Jesus Christ, to Whom be glory for ever and ever. Amen. Hebrews 13: 20-21.

196. A "real breakthrough on the thorny road of intercommunion" was evident in 1966, according to the Rev. Dr. Albert H. van den Heuvel, executive secretary of the Youth Department of the World Council of Churches. He says he knows, as others also do, of "eucharistic acts between Protestants and Roman Catholics" but "since Protestant ministers and Roman Catholic priests could get into trouble with their ecclesiastical authorities over such a breach of their church laws I am in the habit of not disclosing any of the facts," he says in a letter dated March 8, 1966. In the eucharistic realm, although not the eucharistic celebration of a mass or Divine Liturgy, he cites the "Shalom" movement in Holland: "Every Friday night a love feast (Agape—pronounced A-gá-pay, after one of the New Testament's most profound words for sacrificial love) is celebrated between Roman Catholics and Protestants which is described by them as an eucharistic act. [The Last Supper of Jesus with his disciples is considered a "love feast" before the words of institution and breaking of the bread and consecration of the cup.] Although the words of institution are not formally used, stories are read from Scripture in which the meal is undoubtedly a symbol for the closer contact between God and his people, like the instance of the feeding of the multitudes in some of the Synoptic gospels. The story in the Johannine tradition represents the Eucharist while no formal account of the institution of the Holy Communion is given. Agapes are celebrated all around the world in very different forms. . . ."

A booklet put out by Dr. van den Heuvel's department has an article, unsigned, about "An Agape Meal in Manchester":

We decided to hold an Agape on the evening of the last Sunday of the camp. I had been to one at Bossey at the leaders' conference and was able to organize ours roughly on the same lines.

The menu was: Fish, with vegetables; fruit; bread and cheese; wines—Spanish Chablis, Spanish Sauternes, and Mosel.

Order of events: Hymn—*Cantate Domino*; Psalm 104: 1-23 read by leader; Bible readings—Exodus 16: 12-18, 31-32 (Manna); 1 Kings 19: 1-8 (Elijah); John 2: 1-11 (Marriage at Cana); Matthew 14: 13-21 (feeding the five thousand); John 6: 30-35 (the Bread of Life); Revelation 22: 1-5 (The River of Life)—read by six campers, each in his own language, with the others following in their own Bibles; Act of sharing (collection, given to work project); Lord's Prayer; Grace; Meal; Hymn—*Cantate Domino*; Benediction.

It was for all of us the most profound spiritual experience—in the true sense of seeing the material and the holy at the same time. It was therefore virtually sacramental, and a far more vital sacrament than most Communion services, though of course, we knew that liturgically it could not be precisely the Eucharist itself. We all felt it brought out one element at least which is always lacking at Communion services, and yet is the *basic* element of the Eucharist—the Fellowship Meal. Of course it could only be this because it was accurately expressing the close and deep fellowship which really was existing in the camp—and at the same time it deepened the fellowship and sealed it with Christ as none of our ordinary worship had done, however, good it was.

It was in truth the highest moment of the camp, this holy and glorious love-feast.

197. Instances of sharing one another's pulpit in the special services increased. Two bishops, Roman Catholic John E. Taylor and Lutheran Helge Ljungberg, both bishops in Stockholm, shared the pulpit, with others, in a Week of Prayer for Christian

Unity service in the Katarina Church in 1966. The Rev. Father
Thomas Corbishley, S.J., preached in Westminster Abbey, January 21, 1966; the first time a priest had preached in it in 400
years; likewise for the first time since the Reformation, a priest,
Vicar Franz Joseh Fischedick, of Bergen, preached January 18,
1966 from the pulpit of the national Lutheran Church of Norway
in Bergen, Norway; again in a service in connection with the
Week of Prayer for Christian Unity, Episcopal Bishop George L.
Cadigan, of St. Louis, preached from the pulpit during a Week
of Prayer for Christian Unity service in 1966 at the Roman Catholic St. Louis Cathedral. Bishop Ian Willebrands, secretary of the
Vatican Secretariat for the Promoting of Christian Unity,
preached in a Lutheran church in Copenhagen in 1966.

The Rev. Malcolm Matheson, pastor of the Chestnut Street
Congregational Church, preached in a unity service in St. Paul's
Catholic Cathedral, Worcester, Massachusetts, and the Catholic
bishop of Portland, Maine, the Most Rev. Daniel Feeney, preached
from the pulpit of Immanuel Baptist Church, Portland, in an
ecumenical service.

One of the pioneers in speaking from one another's pulpits
was a Roman Catholic priest who preached from the pulpit at the
conclusion of an Episcopal service of Evensong, or evening
prayer, January 3, 1965, Bexhill-on-Sea, Sussex, England. The
Rev. Father Michael Richards, of St. Edmund's, Ware, who is on
the staff of the Westminster Seminary, Hertfordshire, attended
the service wearing his black cassock, but minus the surplice.
In the same congregation at the service in St. Peter's Anglican
Church, were his parents, Mr. and Mrs. R. C. Richards, members
of St. Peter's. Father Richards said:

> I have spent a good deal of time reading Church history, and
> I believe that this is the first time for over 400 years that a
> Roman Catholic priest has spoken to an Anglican congrega-
> tion at an Anglican Church. . . . This evening has been pre-
> pared for over many years, but this is not a stopping place;
> it is another stage in a movement which must go forward
> towards unity, which is something we must all pray for.
> This is not, however, just a drawing together of the

Churches in difficult times, we are renewing ourselves in order that we may renew the faith of the whole country so that all may find faith. . . .

It is now our desire as English Roman Catholics to develop the whole scope of our faith and work in the service of unity. That is what the Council has told us to do and that is why we are coming out of our shells to pray and work for unity. We want to work and prepare for the day when we shall be of one faith. . . .

It is going to be a hard and painful struggle to which men will be required to give their whole lives. . . .

There must be much hard thinking and above all, hard praying, and we must be patient. But at least we all want it and we must work together to find one church once again. But neither must allow the other to flag or to fall behind in work that all may be one and that the world may believe.

198. A Roman Catholic priest and an Episcopal rector exchanged pulpits for special services in Flagstaff, Arizona, February 8, 1965. Two hundred persons crowded the Episcopal Church of the Epiphany to hear the Rev. Father James Lindenmeyer, pastor of Our Lady of Guadalupe Roman Catholic Church in Flagstaff, at the Sunday morning service. He preached for 15 minutes, but did not in any way take part in the Episcopal liturgy. At a Sunday evening service at the Our Lady of Guadalupe Church, the Rev. Robert Lord, rector of the Episcopal Church of the Epiphany, spoke to 225 persons.

a. Father Lindenmeyer said in his sermon:

There are differences of belief in our churches concerning the sacraments, but we do affirm the existence of the sacraments as a means of salvation instituted by Christ. It is this common teaching which we treasure.

b. The Rev. Mr. Lord said in his sermon at the Catholic church:

The significant thing to consider is that the separation of the two communions was not based on religious matters, but rather on political matters. Unfortunate it is that this political division should have incited such gross and sinful excesses on both sides . . . that dialogue has been impossible until now.

199. A Catholic nun almost spoke from a Methodist pulpit in Detroit during a Sunday morning service. Sister Alexine, just back from helping in the Good Samaritan Hospital in Selma, at the height of the civil rights demonstrations there, had hoped to give a five minute talk from the pulpit Sunday morning, April 4, 1965, at the invitation of the Central Methodist Church pastor, the Rev. Dr. James H. Laird. The talk was to precede a special collection for the Selma hospital. She was told by her superiors she could speak after the service, but not during it. Sister Alexine, of the Sisters of St. Joseph, elected to send her voice by tape rather than speak when the service was all over. So during the service for five minutes, on Sunday, at the 11 A.M. service, the Central Methodist congregation listened to a tape recorder staring down to them from the pulpit. Sister Alexine discussed the plight of the Negro economically and medically in Selma, and told of the apathy and fears that filled the Good Samaritan Hospital.

The pastor at Central Methodist, Dr. Laird, brought up an interesting topic in his sermon that morning: Canon Law, concerning ecumenical restrictions, can be circumvented by modern electronic devices such as the tape recorder! He said in his sermon that Sunday morning after the congregation had heard the tape of Sister Alexine's speech to the congregation:

Some days ago we invited a Roman Catholic nun, Sister Alexine, to tell about conditions in the Good Samaritan Hospital in Selma, Ala., so our congregation could be given an opportunity to give to it. Sister accepted but the archdiocesan authorities refused to give her permission to speak. They were very nice about it and explained there were rules against that sort of thing. Roman Catholics sharing in a Protestant service of worship. The fact that she was to help raise money for a Christian enterprise desperately needing help was beside the point. The man-made rule took priority over human need. The claim of love was turned aside because the rule had to be followed. But we invited Sister Alexine to record her plea and this she graciously did, the demand of Christian love for the people in Alabama was that strong. The authorities of the church were nonplussed; they had no rule governing that since the rules had been made before the advent of tape recordings. So love found a way.

200. A nun spoke from the pulpit of St. Mark's Episcopal Church, St. Louis, during layman month commemorations, February, 1966. In a letter of invitation to Sister Ann Patrick Ware, of the department of theology, Webster College, St. Louis, the rector of St. Mark's Episcopal Church, wrote:

During February of each year we invite laymen into the pulpit of our church on Sundays to address the major gathering of the flock at the 10 A.M. service of morning prayer (not a service of Holy Communion). Our purpose is several-fold:

(1) To accent the ministry of the laity (the called People of God);

(2) We of the institutional church ought to listen to those who fight for their daily bread out in the world;

(3) We, the church, are sent to minister to and for the world.

We do not make a false dichotomy between church and world, sacred and secular; yet we recognize a vast abyss between church and world. We are especially interested in listening to the communicators of 1966, of which you are one.

We do not give the guest speaker a subject, but suggest she deal with the relationship or inter-relationship of her work, her religion and her world; or in re the great emphasis on the lay ministry—as a layman, "How do I minister through my work in the world?" We also like a script if possible, as one of our national church papers generally publishes the addresses. We like a presentation of about 20 minutes.

Following the service we adjourn to the parish house where the Autoptos Club (18-25 adults) in round table fashion questions and discusses with one another and the speaker his address. (I submit myself to this each week.)....

This year, for both ecumenical and theological reasons, we would like our speakers to be women. Thus far we've only used men. I've met and heard you once or twice and I know you'll do a fine job. Because we want *you* and because we know you have many demands for extras, we are giving you first choice of dates. Could you come February 13, 20 or 27 at 10 A.M. We'd provide transportation for you and any companions if desired.

Sincerely yours,
Murray Kenny
Rector and Ecumenical Officer,
Diocese of Missouri

201. Protestants and Catholics have on occasion, when there was no danger of mixing the services, shared one another's place of worship for regular services. Example: the interfaith chapel at Selfridge Air Force Base, near Mt. Clemens, Michigan, where as the Catholics come out of an early Mass, the Protestants are coming in. In Taizé, France, the Protestant monks used an ancient Catholic village church at the permission of the diocesan bishop (they now have their own church building). In Wells, Vermont, the Catholic Mass was offered weekly in the local St. Paul's Episcopal Church at 9:30 A.M. on Sundays for the local tourists. Wells, located on Lake St. Catherine, has no Catholic church of its own.

In another approach, there is the demonstration church service in which a complete rite of the other faith can be presented for educational purposes in a church of a different faith. In Berkeley, California, a Roman Catholic priest thus stood before the altar of a Protestant church, sang a hymn written by Martin Luther (the recently adapted "A Mighty Fortress Is Our God—see Section 202), and then led a Catholic Mass predominantly in English. The Rev. Father James Fisher, chaplain of Newman Hall, on the University of California campus, knelt at the altar, or communion table, of the Congregational Church of the Great Commission. Demonstration masses were also held in Colorado at the Holy Cross Abbey, Canon City, and the Episcopal Church of the Ascension, Pueblo.

In East Liberty Presbyterian Church, Pittsburgh, 700 persons, mostly Catholic, including 75 nuns and 12 priests, gathered for a demonstration of a Presbyterian service on Sunday, March 28, 1965.

The order of service at that 2:30 P.M. "demonstration" service was "exactly the same as at the 11 A.M. service that Sunday with the exception that the sermon topic and the New Testament reading were different. A discussion followed the demonstration service.

Comments received by the pastor, the Rev. Charles P. Robshaw, after the service:

I was present at the program at the East Liberty Church yesterday and I want to thank you sincerely for the invitation. The past few years have brought wonderful changes to this community of ours. [Miss Eileen Mawe]

Please accept our grateful thanks for making our day with you possible. We found the afternoon a most instructive one and feel that such opportunities will afford greater understanding and love for all concerned [Sisters of St. Francis, Monongahela, Pa.]

Thank you and all the staff for that very stirring and moving service yesterday afternoon. I did feel it was a very great privilege to be a participant in a service that seemed so alive with a real love of Jesus and what He means to all of us no matter who we are. [Mrs. Henry W. Fulton]

It was with hearts full of thankfulness that we, members of the Roman Catholic faith, sat in a Presbyterian Church and joined our voices to yours in the common effort to approach the Throne of God, as believers in the common brotherhood of man. Tears came to our eyes as the magnificent strains of the Doxology poured out of the throats of over a thousand communicants. [Mr. and Mrs. Maurice G. French]

In speaking to one of your deacons I was greatly impressed by the generosity and dedication of those holding this office. This impression has served to stimulate a like response. May your charity be blessed. [Sister Aimee, C.D.P., Beaver, Pa.]

[Pastor Robshaw himself adds in a letter] Our assumption was that the demonstration service guests would merely observe, but in actual fact they joined with us in the singing of the hymns, the recital of the Apostles' Creed and The Lord's Prayer, and while this may not have been strictly according to the Catholic Church's ecclesiastical regulations it was a remarkable evidence of the spirit which pervaded our service.

202. Music provided a ground for ecumenical expression, although, as indicated in Chapter III, some prelates, such as Bishop John Wright of Pittsburgh, warned of "indifferentism" that might be created in some musical situations as choirs sang church music whose words they could not accept. Yet music, a universal language, was often the same in Protestant and Catholic churches, and the words spoke to both faiths. For example, Protestant choirs sing "Silent Night," written by a Catholic priest, Joseph Mohr; and Plainsong, and anthems by Mozart, Palestrina, and Vittorio. A Protestant favorite had long been "Faith of Our Fathers" (a Catholic hymn, though most Protestants do not know this) by Englishman Frederick William Faber. A sixth stanza of this stirring hymn mentions the Virgin Mary—"Faith of our Fathers! Mary's prayers, Shall keep our Country fast to thee . . ."—though, curiously enough, it is so accepted as a Protestant hymn that now when it is used in interfaith gatherings this sixth verse is still left out. Now Roman Catholics began to use Lutheran Johann Sebastian Bach and began to sing unmistakable Protestant hymns, most notably, Luther's "A Mighty Fortress Is Our God." It was introduced to Catholics at the Catholic Liturgical

Week Conference on August 25, 1964, in the Kiel auditorium, St. Louis. The Mass, celebrated by Joseph Cardinal Ritter, of St. Louis, began with a procession of white-robed priests (no elaborate vestments) marching down the aisle to Luther's stirring battle cry with 16,000 priests, nuns, and laymen joining in. The new *People's Mass Book* included the hymn. Extensive changes in the wording of the hymn simply marked an updating of terminology—references to "guns and nuclear might," for instance, instead of "earthly power," etc.:

> A mighty fortress is our God*
>     A bulwark never failing,
> Protecting us with staff and rod,
>     His power all prevailing.
> What if the nations rage
>     And surging seas rampage;
> What though the mountains fall,
>     The Lord is God of all;
> On earth is not his equal.
>
> The waters of his goodness flow
>     Throughout his holy city,
> And gladden hearts of those who know
>     His tenderness and pity.
> Though nations stand unsure,
>     God's kingdom shall endure;
> His power shall remain,
>     His peace shall ever reign,
> Our God, the God of Jacob.
>
> Behold his wondrous deeds of peace,
>     The God of our salvation;
> He knows our wars and makes them cease
>     In ev'ry land and nation.
> The warrior's spear and lance
>     Are splintered by his glance;
> The guns and nuclear might
>     Stand withered in his sight;
> The Lord of hosts is with us.

203. Protestants were writing Mass music for Catholics, and even excelling at the task. Presbyterian Gordon Young, organist and choir director at First Presbyterian Church, Detroit, wrote Mass music for the Gregorian Institute and for the J. Fischer and Brothers Company, Glen Rock, New Jersey. How

---

* Reprinted by permission of the *World Library of Sacred Music, Inc.*, Cincinnati, Ohio.

well Protestants were welcomed is illustrated by an acceptance
letter to Mr. Young from the Fischer company:

My dear Mr. Young,
. . . .There has been such a steady stream of these things
[English Masses] coming in ever since the Church regulations were changed that we have been perplexed to know
just how to handle them. Somehow in the rush your manuscript got waylayed and it was not until our editorial conference yesterday that it was brought up for attention.

I am very happy to report that everyone present was delighted with it: frankly, it was one of the very few manuscripts received that contained what we feel the Church
wants in this new type of composition—simplicity, musician-
ship, practicality and a good and proper treatment of the
text. There was only one objection, the rather striking
"Abide with me" melody of the introduction; this could
easily be changed, of course, using the same chord progres-
sions. And perhaps a few notations suggestive of possible
congregational directions. But none of these offer any problems whatever, and we are putting it into immediate production. . . .

> Very sincerely,
> Howard D. McKinney

204. The Jesuits began to sound like Protestant spiritual singers. The Woodstock (College) Singers Album included this "The
Lord God":

Ol' Noah call'd the people when the clouds got stormy black
But the people wuz a sinnin' an' dey wuzn't comin' back.
So ol' Noah built a boat,
Got de animals aboard,
An' de waters flooded up an' Noah sail'd to the Lord.

*(Refrain)*
Oh the Lord God He come seekin' out his people
An' a hero from the people led the people to the Lord.) repeat

When ole Pharaoh chain'd the people makin' bricks all
night till dawn

Moses plagued them gypsy slavers till the Pharaoh said begone!
An' he march'd us round the desert
Till the thirst inside us roared;
An' when all of us were bleached ol' Moses led us to the Lord.

*(Refrain same as above.)*
We've run off back to slavery an' our souls an' bodies ache,
So we come beggin' mercy, Lord our hearts it fit t' break.
Bring us home to You and freedom!
Raise a king to lead us in!
God we need a king like You to lead us singin' down the wind.

*(Refrain)*
Will the Lord God still come seekin' out his people?
Will a hero from the people come to lead us to the Lord?) repeat

205. Choirs got together. In Detroit, the Optimist Club sponsored joint interfaith concerts in the Ford Auditorium; the Our Lady Queen of Peace Boys' Choir (Roman Catholic) put on a concert at the Grosse Pointe Memorial (Presbyterian) Church, as part of a choir festival. An interparish hymn sing was held at the Holy Ghost Catholic Church, Milwaukee, with Ascension Lutheran Church members as guests, on All Saints Day, November 1, 1964. An interfaith Christmas candlelight concert involving the same two parishes was held several weeks later at the Ascension church. Twenty nuns, plus priests and Catholic seminarians attended the concert. (Later another Protestant-Catholic hymn-sing was held at Lake Park Lutheran Church under the auspices of the Lutheran Student Center and the Newman Club of the University of Wisconsin-Milwaukee). The Central Methodist choir in Kansas City gave a concert in the sanctuary in front of the altar at the Immaculate Conception Roman Catholic Church. The community orientated Rackham Choir, Detroit, made up of members of all faiths, performed for an evening mass, arranged by the Rev. Father Charles Boyle, of the Oblates of St. Francis de Sales, a high school music teacher and the lone priest member of the Rackham Singers.

A "Hymnal of Christian Unity" was inevitable and it appeared in 1964, published by the Gregorian Institute of America, Inc. The new church unity hymn book, with an imprimatur of the Most Rev. George J. Rehring, bishop of Toledo, contains one-hundred hymns in its wide spiraled pages. Covering all the topics of the church year, the hymnal includes such Protestant stalwarts as "The Church's One Foundation," and "Holy, Holy, Holy," and a version of the Catholic "Veni Creator Spiritus" in English and a new tune, "St. Joseph, Be Our Guide," by the Rev. Father H. F. Bruckner, S.J. "Faith of Our Fathers" is here but follows the Protestant version. The editors, Clifford A. Bennett, president of the Gregorian Institute of America, Inc., and Paul Hume, music director, Georgetown University, explained the new hymnal in the preface:

Someone once made the deeply psychological remark: "Give me but to write the songs of my country and I care not who makes her laws!" The idea is remotely applicable to the broader aspects of the Christian religion. Whatever differences may exist among the various Christian confessions, there is always the great possibility of ever-increasing unity through sacred singing. This compilation represents the most serious sentiments of divine worship which Christians have ever experienced in common, and the editors feel it would be a regretful neglect to ignore the vast treasury of religious thought and feeling which Christian faiths have shared for so long, however much we may have failed to recognize the existence of that fact until comparatively recent times.

In the hymns which typify the common spirit of giving glory to God in this Hymnal of Christian Unity, several texts and melodies are completely new, but with a clearly perceptible warrant in historical worship and an ideal form for strengthening the recognition among the various Christian faiths of a true bond of charity. Other hymns, such as the adaptation of the Psalms, bring us back to man's earliest attempts to formulate his adoration of God, his awe, his love, his contrition. And still other hymns revert to the early days of Christianity when we held a common tradition of worship, bringing us to the comforting realization that here too is a heritage of which all can be proud.

The editors of this Hymnal have made every effort to select a series of hymns which can be used by all faiths without hesitation and yet not play down the essential doctrines by which a true Christian spirit is guided. The great theme throughout the Hymnal is praise of God—so instinctive with the nature of music—and this is the theme which all liturgies have featured from the beginning. Our contact with God in prayer and song is never so assured as when we extol His glory, His preeminence; so thought the ancient psalmist; so thinks the modern worshipper. May this Hymnal go on its way with a warm gospel of Christian love and bring all of us to the feet of our God with deeply-felt union of spirit.

206. Cooperation extended to the marriage rites considerably before Pope Paul VI's *Matrimonii Sacramentum* of 1966. In Warson Woods, Missouri, June 13, 1964, Susan H. Ekberg, an Episcopalian, married Patrick C. Barker, a Roman Catholic, before an Episcopalian clergyman and a Catholic priest at the Ste. Genevieve du Bois Roman Catholic Church. The young couple said they wanted to avoid the situation of Princess Sophia of Greece, a Greek Orthodox, and Prince Juan Carlos, of Spain, a Catholic, who were married in two ceremonies, one in each church. The Rt. Rev. George L. Cadigan, Episcopal bishop of Missouri, and the Rt. Rev. Msgr. William M. Drumm, the Catholic chancellor of St. Louis, worked out the joint arrangement. In the ceremony, the wedding rite from the Roman ritual was used at the start of the ceremony. This includes the invocation by the priest. The Episcopal Book of Common Prayer was used for the rest of the ceremony. Catholic canon law requires that the priest receive the couple's vows and witness the marriage at the precise moment it takes place. The Episcopal minister pronounced the couple man and wife after their vows. Officiating were the priest, the Rev. Father Leonard Jackson, and the Rev. Claudius Miller, the Episcopalian. "While it would be wrong to consider this the general pattern," said the Rt. Rev. Msgr. Joseph W. Baker, canon-law adviser to Cardinal Ritter, "there is no reason to think that such permission would not be granted in the future, given the same set of circumstances. And chief among those circumstances were the bride's sincerity and her allegiance to her faith." However, the ecumenical wedding, in which the

bride agreed to the usual promises of rearing the children as Catholics, was soon the center of controversy. An Episcopal bishop, the Rt. Rev. John S. Higgins, of Rhode Island, in a letter to *The Living Church* (Oct. 4, 1964, p. 38), called the wedding "ecumenical jaywalking" and "indefensible and misguided sentimentality which can only encourage other Anglican brides and grooms to do the same thing. Anglicans in such a situation need help and not betrayal by those who are their leaders." *The Christian Century* (Oct. 28, 1964, p. 1326) also called the wedding a "one-sided capitulation" and not "ecumenicity" and a "betrayal" of the children that might come from the union.

A similar controversy brewed in Holland, but was somewhat lessened by the signing of a more general promise to rear the children as "Christians." A priest and a Dutch Reformed pastor officiated at the mixed marriage in the chapel of the Catholic University of Nijmegen, The Netherlands. The couple were Herman Hebinck, twenty-one, a Catholic and medical student at the University, and Elleke Tenhoopen, twenty, a Protestant majoring in social science. The Rev. Father H. Vanwaesberghe, S.J., a graduate student at the University, conducted the ritual and blessed the rings. The Reformed pastor, the Rev. N. Hefting, preached the sermon during the ceremony.

a. Father Vanwaesberghe outlined the ceremony:

(1) The pastor and I received and welcomed the couple entering the church. The priest said the introit of the Mass and Psalm 127, and the pastor some greeting words from the beginnings of Paul's Epistles.

(2) Community singing.

(3) Ephesians 5: 20-33 (Father Vanwaesberghe).

(4) Sermon by the pastor.

(5) Sacramental celebration of the marriage by priest only according to Catholic liturgy.

(6) Pastor hands the Bible to the young couple.

(7) Community singing.

(8) Benediction by the priest.

It was a co-operation between the pastor, who administered the word of the God and the priest as a minister of the Sacrament.

b. In the aftermath of the ceremony, the *Hervormd Weekblad* (Reformed Weekly) called the ceremony "no ecumenism but capitulation." The Catholic *Volkskrant* ("People's Paper") countered:

The two churches acknowledge their reciprocal baptism. A marriage between baptized Christians of different churches seems to be a logical rounding off, when it is celebrated in a cooperation of the minister of the churches. It is a testimony of respect for the faith, the baptism and the Christianity of the other partner.

207. An Orthodox priest from Toledo, Ohio, performed the Greek Orthodox funeral rite for M. F. Kerbawy, 90 (who wanted his funeral in a Roman Catholic Church) in St. Peter's Roman Catholic Cathedral, Blissfield, Michigan, assisted by the Catholic priest. A Baptist pastor and a Catholic priest cooperated in a funeral in Tacoma, Washington, for a couple, Mr. and Mrs. William Hillock, who were killed instantly in a Thanksgiving weekend accident. The husband was Catholic, the wife a Baptist. The families had requested a joint service. The priest, the Rev. Father Thomas J. Pitsch, of St. Patrick's, Tacoma, and the Rev. Lynn E. Hodges, of Tacoma First Baptist (American) Church, each took 12 to 15 minutes of the service at the funeral home, and the same amount at the graveside.

a. Father Pitsch explained the ceremonies:

I got permission to have the prayers and sermon that I give at the funeral parlor in extraordinary cases and Lynn followed me, 15 minutes later. The bodies of the couple remained together in the chapel during both services, but it was not a "joint service." The people naturally enjoyed hearing both of us, especially since the majority—99 per cent—were Baptists and had never heard a Catholic priest speak before at a service.

b. Pastor Hodges concluded the ceremony at the graveside with these words:

Not only have we conducted the funeral of a young man and a young woman today—but by the very nature of this particular service, we have buried a bit more of the separation which exists among brethren in the Kingdom of God. We have been reminded that the ground is level where the children of men and death meet. So is the ground level at the bottom of the cross where all us sinners and God's saving grace meet. To all of us, men, women, clergy, laity, young, old, Catholic, Protestant—our basic needs and God's forgiveness is one and the same.

As these two bodies have been planted in consecrated ground to await resurrection to immortal state, let us pray that God's word and God's way may also be planted in each of our hearts—and nourished by prayer and devotional attention so as to hasten that day of new hope and blessedness awaiting that time when all who trust in Christ Jesus as Lord and Saviour will unitedly rise to live, die and live again in oneness of faith. Amen.

208. In the special installation services and in consecration and ordination rites, there has been cooperation. The Rt. Rev. Msgr. O. A. Coggiola-Mower, of the Church of the Annunciation, Albuquerque, read the Scripture at an installation service of the New Mexico Council of Churches. Four Catholic representatives attended the installation of the Rt. Rev. John E. Hines, as presiding bishop of the Protestant Episcopal Church, in Washington, January 27, 1965. Methodist Bishop Dwight Loder and Greek Orthodox bishop Germanos marched in the procession and sat in the sanctuary (altar) area of Blessed Sacrament Roman Catholic

Cathedral in Detroit during the consecration of Catholic auxiliary bishop, Joseph Breitenbeck. In the Congo, the Most Rev. Joseph F. Cornelis, Catholic archbishop of Elizabethville, attended the consecration of the Rev. John W. Shungu, first native African bishop of the Congo, in the Springer Auditorium on the campus of Mulungwishi Mission Station. After the service, the archbishop spoke at a dinner honoring the new bishop, and said:

> My dear brothers in Christ, it was with joy that I replied immediately to your very friendly invitation which has permitted me to associate myself with a ceremony which is heavy with consequences for the future of the Methodist communinty. Please receive my brotherly congratulations and the testimony of sympathetic concern of the Catholic community of the country. I join my gratitude with yours for all the spiritual benefits that the Lord, in his mercy, and through every trial, has not ceased to give to this African land.
>
> I must also render homage to all of these generations of missionaries who preceded us, and who in pain and unappreciated labor, sowed seed in the soil and made possible the coronation of today. . . .
>
> I present my sincere wishes to the new spiritual leader of your community. A fragile vessel, he is clothed with an authority about which he must render an account to God. But illuminated as he is by an ardent faith, he will receive the necessary grace to face all of the requirements of his charge. I promise him the aid of my brotherly prayers.
>
> In this land, in which all Christian souls are animated by the Spirit of God, seek dialogue, aspire to unity in the hour in which religious pluralism acquires prominence everywhere in the world, it has become natural that our communinties, distant for a long time, wish to draw closer together on the plane of the heart, and pray together to the Common Father. I am leaving again for Rome next week whore the Council will be continuing. I will find again there

the observers of the Methodist Church and will not fail to tell them of the great event which I have just lived through with you today.

And may the God of Abraham, of Isaac and of Jacob pour forth on you all an abundant shower of heavenly benediction!

209. In Palmyra, Missouri, a Northeast Missouri farming town of 2,900, on December 19, 1964, a Catholic priest read the non-sacramental portion of the preparatory litany in the ordination of an Episcopalian priest. The. Rev. Father John Schultz, curate of St. Pius X Roman Catholic Church, Moberly, took part in the rite for his friend, the Rev. Richard H. Baker. However, the Catholic priest did not take part in the laying on of hands with the Rt. Rev. George Leslie Cadigan, Episcopal bishop of Missouri, during the rite at St. Paul's Episcopal Church. Also, Southern Baptist, Assemblies of God, Methodist, Disciples of Christ, Presbyterian ministers and other Roman Catholic clergy marched in the procession.

Father Schultz understood that he had the permission of his bishop, the Most Rev. Joseph M. Marling, bishop of Jefferson City, before the service, although nothing was in writing. Bishop Marling, however, later said he had not given his permission, and chancery officials said that anything they said could not have even remotely been taken as approval to take part in the ordination. In a letter to his priests, Bishop Marling said: "It is my judgment that the act in question was a serious infraction of Canon 1258," which warns against "participating" in non-Catholic worship services. "And had my permission been sought," the bishop said, "it would have been refused."

The role of Father Schultz, however, was not as "active" as if he had taken another part of the rite. In the Episcopal Church the litany is one of the services which may be read by a lay person, therefore technically freeing Father Schultz of any implied or actual transgression of his faith; depending, of course, on what is meant by "participation," "worship," and even "non-Catholic" in the canon law which most Catholic canonists believe must be understood in the light of the new Decree on Ecumenism. The order of service at the Rev. Mr. Baker's ordination:

*Processional Hymn.*

*Sermon:* The Rev. Samuel Johnston, rector, St. Andrew's
   Church Kansas City.

*Introit Hymn*

*Presentation of the Candidate:* The Rev. Doug Vair, vicar,
   St. Barnabas Church, Moberly.

*The Bishop's Charge to the Congregation.*

*Litany for Ordinations:* The Rev. John Schultz, curate,
   St. Pius X Church, Moberly.

*The Ante-Communion:* Kyrie Eleison, the Collects, Epistle
   (the Rev. Calvin Stuart, curate, Church of the
   Ascension, St. Louis), the Gospel (the Rev. Kirk
   Cresap, rector, St. James Church, Macon).

*The Exhortation and Examination*

*Veni Creator Spiritus*

*The Ordination Prayer*

*The Laying on of Hands*

*Presentation of the Holy Bible*

*The Nicene Creed*

*The Eucharist:* Offering (for diocesan Theological education fund); doxology, prayer for the Church,
   Sanctus, Prayer of Consecration, Agnus Dei, Communion Hymns.

*Prayer and Benediction*

*Recessional Hymn*

210. One of the most interesting of recent Catholic liturgical developments is the "Bible Vigil" service of prayer and Scripture, developed largely for deepening Catholic appreciation for the Scriptures, particularly among laymen. This has ecumenical portents for the future, according to the Rev. Father Michael J. Taylor, S. J., assistant professor of theology, Seattle University, in his half of a book written with the Rev. Romey P. Marshall, founder of the Order of St. Luke and pastor of the Summerdale (Pennsylvania) Methodist Church. Father Taylor says:

> Although Catholics have rigidly avoided worshipping with their separated brothers on the grounds that so doing has a tendency to promote indifferentism and to compromise, the faith of Catholics (cf. Canon 1258, *Communicatio in sacris*), there is cause to belive that a day is coming when these restrictions will be relaxed, precisely because certain forms of common worship can be devised which will not compromise the faith of Protestants or Catholics. Remarkably there is emerging within the Catholic Church a "para-liturgical" service that greatly resembles the liturgy of the Word. It would seem that in the Catholic "Bible Vigil" and in the Protestant "Service of the Word" we have acceptable ground for common prayer. The "Bible Vigil" after all, is just a modern variation of the traditional Christian synaxis service which is mother to both Protestant Worship and the Catholic Fore Mass. It is true that the service is strongly instructional with its emphasis on Scripture and homily; some would say that it has a "catechumenal" quality. But though instruction predominates, there is also community response by means of hymns and prayers; it is therefore true Christian worship and an especially worthy form for divided Christians to use in their prayer for unity. In this service the one Christ proclaims the one Gospel to a flock divided but in search of unity.

211. The purpose of the Bible service, or "vigil," or "devotion," as it is also called, is explained in a handbook, *Liturgy and Laity*, published by the Confraternity of the Precious Blood:

The main purpose of the Bible vigil is to make us more conscious of Holy Scripture, to create a scriptural mentality which will enable us to center the heart of our spirituality on the fundamental structures of Scripture and the Liturgy rather than on secondary devotions. The Bible vigils are not properly liturgy. They are para-liturgical since they are constructed along liturgical lines and dispose us to a deep appreciation of the liturgical response we intend to give God. In many countries, Bible vigils are called Bible devotions. We have deliberately refrained from calling them Bible devotions, since we would like to see them used principally, not exclusively, to prepare for the great liturgical celebrations in our lives, Holy Mass and the sacraments.

The structure of the Bible vigils is based on the broad outlines of the early Lenten Masses. There are two lessons, one from the Old Testament and one from the New Testament in addition to a reading from the Gospel. Each section is followed by a period of silent prayer and the Gospel by a homily when this is possible. Each of these three sections of God speaking to us receives a response, either in psalms or excerpts from His Word. There follows, finally, a litany of petition and a collect based on the theme of the Bible vigil, and the conclusion is a prayer of praise by all of the assembly.

Reading and hearing the Word of God under the aspect of a Bible vigil will be greatly beneficial to "forming this mind in us which is in Christ Jesus." Salvation history is the story of God's divine plan to reconcile man to himself in, with and through Christ. An important part of the plan is the giving of His words in Sacred Scripture. The Bible is God's book. It is special because it is His and in it He speaks to us, instructing, forming, threatening, loving. . . .

212. The structure of the Bible Service, recommended as one kind of popular devotion in the "Constitution on the Sacred Liturgy" of the Second Vatican Council, is suggested in some detail by the Rev. Father Geoffrey Wood, S.A., in his National

Council of Catholic Men's booklet, *Bible Services for the Laity:*

> The Bible Service is a form of instruction and worship that adapts easily to modern needs and conditions. It has freedom and spontaneity and can be conducted almost any time and almost any place. It has unlimited flexibility and appeal. . . .
>
> The participants are a celebrant, three readers (laymen) and laymen to carry the censer and lighted candles.
>
> One person conducts a practice session for the congregation before hand, during which the music is practiced briefly and preparation is made for the action to come later in the service. This practice should take no more than five minutes.
>
> The typical Bible Service begins with an entrance rite. The congregation stands and sings the entrance hymn as the celebrant, the readers and the assisting laymen enter the church.
>
> The readers enter first, followed by the layman carrying the censer. The celebrant, flanked by two men carring lighted candles, enters last. The celebrant reverently carries the Bible. While the congregation sings, this group marches up the aisle to the sanctuary.
>
> The celebrant places the Bible on a lectern in the center of the sanctuary. The Bible should be placed in such a way that the readers face the people when they speak.
>
> The celebrant opens the Bible to the first passage to be read, bows deeply toward the Bible, then incenses the Bible while the two men with lighted candles place them on either side of the Bible lectern. This concludes the entrance rite.
>
> The readers and the other participants then stand near their seats at the side of the sanctuary while the celebrant leads the preliminary prayer, an invocation to God, asking that he

look with favor on the gathering and open minds of the congregation to hear his word.

After this prayer, the celebrant explains the theme of the Bible Service to the congregation. This sets the stage for the Scripture readings to follow.

The celebrant and the congregation then sit to hear the Word of God read from the Bible. The first reader, who has been at the side of the sanctuary, comes to the lectern. He bows before the Bible, then announces the book from which the reading is to come, such as "a reading from the Book of Genesis." . . .

As soon as the first reading is completed, the reader takes his seat and the celebrant rises and comes forward to give his short comment about the passage. In this talk, the celebrant expounds on the Word of God and explains it more fully to the congregation.

After the celebrant's comment on the Scripture passage, he invites the congregation to sing or recite a psalm. . . . If pauses are made *only* at the end of each line, the psalms can be read in perfect unison.

This concludes this portion of the service. This same procedure is then repeated twice more. There is a reading, the celebrant's comment on the reading, and recitation or singing of a psalm.

After the third reading, the celebrant gives a homily. This is longer than the comments after the first two readings and explains fully the relationship between the people who have participated in the service and the three Bible passages that have been read. After the homily, the congregation sings or recites a psalm.

This is followed by a prayer.

After the prayer comes the action. This gives the congregation an added sense of fulfillment to the listening, singing and praying. This action adds a great sense of meaning to the Bible Service. The action may take many forms, such as a procession, blessing, litany or other communal participation.

For instance, if Baptism is the Bible Service theme, sprinkling the congregation with holy water is most appropriate.

The closing rite follows the action. The celebrant steps to the Bible, bows deeply, closes the book and takes it reverently from the Bible lectern. The congregation begins to sing the recessional hymn, and the celebrant, the readers and the assisting laymen march from the church.

The order of march is the same as for the entrance: readers first, thurifer, and the celebrant, flanked by the two men with lighted candles.

213. Booklets on the Bible service with a Christian unity theme began to appear: example, the Graymoor Friars (who started the Unity Octave in the United States) published a "Bible Devotions for Christian Unity." An imaginative effort was a "Bible Devotion on Unity" service prepared by the sisters at Marymount College, Boca Raton, Florida. The service is made up of "excerpts from the various booklets available," said Mother de la Croix, R.S.H.M., president of the college. The Rev. Canon Don H. Copeland, former rector of St. Stephen's Episcopal Church, Miami, and currently director of the World Center for Liturgical Studies, Boca Raton, took part as a lector, or reader, in one of the services.

The Bible devotion services came to the homes. Pioneering in preparing liturgical services that could be used in the home as well as in an auditorium were the Worcester Council of Churches and the Roman Catholic Diocese of Worcester. Five attractive booklets with symbols of the faith in contemporary art on the cover were prepared. A "Guide Sheet for Host Couple for an Evening of Christian Friendship," a supplement to the booklet, says:

It is hoped that this evening will enkindle a new kind of Christian friendship among neighbors that will continue to grow and deepen. . . . The following are some suggestions. . . .

(1) The host couple should open the meeting by leading the group in the singing of the hymn encouraging everyone to join in the singing.

(2) The husband of the host couple should then take the part of the leader and lead the group through the litany.

(3) Next the host should ask a member of the group to read the first Bible reading and to lead the group in the response which follows it. A different member of the group should be selected to read each of the Bible readings and responses which follow.

(4) The section on "Christian Testimony" (Bible commentary and discussion) will require some forethought on the part of the host, for here the host must take on the role of discussion leader. First, he reads aloud the introduction and the discussion question which follows. Then the host should begin the discussion by giving his testimony (commentary and discussion) first. It might help if next he would go around the room quickly and receive a "yes" or "no" answer from each member of the group to the first part of the discussion question and then go back to each for their comment on the second half of the question. It is important that everyone participate in this testimony (commentary and discussion) but the discussion should not be allowed to ramble and a time limit should be set. The testimony (commentary and discussion) should not take more than 30 minutes.

(5) After the "Christian Testimony" the "Choral Prayer," "Scriptural Readings," etc., should be continued and concluded with the closing hymn.

(6) The formal part of the evening should be followed by coffee and cake with friendly informal discussion. The discussion should center on the topics presented. The answers and responses of the group to these topics should be noted by the host couple and a report of them given to the CCD Diocesan office later on.

214. Catholics contributed to the practice of prayer in common by calling for prayers for the World Council of Churches meeting in New Delhi (later to be reciprocated by Protestants praying for Vatican II). A letter by Bernard Cardinal Alfrink, of Utrecht, and the rest of the Dutch hierarchy in November 1961, said:

What happens at New Delhi cannot leave us Catholics indifferent. Distress over the division of Christianity must also be felt by us as a true distress. The objective of unity aimed at by the Second Vatican Council is a vivid evidence of this. Pope John XXIII summons us all to a renewal of thought and life, in order that the pure shape of the Church for which the whole of Christendom is searching may become manifest.

We are asked for an effective interest and a joint, prayerful reflection upon Christ as the Light of the World. We are asked for prayer that is not against the other, but for the other—prayer in which everybody wishes for himself what he asks for the other. And that prayer is that in the Light of Christ all Christians may thus renew themselves, that from this joint renewal may result that unity which Christ wills and that it may be effected along the road He wills.

In that prayer, there will be a true community with all others to profess the name of Christ. Respond, therefore, to this call for prayer and sacrifice, to this call for joint reflection upon Christ as the true Light that must free us from the darkness of division.

215. A spontaneous, colloquial prayer, devoid of some of the more refined and sometimes studied phrases of the clergyman,

was nevertheless a great prayer of unity when uttered by an astronaut, Maj. Leroy Gordon Cooper, Jr., U.S. Air Force, on May
16, 1963. Literally circling the globe, the prayer was a ready
symbol of a common bond with the Creator, and it had universal
appeal in its simplicity (so much so, that not only did Billy Graham's magazine *Decision* quote Astronaut Cooper, a Methodist,
in its March, 1966, issue, but Augustin Cardinal Bea included
the prayer in his book, *Unity in Freedom*. To Bea, the prayer was
significant because it emphasized that man, even an astronaut,
must place his "ultimate hope in God." Maj. Cooper, who later
spent eight days in orbit, in August, 1965, explained his initial
prayer in his first orbital flight in a speech before the two houses
of Congress, May 21, 1963. "I am not too much of a preacher,"
he said, "but on the flight on the 17th orbit, I felt so inclined to
put a small prayer on the tape recorder in the space-craft—it was
over the middle of the Indian Ocean in the middle of the night.
Things had been going so beautifully, everything had been working perfectly, and it was an ideal flight. I was encouraged to read
a little transcript of this prayer as an ending [to his speech].
... " His prayer, repeated at the joint session of Congress:

> Father, thank you, especially for letting me fly this flight.
> Thank you for the privilege of being able to be in this posi-
> tion; to be up in this wondrous place, seeing all these many
> startling, wonderful things that you have created. Help
> guide and direct all of us that we may shape our lives to be
> much better Christians, trying to help one another, and to
> work with one another rather than fighting and bickering.
> Help us to complete this mission successfully. Help us in our
> future space endeavors that we may show the world that a
> democracy really can compete, and still are able to do things
> in a big way, and are able to do research, development, and
> can conduct many scientific and very technical programs. Be
> with all our families. Give them guidance and encouragment,
> and let them know that everything will be OK. We ask in
> thy name. Amen.

216. Paul-Emile Cardinal Leger, of Montreal, led a series of
prayers for unity in an ecumenical service at the University of

Montreal in connection with the World Council of Churches
Fourth Faith and Order Conference, July 21, 1963. He shared
the platform with the Rev. Dr. William A. Visser 't Hooft,
World Council general secretary, and Metropolitan Athenagoras,
Greek primate of Canada (now primate of England). Said Cardinal Leger:

> It is on their knees that men must continue their difficult
> search for peace. In a divided world, where blocs set themselves against each other, where peoples have become restless, Christians must search for truth, practice justice by
> respecting the rights of all men, and seek to establish a
> climate of freedom which is necessary for men who want to
> live in charity.
>
> If the Churches do not bring this peace to the world, if they
> do not give the witness of unity in Christ, the Twentieth
> Century may well lose its opportunity of salvation.

217. Facing differences through prayer was "An Ecumenical
Prayer" of the Rev. Father John A. Carr, C.S.P., given at the
*Catholic World* Associates conference on "The Christian and Religious Liberty on the American Scene" at Carnegie International
Center, New York City, May 8, 1965:

> O God, the unending source of life and wisdom, guide and
> strengthen our efforts to understand better the practical,
> complex religious problems of our pluralistic society and to
> advance to solutions that will be acceptable and beneficial to
> the people of this land of the free. May we always be ready
> to converse with others in friendly fashion, to respect the
> opinions of others and to learn from one another. And when
> we disagree, may we do so with calmness and kindness. May
> our minds and hearts never be closed to truth and love which
> nourish the human spirit. Sweep away our prejudices that
> we may be open and receptive to new insights that will make
> us more like you and more tolerant of our fellow citizens.
> May you, the one true God who gives freedom to everyone,
> bless all of us.

218. From Nigeria, comes this prayer for Christian oneness:

> O God, our Father, we ask Thee to bless our three Churches (Anglican, Methodist, and Presbyterian), as we prepare for our new life together (in the proposed Church of Nigeria).
>
> May every member have a burning desire for that unity which Thou has planned for us:
>
> Give to our leaders special gifts of wisdom and understanding, as they seek to know and follow Thy will:
>
> Make us less concerned about our own interests, and more ready to accept together Thy way for us:
>
> Make us less fearful for ourselves, and more fearless as Thy witnesses:
>
> Make us less anxious to seek power, and more anxious to serve the needs of the world around us:
>
> Fill our Churches with love in every part, that the world may see in us that pattern of fellowship for which it hungers:
>
> Keep our minds open to the guidance of the Holy Spirit that wherever He may seek to lead us, we may always be ready to follow.
>
> We offer this prayer, in the fellowship of Thy people, and in the name of Jesus Christ our Lord and Saviour.

219. What do Catholics and Protestants say when they formulate prayers together?

    a. In the schools:

        (1) Jewish, Catholic and Protestant chaplains jointly composed a prayer for the American Legion's "God and Country"

covers for textbooks. The prayer was presented by the national chaplain of the American Legion, the Rev. Alfred C. Thompson, of Brookyln, in February, 1966, to the NCC Division of Christian Education, meeting in Louisville as a means and example of giving religion a "legal and proper place" in the public schools following the Supreme Court rulings against recitation of a state prepared prayer (Engle v. Vitale, 1962) and then of the Lord's Prayer and Bible reading (Abington Township, Pennsylvania, School District v. Schempp and Murray v. Curlett, 1963). The Legion's prayer, which could be used by children who wished to use it, and when they wanted to, appeared on more than 1,750,000 book covers distributed by the Legion. The prayer said:

> We acknowledge our dependence on Thee, Almighty God, and pray Thee to assist with Thy spirit of counsel and fortitude the leaders of our country. Grant that they may perpetuate to us the blessings of liberty and freedom. Bless our teachers and parents and all the people of our beloved country and may we ever be faithful to Thee. Amen.

(2) In Fairfax, Virginia, this prayer was used in the W. T. Woodson High School (it was challenged, however, by the American Civil Liberties Union):

> Come, Lord God, and be our guest. Let these Thy gifts to us be blessed. For health and strength and daily food, we praise thy name, O Lord, Amen.

(3) In Dar es Salaam, Tanzania, this prayer, in the Kiswahili language, was agreed on by the Education Secretaries of the Tanganyika Episcopal Conference and the Christian Council of Tanganyika for use in all Christian schools:

> O God, our Creator, we greet You, we adore You, we ask You to bless us this day. Help us in our lessons and studies that we may get the education which will be of profit to us during our life here on earth. Enrich us also with the knowledge we need to give You due honour and service, Amen.

b. In the institutions, there was, for example, this inter-faith prayer at the Detroit General Hospital, written by the Protestant chaplain, the Rev. Robert Pattie:

> O Almighty God,
> You know the sin that I have
>         the pain that I feel
>         the fear that I know
>         the hope that I hold
> In thy love and mercy be present with me at this time and in this place. Bless those who serve in this hospital that they may do all for love of thee. I pray this in the faith that is mine. Amen.

220. When two interfaith chapels at two military bases (Fort Dix, New Jersey, September 3, 1964, and Lackland AFB, Texas, September 13) were dedicated, this prayer was used:

> CHAPLAIN: As a reminder of the presence of God with His children;
>
> PEOPLE: We dedicate this house.
>
> CHAPLAIN: As a place of worship for men of every faith;
>
> PEOPLE: We dedicate this house.
>
> CHAPLAIN: As a place of prayer and meditation;
>
> PEOPLE: We dedicate this house.
>
> CHAPLAIN: As an incentive to right living and unselfish service;
>
> PEOPLE: We dedicate this house.

221. Four faiths were represented in the prayers offered at the inauguration of President Johnson, January 20, 1965, as they

had been present at previous inaugurations. Offering the prayers
were the Most Rev. Robert E. Lucy, of San Antonio, Texas; Rabbi
Hyman Judah Schachtel, Congregation Beth Israel, Houston; the
Rev. Dr. George R. Davis, pastor, National Christian Church,
Washington, and Archbishop Iakovos, of the Greek Orthodox
Archdiocese of North and South America. Archbishop Iakovos
prayed this benediction:

> Omnipotent and Omniscient God, Who in Thy Providence
> ordainest that the destinies of men and nations upon this
> earth should be entrusted into the hands of the worthy:
> hearken, we beseech Thee, to our Thanksgiving prayer and
> supplication.
>
> From the time of the pilgrims and founding Fathers of this
> Nation and throughout the course of our entire history, Thou
> hast been our guiding light, our constant inspiration and
> illumination and an inexhaustible source of reinforcement
> and fortitude.
>
> Having our trust in Thee, we have raised, under the splendor
> of Thy skies, the stars and stripes of our exalted ideals and
> national pursuits. And in the measure of Thy loving kind-
> ness, we selflessly served the spiritual, as well as the mate-
> rial welfare, of our fellow men, at home and abroad.
>
> We believe it is Thy Will that we continue in an unbroken
> continuity, this honored tradition, and it is this belief that
> underlies the Inaugural Ceremonies and installation of our
> thirty-sixth President in the person of an honorable and
> dedicated servant of our people, Lyndon Baines Johnson.
>
> This Inaugural Ceremony is a most solemn act of rededica-
> tion. We, therefore, Pray to Thee, O Lord, to empower our
> beloved President, his Vice President and associates in the
> government of our Nation, to ever guard the real image and
> beauty of our commonwealth as the land of the free and the
> home of the brave. Shield and protect them from all ills,

and enable us, O Merciful One, to ever uphold the spirit that made our Nation the hope of the distressed and the joy of the oppressed.

We ask this in the Name of the Father and of the Son and of the Holy Ghost, the all-holy, life-giving Trinity, and for the benefit of our nation and all nations believing in or aspiring for freedom, justice, dignity and peace. Amen.

222. A commonly used ecumenical prayer is Jesus' own, the Lord's Prayer. Pope Paul VI and the observers prayed it together December 4, 1965, in the ecumenical rite with the Protestants and Orthodox at the close of the Vatican Council. (The program listed the "Catholic" version, minus the final words, "For thine is the kingdom, and the power, and the glory, for ever." Actually, there is no monopoly of Protestants on the longer version—Roman Catholics have used it in earlier times, and still do in the Byzantine rite. Missing nearly unanimously in the more reliable of the ancient New Testament manuscripts, the final phrase is left out of the Revised Standard Version of the Bible and the New English Bible. As a common courtesy, at ecumenical gatherings, the Protestants usually stop before the final words, as their Catholic brethren are used to doing, while the Catholics continue on with the full wording. During Pope Paul's visit to the United Nations, he prayed the Lord's Prayer with Archbishop Iakovos, Greek Orthodox archbishop of North and South America—the Pope used Latin, Iakovos prayed in Greek.

(Augustin Cardinal Bea recited the Lord's Prayer as a guest at an Eastern Orthodox Divine Liturgy celebrated by Orthodox Ecumenical Patriarch Athenagoras I in Istanbul.) When the Rev. Father John B. Sheerin, editor of the *Catholic World*, addressed a 12:30 P.M. Lenten service in the Pilgrim Hall of the Broadway Congregational Church of the United Church of Christ, New York City, March 24, 1965, he led the congregation in the Lord's Prayer afterwards.

The leaders of two Lutheran churches of France, the Reformed, the Orthodox churches and the Roman Catholic church issued a new joint version of the Lord's Prayer in the beginning of 1966. Making the announcement were Etienne Jung of the Church of the

Augsburg Confession of Alsace and Lorraine and Marcel Joron of the Evangelical Lutheran Church of France, Joseph Cardinal Lefebvre, chairman of the French bishops' conference, and leaders of two Reformed denominations, and four Orthodox prelates. Translated by the Rev. Father George H. Tavard, of Mount Mercy College, Pittsburgh, a native Frenchman and church unity scholar, here is the English version of the new French common version of the Lord's prayer:

> Our Father, who are in heaven, may your Name be sanctified, may your Kingdom come, may your Will be done on earth as in heaven.
> Today give us our bread for this day.
> Forgive us our offenses, as we also forgive those who have offended us.
> And do not test us through temptation, but deliver us from evil.

## REFERENCES

### Chapter VI

177. Gregory Baum, "Communicatio in Sacris," *The Ecumenist*, II, No. 4 (May-June, 1964), 60.
178. Cyril C. Richardson, "Word and Sacrament in Protestant Worship," Samuel H. Miller and G. Ernest Wright, eds., *Ecumenical Dialogue at Harvard* (Cambridge, Mass.: The Belknap Press of Harvard University, 1964), p. 160.
179. *Proposed Order for Holy Week and Easter*, authorized for experimental use only, pp. 9-11. Prepared by the Commission on Worship, LCA.
180. *Missal for Use of Orthodox:* The Divine Liturgy According to the Western Rite (Mount Vernon: Society of St. Basil, 1963), pp. 13-15.
181. a. Max Lackmann, *The Evangelical Mass*, reprinted from the *Yearbook of Liturgical Studies*, IV (Notre Dame, Ind.: Fides Publishers, 1963), pp. 36 *ff.*
    b. *Ibid.*, pp. 47, 48.
182. a. "A Proposal for a Center for Interfaith Research on Religious Architecture," supplied by the Church Building and Architecture Department of the NCC, p. 6.
    b. *Ibid.*, p. 3.
183. *Religious News Service*, Garrison, N.Y., Aug. 26, 1960.
184. Letter, Massachusetts Council of Churches letterhead, Jan. 1, 1965, signed by the Rev. Albert J. Penner, Council president, and Richard Cardinal Cushing.
185. *Holy Cross News*, Holy Cross Monastery, West Park, N.Y., III, No. 1, 2.

186. Pamphlet, "Week of Prayer for Christian Unity," Jan. 18-25, 1966, sponsored by the NCC and WCC Departments of Faith and Order and recommended by the Bishops' Commission for Ecumenical Affairs.
187. a. and b. Copies of letters to the Most Rev. Charles H. Helmsing, bishop of Kansas City-St. Joseph, dated Oct. 22, 1964, and a reply by the chancellor, the Rt. Rev. Msgr. Joseph V. Sullivan, Oct. 23, supplied by the Rev. Shrum Burton, president of the Council of Churches of Metropolitan Kansas City.
188. Copy of letter from the Rev. Richard D. Isler, executive director of the Council of Churches of Greater Cincinnati, to local clergy, June 17, 1964.
189. From program bulletin, "An Evening of Ecumenical Witness," Municipal Auditorium, San Antonio, Tex., June 2, 1963.
190. Program Bulletin, "A Christian Memorial Service for Civil Rights Workers," Tokyo, Oct. 25, 1964, courtesy of the Rev. Dr. Henry D. Jones, industrial missionary, United Presbyterian Church, Tokyo.
191. Program bulletin, "Ecumenical Advent Service," Christ Church, Cambridge, Nov. 29, 1964, courtesy of the Rev. Gardiner M. Day, rector.
192. From the mimeographed German text of the worship service, courtesy of Helmut Blasche, Schwechat, Austria, Apr. 26, 1965.
193. "Celebration of Prayer for Promoting the Unity of Christians, with the participation of the Holy Father, Paul VI, together with the Fathers of the II Vatican Council and the Delegated Observers and Guests," Basilica of St. Paul Outside the Walls, Dec. 4, 1965, mimeographed text distributed to the press at the Vatican Council.
194. "Experiment in interfaith conversation," *Federation News*, No. 2, 1965, pp. 9, 10; also letter from Dr. Kelley, July 30, 1965.
195. Service No. 5, Cane Ridge Meeting House, *Worship Services*, Consultation on Church Union, Lexington, Ky., 1965, p. 11.
196. "An Agape Meal in Manchester," in *Congregemur*, "A Worship Booklet for Modern Young People," edited by the Youth Department, World Council of Churches, 150 route de Ferney, 1211 Geneva.
197. "Historic Occasion at St. Peter's," *Bexhill-on-Sea Observer*, Bexhill-on-Sea, Sussex, England, Jan. 9, 1965.
198. a. and b. *Associated Press*, Feb. 8, 1965, Flagstaff, Ariz.
199. Sermon excerpt, Apr. 4, courtesy the Rev. Dr. James H. Laird, minister, Central Methodist Church, Detroit.
200. Letter, the Rev. Murray Kenney, rector and ecumenical officer, Diocese of Missouri (Episcopal), to Sister Ann Patrick Ware, Webster College, Webster Groves, Mo., Nov. 4, 1965.
201. The Rev. Dr. Charles P. Robshaw, from his column "The Service for Observers" in the East Liberty Presbyterian *Church Week*, XVIII, No. 29 (Apr. 9, 1965), and from a letter from Dr. Robshaw, Aug. 3, 1965.
202. "A Mighty Fortress Is Our God," opening lines by Martin Luther; remainder of hymn by J. Clifford Evers, in *People's Mass Book* (Cincinnati: World Library of Sacred Music, 1964), No. 111, p. 156.
203. Letter, June 25, 1965, from Howard D. McKinney, of the J. Fischer and Brothers Music Publishers, Glen Rock, N.J., to Gordon Young, Detroit composer.
204. Leslie Schnierer, William O'Malley, "The Lord God," 1963.
205. Clifford A. Bennett, Paul Hume, eds., *Hymnal of Christian Unity* (Toledo, O.: Gregorian Institute of America, Inc. 1964), p. 2.
206. a. From letter from the Rev. Father H. Vanwaesberghe, S.J., University of Nijmegen, The Netherlands, Mar. 30, 1965.

b. *Volkskrant*, Dec. 11, 1964.
207. a. From Letter from the Rev. Father Thomas Pitsch, St. Patrick's Roman Catholic Church, Tacoma, Mar. 3, 1965.
 b. "Letters" column, *Crusader*, American Baptist national monthly, Feb., 1965, p. 10.
208. Text supplied by the Board of Missions of The Methodist Church, Sept. 15, 1964.
209. From program bulletin, "The Ordination to the Priesthood of the Rev. Richard Henry Baker," St. Paul's (Episcopal) Church, Palmyra, Mo., Dec. 19, 1964.
210. Romey P. Marshall, Michael J. Taylor, S.J., *Liturgy and Christian Unity* (Englewood Cliffs, N.J.: Prentice-Hall, Inc., 1965), p. 168.
211. Peter A. Chiara, *Liturgy and Laity* (Brooklyn: Confraternity of the Precious Blood, 1964), pp. 149, 150.
212. Geoffrey Wood, S.A., *Bible Services for the Laity* (Washington: National Council of Catholic Men, 1964), pp. 10-12.
213. "Guide Sheet for Host Couple for an Evening of Christian Friendship," mimeographed, courtesy of the Rev. Father Mederic J. Roberts, director, Confraternity of Christian Doctrine, Diocese of Worcester.
214. *Religious News Service*, Utrecht, Nov. 16, 1961.
215. Major Leroy Gordon Cooper, Jr., U.S. Air Force, Joint Meeting of the two Houses of Congress, *Congressional Record*, May 21, 1963, p. 9156.
216. *Presbyterian Life*, Sept. 1, 1963, p. 26, with approval of this text from Cardinal Leger.
217. John A. Carr, C.S.P., "An Ecumenical Prayer," *The Catholic World*, CCI, No. 1, 206 (Sept., 1965), 366.
218. "A Prayer of Preparation for the Union of the Anglican, Methodist, and Presbyterian Churches" in Nigeria, *Church Union News*, No. 4, Jan.-Apr., 1964, Lagos, Nigeria, p. 16.
219. a. (1) From American Legion "God and Country" textbook cover.
 (2) *Religious News Service*, quoted in *Michigan Christian Advocate*, Nov. 26, 1964, p. 9.
 (3) Release, Catholic Secretariat, Tanganyika Episcopal (Catholic Bishops') Conference, Dar es Salaam, PNB 14/64, FvD/rpa, July 11, 1964.
 b. Receiving Hospital "Chaplaincy Service" card, Detroit, Rev. Robert Pattie, chaplain.
220. *The Chaplain*, Feb., 1965, p. 46.
221. "Inaugural Benediction," the Most Rev. Iakovos, archbishop of the Greek Orthodox archdiocese of North and South America, release from the Office of the Public Relations (Greek Orthodox, New York), Jan. 19, 1965.
222. French text, Lutheran World Federation release, Paris, Jan. 18, 1966. Translation by the Rev. Father George H. Tavard, Mount Mercy College, Pittsburgh. The French text: "Notre Pere qui es aux cieux, que ton nom soit sanctifie, que ton regne vienne, que ta volonte soit faite sur la terre comme au ciel. Donne-nous aujourd'hui notre pain de ce jour. Pardonne-nous nos offenses, comme nous pardonnons aussi a ceux qui nous ont offenses. Et ne nous soumets pas a la tentation, mais delivre-nous du mal."

# seven

# Fruits of Cooperation

Once the seeds of inter-Christian relations had begun to grow, and conversation was a reality on all levels, the new activity began to bear fruit. As people talked with one another they began to help one another, and more, to become aware of greater needs in the world and ways they could meet the challenges cooperatively. "By their fruits ye shall know them," said Jesus (Matt. 7: 20). The fruits of genuine interfaith contacts were many: in the international sphere, in the nation, and in the community. Not only were there advancements in study and research efforts, such as plans for developing a common Bible (see Chapter IV), but there was new fresh fruit of cooperation in the practical, social action field.

223. Yet there was still another side of the picture. For dialogue not only brings cooperation, but cooperation brings more dialogue and togetherness, a measure of unity, noted the Roman Catholic bishops of Canada. Social action also gives birth to the tree of faith. The seed was indeed in the fruit:

> Probably at no time in our history have men united to the same degree in meeting the needs of the hungry, the sick, tho unlettered, and the unaccepted.

410

And even though, in doing so, we have not always shared the common ideal of uniting all in Christ, a great measure of unity has resulted.

When men of goodwill work together to serve the needs of all, they are responding to God's will that all men unite. And so social action, in building the community of man, prepares the way for perfect community in the city of God. . . .

Only when all things are united in Christ will all men have their share. We Christians, who are nearly one third of humanity, can hasten that day by uniting with one another to this end.

224. Linking love and unity in religion, Patriarch Vasken I, Etchmiadzin, Armenia, head of the Ancient Church of Armenia, said in an encyclical letter:

Let us pray that our Lord shall cause the light from His universe of love to shine into our hearts, our life and on the work of our hands, so that we all, all Christians of the world, learn to walk on the road of peace and brotherly cooperation. "For love is of God" and "God is love" (1 John 4: 7, 8).

It was with this spirit of love that Christ and the Apostles founded the Church. It is with this spirit of love alone that all Christian churches may unite in the Universal Church of Christ.

With this spirit of love, the churches and the faithful are "no more strangers and sojourners, but fellow citizens with the saints, the household of God, built upon the foundation of the apostles and prophets, Christ Jesus himself being the cornerstone" (Eph. 2: 19, 20). . . .

We urge and invite you, our beloved people, to proceed, without deviation on the luminous path bequeathed to us by our forefathers, our National Apostolic Holy Church, and to work sincerely and joyously so as to see the realization of the unity and fraternity of all Christian churches through the life giving love of Christ.

"Remember them that had the rule over you, men that spake unto you the word of God and considering the issue of their life; imitate their faith" (Heb. 13: 7).

Love, peace and unity to all Christian churches.
Love, peace and unity to the Armenian Church, now and forever.

The mercy of God and grace of our Jesus Christ be with you, Amen.

VASKEN I, Supreme Patriarch and Catholicos of all Armenians

225. Behind the scenes, church representatives met in small groups to consider steps of cooperation in practical areas. Thirty Roman Catholic representatives and WCC officials met in Geneva in February, 1966, to discuss measures for more cooperation in emergency aid around the world. Chairmen of the meeting were Anglican Archbishop Campbell MacInnes, of Jerusalem, and Msgr. Jean Rodhain, of Paris, president of the International Conference of Catholic Charities. Eleven representatives of the WCC and eight Roman Catholics from the Vatican's Secretariat for the Promoting of Christian Unity, met in Pinner, England, in the same month to outline areas of "consultation" and "collaboration" in services areas.

Christians planned to demonstrate their common concern for humanity by planning only one exhibit together at the 1967 World Exposition in Montreal. Leaders of seven Christian groups signed the agreement: Paul-Emile Cardinal Leger, Montreal (Roman Catholic); the Rev. Dr. E. M. Howse, Toronto (moderator, United Church of Canada); the Rt. Rev. R. Kenneth Maguire, Anglican bishop of Montreal; the Rev. Dr. C. Ritchie Bell, (stated clerk, Presbyterian Church in Canada); the Rev. Emrys Jenkins (moderator, Baptist Convention of Ontario and

Quebec) ; the Rt. Rev. Timotheus (bishop, Greek Orthodox Diocese of Canada), and the Rev. Dr. Earl J. Treusch, Winnipeg (executive director, Canadian Lutheran Council). Their common declaration of purpose said:

> Joined together through their baptism in a same faith in Jesus Christ and in a same hope, the Christians of Canada on the occasion of the 1967 World Exhibition of Montreal, wish to express their love to their fellowmen throughout the world, and to alleviate the anxieties and fulfill the expectations of our century by a common proclamation of the Gospel. Beyond the cleavages imposed by history, the Christians of the whole world will rejoice at the news of the following decision that we have reached as a result of many months of meetings and exchanges of views: together we will erect a Christian Pavilion capable of showing the world that God was made Flesh to dwell among us and that He is present in all that is happening concerning "Man and his World."
>
> In spite of those things that separate us, we believe that we can and must humbly bear witness together to our faith in Jesus Christ and to our intent to be, like Him, servants of our fellowmen. Before God we wish to carry out this work together, in order to implore perfect Christian unity which His divine grace can give. To the world in which we live this gesture is an invitation to meditate upon the salvation offered to our free will and upon the hope that goes out to meet the world in its forward march.

226. The spirit of oneness propelled the churches to seek answers to man's political dilemmas and the continued threat of nuclear war. Jointly-sponsored prayers were held for peace in Chicago during the 1965 Christmas holidays in the Dixon Chapel of the Chicago (Methodist) Temple and the Calvert (Roman Catholic) House, a student center. Also in Chicago, top-rank Catholic, Protestant, and Orthodox officials took part in an "hour of prayer for peace and unity" on New Year's eve 1965, co-sponsored by the Catholic Peace Fellowship, an affiliate of the Fel-

lowship of Reconciliation, and the Chicago Church Federation's Christian Citizenship Department. The invitation was issued by the Most Rev. John P. Cody, archbishop of Chicago. A year previously, in February, 1965, men of all faiths had rallied for a study conference of world leaders on the theme of Pope John's encyclical, *Pacem in Terris*. That conference, meeting for the most part in a New York hotel, went to the United Nations General Assembly for its opening night and heard Vice President Hubert Humphrey and the late UN Ambassador Adlai Stevenson praise the memory of Pope John and his quest for peace.

In the same year, on October 4, Pope Paul, in his first visit to the United Nations in the first trans-Atlantic papal trip, recalled the memory of Pope John XXIII and exhorted the nations, not only in his own name, but in the name of all Christians to work for peace:

> We are the bearer of a message for all mankind. And this we are, not only in our own personal name and in the name of the great Catholic family; but also in that of those Christian brethren who share the same sentiments which we express here, particularly of those who so kindly charged us explicitly to be their spokesman here. . . .
>
> No more war, war never again; Peace, it is peace which must guide the destinies of peoples and of all mankind. . . .
>
> Peace, as you know, is not built by means of politics, by the balance of forces and of interests. It is constructed with the mind, with ideas, with works of peace. You labor in this great construction. But you are still at the beginnings. Will the world ever succeed in changing that selfish and bellicose mentality which, up to now, has been interwoven into so much of its history? It is hard to foresee; but it is easy to affirm that it is towards that new history, a peaceful, truly human history, as promised by God to men of good will, that we must resolutely march. The roads thereto are already well marked out for you, and the first is that of disarmament.

If you wish to be brothers, let the arms fall from your hands. One cannot love while holding offensive arms. Those armaments, especially those terrible arms which modern science has given you, long before they produce victims and ruins, nourish bad feelings, create nightmares, distrust, and sombre resolutions; they demand enormous expenditures; they obstruct projects of union and useful collaboration; they falsify the psychology of peoples. As long as man remains that weak, changeable and even wicked being that he often shows himself to be, defensive arms will, unfortunately, be necessary. You, however, in your courage and valiance, are studying the ways of guaranteeing the security of international life without having recourse to arms. This is a most noble aim: this the peoples expect of you. This must be obtained! Let unanimous trust in this institution grow, let its authority increase; and this aim, we believe, will be secured. . . .

Indeed, it seems to us that here we hear the echo of the voice of our predecessors, and particularly of that of Pope John XXIII, whose message of *Pacem in Terris* was so honorably and significantly received among you.

You proclaim here the fundamental rights and duties of man, his dignity, his freedom—and, above all, his religious freedom. We feel that you thus interpret the highest sphere of human wisdom and, we might add, its sacred character. For you deal here above all with human life; and the life of man is sacred; no one may dare offend it. Respect for life, even with regard to the great problem of birth, must find here in your assembly its highest affirmation and its most reasoned defense. You must strive to multiply bread so that it suffices for the tables of mankind, and not rather favor an artificial control of birth, which would be irrational, in order to diminish the number of guests at the banquet of life.

It does not suffice, however, to feed the hungry; it is nec-

essary also to assure to each man a life conformed to his
dignity. This, too, you strive to perform. We may consider
this the fulfilment before our very eyes, and by your efforts,
of that prophetical announcement so applicable to your institution: "They will melt down their swords into plough-
shares, their spears into pruningforks." . . .

227. Just a few weeks after Pope Paul's plea at the United
Nations the Sixth World Order Study Conference, under the
auspices of the National Council of Churches' International Affairs Commission, recommended in St. Louis that new initiatives be made by the churches cooperatively to study the issue
of world peace. The World Order Conference recommended:

> (a) That there be the fullest co-operation with na-
> tional and international non-governmental organizations
> which share our concern for the development of peace in-
> cluding economic and social co-operation and cultural ex-
> change.

> (b) Exploration be undertaken with the World Coun-
> cil of Churches, the Vatican, the Ecumenical Patriarchate
> of the Eastern Orthodox Church and the representatives
> of such other faiths as are interested regarding the conven-
> ing of a conference to discuss a religious approach to world
> peace.

> (Concerning future World Order Study conferences):

> We recommend that the National Council of Churches in-
> vite Roman Catholic, Jewish, and other religious commu-
> nities to share in the planning and sponsorship of future na-
> tional study conferences on world order.

228. Churches in 1966 expressed themselves in joint statements on war and peace in more specific terms than before. On
the nation's conscience was the war in Vietnam, right or wrong,
and the voices of Christians, some of whom had marched on
Washington in November, 1965, in protest of United States policy

in Vietnam, under the auspices of the National Committee for a sane nuclear policy, and others, were heard in a united refrain of concern, although they did not always agree in specifics. They generally supported negotiations in Vietnam, and in some cases, specified negotiations with the Viet Cong in South Vietnam, an unrecognized political entity, and there was general consensus against continuing bombings of North Vietnam. Twenty-five hundred Protestant, Jewish and Roman Catholic clergy reportedly supported the newly formed International Committee of Conscience on Vietnam sponsored by the pacifist Fellowship of Reconciliation.

a. Another newly-formed group, the National Emergency Committee of Clergy Concerned about Vietnam, attracted leading men of all faiths and was more conciliatory in its demands; but nevertheless the group underscored a discontent, if not dissatisfaction, with United States policy in Vietnam. On January 12, 1966, the Committee wired President Johnson, its protest of the "inhumanity" in the Vietnamese war, but later followed with a wire of appreciation for the President's "persistence in seeking a negotiated peace." In its initial wire to the President, the Committee said:

We are appalled by the inhumanity of the war in Vietnam and the extension of hostilities to neighboring countries. Impending national decisions about Vietnam will fundamentally influence the political, military and, above all, the moral future of our nation and world. We are heartened by your recent efforts for peace and we urge:

(1) That the cessation of bombing in North Vietnam be maintained.

(2) That you continue to press for a negotiated peace, and that the National Liberation Front be given direct representation in all discussions.

(3) That you vigorously resist all pressures toward further escalation.

(4) That economic development for humane purposes at home and abroad be given budgetary priority over military spending.

b. The National Inter-Religious Conference on Peace billed as the first "religious summit for world peace," with its co-chairmen drawn from the Catholic, Orthodox, Protestant and Jewish ranks proposed a ceasefire of indefinite length that could begin on Good Friday, 1966. The leaders also asked for the admission of the People's Republic of China to the United Nations. The statement on Vietnam said:

> We, the members of this National Inter-Religious Conference on Peace,
>
> Ever mindful of the important formal statements on the war in Vietnam which have been made separately and recently by Pope Paul, by the Synagogue Council of America, by the National Council of Churches, and by other official groups;
>
> Deeply concerned by the continuing and increasingly tragic consequences of that war;
>
> Keenly sensitive to the moral issues involved in this entire sad situation, and especially in the consequential taking of many lives of innocent civilians;
>
> Fully aware that the matter is complex and intense and solutions are not easy;
>
> Do request and authorize the co-chairmen [Rabbi Maurice Eisendrath, Catholic Bishop John Wright, Methodist Bishop John Wesley Lord, Episcopal Presiding Bishop John Hines, Orthodox Archbishop Iakovos, Unitarian Dan Greeley] of this Conference to ask a number of other major leaders of American religious bodies to join with them and together to seek a personal conference with the President at the White House for the purpose of respectfully urging upon the President that he:
>
> (1) Consider respectfully an immediate halt to the bombing in Vietnam;

(2) Announce the readiness of the United States to join in a ceasefire of indefinite duration, beginning Good Friday, 1966, with no continuation of the build up on either side;

(3) Pursue every possible avenue, including channel of the UN that may create more favorable circumstances under which negotiations can begin;

(4) Adhere steadfastly to the principle that there can not be a satisfactory military solution to this problem, and until a negotiated settlement is achieved, not to permit a change in the character of the conflict through military escalation;

(5) Agree to the direct representation of the National Liberation Front [Viet Cong] as well as the other concerned parties in any negotiations;

(6) Maintain a determination to promote social and economic change and progress in South Vietnam and to provide the people of that land an opportunity, at an early date, to choose their own government;

(7) Continue providing reconstruction assistance and long range economic development funds for southeast Asia;

(8) Direct that high priority be placed in Vietnam upon patient, persistent, peace building programs, to overcome the dehumanizing and brutalizing effect, especially upon youth, of the 20-year war.

We do further state expressly that this delegation of religious leaders will make their presentations to the President with the thoughtful and understanding knowledge of the conflicting advice and pressures to which he is ever subject and of the awesome responsibility and heavy burden which he now carries in the White House. For him, and all sharing his onerous responsibilities, we pledge our prayers.

We further suggest that most Congressional leaders would

welcome similar conversations and representations in which
the delegates here bring to bear the rethinking and moral
guidance which legislators need in groping with the problems of maintaining the peace of the world.

229. Sometimes the involvement of churchmen in issues of
war and peace reflected their culture and political ideologies.
Nevertheless, reconciliation was on the mind of the churchmen.

a. In Vienna, September 7-9, 1964, the annual Congress
of the International Committee for the Defense of Christian
Culture, representing churchmen and statesmen of all faiths,
mostly in the West, expressed its concern by calling for:

(1) Affirmation and defense of Christian principles, the
ethics of the West and a search for forms of coexistence
that will guarantee to all nations human dignity, freedom,
justice and social development under improved world conditions;

(2) Resistance against regimes and political concepts that
are contrary to the Christian spirit and the ethics of the
West;

(3) Cooperation of Western peoples and persons in responsible positions, to promote progress toward these aims.

b. At the other pole of the political spectrum, 60 representatives of religious groups among 1,500 delegates to the World
Congress for Peace, National Independence and General Dis-
armament, meeting in Helsinki, issued an "appeal . . . to all people of good will, to work for peace." The terms of peace, however,
reflected anti-American sentiment, particularly in regard to Vietnam. Six of the clergy were from the United States and at least
three of them raised a voice of protest against what they called
the one-sidedness of the statement. The appeal of the larger
group, the sixty, said:

Our religious responsibilities for the destinies and ways of
mankind in the contemporary world had caused us who represent different countries and peoples and numerous reli-

gious creeds to rally for joint efforts with those who treasure
peace and who dedicate their lives to serving their neigh-
bour and protecting him.

In the name of God and His love for the human race we appeal to you to raise your voices and to unite in order to avert
death and destruction of the world.

We are divided by distances, various boundaries and political barriers but thanks to the intimacy of our hearts and
with the almighty help of God we can unite in our service
to the people. Age-old alienation and religious division still
exist among us but we are all children of One God, and
brothers, and precisely at this time we should open our arms
to each other in the name of God and in the spirit of His
Love. When innocent blood is being shed and we ignore
the sufferings of mankind our prayers cannot please the
Lord, for our inaction and silence put a deadly sword into
the hands of war-mongers. Therefore, in sending our ardent
prayers to God to pacify mankind we, as citizens of the
Earth, do everything in our power in order to rule enmity,
hatred and fratricidal wars out of human life. We urge you
to take active steps conducive to an immediate end to the
murderous war on the longsuffering land of Vietnam, in
the Dominican Republic and other parts of the world where
dangerous hotbeds of war arise. We urge you to become
aware of the fraternal bonds that unite us as human beings
in order to defend and secure the right of every man to
live and in order to uphold his dignity. . . .

230. Churches continued to maintain they had a right to speak
on international issues, from Poland, where Stefan Cardinal
Wyszynski was kept from going to Rome on account of allegedly
political views expressed in 1965, to the United States churches
faced with a growing right wing extremism, especially during
the Presidential election campaign.

Some denominations combatted growing criticism that the
churches were soft on Communism with anti-Communist statements of their own. The Church Council of The American

Lutheran Church, for instance, came out with a ringing condemnation of Communism in a statement on October 27, 1961:
"Marxist-Leninist Communism" breeds "hate" and "must be condemned." But Protestants and Catholics were facing head-on
and together a common challenge from the extreme right ex-
tremists. An 80-page treatise on "Communism: Threat to Freedom" by John F. Cronin, assistant director, Department of Social
Action of the National Catholic Welfare Conference, warned of
"hysteria or unreasoned fear," and gave Protestant clergy a clean
bill of goods, as well as Catholics. The rightists, Father Cronin
said, "would be hard pressed to name 200 living clergy who are or
have been Communist sympathizers." A National Council for
Civic Responsibility, backed by 80 leading clergy of all faiths
(the president of the National Council of Churches and the presiding bishop of the Protestant Episcopal Church were included)
was formed September 22, 1964, by Dr. Arthur Larson, former
under-secretary of Labor and special assistant to President Eisen-
hower. In announcing the formation of the group, Larson said:

> . . . The National Council for Civic Responsibility [is] an
> organization whose purpose is systematically to bring to the
> American people, through the mass media, the truth about
> the John Birch Society and related radical reactionary
> groups, and about the mis-statements on public issues and
> personalities that they are spreading on a rapidly increasing
> scale. . . .
>
> What they [members of the new organization] have in com-
> mon is a growing concern about the damage that will be
> done to American standards of public discussion and respon-
> sible behavior in a democratic society, unless a methodical
> and continuing program is launched to expose both im-
> propriety of methods and falsity of substance as they appear
> in radical reactionary broadcasts and publications.

231. Church World Service, relief arm of the National Council of Churches, and Catholic Relief Services cooperated in re-
settling Cuban refugees. "We're not concerned with who is a
member of what church," said one typical sponsor, the Rev. D.

Allan Easton, rector of St. Paul's Church in Wood-Ridge, New Jersey, and world relief secretary for the Episcopal Diocese of Newark. A fact sheet of the Cuban Refugee Center, Miami, explained one phase of the cooperation in 1962:

> Nearly 2,000 Cubans, escaping communist tyranny, continue to arrive in the United States each week. Miami, Florida, 90 miles from their communist-dominated homeland, is a generous host, serving as the port of entry that receives this great number of refugees week after week.
>
> But the time has come for a greater sharing in this example of traditional American hospitality to freedom-seeking Cubans. You, in communities throughout this free land, have opportunity to join in extending this welcome.
>
> Sponsors and jobs are the immediate need. Every state, every city has an obligation to provide jobs if full success is to attend the federal government's plan for refugee assistance. The United States program is administered by Secretary Ribicoff's Department of Health, Education, and Welfare, under a directive from President Kennedy.
>
> Our Cuban guests are eager to earn livelihoods in our free country. How you welcome them and provide job opportunities has a direct bearing on their evaluation of the United States way of life. Other peoples in our hemisphere, too, are observing the experiences of the Cuban refugees among us. Write to: The Cuban Refugee Center, Miami, Florida. . . .
>
> Represented at this Center, ready to fill orders of sponsorships and jobs for refugees, are these Voluntary Agencies experienced in resettlement: Catholic Relief Services, Church World Service, Hebrew Immigrant Aid Society, International Rescue Committee (Non-sectarian). Each may be reached through its representative in your community— priest, minister, or rabbi—or directy by addressing the Agency of your choice at the Refugee Center, Miami.

232. Responding to estimates that more than 12 million persons faced starvation in India in 1966, Protestants and Catholics pledged to raise funds together for India. In the Netherlands, for example, Catholics, Old Catholics, and Protestants teamed up with five TV and Radio networks and other organizations to raise 18,000,000 Guilders ($4,998,600) to aid famine victims in India. In the United States, the Rev. Dr. David M. Stowe, associate general secretary of the NCC and head of the NCC Division of Overseas Ministries, and Bishop Edward Swanstrom, executive director of Catholic Relief Services of the NCWC, issued a joint statement for Christians to raise their "collective voices" on behalf of the hungry in India.

A five-point recommendation, enabling the World Council of Churches to coordinate its relief projects with Roman Catholic agencies for famine victims in India and Africa was approved February 11, 1966, by the WCC's Central Committee meeting in Geneva. The recommendation asked Roman Catholic and WCC agencies to:

—Plan synchronized efforts within their nations for famine victims of India and Africa;

—Feature in their appeals not only needs for immediate relief and rehabilitation, but also for projects which will seek to prevent the recurrence of such disasters;

—Urge them in areas of need to consult together, to plan together and to take common action as far as is possible and desirable in their service to manifest the concern and care of the whole Christian community for those who are suffering;

—Urge the Roman Catholic Church and World Council of Churches at the international level to keep in closest touch with each other in order to provide the maximum continuing coordination possible for this Christian action; and,

—Urge Roman Catholic and World Council agencies to act in partnership in their collaboration with governmental and inter-governmental agencies involved in dealing with this emergency.

233. Ecumenical work camps developed under the auspices of the World Council of Churches. Originally engaged mostly in construction projects, the work camps have now reached over into providing special services for the handicapped and needy children and the aged. Although Protestant orientated, the camps have been open to anyone "who understands the nature of ecumenical work camps and who wishes to enter wholeheartedly into their life (even if he does not consider himself a Christian)." The philosophy of the camps is described in a leaflet published by the Youth Department of the World Council of Churches:

> ... Youth did not make this world; but it is theirs as well, and they have to decide whether they want to live with division or work for wholeness. One of the possibilities for young Christians to experience such wholeness is the ecumenical work camps programme of the World Council of Churches. Originally an undertaking to aid post-war Europe, this programme today involves more than 1,000 youth annually from all over the world in camps in Asia, the Middle East, Africa, Europe, and North and South America.
>
> An ecumenical work camp is a carefully selected international, interracial community of some fifteen to 25 Christian youth from a variety of denominational backgrounds who volunteer their time and labour to live and give service together. The average camp lasts from three to four weeks. It is a working vacation, where youth have a chance to test their faith in a common life of service to others.
>
> The kinds of work projects vary considerably and each camp establishes its own methods and rhythm of work. The average daily camp programme consists of six hours simple manual labour, of worship and Bible study, discussion and recreation. Work camps are laboratories of ecumenical experience. The manual labour is the kind that unskilled workers can do or learn to do with professional direction. Campers have the opportunity of getting to know the churches in the area and the country where they work.

Camps are held annually in some 40 countries. In recent years they have included these:

—Construction of a house and clearance of grounds for a church-sponsored home for refugee and orphan children in Jordan.

—Reconstruction work in a typhoon-damaged area of Japan.

—Construction of hospital rooms for the only hospital serving the rural population in the vicinity of Primavera, Paraguay.

—Provision of a recreational and educational service for migrant farm labourers in upper New York State, USA.

—Development of a holiday-play-scheme for children in the East End of London.

—Construction of a training centre for literacy campaigns in Togo.

Whether the camp fulfills its purpose is not determined solely by the work done at the camp site. Important as this is, of equal importance are the new attitudes and broadened views each camper takes back to his home community and church.

Through Bible study and particularly in the discussion groups, campers are brought face to face with the implications of the Christian faith and with a set of new ideological, cultural, and religious points of view, often in conflict with their own. For many the frustration of not being able to take part in the service of Holy Communion with other campers represents their first personal encounter with the depth of the tragedy of Christian disunity. For many also the experience is a breakthrough of deep-seated racial and cultural prejudices. For all, a work camp provides a unity of life, work, worship, and fellowship, which is rare in a modern society.

234. The youth village, Agape [pronounced "ah-gáh-pay"], in northern Italy, near Turin, has drawn young people from all over the world to live together and to work on common projects. By 1965, the village, built largely by the youths themselves, had developed a full camp and conference program which "will take place in the context of a wider activity of dialogue, study, brotherly understanding and research for community life," said the 1965 Agape booklet. "Agape is open to everyone. It is the village without enclosures, the village which welcomes young people of every nation, every religious denomination, and every culture, with no discrimination. . . ." Just what is Agape is explained in the January 1957 bulletin of the Agape community:

It is a village built for the youth of all the churches (without confessional distinction). Young Christians, be they Protestants, Catholics or Orthodox, are all equally welcome, so that they can get to know each other better and together seek after the will of their common Lord—Jesus Christ. In this village, as they live together and learn to love each other, they will realize that, despite traditional divisions, the Church remains one, and that in Christ barriers of class, nationality and culture are meaningless. They will furthermore learn that our worship of the Lord and our service to Him cannot be performed merely in words or ceremonies, but must be expressed through a life given up to helping and serving our neighbours. In serving each other, here at Agape, they will learn a lesson important for all their lives as Christians. Loving means giving oneself, not keeping oneself for oneself and one's own purposes. Furthermore, in this village, they will seek together, in the light of the Gospel, to know what is the Lord's will in the present time, and how best to plan their lives so that they may be well and truly employed in His service.

All this, indeed, is summed up in the name that the village bears: Agape. Agape is a Greek word used by the writers of the Bible to refer to the love with which God loves us, the love which was incarnate in Jesus Christ.

How did Agape begin? The story of the building of this village begins with a group of young people who desired to follow the calling with which God had confronted them. They had suffered greatly during the war, both at the front and in concentration camps, either as partisans or as anti-fascists. In 1945 they felt that there was only one way open to men if what had passed was not to be repeated—namely the love of Christ. This love they resolved to proclaim to everyone through their own brotherly love. They had neither financial resources nor experience; but they didn't wait to get either one or the other before beginning. While some began to collect funds, others started work on a plot of land, which was partially given to them by the local council and partially bought. In the first summer (1947) the work was very arduous; however, others came and joined them; and gradually the project became known throughout Italy and abroad.

The press, the wireless and the cinema all mentioned Agape, and a growing number of young people from many countries came up to the village in order to make real their common calling. In all, the youth of 32 countries, from Sweden to New Zealand, from Canada to Africa, joined the small initial group of Italians, and, at the same time, the first group of Waldensians was enlarged by others who came at the calling of the one Lord, Jesus Christ, from all the branches of the Church—Anglicans, Lutherans, Catholics, Reformed, Orthodox, etc. At last after five years' work the building was completed, 90 per cent of it built by volunteers —skilled and unskilled. And what counts most in the life of Agape is not the good intentions of those who built it, nor the goodwill of those who direct it or use it. What counts is that in it Christ's love is affirmed as a fact experienced in history.

235. The churches experimented with many cooperative proj-

ects to aid underprivileged peoples around the world. In Car-
cavelos, Portugal, near Lisbon, Protestant seminarians and
Roman Catholics joined their forces to teach 100 children in
an underprivileged community. In Niederalteich, Germany, Orthodox, Protestants and Roman Catholics planned to set up a
"circle of friends for ecumenical fraternal service" to help the
poor. Mennonites and Catholics worked together in camps for
the homeless in Bonn. Catholic Maryknoll priests and Pentecostals in Chile consulted concerning joint literacy drives. In
Denmark, the churches banded together to help distribute a
surplus of pork to nine nations. Involved were Danish Lutheran
charities, several smaller Protestant churches, and the Catholic
Relief Service. Roman Catholic Bishop Hans Martensen, of Copenhagen, gave collections of the parishes on July 18, 1965, to
the project. In New Mexico, the New Mexico Council of Churches
and the Catholic Archdiocese of Santa Fe jointly sponsored a
widespread collection of clothing for distribution through Church
World Service and Catholic Relief Services.

To bring cooperative efforts more to the local level where the
real work is done to aid the underprivileged, the Rt. Rev. Msgr.
Joseph B. Gremillion, director of socio-economic development for
Catholic Relief Services of the National Catholic Welfare conference proposed a new national inter-religious committee to
battle world poverty. He spoke to the annual meeting of the
Catholic Association for International Peace in New York, in
December 1965. His proposal was largely realized when the
major faiths participated in organizing the Inter-Religious Committee Against Poverty, January 18, 1966. The 45-member committee of Jewish, Protestant, Orthodox and Roman Catholic leaders said its function was to "encourage, evaluate, and coordinate
efforts" rather than launching new anti-poverty projects. A statement of purpose of the Inter-Religious Committee Against Poverty said:

> The leaders of churches, synagogues and organizations co-
> operating through the Inter-Religious Committee Against
> Poverty are committed to the proposition that the persist-
> ence of massive poverty in our society is a moral blight
> which can and must be eradicated. . . .

Hundreds of thousands of the poor are now participating in governmental anti-poverty programs. Their opportunities must not be wasted or thwarted. Those now being assisted and the millions not yet being assisted must be helped to escape from poverty and to make their contributions to the strengthening of our society.

We urge that increased appropriations be provided to strengthen and broaden the nation's programs to eliminate poverty.

Our country has both the material and human resources to expand and strengthen these programs. It would be a cruel injustice to require that the poor—the young, the old, the sick, the disadvantaged—should be the ones to make the major sacrifice for the other problems we must solve.

The Congress has wisely emphasized the importance of Community Action programs to encourage local initiative and responsibility for devising and administering programs best adapted to differing needs, problems and circumstances.

Greater awareness of poverty in each community, deeper understanding of its causes, a firm resolve to overcome it, and the strengthening of community-wide bodies, with the fullest participation of voluntary agencies, are vital goals of anti-poverty programs.

We urge continuing and increased support for Community Action programs.

One of the most challenging aspects of the Community Action programs is the requirement that they be "developed, conducted, and administered with the maximum feasible participation of residents of the area and members of the groups served."

This basic concept is an integral part of the religious and

democratic commitment to help people help themselves. We deplore any attempt, national or local, to dilute the concept of maximum participation of the poor. We affirm our faith in the fact that their involvement is feasible, and should be viewed as a creative utilization of the natural human resources found in the community of the deprived who are themselves dedicated to ridding the nation of poverty. Constructive participation of the poor in the conduct of these programs is achievable. The difficulties of accomplishing this purpose should not lessen our striving for its realization. We urge a redoubling of the efforts to encourage the full involvement of the poor in anti-poverty programs.

The commitment to our anti-poverty programs must not only be maintained, but must be increased to achieve its noble purpose—the development of a just society.

236. Church women around the world were organizing to make themselves heard on world social and religious issues. Under the joint sponsorship of the World Council of Churches and the Secretariat for Promoting Christian Unity, 30 women of Catholic, Protestant, and Orthodox backgrounds met October 22-29, 1965, at Vicarello di Trevignano, near Rome. Nuns, Anglican and Lutheran deaconesses and lay women, many of them heads of church women's organizations discussed a wide variety of topics: family life, role of women in the world, marriage and celibacy, current theological thinking concerning women, and new trends in religious orders.

More specifically, in the United States, a woman's group was formed to serve in community projects, particularly to combat poverty. Called Women in Community Service (WICS), the new organization with 3,500 members in 1966, is sponsored by the National Council of Catholic women, the National Council of Jewish Women, the National Council of Negro Women, and United Church Women of the National Council of Churches. An introductory WICS flyer says:

In January 1965, WICS, now formally incorporated as Women in Community Service, signed a government contract to provide the Job Corps Training Centers with their first women enrollees. . . .

The federal government's Women's Job Corps program provides residential centers across the country in which 16-through 21-year-old girls from economically and culturally deprived families will have the opportunity to learn how to move themselves up from poverty. Out of school and out of work, these girls will receive occupational training, basic remedial education and training in family responsibilities and citizenship at the centers. Emphasis will be on preparation for service jobs that cannot be easily automated.

WICS contracted only to screen girls for the Job Corps. But it undertook, on its own, a much broader commitment: to do a *total* job of continuing community service for every girl its members urge and help to leave home and join the Job Corps.

This means nationwide planning and community-by-community implementation. In down-to-earth detail, here's how it works. . . .

A small staff of professionals helps local groups to: set up screening centers, maintain contact with organizations serving underprivileged youth, distribute information about Training Centers, and provide training for women volunteers.

In many cities, towns and rural areas, community WICS have already been set up to rush this program into operation. Trained volunteers from active chapters or sections of the four women's groups are devoting hundreds of thousands of hours to the urgent threefold task before them: recruitment . . . screening . . . follow-up. In short: WICS calls on all women, of every faith and race, to reach out in their communities to the young girls and women who most need help.

237. The Archdiocese of Philadelphia launched its own war on poverty through a newly established Commission on Economic Opportunity Program under the direction of the Most Rev. John J. Krol, archbishop of Philadelphia. While the action was largely unilateral, the Program is open to all religions and presupposes a consensus of support from the entire religious community. The Chancery in Philadelphia supplied this report on its community project:

> Under Title II of the Economic Opportunity Act of 1964, the Archdiocesan Community Action proposal is designed to operate essentially from two community centers located in parish facilities in the two areas of the city with the highest incidence of poverty. The services of the Center will be extended to subcenters in neighboring parishes thus serving a larger geographical area than is covered by one parish. Services will be offered to all members of the community regardless of race, religion or national origin. . . .
>
> A comprehensive program is set up for the community centers encompassing tutorial and remedial programs, study hall facilities, home economics programs, carpentry and electrical shop facilities, sewing shop, psychiatric services, referral services, housekeeping services, home visiting services for the aged and ill, and case worker services.
>
> Many of the services of the Center will be offered for the first time, but already proven projects undertaken by the Archdiocese in the past form the basis for many of the proposed programs in the Community Centers.
>
> One such successful program is "Operation Incentive." This is a flourishing program in eight parishes offering educational, athletic and cultural opportunities for disadvantaged children. Study halls are operated from 7 to 9 p.m. two to four nights a week and tutoring services are not only offered but actually sought by many of these youngsters whose home environment is not conducive to study. Volun-

teers provide scholastic tutoring, athletic coaching and musical and dramatic training. We plan to incorporate the same programs in the community centers. . . .

Working mothers in North Philadelphia have had great difficulty in securing proper care for their children during the working day. In the past five years, 25 per cent of the first grade pupils in the Gesu Catholic School have had to repeat first grade. Sad experience indicates that the children in the area are badly in need of adequate pre-school learning experience. To help remedy this situation, the Bambino Gesu Day Nursery was recently opened and it is hoped that it will qualify for federal funds under the Archdiocesan Community Action Program.

Professional staff for the nursery will include three Oblate Sisters of Providence who have had considerable experience in teaching Negro children. The Sisters have had some instruction in the Montessori Method of teaching and will strive to adapt it in some measure to the needs of the poor children in the area. Although the Sisters are Negro and Roman Catholic, their services will be provided for any and all needy families regardless of race, creed or national origin.

238. Across the United States there was constant probing for ways to augment the President's poverty program. Participating in one conference under the sponsorship of the Maryland Council of Churches were the Rev. Dr. Cameron P. Hall, executive secretary, Church and Economic Life Department, of the National Council of Churches, and the Rev. Father Harry Maloney, S.S.J., of St. Francis Xavier Church, and others. Tne meeting in Baltimore brought a commendation from the White House February 20, 1965:

Dear Dean Peabody: [The Very Rev. John N. Peabody, president, Maryland Council of Churches]

President Johnson has asked me to thank you and your associates for your early and enthusiastic support of the War on Poverty.

He is most gratified at the initiative displayed by the Maryland Council of Churches and its Christian Social Relations Division in summoning the first state-wide religious conference on the national effort to eliminate poverty.

He has asked me to extend to you his sincere congratulations on the efforts of the council and the success of your conference, for, as you know, the success of the anti-poverty effort is largely dependent on local initiative.

He noted in one of your conference leaflets, "Facts on Poverty in Maryland," apathy on the part of individuals and of society in general poses one of the great problems we all face in our efforts to overcome poverty.

This fact is paramount, and your confidence stands as a model in making the public aware of the existence and complex nature of poverty.

> Sincerely yours,
> Douglass Cater,
> Special Assistant to President

239. The Salvation Army and Catholic Charities of the Diocese of Rockville Centre, New York, joined in a program to help 150 migrant families in 1964. The joint effort came as a result of county officials seeking emergency aid to meet conditions in a "very bad" and "unbelievable" slum. Overall director was the Rev. Father Robert Emmet Fagan, associate director of Catholic Charities for the diocese. The Suffolk Council of Churches, the Diocesan St. Vincent de Paul Society, and local parishes also assisted in the housing, educational, medical, and community service phases.

Father Fagan explained the attitude of the Diocese:

We in Catholic Charities were more than willing to cooperate with the Salvation Army in uniting our resources in attempting to answer this social problem.

Several excellent meetings were held with the executives

and local directors of the Salvation Army as well as the executive director of the Suffolk Council of Churches. A working arrangement was agreed upon to prevent duplication of services. Reverend Buck Jones of the Council of Churches would handle any religious problems since 97 per cent of the families were Protestant, for example, such as informing the families of their local church denomination, etc.

Salvation Army and Catholic Charities worked at providing furniture for their new homes, clothing for the children and adults.

Catholic Charities has no policy statement as such except that of the [Second Vatican] Ecumenical Council which encourages our faithful to work with other religious denominations on social problems of the community.

I can speak both for myself and the other directors of Catholic Charities in stating that we felt this joint venture with the Salvation Army was a very good thing.

In our meetings, there was always an open and charitable sharing of opinions, as a result there is a better appreciation of the contribution both agencies can make in meeting very difficult community problems; and a friendship now exists between us which before for the most part was only a knowledge of the name and title of the personnel in the agencies.

240. The church's voice was heard cooperatively concerning the plight of migrant workers. In California, an interfaith committee was organized to help support a strike of grape pickers, many of them migrants, in a 400-mile square area centering on Delano, California. Most of the workers were earning under $1,500 annually. Although the Delano Ministers' Association (made up of a Lutheran, an Episcopalian, a Methodist, three Baptists, and an Assembly of God pastor) opposed the effort, other churchmen—Protestants, Catholics and Jews—gave official and active support. The National Catholic Rural Life Conference,

the National Council of Churches Commission on Economic Life
and the Synagogue Council of America all supported the strikers.
In San Francisco, in a meeting called by Protestants who had
been to Delano, more Roman Catholics showed up than Protestants.

In Michigan, far-sweeping support for migrants in orchards,
tomato and beet fields, was organized on a dramatic state-wide
level. The Michigan Council of Churches and the Michigan Catholic Conference received a $1.3 million poverty grant from the
Federal government to operate four migrant training and welfare centers together. Their interfaith corporation, Michigan
Migrant Opportunities, Inc., is headed by the Rev. Wendell Bas-
sett, executive secretary of the Michigan Council of Churches,
chairman of the board, and Francis J. Coomes, executive director
of the Michigan Catholic Conference, president. The rest of the
board consists of seven members from each group. A later report with proposals for 1966-1967 outlined plans for 15 families
to "form a Migrant Association for the purpose of helping one
another build new homes or renovate older homes."

Types of services provided in this interfaith Michigan Migrant
Opportunity, Inc., are illustrated in the first three-month report,
July 12, 1965:

> — Since the opening of our first youth education-day care
> center on June 14, 1965, we have enrolled 1,051 youngsters
> (concentrated in the 2 through 11 age bracket) at 23 cen-
> ters in our four regions as of July 12, 1965. This enrollment
> figure reflects the average number of youngsters enrolled
> and does not indicate the total numbers that have had con-
> tact with our program. Because of the regular turnover of
> migratory labor, we have not been able to process enroll-
> ment cards rapidly enough to secure an accurate count of
> the total number of youngsters participating in our pro-
> gram.
>
> Much of the efforts of the central staff have been directed
> to assisting in the orientation of youth education-day care
> center staff personnel, selecting and distributing in excess
> of $3,000.00 worth of educational materials, and securing

800 books from the Michigan State Library for loan to our regional centers. . . .

—A wide variety of surplus commodities have been made available to the MMOI regional day care and youth education centers. These commodities were distributed according to the rates shown below: Dry beans, 1 pound per child; canned beef, 1 can per 2 children; butter, 1 pound per child; cheese, 1 pound per child; chopped meat, 1 can per 2 children; cornmeal, 1 five-pound bag per 10 children; flour, 4 pounds per child; milk, four half-pound packages per child; peanut butter, 1 can per eight children, etc.

—To date, work has been provided by MMOI for 521 migrants or ex-migrants. Wages of $22,247.79 have been paid, $313.75 for tools, $6,481.90 for supplies and paint, and $280.60 for foreman travel. The work has improved the housing of 3320 migrants. The work has included painting, cleaning up of the housing and surroundings, repairs of the roofs, floors, screens, doors, steps, and outhouses.

241. Cooperatives were also launched. In Canton, Ohio, eight Protestant and Roman Catholic churches formed Heritage Housing, Inc., to build a 100-unit home for the aged in the inner city. The Protestant monks of the Taizé Community in France pooled their farm land with five young Roman Catholic couples in the Burgundy countryside to form a new cooperative. Previously the Protestant brothers had organized a dairy cooperative which now has 1,200 farms participating. Credit unions, serving men of many faiths, gained popularity in South America and other underdeveloped areas. A grand old man of the credit union movement, the Rev. Allen R. Huber, father of credit unions in the Philippines, described the philosophy of the credit union movement:

The church credit union trains its members in the wise use of money; it encourages them to save something each pay day; it lends to them, at a fair rate of interest, the funds necessary to meet their provident and productive needs; and it gives them a new appreciation for the security that comes from membership in a mutually responsible Christian group. They see, in many cases for the first time, the church as a redemptive fellowship concerned with the total needs of man, whether they be spiritual, mental, physical or economic. They hear again the thrilling words of Dr. Luke in Acts 4: 33-34, "And with great power the apostles gave their testimony to the resurrection of the Lord Jesus, and great grace was upon them all. There was not a needy person among them. . . ." We who are active in credit unions believe that we please God when we serve man.

242. Special attention to the needs of workers among the churches was evident in India, where Protestants and the Catholic Young Christian Workers' Chaplains shared problems and techniques in Ranchi, Bombay and Bangalore. The Inter-Church Trade and Industry Mission, of Melbourne, is an interfaith team of clergy counseling workers in plants in the Province of Victoria, Australia. Participating are the Anglicans, Roman Catholics, Presbyterians, Methodists, Baptists, Congregationalists, Greek Orthodox, the Churches of Christ and the Salvation Army. The I.T.I.M. training manual outlines eight steps in the interfaith approach:

(1) There must be inter-church co-operation in the selection, training and use of industrial chaplains whether they be part-time or full-time.

(2) Co-operation between chaplains. It early became clear that industry would not take kindly to a 'procession of chaplains' through any one plant—nor on the chaplain's side would he ever get to know intimately the men in his plant if he only visited occasionally in turns with other chaplains. The practical solution being used by I.T.I.M. is for one chaplain to be attached to one plant and for that chaplain to be one of a group of chaplains working in that area, representing as many of the member churches of I.T.I.M. as possible. The plant chaplain will, therefore, be able to make

the necessary contact with the men in his particular plant and will have available in his area the service of chaplains of other churches as such services become necessary.

(3) The appointment of chaplains should ensure: (a) suitability; (b) payment by I.T.I.M. and not by management. It is essential that the chaplain is independent of all parties. He must not be a boss's man which he would seem to be in the eyes of the work-force if he were "on the staff"; (c) adequate training for both part-time and full-time chaplains.

(4) Introduction of a chaplain. Before commencement of visiting at any plant a consultation must take place with the local works manager as to the best method of visiting. The chaplain must be fully trained in safety requirements. Each industrial unit will need its own plan of visitation. It is essential, however, that no plant be accepted for industrial chaplaincy work unless there is freedom of entry consistent with the working of any particular plant. . . .

(5) *Every effort must be made to achieve the good-will and guidance* of both management and trade unions. I.T.I.M. must NOT SEEK IMMEDIATE OFFICIAL APPROVAL of a service that only experience will prove to be of value. What we ask is co-operation whilst such experience is gained. What is required on the part of I.T.I.M. is to keep both the management and trades unions concerned fully aware of what is being attempted. The chaplains have already discovered a wealth of good-will amongst all sections of the industrial community—amongst men, many of whom are proud to call themselves Christian although they rarely see the inside of a church.

(6) "Tramping the rounds." Just as visiting is the pastoral basis of parochial life, so is visiting the basis of the work of the industrial chaplain. Only by his being constantly on the factory floor will he be able to: (a) listen and learn; (b) listen and help; (c) become part of a scene and no longer a visitor from outside; (d) to keep in touch with such people

as personnel officers, foremen and shop stewards who are
themselves close to their men and who can often tell the
chaplain where he is needed. . . .

(7) Non-interference in industrial disputes by industrial
chaplains. Whilst, as a long term programme, the industrial
mission will work for good human relationships within industry based on truth and justice, it is necessary to stress
that an individual chaplain should never interfere in an
actual dispute. . . .

(8) Use of part-time parochial clergy to supplement the
work of the full-time chaplains. The use of part-time chaplains would not only help I.T.I.M. but also extend the experience and understanding of the parochial clergy; but they
need to be as carefully selected and trained as the full-time
men and there needs to be an assurance of continuity and
regularity of visiting.

243. In the inner city, there were dynamic new joint efforts,
especially in the way of new community organizations. Chicago
Protestants, Catholics, Jews affiliated with the Interreligious
Council on Urban Affairs gave $20,000 to launch a program of
building community leadership in the West Side Negro slum area
in West Garfield Park. In Kansas City, Saul Alinsky's Industrial
Areas Foundation which launched the organization for the Southwest Community (OSC), the temporary Woodlawn Organization
(TWO), and the Northwest Community Organization (NCO) in
Chicago, with Protestant and Catholic funds and personnel, en-
tered into an agreement with a group of Protestants (Disciples,
United Presbyterians, Episcopalians) and Roman Catholics to
develop an action program in "ghettoed" neighborhoods.

An interfaith store-front center, with full backing of Catholic
and Protestant organizations, was established in a changing
neighborhood of Detroit. Called the Inter-Faith Center, on the
near northeast side, the center has staffers and money from the
Catholic Youth Organization, Protestant Community Services
and Catholic Social Services of Wayne County. The project grew
out of the friendship and common parish needs of Grace Lutheran

Church and St. Anthony's Roman Catholic Church, ten short
blocks apart. First co-ordinator of the project was Richard Peck,
on loan from the Catholic Social Services, who died in the fall of
1965. Another young Catholic social worker, John Peters, heads
the project now. In the first annual report, in the summer of 1965,
Mr. Peck outlined what the Inter-Faith Center accomplished in
its first year:

> (1) We began with our 500 interviews in the community,
> mostly conducted by the young first-year priests at St.
> Anthony's. If our program did nothing more than to intro-
> duce social problems and people to these priests, I feel it
> would have been worth it. Half of the priests worked on
> their own with periodic Inter-Faith consultation on projects
> that they themselves picked up during the surveying. All
> 10 of the priests in my judgment had become in a very quick
> time an emotional part of the community.
>
> (2) Our building was remodeled using people hired right
> from the community and the offices were furnished mostly
> with agency donations.
>
> (3) A secretary who lives in the community was hired.
>
> (4) Thirteen groups of fairly disturbed youngsters were
> served and one group of ADC mothers was organized. All
> the youngster groups were made up of police or school re-
> ferred youngsters or the street gang kids who have collected
> at Grace.
>
> (5) Approximately 70 families received short term case-
> work service, with another 15 families being seen exten-
> sively over a period of time.
>
> (6) Approximately a dozen people were placed in jobs de-
> veloped through friends of the Inter-Faith staff members.
>
> (7) Children of 17 families received presents at Christmas.

(8) The Community Council received a tremendous amount of help during the year. Working through and with the Council, the following specific things were accomplished:

(a) Two of our worst houses were torn down early in the year.

(b) Over 800 signatures were obtained from residents of the area who were disturbed over the abandoned cars and dilapidated vacant housing. Twenty people who had only limited involvement in the Community Council, circulated the petition.

The Common Council [of Detroit] ordered a representative of housing to tour the area with us to evaluate our complaints. A strong report was then sent to the Council President, who forwarded it to the proper departments and gave us dates by which our complaints were to be handled.

Since then most of the abandoned cars have been removed and Building and Safety has given us July 1 as the date the houses will begin to be torn down. The Health Department has also been more responsive to complaints from the area.

We are still in possession of our petitions and photographs and may yet press for a public hearing if the housing is not tended to.

(c) A Tot Lot that the Community Council has been after for four years was obtained when we helped the Fishers go over the head of the person who has been saying NO for four years. To our surprise, they have also supplied a play leader.

Parks and Recreation has also sent a female staff person out to the St. Anthony Playground, and did some work on drains on that playground. . . .

(d) The Council has been attracting much larger audiences at their public meetings. From 20 people, at several meetings I attended when I first came to Inter-Faith, the Council has had 200 at Inter-Faith's Open House, 300 at a meeting around the Board of Education's plans for the area, and 75 at a Police Community meeting. . . .

(9) A Retiree's Advisory Committee was formed in February by our second CO student, and this is currently really producing.

The Committee has settled on three main areas of need to work on; Housing, income and organization, through which the Seniors can realize their potential force in the community, get over their feelings of alienation, and begin to work for its betterment. . . .

(10) [There is interest in] increasing income of Seniors by part-time work. . . . A small business loan through TAP is very possible, and a volunteer consultant from the Small Business Administration, who has had experience in cooperatives in foreign countries, has met with us and expressed a good amount of interest in the possible project. . . .

(11) In response to a request from Housing, Inter-Faith has submitted a list of empty lots privately owned which have become a refuge for abandoned cars and junk of all kinds. Housing intends to use these properties as examples, and to draw up new legislation which will correct this problem of privately owned, but unkept lots.

(12) Since Fall, Inter-Faith has been assisting Grace Lutheran in a Teen Canteen, which draws 75 to 125 teens every Tuesday. The Canteen is run primarily by a Teen Council, made up of representatives from the gang groups at Grace. It is staffed at the moment by an ACSW Social Worker and a psychologist from Hawthorn Center, who are Inter-Faith volunteers, and they are aided by our staff.

(13) This summer University of Detroit placed a graduate student in sociology who is a life-time resident of the area at Inter-Faith for six weeks of directed study by myself. During this time Miss Brooks will be making a detailed examination of the Real Estate practices in the area, with the goal being to document actual transactions which are either illegal or highly questionable.

(14) During the summer, PCS has placed a Sweep worker in the area who will be providing services for teens who otherwise might be creating trouble.

(15) During the summer some work is being done in preparation for the PCS Vista Volunteer Program in Cultural Arts and Rose School Teacher Aids. Also some preparation is being done for the NYC—Federation of Settlement Program.

(16) Throughout the year one of Inter-Faith's biggest contributions has been its availability to the teachers of St. Anthony's, Rose and Barbour Schools and to our two pastors, Father Langhols and Pastor Gotts.

(17) Inter-Faith is beginning to be a focal point for outercity groups interested in knowing about Poverty. One month alone staff gave seven talks to 450 people. These included 200 Dominican nuns, Grosse Pointe Woods CFM group. . . .

(18) Inter-Faith was also the focal point of two business donations this year. The first because we were in the neighborhood. The second of $1,500, because we represented religion and the spirit of Christmas in the modern world. . . .

244. Cooperative action in the inner city extended to existing organizations. A merger of the YMCA and the Catholic Youth Organization was suggested by the Rev. Father George Hagmaier, C.S.P., professor of religious education at Catholic University in Washington:

... One of the best tests of our readiness to approach common causes with confidence is the willingness of the churches to involve themselves in closer collaboration within the areas of social justice and community welfare—in short, a more unified dissemination of the corporal works of mercy.

In these areas, we face no deep dogmatic impasse. In meeting the pressing social needs of people in want, or in pain, or in distress of many kinds, we dispense together the same merciful solicitude of Christ. And yet there are unexplored opportunities for ever closer fraternal collaboration. Old rivalries and prejudices still hold us back from an effective social apostolate. And it may be precisely on this pastoral level, rather than on the more sensitive theological plane, that Christianity in our time will rise and fall.

One eminently practical area for immediate consideration ... is the possibility of amalgamating the major religious organizations serving our nation's youth. In these ecumenical times I feel certain that the worthy objectives of both the YMCA and the CYO could be achieved in one facility, under one roof, with clergymen of all denominations ministering each to their own youngsters in a non-proselytizing effort to deepen the spiritual and formative values which all hold dear.

Dare I even suggest that a reexamination of the present state and purpose of Masonic organizations might reveal grounds upon which Catholics and other Christians could collaborate in the many worthy humanitarian enterprises these currently forbidden societies sponsor.

245. About the time that Father Hagmaier was making his bold suggestion for joint fraternal cooperation, the "miracle" occurred in Pittsburgh. The Knights of Columbus Bishop Wright Project of the Roman Catholic Diocese of Pittsburgh and the Pittsburgh Shriners' Syria Temple filed corporation papers setting up a Nobles and Knights Charities, Inc. The two traditional rivals would work together to raise funds for needy children. The

charter approved September 24, 1964, by the Court of Common
Pleas of Allegheny County said the purpose of the new alliance
was:

> To jointly promote and foster the Christian ideal and con-
> cept of the charitable activities of its members in the com-
> munity in which they live and for these purposes to have,
> possess and enjoy all the rights, benefits and privileges of
> the said act of assembly and its amendments.

246. A bid for the cooperation of fraternal organizations was
heard on the national level. Calling for a development of "the
ecumenical spirit in fraternalism . . . between the Knights of
Columbus and the members of the Masonic Order" was the supreme officer of the Knights of Columbus, John W. McDevitt.
He spoke to a jointly sponsored breakfast meeting of the Knights
and Masons in Sharon, Massachusetts, February 27, 1966:

> Now is the time for us to become concerned with the goals
> and principles our fraternal organizations have in common.
> Jointly we must try to foster and strengthen these in a civ-
> lization where traditional values and objectives are being
> questioned and rejected.
>
> As I look over the guiding principles that form the founda-
> tions of the Masonic and Columbian societies I find we have
> a number in common. I propose that in these areas joint
> efforts can and should be made so these ideas can be pro-
> moted by our societies with greater effectiveness.
>
> This collaboration can be carried on at all levels of our or-
> ganizational structure, but I believe it is always most effec-
> tive when conducted at the local council and lodge level.
>
> Among the guiding principles of masonry are belief in a
> Supreme Being and in the immortality of the human soul;
> a belief in the supreme fatherhood of God and the universal
> brotherhood of man.

The Knights of Columbus, as you all know, must be practicing members of the Catholic Church and must hold to its religious beliefs and moral practices.

The great bond I see between our societies is our mutual belief in God and the paramount importance and eternal destiny of the human soul.

Here are values of the highest import which are receiving serious challenge in our present civilization. A professedly atheistic political and economic philosophy has seized control of the minds and destinies of a billion people covering vast stretches of the earth. The infection of this philosophy has spread even to our own country where it is finding its most dangerous expression in a creed of absolute secularism which would extirpate all theistic or religious influences and values from our national life. . . .

Here . . . are three lofty objectives in which our two fraternal orders can cooperate: the spread and defense of a belief in God; the promotion of patriotism; and the safeguarding of a national morality.

Recalling . . . the noble example of Pope Paul VI and Patriarch Athenagoras [withdrawing the historic mutual excommunications], I say that the Knights of Columbus are eager to extend to brothers of the Masonic order an embrace of friendship, an embrace of understanding, an embrace of trust, an embrace of charity that will bring us to new heights of ecumenism in fraternalism.

247. There was a proposal—and a plan—that the churches build on a cooperative basis in a new community, with a view to conserving funds and centralizing worship in the community, and also to place the churches at the heart and life of the community. The experimental project in a new area was Columbia, Maryland, a residential community on 14,000 acres:

This proposal suggests that a non-profit corporation be established by religious groups to build, own, and manage facilities in the new town [Columbia] in Howard County. The facilities would be used by various religious groups on a combination of lease, rent, and fee basis with some facilities shared in common by all groups.

Such a corporation would have several advantages:

(1) The serious problem of "lack of facilities fit" which plagues churches could be largely overcome since it would be possible for any given congregation to obtain more facilities in the common center or to reduce its facilities as the need arises.

(2) Excellent facilities would be available for each congregation even in its earliest stages of development.

(3) Sharing of many facilities would greatly reduce their cost to each group (this might include a lounge, dining area, central office space which could be equipped, theatre, etc.)

(4) The facilities could be so designed that they are informal and do not have that "institutional look."

(5) The burden of construction, management and financing of the facilities would be largely removed from the local congregation with very considerable savings in the amount of time needed for internal maintenance plus the economies that could be achieved in having specialists control construction and building maintenance.

(6) The competition between churches for status which occasionally reflects itself in exorbitant expenditures on buildings would be largely overcome since a common religious center would be shared by all.

Such a corporation might sell bonds either to the participating denominations or bonds backed by the denominations. A lower interest rate might thereby be achieved than is the usual case in church mortgages.

A local congregation would lease a part of a building to fit its particular needs, might share on a rental basis some of the other facilities, and would have access to still other facilities (such as a large dining room) on a fee basis.

A local congregation could have a building fund drive (or this might be conducted on a community wide basis) with the amount of money raised used to purchase the bonds of corporation. The interest from the bonds would then be used as part of the payment of the rent or lease of the particular congregation.

The facilities held in common could be supplemented (probably at a later time) by the construction of sanctuaries. Such sanctuaries could be so located as to relate readily to the multi-purpose building, and they might be owned and operated by local congregations. However, provision should be made in the initial facility design to accommodate congregations for perhaps the first ten years.

A worship facility in the town center might be constructed for common use. It might be useful for the corporation to purchase land at an appropriate spot (perhaps on the lake) for future development of a sanctuary.

248. A "United Christian Hall" for youths was planned by Anglicans, Roman Catholics, Methodists, Quakers, and Christadelphians in Bewdley, Worcestershire, England. Among guests taking part in the opening of the hall in December 1964, were the Rev. B. O'Gorman, chairman of the Methodist District, Rt. Rev. Mervin Edwards, Anglican bishop of Worcester, and the Very Rev. Msgr. H. Francis Davis, Roman Catholic representative from St. Gregory's, Birmingham, and the mayor and members of the Borough Council.

a. A brochure describes the project:

Five Christian Churches in Bewdley, Worcestershire, inspired by the strong current desire for Christian Unity, have realized that their town's lack of an adequate Hall provides them with a unique opportunity of working together for the common good.

Further need for such a Hall is caused by a building programme planned to double the population of this little Severnside town in five years.

The Interdenominational Committee have acquired St. George's Hall, which has long been standing empty beside Bewdley's central Car Park in Load Street. It has been paid for by the kindness of a member of one of the Churches concerned.

This building will now be called the Christian Community Hall. It will be equipped for drama, music, receptions, meetings, games, dancing, etc. The hall will be used by the churches individually and for their combined social occasions. It will also be available for hire. Facilities for large-scale catering are planned. . . .

b. The Rev. W. G. Harwood, the Anglican rector in Bewdley, who first suggested the interfaith hall, explains how some of the problems are overcome:

We include Roman Catholics, who are very keen to dance and meet together socially when we cannot yet worship together. We are already holding united dances (in other hired rooms) for money-raising.

There was difficulty over the fact that Methodists officially disapprove of dancing. And drink was a problem. So we have included an Escape Clause in the Constitution, stating that a majority decision does not imply approval by all.

Our committee consists of two voting members from each of the five churches, irrespective of the size of church membership; plus other non-voting members as required.

We also have an item in the rules about finance: Initial capital contributions from the churches are distinguished from other money raised by united efforts. In the event of a winding-up and sale of the property, proceeds will be divided among the churches in proportion to their initial capital contributions. But any church withdrawing unilaterally, not by a final wind-up of the project, gets no compensation.

249. Developments on the campus were many: (1) Catholic University of America established an Institute of Ecumenism, inviting scholars "both Catholic and non-Catholic" to "inform direct and inspire the absorption of the vital teachings of Vatican II into the lifestream of American thought." (2) Inter-Christian colloquiums were held, for instance, in India at St. Mary's College, Kurseong, and Serampore College, West Bengal, on the subject of the Cosmic Christ. (3) Interfaith seminars replaced or supplemented the usual religious special activities on the campuses. The Rev. Father T. A. McGoldrick a Catholic chaplain at the University of Liverpool, England, said "the Christian societies in the University form a federation known as the Associated Christian Societies. They hold a certain number of meetings jointly and the chaplains co-operate in providing a counselling service, sitting down for their own meal among the students." (4) A full year of study of the Bible was ordered for the fulltime Catholic students at Barry College, a Catholic girls school, Miami, but optional for the non-Catholics—the approach, however, reportedly created a new ecumenical spirit among the Catholic students and students from Baptist and Bible-belt churches. (5) There were Ecumenical study tours, such as the "European Study Seminar" of Eastern Michigan University, the University of Michigan, and Wayne State University during the summer of 1966, with visits to Catholic and Protestant theologians in Europe. (6) The Catholic Newman Center and a dozen other religious groups, most of them Protestant, are to be housed under the same roof in a new student union center planned at Wayne State University, Detroit; a similar arrangement exists at Portland State College, Portland, Oregon. (7) Schools saw the value of dialogue not only with one another but together with the secular campus. Paulist fathers writing in *The Catholic World*

called for Catholic seminaries to be in the world rather than in isolation, and to be located near secular universities. Protestants had the same idea. Example: Five Lutheran Church of America theological schools voted to merge and relocate on a new campus adjoining the University of Chicago.

In August, 1965, twenty-two Newman chaplains from secular campuses met in Atlanta, and issued this ecumenical and inter-cultural "manifesto":

(1) Because the university is a significant institution in the shaping of our world, the church must be concerned about its relationships with it.

(2) As chaplains, our concern is with the university, not simply the administration but the whole collection of persons and structures. We respect the integrity of the university's own life, without seeking to impose on it preconceived religious images. We seek to cooperate with the university in its continuing search for self-understanding. We seek to cooperate with it in providing occasions for inter- and intra-disciplinary dialogue. At times we must be creative critics of the university, without standing over against it. We see the teachings of theology as an academic discipline to be the responsibility of the university.

(3) It is not necessary to define but to develop our position in the structure of the university, though in many instances the position we are seen to occupy hinders and frustrates the vitality of our work.

(4) A Christian ecumenical ministry is not only possible now but imperative, and we are committed to it. We can no longer tolerate sectarianism, and we should work to modify the structures which perpetuate a sectarian stance. This does not suggest that we are all of single mind regarding revelation as it relates to belief and practice, but it does suggest that we must continue to seek that consensus consistent with intellectual integrity. We shall seek to be re-

sponsible to one another. In such matters as religious counseling there is already a climate for mutual acceptance of
each other's work.

(5) As we seek within the university a ministry consonant
with our possibilities in an ecumenical age, so we seek from
the church freedom to discover forms of the church which
best serve the campus community and freedom to experiment with forms of worship and service which best celebrate the presence of Christ there.

(6) Though the precise forms of the church on campus
are not clear, it is clear that they cannot be along denominational lines. They will more than likely be flexible enough
to follow natural university groupings which suggest small
communities which may be brought together on occasion.

(7) We must seek from the community of scholars the
ideas, insights and research which can and should be re-
shaping the life of the church.

(8) College and university chaplains must be intellectually
and academically competent.

250. Facilities—and faculties—were shared, sometimes dra-
matically, as in Leopoldville, Republic of the Congo, where the
new Protestant "University Libre," nearly wiped out by rebels
in 1964, used borrowed headquarters in the Catholic Louvanium
University.

Significant was the growing cooperation in instruction. Catholic priests not only took teaching assignments on the secular,
composite campus (example, a priest at Western Michigan
University; a nun, at Wayne State University), but priests could
be found on the faculties of Protestant seminaries, and Protestants on the faculties of Catholic seminaries. At McCormick
(Presbyterian) Seminary, Chicago, the Rev. Father Eugene C.
Kennedy, of the Maryknoll Seminary, Glen Ellyn and Loyola,
was a visiting lecturer, and the Rev. Father John J. Begley, S.J.,
of Boston, was studying Protestant theology. At the Catholic

PIME Fathers' Maryglade College, Memphis, Michigan, a young Congregationalist from the Port Huron (Michigan) school system taught English. Professorships in Roman Catholic theology were established in Protestant schools—one of the first in the United States was Harvard where the Charles Chauncey Stillman Guest Professorship since 1958 has brought Catholic scholars to the school—among them: Christopher Dawson, Astrik Gabriel, Père Roland de Vaux, Joseph H. Fichter, S.J. Yale had John Courtney Murray, S.J., and in its Divinity school, Carmelite Father Roland Murphy, of Catholic University. At the University of Chicago, was the Rev. Father John McKenzie, S.J.

A Southern Baptist, Dr. James William McClendon, professor at Golden Gate Baptist Theological Seminary, near San Francisco, joined the faculty of the Roman Catholic University of San Francisco as an associate professor in theology in the Fall of 1966. A Missouri Synod Lutheran, Rev. Dr. Ross P. Scherer, joined the department of sociology at Loyola University, Chicago, in September, 1966. Dr. Toney P. Brown, a member of the Church of Christ, became president of the Sacred Heart Dominican College for Women (500-member student body) Houston, Texas, in June 1966.

Joint curricula emerged, first with credit courses taught by a member of another faith, then joint registration in several schools. A Catholic seminary and a Protestant seminary offering, jointly, a credit course on contemporary Protestant theology were Seabury-Western (Episcopal), Evanston, and Bellarmine (Jesuit), North Aurora, Illinois. Teachers were the Rev. J. V. Langmead Casserley, of Seabury-Western, and the Rev. Father John A. Hardon, S.J., of Bellarmine and Western Michigan University.

The University of Dallas (Catholic), five Protestant universities (Southern Methodist, Texas Christian, Austin, Bishop, and Texas Wesleyan) and a private center of research (Graduate Research Center of the Southwest) inaugurated an association to bolster and expand their graduate doctoral programs. Fordham University (Catholic) and Union Theological Seminary (Protestant), New York, worked out a "permanent relationship" which includes an exchange of professors and a mutual acceptance of academic credits. Each school lists five courses available to a student from the other school. The University of Windsor, Windsor, Ontario, Canada, which has offered courses by clerics of different faiths, ceased to list whether a religion course would be taught by a Protestant or a Catholic.

In Dubuque, Iowa, three of Dubuque's seminaries— Lutheran, Presbyterian and Roman Catholic—signed a pact creating the Association of Theological Faculties in Iowa, Inc. The agreement allows all three seminaries—Wartburg Lutheran Seminary, the University of Dubuque Theological Seminary (Presbyterian), and the Aquinas Institute School of Theology (Roman Catholic)— to schedule clergymen of all denominations for lectures, Bible study and general conversation. Also a student enrolled in one school can attend classes for credit at any other member school without additional tuition. When one class from one seminary studies the teachings of one of the other religious faiths, professors of that particular faith can be brought in from one of the other schools for a special lecture.

One of the first and most ambitious graduate projects emerged in the San Francisco Bay area where seven seminaries, ranging from Unitarian to Roman Catholic, formed the Graduate Theological Union. Twenty-four students signed up for the 1964-65 year in the entirely new Th. D. and Ph. D. program that pools library, classrooms, and teaching resources.

a. The first dean of the new Graduate Theological Union program in Berkeley, the Rev. Dr. John Dillenberger, who once directed doctoral graduate programs in divinity at Harvard University, described the new interfaith arrangements:

By its Articles of Incorporation the Graduate Theological Union was formed "to conduct an educational institution offering instruction on the graduate theological level; to participate with theological seminaries and other institutions of higher learning in co-operative programs in universities and seminaries of learning, either in its own name only, or in conjunction with another such institution." It is clear that the charter of the GTU is broadly conceived; it was specifically formed to combine the theological and, indirectly, the university resources of the Bay Area at the doctoral level in the field of religion. But its Articles of Incorporation could also cover other cooperative developments.

The initial and currently participating schools are Berkeley Baptist Divinity School, The Church Divinity School of the Pacific (Protestant Episcopal), The Pacific Lutheran Theological Seminary, Pacific School of Religion (Interdenominational), Saint Albert's College (Dominican), San Francisco Theological Seminary (Presbyterian), and Starr King School for the Ministry (Unitarian Universalist). A cooperative working relation has been established with the University of California at Berkeley in connection with the Ph. D. program, and the first students have been admitted to this program. Conversations are under way with two additional Roman Catholic institutions and with representatives of Jewish and Eastern Orthodox scholarship. It may not be possible to relate these institutions in one pattern, but the resources of all might be available through schools becoming participating institutions, through relating the GTU to a center, and through the creation of specific chairs in definite fields. Adequate representation on the Board of Trustees would, of course, also be implied by any action with reference to each of these possibilities. Our hope is to create nothing less than a theological university—although we do not use the term—alongside of, but in close working relation with, the University of California at Berkeley and with other universities in the area.

We are immersed in a situation in theological and university education where the older isolation is neither defensible or desirable. In the American scene, the scholarly and intellectual endeavors across confessional lines are only now beginning to come to fruition. Not since the days of the seventeenth century has the general climate been so auspicious or the potential gains so promising. In light of this, it would seem important to find ways of overcoming the spatial distances which do inhibit the routine exposure to each other which is so necessary for potential development.

The day is at hand when our human and scholarly concerns can feed each other and when, in this sense, we desparately need each other. It is highly important that scholarly and academic communities be created in which this becomes a natural ethos. It is not that any theological group, Protestant denomination, Roman Catholic, Judaic, or Eastern Orthodox, or university group—agnostic or believing—dominate or tolerate any of the others, but that all must unite in pursuing issues as issues. Some issues will evaporate, and new ones will emerge. The enterprise of exploration and affirmation for the sake of truth may find new patterns.

Naturally we think that the Berkeley situation is exceptionally ideal for moving in this direction. . . . It functions at the doctoral level but, obviously, in such a way as to affect the various levels of the life of all the institutions and participants.

b. The Graduate Theological Union's bylaws explain the relationship of its member institutions, students, and faculty:

Article II: *Participating Institutions:* Any academic institution providing professional training for the Bachelor's Degree in Divinity or substantially equivalent instruction in the field of Theology may, by formal action of its Board of Trustees or other governing body, apply for acceptance as a participating institution in the Graduate Theological Union. . . .

Institutional participation shall be for a minimum of five years. Thereafter, notice of intention to withdraw shall be given two years before the July first on which the withdrawal is to become effective.

Article VIII: *The Dean:* The Dean shall be the chief executive officer of the Union and shall be elected by the Trustees (representing the institutions), to serve at the pleasure of the Board. He shall recommend to the Trustees persons to be elected as members of the faculty. He shall preside over meetings of the faculty.

251. An Academic Council of an ecumenical institute for advanced theological training was planned for Jerusalem. Groundwork for the project involving Protestants, Roman Catholic and Orthodox was laid in December 1965, at a preliminary meeting at Villa Serbelloni, Lake Como, Italy. The Rev. Father Theodore M. Hesburgh, C.S.C., chairman of the project and president of both the University of Notre Dame and the International Federation of Catholic Universities, said full plans were expected to be developed by September 1966, after further meetings at Notre Dame, Zurich and Jerusalem. "Meanwhile we are faced with the problem of formulating the program and building the buildings and library required," he said in a letter. The initial announcement of the Academic Council said:

> This action was taken in response to an invitation from the International Federation of Catholic Universities, which had been entrusted by Pope Paul VI with responsibility for initiating the project. In recent ecumenical encounters, the desire has been expressed for a program of common theological research, with special emphasis on the theme of the redemptive acts of God in history and their meaning for the men of our day. The institute is being planned to serve this purpose.

> The members of the Academic Council considered the academic, administrative, and financial problems involved in setting up the ecumenical institute, as well as questions of program and personnel. It was agreed that the program should be of a substantial academic character. The institute will be concerned first and foremost to provide established scholars and post-graduate theological students with the means for common research. It is expected that it will serve further as a center for the development of an ecumenical outlook among both the clergy and the laity, through individual study, seminars, and conferences. It is also the intention of the Academic Council that the program

of studies should be carried on in an atmosphere of prayer and worship.

The institute is to be fully ecumenical in spirit and structure. Members of the Academic Council have been invited to serve on the basis of their ecumenical experience, as well as their academic qualifications. The Council will assume full responsibility for the academic direction of the institute.

252. The faiths explored the problems of morality together. In Lake Charles, Louisiana, the Rev. Bill Pinson, assistant professor of ethics at the Southwestern Baptist Theological Seminary, addressed the St. Charles Academy at the invitation of the Academy—Immaculate Conception PTA. He warned youths of the dangers of petting and "second hand sex" in the book stores and in conversation.

In a different area and on a more formal level, nine clergymen representing major faiths made a joint appeal to President Johnson to battle pornography:

The pornography syndicate pours out an estimated one to two billion dollars worth of poison each year. The alarming, dangerous and all-too-true fact is that between 75 per cent and 90 per cent of it ends up in the hands of children. Police have observed a definite interrelation between the stimulus of pornography, and narcotics using, juvenile sex crime and violence. In addition, America has become the world leader in exportation of filth. British customs officials, in the past throo years, have seized 826,454 paperbacks, most of which they say were published in this country. . . .

These are facts, Mr. President, and a very sad and shocking fact is that little has been done about it. There are laws on the books in every state. There are national laws. But police and prosecutors, and recently even legislatures, have been hamstrung by the interpretation of these laws; by too-doctrinaire readings of the First Amendment by members of the judiciary. While this situation prevails, the constitutional rights of parents to protect their young are being violated, and a generation of Americans is being weakened by creeping decay and rot.

We have and must always have a moral basis to all our law. . . . May we suggest . . . in the name of the millions in our flocks, that a Presidential Commission of experts be formed to study this hazard which could eventually spell the ruin of our country; and that it make recommendations for a swift and permanent solution.

May we further suggest, as in the case of the recent race riots, that an FBI investigation be initiated to find the sources of pornography production: and that the facts be made public so that the American people will know who is responsible for this corruption.

We believe that the situation is in the crisis stage and we cannot emphasize too strongly the pressing need for these two actions. May we respectfully urge that they be initiated immediately, for we are convinced that the survival of our nation depends upon direct, definite, firm action *now*.

[*Signed by:* The Rev. Arthur Lee Kinsolving, rector of St. James' Episcopal Church and president of the Protestant Council of the City of New York; the Rev. Wilburn C. West, president, Eastern States Mission, Church of Jesus Christ of Latter-Day Saints; the Rev. W. Scott Morton, executive director, University Christian Foundation, New York University (United Presbyterian), Catholic bishops, the Most Rev. Leo A. Pursley, Fort Wayne, chairman of the U.S. Bishops' National Office of Decent Literature; the Most Rev. Aloysius J. Willinger, Monterey-Fresno Diocese; the Most Rev. John King Mussio, Steubenville, Ohio, diocese; Rabbi Chaim U. Lipschitz, editor *Jewish Press*; Rabbi Jehuda Melber, Briarwood Jewish Center, Queens, New York; Rabbi Dr. Julius G. Neumann, Congregation Zichron Moshe, co-founder of Operation Yorkville.]

253. Episcopalians, Catholics, and Lutherans sought to pro-

vide ethical counsel together for businessmen in Boulder, Colorado. The plan follows an interfaith panel set up by American Motors. The Rev. Dr. Paul Musselman, who had been a member of the original American Motors panel, suggested the panel in Boulder when he was visiting with the Rev. Jack Lundin, pastor of Trinity Lutheran Church, Boulder. Pastor Lundin interested three others: the rector of St. John's Episcopal Church, the director of the Newman Center, University of Colorado, and a local Methodist pastor. Pastor Lundin writes:

> The four of us mainly ask questions and try awfully hard to stay away from "preaching." We have found evidence to support the fact that many businessmen indeed feel "preached to" but not "talked with." Many of the men have told us that they appreciate knowing that our concern for ethics goes far deeper than a superficial moralistic concern for abstinence in the area of "smoking, drinking, dancing and wild, wild women."

> Our ultimate aim is to be of service to our own immediate community and to act by invitation only as a kind of Christian conscience; i.e., the Board of Directors of "X" Company may have decision making dilemmas concerning advertising, employee-employer relations, price fixing, etc. Ethical Counsel (as the clergy team is called) would not determine solutions but help in the formulation of objective observations, with the possibility of pointing out other ethical dilemmas not yet seen.

> After two years of interviewing everyone from psychiatrists to professional politicians, we have started getting some invitations. Our first invitation came a little late, however, and before we had the opportunity to counsel with this particular national organization, they very noisily slipped into the hands of receivers, as well as a number of court cases.

> Whatever we've learned, I think we have at least become

a bit more empathetic toward the world of the professional man and of the man in business and industry.

I must add that the by-products for the four of us in this joint venture have been enormous. Our parishes are now meeting together on a quarterly basis with our laity coming to understand one another within the proper bounds of ecumenicity.

254. In the struggle for human rights for the American Negro, the dialogue perhaps brought its most noticeable fruits. Both Senator Hubert H. Humphrey, D.-Minnesota, who was Senate floor manager for the Civil Rights Bill, and Senator Richard B. Russell, D.-Georgia, who led the Southern filibuster against it, said that churches played a decisive role in the legislative battle.

Protestant activity was shaped and correlated largely through the new Commission on Religion and Race of the National Council of Churches. Its first director, the Rev. Dr. Robert W. Spike, speaking before the United Presbyterian General Assembly in Columbus in 1965, noted the cooperation of the major faiths, and proposed development of further links:

The persuasive witness of the church in racial justice these past few months could not have occurred without the united ecumenical front that was presented to the country. The Commission on Religion and Race was a creation of the major Protestant bodies in this country, and all the top leaders of the communions have personally been committed to its work. Roman Catholics and Jewish leaders have from time to time stood solidly with our patriarchs, at police barricades, before Congress, before great assemblies in Washington. Effective Christian witness in a complicated mass society demands Christian unity. We will continue to need it in the days ahead. Why cannot the major Protestant social action and mission bodies of the churches discussing union immediately form a single working agency of witness, without waiting for the doctrinal necessities to be settled. We have had that in effect, on a pragmatic basis, in the spe-

cialized race relation staffs of the denominations and the
National Council Commission these past two years. It has
worked very well. We must expand that operating unity,
and come to see it as a long time necessity, not just a temporary expedient brought on by the racial crisis.

Also the strong Protestant witness in racial justice would
not have occurred probably without innovation in organization and procedures, without the development of some
new agencies of missions, free and flexible enough to work
in local crisis situations, but also with government in Washington and other powerful private movements for justice in
this country. Effective Christian witness demands ecumenical strength and new missionary structure.

By the same token, Christian unity will disintegrate into
arid discussion groups or worse, organizational gameman-
ship, if it is not for the purpose of mission. There is no
question in my mind but that closeness between Romans
and Protestants in this country has developed more lasting
roots because we have walked on picket lines, and planned
together for joint program action. We find how deeply
kindred we are when we are following our common Lord
into the same place of need, there to serve and witness.
This is true *koinonia* (Fellowship), common obedience to
Christ in a real struggle.

255. Catholic activity in interfaith efforts to achieve equal
rights and opportunities for the Negro received momentum from
the Catholic bishops' statements in 1958 ("We may well deplore
a gradualism that is merely a cloak for inaction" in race relations) and in 1962 ("Every man and woman has equal rights
before the law, notably rights to equal opportunity. . . ."). One
of the strongest pleas for racial justice, cast in the mold of interfaith relations, was made by the Most Rev. Patrick J. O'Boyle, of
Washington, D.C., on October 28, 1964, before the Second Vatican Council, during the debate on Schema 13 on "The Church in
the Modern World" (that document, and the religious liberty,
and non-Christian religion declarations, among others, carried

references eventually, directly or indirectly, concerning the
equality of all races) :

> I wish to propose the addition of a separate section in Chap-
> ter IV on the problem of racial injustice. Racism, which in
> various forms and in varying degrees, is to be found in al-
> most every region of the world, is not merely a social or
> cultural or political problem. It is, first and foremost, a
> moral and religious problem and one of staggering pro-
> portions.

> The present text of Schema 13, refers to the problem two
> or three times, but only incidentally and in passing. What
> I am proposing is that it be treated formally and explicitly
> as a separate problem, not merely from the sociological
> point of view, but from the point of view of morality and
> religion.

> Our treatment of this problem in Schema 13 need not be
> very long, nor should it attempt to offer detailed solutions
> to specific problems in particular countries or regions of
> the world. At the very least, however, it should include a
> forthright and unequivocal condemnation of racism in all
> its forms and should outline, if only in general terms, the
> theological basis for this condemnation.

> It should also emphasize the obligation which rests upon all
> the members of the Church to do everything within their
> power to eliminate the cancerous evil of racial injustice
> and to advance through all available means, the cause of
> interracial brotherhood under the fatherhood of God. I
> might add, in this connection, that our own experience in
> the United States suggests that this is one area of social
> action which calls for the closest possible cooperation be-
> tween Catholics, Protestants, and Jews and all other men
> of good will.

> In our judgment, racism is one of the most serious moral
> and religious problems of our times. If we fail to give it

separate and adequate treatment, I fear that the world will conclude that we are very poorly informed about the signs of the time, or, worse than that, that we are insensitive to the tragic plight of the millions of innocent men and women all over the world who are the victims of racial pride and racial injustice.

In closing, permit me to quote, in my own native language, a brief excerpt from an address delivered in that language by Pope Pius XII, of happy memory, to a group of Negro publishers from the United States: "All men are brothered in Jesus Christ: for He, through God, became also man, became a member of the human family, a brother of all. This fact, the expression of infinite universal love, is the true bond of fraternal charity which unites men and nations. May it be welded even more firmly through the efforts of all men of good will."

Unless I am mistaken, the whole world is looking to us to reaffirm this simple, but very profound truth in a solemn conciliar statement and to do so unequivocally and with all the clarity, precision, and forcefulness at our command.

256. A National Conference on Religion and Race was convened in Chicago among the major faiths in January 1963. The 670 delegates adopted this joint "Appeal to the Conscience of the American People":

We have met as members of the great Jewish and Christian faiths held by the majority of the American people, to counsel together concerning the tragic fact of racial prejudice, discrimination and segregation in our society. Coming as we do out of various religious backgrounds, each of us has more to say than can be said here. But this statement is what we as religious people are moved to say together.

Racism is our most serious domestic evil. We must eradicate it with all diligence and speed. For this purpose we appeal to the consciences of the American people. . . .

Our primary concern is for the laws of God. We Americans of all religious faiths have been slow to recognize that racial discrimination and segregation are an insult to God, the Giver of human dignity and human rights. Even worse, we all have participated in perpetuating racial discrimination. . . .

We repent our failures and ask the forgiveness of God. We ask also the forgiveness of our brothers, whose rights we have ignored and whose dignity we have offended. We call for a renewed religious conscience on this basically moral evil.

Our appeal to the American people is this:

SEEK a reign of justice in which voting rights and equal protection of the law will everywhere be enjoyed; public facilities and private ones serving a public purpose will be accessible to all; equal education and cultural opportunities, hiring and promotion, medical and hospital care, open occupancy in housing will be available to all.

SEEK a reign of love in which the wounds of past injustices will not be used as excuses for new ones; racial barriers will be eliminated; the stranger will be sought and welcomed; any man will be received as brother—his rights, your rights; his pain, your pain; his prison, your prison.

SEEK a reign of courage in which the people of God will make their faith their binding commitment; in which men willingly suffer for justice and love; in which churches and synagogues lead, not follow.

SEEK a reign of prayer in which God is praised and worshipped as the Lord of the universe, before Whom all racial idols fall, Who makes us one family and to Whom we are all responsible.

In making this appeal we affirm our common religious commitment to the essential dignity and equality of all men under God. We dedicate ourselves to work together to make this commitment a vital factor in our total life.

We call upon all the American people to work, to pray and to act courageously in the cause of human equality and dignity while there is still time, to eliminate racism permanently and decisively, to seize the historic opportunity the Lord has given us for healing an ancient rupture in the human family, to do this for the glory of God.

257. Churches stood together to combat discrimination in housing, but at times faced difficulties at the polls. In California in 1964, voters approved Proposition 14 which overruled existing fair-housing legislation, and again the churches failed in Akron and in Detroit in 1964 despite considerable effort on an interfaith basis to achieve open housing. The churches fought on in their joint crusade in the north for open housing. In Chicago, "An open Letter to the Members of the Real Estate Industry" to assure non-discrimination and to begin "constructive" efforts were mailed by the interfaith Chicago conference on Religion and Race. In Baltimore, the major faiths distributed 30,000 pamphlets and pledge cards that said the signer would welcome responsible persons of any race in his neighborhood. Sponsors were the Maryland Council of Churches, the Baltimore Board of Rabbis, and the Baltimore Roman Catholic Archdiocese through its Women's Committee for Civil Rights and the Catholic Interracial Council. Individuals receiving the pledge cards were asked to agree to these propositions:

*I believe* that every person is endowed with the inalienable right to purchase or rent a home anywhere without limitations based upon race, religion, or national origin.

*I believe* that discrimination on the basis of race, religion, or national origin is evil, and that obedience to God compels me to love my brother in word and deed.

*I believe* that it is imperative within our Baltimore metro-

politan area for all persons of good will to take an active
role in helping to achieve freedom of opportunity in housing.

*Therefore*, I will welcome into my neighborhood responsible persons of any race, religion, or national origin, and I
will work with them and other neighbors to maintain a desirable community for all. (It is the understanding of the
person signing this pledge that the sponsoring organizations may publish his name and neighborhood with not less
than 10,000 others.)

258. Fifty clergymen of all faiths in Little Rock, led by the
Episcopal bishop of Arkansas, marched on Gov. Orville Faubus'
office and asked him to reopen the Capitol cafeteria to all races
on March 23, 1965. The cafeteria, operating as a "private club"
to avoid integration, was closed after three demonstrations by
the Student Non-violent Co-ordinating Committee. The Rt. Rev.
Robert R. Brown was the only bishop present, but a petition
bore also the signatures of the Most Rev. Albert L. Fletcher,
Roman Catholic bishop of Little Rock; Bishop Paul V. Galloway,
of the Methodist Church of Arkansas, and Bishop George N.
Collins, of the Arkansas and Oklahoma Districts of the African
Methodist Episcopal Church. The petition said:

Motivated by the love of peace and justice and in antipathy
to violence and brutality we ministers of Little Rock present ourselves before you with this petition. . . .

The Capitol cafeteria is one of the few remaining segregated eating places in the entire city of Little Rock. As
long as any of its facilities remain segregated our Capitol
stands as a symbol of division and injustice. . . .

The moral issue takes precedence over the legal aspects.
We therefore petition you to use your office to direct that
the cafeteria in the state Capitol be opened immediately
to all the citizens of Arkansas irrespective to race, color or
creed.

259. Among the more concrete efforts in race relations is the interfaith "Project Equality." Initiated by the Roman Catholic Archdiocese of Detroit in May 1965 and the St. Louis Archdiocese, Project Equality seeks to secure compliance from employers to a covenant that they will not discriminate in hiring or employment practices. (Project equality in 1966 comprised Detroit, St. Louis, San Antonio, Hartford, with an interfaith national Advisory Council.) Affirmative action—signing of assurances of equality—is sought from all businesses and firms servicing a diocese or archdiocese with its multi-million dollar consignment through various institutions. In November 1965, the Detroit Council of Churches and the Jewish Community Council voted to join the Detroit Project Equality at the invitation of the Archdiocese of Detroit, and in December, the Eastern Orthodox community joined. The budget of an estimated $27,000 was split among the groups, with the Archdiocese, which has by far the biggest expenditure (the other groups do not represent the buying power of their local constituency), bearing more than half the cost. For the tightly budgeted Detroit Council of Churches it meant foregoing raises of the Council's staff to join in the project at an estimated share of $9,000 a year. A common office for Project Equality was set up in the Archdiocesan office building. Officials estimate that about 60 other areas in the nation are expected to have a similar Project Equality, with many of them also going on an interfaith basis.

a. At the expansion of Project Equality to an interfaith basis, the archbishop of Detroit, the Most Rev. John F. Dearden, said:

The Archdiocese of Detroit is happy to join with the Metropolitan Detroit Council of Churches, the Council of Eastern Orthodox Churches, and the Jewish Community Council of Metropolitan Detroit in this practical expression of our common belief in the dignity and rights of all men. Project Equality is a program of action aimed at giving all men an equal opportunity to obtain employment, to advance in it, and to develop to the fullest their God-given potential. By undertaking this program together, the religious groups of the Metropolitan Detroit areas are giving an example of the way in which all religious convictions must influence men's lives; an example which will be seen by all the people of the community. Today we are preaching together a significant sermon.

The acceptance of Project Equality across the nation by government, management, and labor as well as by religious groups guarantees that it will be an effective tool in helping us to overcome patterns of discrimination deeply ingrained in our society. The fact that the whole religious community of the Detroit area is the first to join together in this effort under Project Equality is an indication of our ecumenical maturity. The Catholics of the Archdiocese are proud to be a part of it.

b. The president of the Detroit Council of Churches, the Rev. Dr. Joseph L. Roberts, pastor of the Bethel A.M.E. Church, concurring, issued this statement:

The Metropolitan Detroit Council of Churches participates wholeheartedly in the interfaith movement, "Project Equality." The name "Project Equality" is descriptive of its purpose. It concerns itself with the practical application of equality of opportunity and responsibility for every person, in every aspect of life. This position is rooted and grounded in our mutual faith in God: in pronouncements of the governing bodies of the denominations which constitute the Council: in our democratic stance: and in our recognition that this is a must for existence. No nation, nor even the world itself, can long survive half slave and half free. Our interfaith initiation and implementation of this project suggests that we accept "Project Equality" as one of our fundamental imperatives.

In the light of the above stated facts, the Board of Directors of the Council in stated meeting voted unanimously to participate in "Project Equality." The vote was in essence a vote to implement positions already taken by many of the denominations of the Council. . . .

Our common faith demands action, on every level of life. Through "Project Equality" we hope to alert each pastor and layman of our divine obligation to work with God in his effort to see that our creeds may become deeds and that our pronouncements may progressively become incarnations. As together we make a united trust our witness will be stronger and the fruits of our labors will be more abundant.

260. A "Committee of Concern" in Mississippi, including Catholics, Jews and Protestants, headquartered in Jackson, sought to rebuild 36 Mississippi churches damaged or destroyed by fire. A flyer published by the Committee explained its purposes:

The Committee wishes to make it possible for men, women and children of goodwill to respond to violence, hatred and destruction with concern, compassion and construction. With this motivation we initiated a united effort for concrete and personal action in response to the physical losses and personal injustices and indignities suffered by Negro congregations whose buildings have been set fire by unknown arsonists.

We feel that these attacks are attacks on *all* houses of worship, on religion itself, indeed upon our Constitutional guarantee to assemble and worship. We accept the losses and suffering as *our own*. A fund for rebuilding and refurnishing is already in existence under the care of the treasurer of the Mississippi Baptist Convention Board. Materials, labor, equipment and financial aid will be accepted and dispersed by the Committee only when requested by a congregation and then after a responsible investigation. Every attempt will be made to allow the local community to answer the needs of the deprived congregation first.

The Committee will determine which congregation will receive funds and donated equipment, and all aid will be offered irrespective of denomination.

> Contributions from individuals, churches and synagogues are urgently needed to restore the estimated $100,000 to $300,000 loss which these 36 congregations have suffered. . . .

> Through personal acts of concern and compassion by Jews and Christians throughout our state we hope that a new spirit of goodwill springs up to "let justice roll down like waters, and righteousness like an overflowing stream." It is our prayer that all people will be guided by a sense of wisdom and justice which will destroy the will to violence of any sort.

261. From Los Angeles to St. Augustine, from Montgomery to Chicago, priests, nuns, pastors marched arm in arm for civil rights. They were at the forefront of the big marches:

a. In Washington, D.C., August 28, 1963, Presbyterian Eugene Carson Blake and Catholic Archbishop of Washington, the Most Rev. Patrick A. O'Boyle, spoke to the 200,000 who marched on the capitol. Train-and plane-loads of clergy and church delegations had helped to swell the numbers. Principal speaker was a clergyman himself, the Rev. Dr. Martin Luther King, Jr., who has spent much of his time in recent years in jails as he has led the struggle for civil rights. Departing from his prepared text, he said:

> I still have a dream, a dream deeply rooted in the American dream—one day this nation will rise up and live up to its creed, "We hold these truths to be self-evident, that all men are created equal."

> I have a dream that one day in Alabama little black boys and little black girls will be able to go hand in hand together with little white boys and little while girls as brothers and sisters.

> This is the faith that I will take down to the South—that out of this mountain of despair, I can find a soul of brotherhood.

Let freedom ring from every hill and molehill in Mississippi, from every city and state in the country.

b. In Selma, Alabama, on March 9, 1965, the Rev. Father Geno Baroni, one of more than forty Catholic priests marching with Protestant and Jewish clergy, championing voting rights for Negroes, gave this account:

As we came over the bridge we saw the state troopers lined up about 200 yards ahead. I was marching in the second line just behind Dr. King and other leaders, and from where I was it looked like a whole regiment waiting for us.

All of us had already made our commitment in mind and conscience. As some of the clergymen put it, we were going to Golgotha without the cross.

Still, as we marched we couldn't help asking each other what tear gas felt like and hoping that, if there was going to be violence, at least the older clergy wouldn't be badly beaten.

I suppose some people were surprised at the spectacle of priests and ministers and rabbis—there were perhaps 300 or 400 of us in that body of 2,000 marchers—coming out to demonstrate in defiance of a federal court's injunction.

But we didn't make the decision lightly.

During a meeting back at Brown's chapel, the A.M.E. church in Selma that was the focal point for our activities, speaker after speaker rose to say that the law of conscience is higher than Federal law. If a man is not free to follow his conscience, we agreed, he is already dead in spirit.

262. Charity—works—deeds—brotherhood—love for one's fellowman—these were the visible signs of dialogue. In the background, these formed the molds for talk of unity—and these were also the fruits of existing bonds. The seeds in the fruit were assurances of more dialogue to come, and assurances that

strands of faith—the fibers of a deeper unity—would begin to form a more excellent growth. Said the Rev. Patrick C. Rodger, former executive secretary of the World Council of Churches' Department of Faith and Order and now canon and vice-provost of St. Mary's Cathedral (Episcopal Church of Scotland), in Edinburgh:

> If "faith without works is dead," assuredly Faith and Order without the actual wrestlings for reconciliation and re-newal in the lives of churches is dead also. To take a meta-phor: Faith and Order may be compared to a group of those who sit and patiently unravel a large mass of tangled ropes (and the ropes frequently cross and recross one another, so that even the most eagle-eyed confessionalist cannot al-ways distinguish the Baptist rope or the Lutheran rope or the Anglican rope in the process of sorting them out). And from time to time ropes will be called for, even with some urgency, so that they may be knotted together for use—and this is the work of church union in the world (and I do not use "the world" simply in a geographical sense here, but in a Biblical one also). Whether the ropes will be available when wanted, and whether they will be able to bear the strain of constant use and theological tug-of-war, will de-pend a great deal on the quality of the work being done in the background.

## REFERENCES

### Chapter VII

223. "Unity Through Social Action," Canadian Catholic Conference Statement, for Social Action Sunday, May 10, 1964, *Social Action Notes for Priests*, May, 1964, p. 16.
224. Vasken I, Patriarch and Catholicos of the Ancient Church of Armenia, encyclical, "Unity in Diversity," *The Armenian Church*, XIII, No. 4 (July, 1965), 2.
225. From photostat of "Common Declaration," an agreement of seven Christian churches to share a common pavilion at the 1967 World Exposition in Montreal; courtesy Sydney Morrell and Company, Inc., New York.
226. Pope Paul VI, speech at the United Nations, Oct. 4, 1965, in *Pope Paul VI in New York*, texts of Pope Paul's speeches in New York, NCWC, n.d., pp. 6-11.

227. Final Recommendations, Sixth World Order Study Conference, "International Organization and Peaceful Change, "Section II, VI and VII, Oct. 23, 1965, in St. Louis.

228. a. "National Clergy Group Fights War Escalation," *The National Catholic Reporter*, II, No. 12 (Jan. 19, 1966), 1.

    b. "A Declaration of the National Inter-Relations Conference on Peace," March 17, 1966, subsection "A Statement on Vietnam," courtesy of Gunther Lawrence, director of Public Information, Union of American Hebrew Congregations, from a carbon copy.

229. a. "International Committee for Defense of Christian Culture," *The Ukrainian Bulletin*, Nov. 1-15, 1964, p. 91.

    b. "An Appeal of Religious Leaders to All Believers, to All Churches and Religious Organizations, to All People of Good Will," religious delegates, World Congress for Peace, Helsinki, July 10-15, 1965.

230. *Information Service*, National Council of Churches, XLIII, No. 16, Oct. 10, 1964, 3.

231. Fact sheet of the Cuban Refugee Center, Miami, Fla.

232. Release, WCC, New York Office, No. 7-66, Feb. 11, 1966.

233. Ecumenical Work Camps leaflet, Youth Department, World Council of Churches, Geneva.

234. *What Is Agape?* Tullio Vinay, booklet distributed by Segretaria d'Agape, Perrero per Prali, Torino, Italia, pp. 2, 4.

235. "Statement of Inter-Religious Committee Against Poverty," Washington, D. C., Jan. 18, 1966, NCC Release, 4DCLM.

236. *WICS*, Women in Community Service, Inc., flyer, courtesy, Margaret Mealey, executive director, National Council of Catholic Women, May 3, 1965.

237. "War on Poverty in Philadelphia," submitted by Office of Archbishop's Commission—Economic Opportunity Program, Philadelphia, Pa., pp. 4-6, 8, 9.

238. Copy, letter to the Very Rev. John N. Peabody, Douglass Cater, special assistant to the President, Feb. 20, 1965.

239. Letter, from the Rev. Father Robert Emmet Fagan, associate director, Catholic Charities, Diocese of Rockville Centre, N.Y., Apr. 27, 1965.

240. Michigan Migrant Opportunity, Inc., Operational Progress Report Summary, Apr. 12-July 12, 1965, pp. 1, 2, 4.

241. Allen R. Huber, *Church and Community*, IV, No. 2 (Mar.-Apr., 1964, United Church of Christ in the Philippines), 13.

242. Lawrence E. Styles, *Industrial Chaplaincy*, Inter-Church Trade and Industry Mission, Victoria, Australia, Melbourne, pp. 4-7.

243. Annual Report, 1965, Inter-Faith Center, Detroit, Richard Peck, executive director.

244. The Rev. Father George Hagmaier, C.S.P., Catholic University, quoted in the *U.S. Catholic*, Aug., 1964, p. 58.

245. *Articles of Incorporation*, Nobles and Knights Charities, Inc., chartered Sept. 24, 1964, by the Court of Common Pleas of Allegheny County, Pa.

246. Supreme Knight John W. McDevitt, from release, Sharon, Mass., Feb. 28, 1966, by Knights of Columbus, Supreme Headquarters, New Haven, Conn.

247. *Working Papers in Church Planning*, Columbia, Md., prepared by The National Council of Churches, Stanley J. Hallett, n.d., pp. 25, 26.

248. a. Brochure, *A United Christian Hall? Yes*, Christian Hall, Bewdley, Worcestershire.

   b. Letter from the Rev. W. G. Harwood, Anglican rector, Bewdley, Worcestershire, England, May 25, 1965.

249. "The Atlanta Statement," *The Catholic World*, CCII, No. 1, 211 (February, 1966), 302-305.

250. a. John Dillenberger, "The Graduate Theological Union in the San Francisco Bay Area," *The Journal of Bible and Religion*, XXXIII, No. 1 (Jan., 1965), 49, 50.

   b. Bylaws of Graduate Theological Union, adopted Nov. 19, 1963; revised Mar. 11, 1964, pp. 4, 6.

251. Announcement, Dec. 15, 1965, from the Rev. Father Theodore M. Hesburgh, C.S.C., Notre Dame, Ind., on behalf of the new Academic Council.

252. "Nine Clergymen Appeal to President," *Operation Yorkville Newsletter*, III, No. 8, 1, 3.

253. Letter, from the Rev. Jack W. Lundin, Trinity Lutheran Church, Boulder, Colo., May 11, 1965.

254. Robert W. Spike, text of address before the Ecumenical Service of Worship, United Presbyterian General Assembly, Columbus, O., May 23, 1965, pp. 9-11.

255. *The Josephite Harvest*, Nov.-Dec., 1964, NCWC p. 1.

256. Mathew Ahmann, ed., *Race: Challenge to Religion* (Chicago: Henry Regnery Co., 1963), pp. 172, 173.

257. Pledge Card, "The Baltimore Area Inter-Religious Campaign for the Good Neighbor Pledge," courtesy Maryland Council of Churches.

258. "Clergymen Petition Governor . . .", by Richard Allin, *Arkansas Gazette*, CXLVI, No. 125 (Mar. 23, 1965), 2.

259. a. Archbishop John F. Dearden, archbishop of Detroit, statement launching "Project Equality" on an interfaith basis, in cooperation with the major faiths in Detroit, Dec. 16, 1965.

   b. The Rev. Dr. Joseph L. Roberts, president, the Metropolitan Detroit Council of Churches, statement concerning the Council's joining "Project Equality," Dec. 15, 1965.

260. "Beauty for Ashes," flyer, Committee of Concern, Jackson, Miss.

261. a. Detroit *Free Press* Wire services, Aug. 29, 1963.

   b. "Selma—'Golgotha without the Cross,'" the Rev. Father Geno Baroni, *The National Catholic Reporter*, I, No. 20 (Mar. 17, 1965), 1.

262. Patrick C. Rodger, "Towards the Wholeness of the Church," Central Committee. No. 15, report given at the Committee's meeting in Enugu, Nigeria, Jan. 14, 1965, courtesy of the World Council of Churches.

# Bibliography

Books of the Protestant-Roman Catholic
Dialogue 1956-1966

## I. *Rules and Means of Dialogue*

Busetti, Charles, F.S. C.J., *Praying for Unity* (Glen Rock, N.J.: Paulist
Press, 1966), an eight-day "unity octave" with content for each day.
Howe, Reuel L., *The Miracle of Dialogue* (Greenwich, Conn.; Seabury,
1963), rules and guidelines for effective communication among the
faiths.
Mackay, John A., *Ecumencies: The Science of the Church Universal*
(Englewood Cliffs, N.J.: Prentice-Hall, Inc., 1964), procedures and
methods in the science of ecumenism.
National Council of Catholic Men and the National Council of Catholic
Women, *Grass-roots Ecumenism*, 1966, a kit of five booklets—first
steps in dialogue, the text of the Decree on Ecumenism, practical
project ideas, how to plan an open house in Catholic churches, plus
ideas for contacts wth Jewish groups.
O'Brien, John A., ed., *Steps to Christian Unity* (Garden Cty, New York:
Doubleday, 1964), 24 Protestant-Roman Catholic leaders, including
Karl Barth, Karl Rahner, Cardinal Cushing, Cardinal Meyer discuss
problems of unity and practical approaches to it.

## II. *Background and History*

Bainton, Roland Herbert, *Christian Unity and Religion in New England*
(Boston: Beacon Press, 1964), factors in early U.S. history contribut-
ing to ecumenical movement.
Baum, Gregory, *That They May Be One: a study of papal doctrine* (Leo
XIII-Pius XII), (Westminster, Md.: Newman Press, 1958).
Bea, Augustin, *The Unity of Christans*, edited by Bernard Leeming
(New York: Herder and Herder, 1963), lectures on Christian union.
Bevan, R. J. W., ed., *The Churches and Christan Unity* (London: New
York: Oxford University Press, 1963), Orthodox, Methodist, Baptist
and other historians trace history of ecumenical movement.
Beaver R. Pierce, *Ecumenical Beginnings in the Protestant World Mis-*

*sion: A History of Comity* (New York: Thomas Nelson & Sons, 1962),
various types of agreement on jurisdiction in missions.

Biot, Francois, *The Rise of Protestant Monasticism* trans. W. J. Ker-
rigan, (Baltimore: Helicon, 1963), a priest reviews Catholic roots in
Protestantism's new monasticism.

Boyer, Charles, *Christian Unity*, trans. Jill Dean (New York: Hawthorn Books, 1962), Twentieth Century Encyclopedia of Catholicism,
Vol. 138, Sec. 14.

Bridston, Keith R. with Walter D. Wagoner eds., *Unity in Mid-Career:
An Ecumenical Critique*, (New York: Macmillan, 1963), an attempt
to identify an ecumenical theology on the current scene.

Cavert, Samuel McCrea, *On the Road to Christian Unity*; an appraisal
of the ecumenical movement (New York: Harper, 1961), history,
main themes of developments.

Curtis, Geoffrey, *Paul Couturier and Unity in Christ* (London: SCM
Press, 1964), study of the development of the Week of Prayer for
Christian Unity and the man responsible for it.

Dawson, Christopher, *The Historic Reality of Christian Culture: A Way
to the Renewal of Human Life* (New York: Harper, 1960), study of
Christianity and civilization and implications for unity through renewal.

Ehrenstrom, Nils and Walter G. Muelder, eds., *Treasure in Earthen
Vessels* (New York: Harper, 1961), discussion of cultural factors
and the role of institutions in unity.

Garrison, Winfred Ernest, *The Quest and Character of a United Church*
(Nashville: Abingdon Press, 1957), history of ecumenical and
Christian union movements.

Goodall, Norman, *The Ecumenical Movement* (London: New York:
Oxford University Press, 1961), what the ecumenical movement is and
does.

Grant, Frederick Clifton, *Rome and Reunion* (New York: Oxford University Press, 1965), history of papacy as relates to Christian union.

Hrodmadka, Josef L., *The Church and Theology in Today's Troubled
Times* (Praque: Ecumenical Council of Churches in Czechoslovakia,
1956), a Czech theologian's views of church history and twentieth
century ecumenism.

Hunt, George L., *Guide to Christian Unity* (St. Louis, Mo.: Bethany
Press, 1958), procedures in Christian unity by secretary of the Consultation on Church Union that started two years later.

Jones, Ilion T., *A Protestant Speaks His Mind* (Philadelphia: Westminster Press, 1960), a San Francisco Seminary professor argues that
the ancient church, which is a model of much ecumenical discussion, is
not really a prototype to follow.

Jungmann, J. A. *The Early Liturgy* (Notre Dame, Ind.: University of
Notre Dame Press, 1959), a look at primitive common liturgy.

Landis, Benson Young, *Ecumenical Movement* (New York: World
Council of Churches, 1965), doctoral dissertations relevant to ecumenism compiled by research executive of the NCC.

Lee, Robert, *The Social Sources of Church Unity: An Interpretation
of Uniting Movements in American Protestantism* (New York: Abing-

don Press, 1960), review of cultural and social influences on union efforts in the U.S.

Mackie, Robert C., with Charles C. West, eds. *The Sufficiency of God: Essays on the Ecumenical Hope in Honor of W. A. Visser 't Hooft*, (Philadelphia: Westminster Press, 1963), essays on theology and problems of social ethics in the ecumenical movement by Congar, Florovsky, Nissiotis, Niebuhr, Bliss, etc.

—————— *Layman Extraordinary* (New York: Association, 1966), life of ecumenical pioneer John R. Mott.

Macy, Paul Griswold, *If it be of God* (St. Louis: Bethany Press, 1960), story of the WCC.

Mascall, Eric Lionel, *The Recovery of Unity* (London: New York: Longmans, Green, 1958), a theological study.

Minear, Paul S., *Images of the Church in the New Testament* (New York: Westminster 1960), a theologian's discussion of unity in the New Testament.

—————— *Nature of the Unity We Seek* (St. Louis: Bethany Press, 1958), outline of unity requirements.

Mudge, Lewis S., *One Church: Catholic and Reformed—Toward a Theology for Ecumenical Decision* (Philadelphia: Westminster Press, 1963), theology of ecumenism.

Neill, Stephen Charles, bishop of Tinnevelly, *Brothers of the Faith* (New York: Abingdon Press, 1960), ecumenical biographies from John R. Mott to John XXIII (London edition: *Men of Unity.*)

—————— *Twentieth Century Christianity* (Garden City, N. Y.: Doubleday, 1963), background concerning the forces of modern ecumenical developments by WCC leaders and others.

Nelson, John Robert, *Christian Unity in North America*, a Symposium (St. Louis: Bethany Press, 1958), views of ecumenical leaders plus views of Southern Baptists and various evangelical groups.

—————— *One Lord, One Church* (New York: Association 1958), history of the ecumenical movement and church union.

—————— *Overcoming Christian Divisions* (New York: Association, 1962), theology of unity.

Newbigin, Lesslie, *The Household of God* rev. ed., (London: SCM Press, 1964), widely circulated lectures on the nature of the church by a bishop of the Church of South India, an important church merger in 1947.

—————— *Is Christ Divided?* (Grand Rapids, Mich.: Eerdmans, 1961), a plea for Christian unity in a revolutionary age.

Nuttall, Geoffrey F., and Owen Chadwick, eds., *From Uniformity to Unity*, 1662-1962 (London: SPCK, 1962), historical problems in nonconformity and consensus.

Outler, Albert C., *Christian Tradition and the Unity We Seek* (New York: Oxford, 1957), discussion of the relation of tradtion and traditions by a Methodist scholar who became an important Protestant observer at Vatican II.

Paul, Rajaiah D., *The First Decade: An Account of the Church of South India* (London: Lutterworth Press, 1958), structure and experiences of a wide Protestant-Anglican merger plan.

Piper, Otto A., *Protestantism in an Ecumenical Age* (Philadelphia: Fortress Press, 1965), roots and responsibilities of the ecumenical movement in the twentieth century.

Riga, Peter, *John XXIII and the City of Man* (Westminster, Md.: The Newman Press, 1966), a look into the thinking of Pope John on various issues before the church.

Rogers, Francis, *The Quest for Eastern Christians* (Minneapolis: University of Minnesota Press, 1962), history, relations of Eastern and Western Christianity.

Romeau, Luis V., ed., *Ecumenical Experiences* (Westminster, Md.: The Newman Press, 1965), testimonies of leading ecumenical figures, such as Cullmann, Guitton, Congar, Suenens, etc.

Sheppard, Lancelot, *Twentieth Century Catholicism*, Vol. 4 (New York: Hawthorn Books, 1966), deals with Vatican Council and Ecumenism.

Skoglund, John E., and J. Robert Nelson, *Fifty Years of Faith and Order* (New York: The Interseminary Movement, 1963), brief history of twentieth century ecumenism by a Methodist and a Baptist. Paperback.

Slack, Kenneth, *The Christian Conflict* (London: Edinburgh House Press, 1960), history of twentieth century ecumenical movement.

Spinka, Matthew, *The Quest for Church Unity*, (New York: Macmillan, 1960), an Orthodox view of the road to unity.

Swidler, Leonard J., *Dialogue for Reunion* (New York: Herder & Herder, Inc., 1962), progress toward unity.

———— *The Ecumenical Vanguard* (Pittsburgh: Duquesne University Press, 1966), tracing of German ecumenism through the Una Sancta movement.

Strawley, J. H., *The Early History of the Liturgy* (New York: Macmillan, 1956), roots of unity discussion in liturgy.

Tavard, George Henry, *Protestant Hopes and the Catholic Responsibility* (Notre Dame, Ind.: Fides Publishers, 1960), Catholic role in ecumenism.

———— *Two Centuries of Ecumenism*, trans. Royce W. Hughes (Notre Dame, Ind.: Fides Publishers, 1960), history of contemporary ecumenical movements.

Todd, John, *Catholicism and the Ecumenical Movement* (London: Longmans Green, 1956), Catholic attitudes toward the ecumenical movement.

Tomkins, Oliver S., *A Time for Unity* (New York: Morehouse-Barlow Co., 1964), lectures and essays on Christian union.

Villain, Maurice, *Unity: A History and Some Reflections*, trans. J. R. Foster (Baltimore: Helicon, 1963), history and appraisal of twentieth century unity movements by the successor to Abbé Paul Couturier, unity pioneer of Lyon.

### III. *Comparing Beliefs*

de Albornoz, A. F. Carrillo, *The Basis of Religious Liberty*, (New York: Association, 1963), review of ecumenical thinking concerning religious liberty.

Bauman, Harold E., *The Price of Church Unity* (Scottdale, Pa.: Herald Press, 1962), requirements of church union from the faiths.

Benoit, J. D., *Liturgical Renewal: Studies in Catholic and Protestant Developments on the Continent* (London: SCM Press, 1958), development in worship in Europe.

Bosc, J., J. Guitton, and J. Danielou, *The Catholic Protestant* (Baltimore: Helicon, 1960), French scholars interpret differences.

Bouyer, Louis, *The Spirit and Forms of Protestantism*, trans., A. W. Littledale, (Westminster, Md.: The Newman Press, 1957), leading Catholic expert on church union discusses essential forms of Protestantism.

————, *The Word, the Church and the Sacraments in Catholicism and Protestantism* (New York: Desclee Co., Inc., 1961), comparison and similarity of the faiths in the sacraments.

Bromiley, Geoffrey William, *The Unity and Disunity of the Church* (Grand Rapids, Mich.: Eerdmans, 1958), differences and creative factors.

Brown, Robert McAfee, and Gustave Weigel, *An American Dialogue* (New York: Doubleday, 1960), a Presbyterian and Jesuit team up to discuss their differences and the essence of the ecumenical movement.

Callahan, Daniel, ed., *Christianity Divided* (New York: Sheed & Ward, 1961), layman leads discussion on problems of a diverse Christianity.

Cassels, Louis, *What's the Difference?* (New York: Doubleday, 1965), a comparision of the world's major faiths and their subgroups and denominations by a newsman.

*Christians in Conversation*, (Westminster, Md.: The Newman Press, 1962) papers of a colloquy held at St. John's abbey, Collegeville, Minn., 1961, by the American Benedictine Academy.

Cowan, Wayne, ed., *Facing Protestant-Roman Catholic Tensions* (New York: Association, 1960), review of key trouble spots.

Cristiani, L., and J. Rilliet, *Catholics and Protestants: Separated Brothers* (Westminster, Md.: The Newman Press, 1960), comparison of beliefs.

Cullmann, Oscar, *Message to Catholics and Protestants* (Grand Rapids, Mich.: Eerdmans, 1959), a plea for sharing of offerings.

Dumont, Christopher Jean, *Approaches to Christian Unity*, trans. Henry St. John (Baltimore: Helicon, 1959), special attention to doctrine and prayer.

Ehrlich, Rudolf J., *Rome: Opponent or Partner?* (Philadelphia: Westminster Press, 1966), survey of Catholic-Protestant contracts since the Reformation, concluding they are still at odds in several important areas.

Englert, Clement, C. C. SS. R., *Catholics and Orthodox: Can They Unite?* (Glen Rock, N.J.: Paulist Press, 1966), detail review of issues that have separated East and West.

Gardner-Smith, Percival, *The Roads Converge*, (New York: St. Martin's Press, 1963), a contribution to the question of Christian reunion by members of Jesus College, Cambridge, includes articles on the Synoptic Gospels, the Reformation, mission of the Church.

Hardon, John A., *The Protestant Church of America* (Westminster, Md.: The Newman Press, 1956), outline of American denomnations by a Catholic scholar who has taught in Protestant schools.

Hedegard, David, ed., *Ecumenism and the Bible* (London: the Banner of Trust, 1964), Lutheran teacher from Sweden offers critical views of the ecumenical movement.

Küng, Hans, *The Council, Reform and Reunion* (New York: Sheed & Ward, 1961), a young German theologian and expert, looking to the Second Vatican Council, outlines the wider dimensions of Catholic renewal responsibilities.

Lackmann, Max, *The Augsburg Confession and Catholic Unity,,* trans. Walter R. Bouman (New York: Herder & Herder, 1963), comparison of creeds, etc., by the head of an unofficial German-based Lutheran movement for reunion with Rome.

Lawrence, John, *The Hard Facts of Unity* (London: SCM Press, 1961) a layman reviews the ecumenical movement.

Leeming, Bernard, *The Churches and the Church* (London: Darton, Longman, & Todd; Westminster, Md.: Newman, 1960) a study of ecumenism developed from the Lauriston lectures for 1957. Catholic church relations in the ecumenical movement.

Leenhardt, Franz J., *Two Biblical Faiths: Protestant and Catholic,* trans. Harold Knight (Philadelphia: Westminster Press, 1964), comparison of Catholic and Protestant on biblical grounds.

Marshall, Romey P., and Michael J. Taylor, S. J., *Liturgy and Christian Unity* (Englewood Cliffs, N.J.: Prentice-Hall, 1965), comparative study of worship by a Catholic and a Protestant.

Miller, Samuel, and G. Ernest Wright, *Ecumenical Dialogue at Harvard: the Roman Catholic-Protestant Colloquium* (Cambridge, Mass.: Belknap Press of Harvard University Press, 1964), the Charles Chauncey Stillman lectures on Christian unity by Augustin Cardinal Bea; also articles by Protestants and Catholics on Scripture, sacraments, problems of conscience, the ecumenical movement, etc.

Moeller, Charles, *The Theology of Grace, and The Oecumental Movement* (London: A. R. Mowbray, 1961), with G. Philips, and trans. from French by R. A. Wilson, study of grace and unity.

Mooneyham, W. Stanley, *The Dynamics of Christian Unity* (Grand Rapids, Mich.: Zondervan, 1963), a symposium on the ecumenical movement reflecting views of evangelical leaders who prefer less visible expressions of church unity; nature of church, Scripture, history, salvation.

Moss, Basil S. *Crisis for Baptism* (New York: Morehouse-Barlow Co., 1966), views of Methodists, Baptists, Roman Catholics, Quakers, Orthodox and others in a recent ecumenical conference.

O'Meara, Thomas, O.P., *Mary in Protestant and Catholic Theology* (New York: Sheed & Ward, 1966), analysis of signs of convergence in thinking on Mary.

Persson, Per Erik, |*Roman and Evangelical,* trans. Eric H. Wahlstrom (Philadelphia: Fortress Press, 1964), the Gospel and ministry as an ecumenical problem.

Pittinger, Norman, *The Church, the Ministry, and Reunion* (Greenwich,

Conn.: The Seabury Press, Inc., 1957), church unity and the nature of the church and orders.

Schilling, S. Paul, *Contemporary Continental Theologians* (Nashville: Abingdon, 1966), review of key lines of thought of 11 leading ecumenical and other scholars of Europe: Barth, Congar, Bultmann, Rahner, Nissiotis, etc., by the professor of systematic theology at Fordham University.

Sherrard, Philip, *The Greek East and the Latin West: A Study in the Christian Tradition* (New York: Oxford University Press, 1959), the philosophical mold of early Christianity related to similar molds in contemporary society.

Stuber, Stanley I., *Primer to Roman Catholicism for Protestants* (New York: Association, 1965), revision of 1960 book; how Protestants and Catholics agree and disagree.

Subilia, Vittorio, *The Problem of Catholicism* trans. Reginald Kissack, (London: SCM, 1964), a Waldensian professor in Rome compares Reformed beliefs with Roman Catholics and directions they should take in dialogue.

Swidler, Leonard J., ed., *Scripture and Ecumenism* (Pittsburgh: Duquesne University, 1966), a scholarly symposium on Scriptural problems in ecumenism.

Torrance, Thomas Forsyth, *Conflict and Agreement in the Church* (London: Lutterworth Press, 1959-60), Vol. 1 Order and Disorder, Vol. 2 The Ministry and the Sacraments of the Gospel.

Vassady, Bela, *Christ's Church: Evangelical, Catholic and Reformed* (Grand Rapids, Mich.: Eerdmans, 1965), discussion of union and the U.S. Consultation on Church Union.

Whitson, Robley Edward, *Mysticism and Ecumenism* (New York: Sheed & Ward, 1966), former chairman of the theology department of Fordham reviews common strains of mysticism within Christianity and other faiths.

Willebrands, J. G. M., et al, *Problems Before Unity* (Baltimore: Helicon, 1963), papers presented at the closed clergy conference held at Garrison, N.Y., under the auspices of the Fracniscan Friars of the Atonement, Graymoor, with foreworl by Augustin Cardinal Bea; reunion and liturgy, Bible, laymen, etc.

## IV. *Documents*

Abbott, Walter M., S.J., gen. ed., *The Documents of Vatican II* (New York: Guild Press, America Press, Association Press, 1966), 16 official texts of the Second Vatican Council with comment by Catholic and Protestant theologians.

*All-Africa Church Conference*, Ibadam, Nigeria, 1958 (New York: International Missionary Council, 1958), reports.

Baum, Gregory, *The Teachings of the Second Vatican Council* (Westminster, Md.: The Newman Press, 1966), Second Vatican Council texts.

Cranny, Titus, *Father Paul and Christian Unity* (Garrison, N.Y.: Chair of Unity Apostolate 1963), an anthology on Christian reunion from

the writings of Unity Octave pioneer Father Paul James Francis,
S.A., with foreword by Gregory Peter Cardinal Agagianian.

Ehrenstrom, Nils, and Walter G. Muelder, *Institutionalism and Church
Unity: A Symposium* (New York: Association, 1963), transmitted to
the churches from the Study Commission on Institutionalism to the
Fourth Conference on Faith and Order, Montreal, July, 1963.

Hudson, Winthrop, *Understanding Roman Catholicism* (Philadelphia:
Westminster Press, 1959), the professor of church history at Colgate-
Rochester Divinity School describes Roman Catholic teaching with
papal documents and encyclicals.

Küng, Hans; Yves Congar; Daniel O'Hanlon, eds. *Council Speeches
of Vatican II* (Glen Rock, N.J.: Paulist Press, 1964), 51 of the more
popular earlier speeches of the Second Vatican Council through the
Second Session.

Lindbeck, George A., *Dialogue on the Way* (Minneapolis: Augsburg,
1965), reports from official Protestant observers at the Second Vatican
Council.

Oldham, J. H., *Foundations of Ecumenical Social Thought* (Philadelphia: Fortress Press, 1966), Oxford Conference reports, with a new
introduction that traces the importance of this 1937 precursor to
the WCC.

Rodger, Patrick C., and Lukas Vischer, *The Fourth World Conference
on Faith and Order* (New York: Association, 1964), reports from
Montreal, 1963, latest findings on the theology of unity of the WCC
Faith and Order Commission.

Visser 't Hooft, W. A., *The New Delhi Report* (New York: Association,
1962), full reports, including debate and action on definitions of unity,
at the Third Assembly of the WCC in 1961 in New Delhi.

———, *The Pressure of Our Common Calling* (Garden City, N.Y.:
Doubleday, 1959), working document for the world conference on the
Life and Mission of the Church in Strasbourg, July, 1960, and for
several other related national and international meetings.

## V. *Confessional Viewpoints*

DeGroot, Alfred Thomas, *The Nature of the Church and Other Studies*
(Birmingham Printers, 1960), a study of church unity from the viewpoint of the Disciples looking to the WCC General Assembly of 1961.

Gilmore, A., *Baptism and Christian Unity* (Valley Forge: Judson,
1966), American Baptist.

Heenan, John, ed. *Christian Unity: A Catholic View* (London: Sheed &
Ward, 1962), a future Cardinal looks at unity.

Holt, Ivan Lee, co-author with Elmer T. Clark *The World Methodist
Movement* (Nashville: The Upper Room, 1956), the World Methodist
Council and the ecumenical movement.

Kean, Charles Duell, *The Road to Reunion* (Greenwich, Conn.: Seabury
Press, 1958), Protestant Episcopal Church and its relation to the
ecumenical movement.

Kik, Jacob Marcellus, *Ecumenism and the Evangelical* (Philadelphia:
Presbyterian and Reformed Co., 1958), viewpoint of the conservative
Protestant.

Lewis, Arthur James, *Zinzendorf, the Ecumenical Pioneer* (Philadelphia: Westminster Press, 1962), the Moravian contribution to mission and unity.

Paton, David MacDonald, *Anglicans and Unity* (London: A. R. Mowbray; New York: Morehouse-Barlow, 1963), the Anglican position.

Routley, Erik, *Congregationalists and Unity* (London: A. R. Mowbray, 1962), a view of autonomous, free church body.

Skydsgaard, Kristen E., *The Papal Council and the Gospel* (Minneapolis: Augsburg, 1961), views of Lutheran World Federation scholars.

Weigel, Gustave, *A Catholic Primer on the Ecumenical Movement* (Westminster, Md.: Newman Press, 1959), revision of article originally in the Thomist Reader.

Zernov, Nicolas, *Orthodox Encounter* (London: J. Clarke, 1961) the role of Eastern Orthodox in the ecumenical movement with special attention to Orthodox-Anglican relations.

## VI. *Trends and Expectations*

Baum, Gregory, *Progress and Perspectives: the Catholic Quest for Christian Unity* (New York: Sheed & Ward, 1962), the direction of the Catholic church in Christian union and the ecumenical movement.

Bea, Augustin Cardinal, *Unity in Freedom* (New York: Harper, 1964), "reflections" on the oneness of the human family in light of growing oneness in space travel, ideologies, church unity.

Blakemore, William Barnett, *The Challenge of Christian Unity* (St. Louis: Bethany Press, 1964), mission and Christian unity, local church government in an ecumenical age.

Burgelin, Pierre, *Unity and Mission of the Church* (Geneva: John Knox, 1960), perspectives in Christian union.

Cornell, George, *Voyage of Faith: The Catholic Church in Transition* (New York: Odyssey Press, Inc., 1966), Associated Press religion writer traces recent developments in the Catholic Church in regard to the ecumenical movement. His thesis is that all of Christianity is in a state of flux and moving toward stronger forms of association.

Glover, Christopher, *The Church for the New Age*: a dissertation on church unity (New York: Expositon Press, 1956), characteristics of a twentieth century church.

Hogg, William Richey, *One World, One Mission* (New York: Friendship Press, 1960), missions and the ecumenical movement.

Jenkins Daniel, *Beyond Religion: The Truth and Error in 'Religionless Christianity* (Philadelphia: Westminster Press, 1962), principles of "true" Christianity versus overemphasized institutionalism.

Morris, William Sparkes, *The Unity We Seek* (New York: Oxford University Press, 1963), Catholic, Orthodox, Protestant authors on tradition, common witness, Reformation, sacraments.

Motter, Alton M., ed., *Preaching on Pentecost and Christian Unity* (Philadelphia: Fortress Press, 1966), sermon collection.

Newman, Jeremiah, *Changes and the Catholic Church* (Baltimore: Helicon, 1966), the Second Vatican Council and ecumenism.

Outler, Albert Cook, *The Christian Tradition and the Unity We Seek*

(New York: Oxford University Press, 1957), early tradition and unity.

Sartory, Thomas A., *The Oecumenical Movement and the Unity of the Church* (Oxford: B. Blackwell, 1963), goals of the ecumenical movement.

Schmucker, Samuel Simon, *Fraternal Appeal to the American Churches* (Philadelphia: Fortress Press, 1965), a plan for Catholic union on apostolic principles.

Schutz, Roger, *Unity: Man's Tomorrow* (New York: Herder & Herder, Inc., 1962), the prior of the Taizé Community looks ahead.

Van Deusen, Henry Pitney, *One Great Ground of Hope* (Philadelphia: Westminster Press, 1961), chronology and direction of Christian unity, 1795-1960.

Wilburn, Ralph Glenn, *The Prophetic Voice in Protestant Christianity* (St. Louis: Bethany Press, 1956), revelation and the ecumenical movement.

## VII *Practical Questions*

Bennett, John C., ed., *Christian Ethics in a Changing World* (New York: Association, 1966), attention to social action and world peace and other areas of Christian ethics with all segments of the "worldwide Christian community" represented.

Cate, William B., *The Ecumenical Scandal on Main Street* (New York: Association, 1965), executive of a local church council discusses principles that apply to local church ecumenism.

Fey, Harold E., *Cooperation in Compassion*: the Story of Church World Service (New York: Friendship Press, 1966), co-operative work of the CWS in meeting world needs.

Fackre, Gabriel, *Under the Steeple* (New York: Abingdon Press, 1957), ecumenical movement and evangelistic work.

Greenspun, William B., C.S.P., and William A. Norgren, *Living Room Dialogues* (New York: Glen Rock, N.J.: National Council of Churches and Paulist Press, 1965), program guide to ecumenical Bible study and discussion in the home.

Jackson, Joseph H., *Many But One* (New York: Sheed & Ward, 1964) leader of the National Baptists discusses ecumenism and charity.

Jones, Douglas Rawlinson, *Instrument of Peace* (London: Hodder and Stoughton, 1965), biblical premises for Christian harmony and unity.

Jurji, Edward Jabra, *The Ecumenical Era in Church and Society*: a symposium in honor of John A. Mackay (New York: Macmillan, 1959), new frontiers of the church, evangelism, Latin America, Americans and Eastern culture, science and religion.

Knapp, Forrest L., *Church Cooperation: Dead-End Street or Highway to Unity?* (Garden City, N.Y.: Doubleday, 1966), discussion of the role of cooperation through 1,000 local United States councils of churches and their relation to larger unity movements by the general secretary of the Massachusetts Council of Churches.

Küng, Hans, ed. *The Church and Ecumenism* (Glen Rock, N.J.: Paulist Press, 1965), Vol. IV of Concilium, mixed marriages, Catholic education, confession, the priesthood, catechism in Africa, sociology in Spain, and other topics by Catholic and Protestant authors.

Margull, Hans Jochen, *Hope in Action: The Church's Task in the World* (Philadelphia: Muhlenberg Press, 1962), evangelical work, mission and ecumenical movement.

Marty, Martin E., *Church Unity and Church Mission* (Grand Rapids, Mich.: Eerdman's, 1964), destiny of church related to its calling in the world.

Miller, J. Quinter, *Christian Unity: Its Relevance to the Community* (Strasburg, Pa.: Shenandoah Publishing House, 1957), lectures before the Association of Council Secretaries on ways to work for unity at the local levels and means of achieving some practical goals through local church councils.

Neill, Stephen, *Creative Tension* (London: Edinburgh House, 1959), outlines of tensions of Christian and non-Christian, church and state, mission and other areas with constructive suggestions.

Nolde, O. Frederick, editor, *Toward World-Wide Christianity* (New York: Harper, 1964), study of international implications of the Gospel by the WCC's expert on world affairs, prepared for the Inter-seminary movement.

Than, U. Kyaw, *Witnesses Together*: (Rangoon, Burma: East Asia Conference, 1960), official report of the inaugural assembly of the East Asia Christian Conference, 1959.

Thompson, Betty, *Turning World* (New York: Friendship Press, 1960) account of ecumenical projects around the world for senior high and adult church study.

## Ecumenical Periodicals

*Bulletin,* Division of Studies of the World Council of Churches 150, Route de Ferney, 1211, Geneva 20. Also *Study Encounter.*

*Communio Viatorium,* Ecumenical Institute of the Comenius Faculty of Protestant Theology and the International Secretariat of the Christian Peace Conference, Jungmannova 9, Prague 1, Czech.

*Concept,* Department of Studies in Evangelism, WCC, *ibid.*

*Dialog,* 315 Fifth Ave. S., Minneapolis, Minn. 55415

*Direction: Unity,* Bureau of Information, National Catholic Welfare Conference, 1312 Massachusetts Ave., N.W., Washington, D.C., 20005

*Eastern Churches Quarterly,* "an Ecumenical Catholic Quarterly," Benedictine Priory, 29 Bramley Road, London, N. 14.

*Ecumenical Courier,* WCC, 475 Riverside Drive, New York, N.Y. 10027

*Ecumenical Notes,* Grailville, Loveland, Ohio.

*Ecumenical Press Service,* WCC, Geneva, *ibid.*

*Ecumenical Review,* WCC, Geneva, *ibid.*

*Ecumenist,* Glen Rock, N.J.

*Faith and Order Trends,* National Council of Churches, 475 Riverside Drive, New York, N.Y. 10027

*Federation News,* World Student Christian Federation, 13 rue Calvin, Geneva.

*IDO-C*, Information Documentation on the Conciliar Church, via S. Maria dell'Anima 30, Rome.

*Image*, Journal of the Ecumenical Institute, a division of the Church Federation of Greater Chicago, Evanston.

*Information Service*, Bureau of Research and Survey, NCC, *ibid.*

*Interchurch News*, NCC, *ibid.*

*Japan Missionary Bulletin*, Oriens Institute for Religious Research, 48, Isaragomachi, Minatoku, Tokyo.

*Journal of Ecumenical Studies*, Duquesne University, Pittsburgh.

*Listening*, Dominicans of Aquinas Institute, "Current Studies in Dialogue," 2570 Asbury Ave., Dubuque, Iowa, 52002

*Lumen Vitae*, International Review of Religious Education, International Centre for Studies in Religious Education, 184, rue Washington, Brussels, 5, Belgium.

*New Christian* (this has a Catholic, Protestant, Quaker editorial board), London.

*One in Christ*, Catholic ecumenical review, 58 Bocking Lane, Sheffield, 8, England.

*Polish Ecumenical Review*, Polish Ecumenical Council, Al. Swierczewskiego 76a, Warsaw.

*Religious News Service*, 43 W. 57th St., New York, N.Y., 10019

*Sorbornost*, St. Basil's House, 52 Ladbroke Grove, London, W. 11.

*Student World*, World Student Christian Federation, Geneva, *ibid.*

*Studia Liturgica*, "ecumenical quarterly for liturgical research and renewal," Mathenesserlaan 301, Rotterdam.

# Glossary

(Selected words from Documents of Dialogue)

*Aggiornamento*—A renewal; Pope John popularized this Italian term when he called for a Vatican Council to update and revitalize the church (from *Italian*: update).

*Ante-communion*—section of a rite "before" communion.

*Antiphon*—a verse sung or stated by a section of a choir in response to another section of the choir (from *Greek*, a response, or literally, "sounding against").

*Apostle*—one who is sent (*Greek, apostolos*); originally the Twelve sent by Jesus; today, usually one who fills the same shoes, such as bishops of the church.

*Apostolic succession*—the continual line of ordination by the laying-on of hands traceable to the Apostles and Christ.

*Appropriation*—the attributing to a member of the Godhead a special quality that appears to be distinctive from the other members of the Godhead, a distinction occuring because of the limitation of language.

*Asceticism*—the practice of self-denial and stern discipline, sometimes but not necessarily a withdrawal from usual pace of life (from *Greek, askein*, to exercise).

*Aula*—a "hall or court" (*Latin*); in the Second Vatican Council, the nave of St. Peter's Basilica with its tier of seats.

*Autocephalous*—independent or self-governing, applying to a church or wing of a church with "its own head" (*Greek*) or authority.

*Autonomy*—the right and practice of self-government for a community. church, or other groups, or in philosophy, the right of the individual to decide by his reason; a church authority invested in local congregations without direction from a central structure (from *Greek, autos*, self, and *nomos*, law).

*Benediction*—a blessing, or "good saying" (*Latin*); words of prayer and petition to God at end of a service or special gathering. Benediction of the Blessed Sacrament: a blessing of the people with the Blessed Sacrament exposed in a monstrance, a vessel which takes several forms, e.g., a cruciform, in which the Host is exposed for adoration.

*Bidding prayer*—a clergy prayer of exhortation, particularly in an Anglican church, before the sermon.

*Byzantine*—from Byzantium, a Greek city, founded by Byzas in 657 B.C. on one of the hills of modern Constantinople; name for Eastern empire headquartered in Constantinople; Eastern rite, church.

Canon (Law)—the laws that govern the Roman Catholic Church. The current Code of Canon Law with 2,414 canons was last revised in 1918 (*Greek, canon,* rule).

*Canticle*—a hymn or psalm taken from the Bible (*Latin, canticum,* song).

*Cassock*—one piece, plain garment reaching almost to the feet. It is close-fitting and buttons down the front. Colors: priest wears black; bishops, purple; cardinals, red; pope, white (*Latin, casacca,* great coat).

*Catechumen*—one who is receiving basic instruction in the faith (*Greek, katechein,* to teach).

*Catholic—catholic*—Roman Catholic Church (capital letters); (lower case and/or used alone) universal, consistent with tradition of the church; one who holds to early creeds; in Protestant unity talks, that which incorporates the continuity of the church—namely, a historic succession in ordination, forms from an ancient liturgy, and acceptance of the earliest creeds of the church (from *Greek, kata,* completely, *holos,* whole).

*Catholicos*—a title of some patriarchs or heads of Eastern churches, particularly in non-Roman Catholic, non-Eastern Orthodox churches, such as in the Ancient (Apostolic) Church of Armenia.

*Celebrant*—the priest who conducts or officiates at Mass.

*Celibacy*—the state of those under vow to remain single. Theologians question whether a diocesan priest takes a vow of celibacy or if he is merely bound by Church law (*Latin, caelebs,* unmarried).

*Censer*—a tray or vase-like vessel in which incense is burned at Mass and other rites. Usually tall, narrow, and suspended by a small chain by which it is waved throughout the congregation (*Latin, incensus,* set on fire).

*Chauvanism*—undue, blind commitment to a dead cause. (From Nicolas Chauvin, French soldier who continued devoted to Napoleon with great zeal even after Napoleon had been exiled.

*Chrismation*—act of anointing; among Orthodox, it is an act of confirmation administered immediately after baptism (*Greek, chrisma,* an annointing).

*Ciborium*—a metal goblet-shaped cup, with cross on top (must be lined with gold) in which the communion host (altar bread) is kept during Catholic Mass (*Latin,* a cup).

*Cloister*—a specially prescribed place for members of religious orders closed off from the world; also, the corridors surrounding an inner garden in a monastery.

*Collect*—a short, inclusive prayer, which is adaptable to the feast day and liturgical season; it is a part of every Mass and is read just before the Epistle. The term comes from the petititions of the congregation being "collected."

*Collegiality*—concept of shared authority of bishops with and under the pope. See "Episcopal College."

*Colloquium*—a mutual exchange of views; discussion; a dialogue, usually of an academic or learned nature on campus among scholars (*Latin*, conversation).

*Communion*—the receiving of the consecrated elements (bread, and in some cases, wine or juice); also synonymous with a denominational grouping, such as the Anglican Communion, an organization of 18 world-wide Anglican regional churches.

*Compline*—a night prayer of the Latin rite said before retiring.

*Concelebration*—the celebration of Mass at the same time by two or more priests together; an ancient custom restored to greater use by Vatican II to emphasize the unity of the priesthood.

*Conciliar*—pertaining to a document of an ecumenical council.

*Confession*—now often synonymous to denomination or grouping of denominations; a European usage deriving from the fact that various denominations are based largely on differing historical confessions of faith—Augsburg, Westminster, Heidelberg, etc. Among Roman Catholics, refers to the Sacrament of Penance which implies sorrow for sin, confession, and satisfaction followed by absolution.

*Congregation*—a committee of prelates at the Vatican in charge of a specified area of the life of the church, such as the Congregation of Religious, Congregation of Ceremonies, Congregation of Seminaries, etc.; also a religious group or order; a local group worshipping together.

*Constitution*—the most solemn of an ecumenical council document, and has greater importance than any other. A decree or declaration (usually very short) are names for lesser documents, in regard to the theology of the church.

*Curate*—assistant to a pastor of a parish; originally any clergyman who had the "care" of a parish.

*Curia*—the court and offices that advises a pope or diocesan bishop; originally, curia was the name for the house of the Roman Senate.

*Deacon*—a step in ordination to the priesthood to which one is ordained sometimes a year before final ordination; a layman with official duties in the church, among Protestants, often has a dual role of assisting in administrating the church and serving communion. Originally, a deacon in the Book of Acts (Chapter 6) served tables (*Greek, diakonos,* servant).

*Deutero-canonical*—the "second" canon; books questioned by some Greek fathers, but considered inspiring and admitted to the canon of the Bible later than the other books in the Roman Catholic Bible. Protestants call them "apocrypha" (or "hidden" books) because they did not appear in the Hebrea canon at Jamnia in 70 A.D. (*Greek, deutero,* second).

*Dialogue*—a conversation, usually formal and scheduled, implying comparison and reasoned evaluation; an exchange of words, often of views (see introduction of book).

*Dogma*—a doctrine, in the Roman Catholic Church, about faith and morals that has been officially proclaimed by the Church as revealed truth; a permanent truth and unquestionable article of faith, declared through authority (*Greek, dogma,* what one believes to be true).

*Ecclesial*—churchly; see "ecclesiology."

*Ecclesiology*—the study (*Greek, logos*) of the church (*ekklesia*) in terms of its theology and history and mission apart from the church as an organization or institution.

*Eclecticism*—a philosophy of selecting doctrines at will from various faiths and philosophies to form a system attempting to combine all truths with the best from each group (*Greek, ekleigein,* to choose).

*Ecumenical*—universal, world wide, all encompassing, referring to the wholeness or complete church (*Greek, oikumene,* the inhabited world).

*Efficacious*—having power to do or "bring to pass" that which one set out to do; e.g., an efficacious solution to a problem (*Latin, efficere,* to accomplish).

*Eminence, your*—title of honor reserved for cardinals and the Grand Master of the Knights of St. John of Jerusalem.

*Epiklesis (epiclesis)*—a prayer in the Eastern Divine liturgies invoking God to send down the presence of the Holy Spirit on the bread and wine following the consecration, and completing the consecration in the Eastern Orthodox rites (*Greek, epikaleo,* to call on).

*Epiphany*—January 6. In the West, it commemorates the appearing of Christ to the Wise Men; in the East, it commemorates, the birth, and the baptism of Christ (His "manifestation" to the world) and the beginning of His ministry (*Greek, epiphanein,* to make to appear).

*Episcopal College*—a collection or group of bishops who are successors of the "college" or group of the Twelve Apostles with and under Peter, and his successor, the pope (*Latin, collegium* a society, *Greek, episcopos,* bishop).

*Eschatology*—a study of last things, such as the end of the world, judgment, etc.; some, such as C. H. Dodd, hold there is a "realized" eschatology in the day by day life process (*Greek, eschatos,* last, *logos,* study).

*Eucharist*—the sacrament of the Lord's supper; "That the Lord Jesus the same night in which he was betrayed took bread: and when he had given thanks (*eucharistesas*), he brake it" (1 Cor. 11: 23, 24). In Roman Catholic usage, Eucharist is used for both the sacrament and sacrifice of Christ whose being is present in the consecrated Host; also the consecrated Host or wine.

*Evangelical*—usually applied to more "conservative" Protestant churches, emphasizing use and importance of the Bible, as compared to more liberal, or world-orientated emphases of other Protestants, and contrasted to an emphasis on use of tradition (Greek, *eu,* good, *angelion,* message).

*Excommunication*—spiritual penalty which deprives a baptized person of the sacraments and fellowship of the church.

*Exegesis*—a detailed, close, critical look at a segment of Scripture to determine its precise form and meaning (*Greek, exegesis,* an explanation, *exegeisthai,* to show the way).

*Existentialism*—popular philosophy, particularly after World War II which declares that existence precedes essence; therefore, what counts are not the traditions, standards and absolutes of one's inherited culture but the intrinsic values of the moment.

*Faith*—a response, with varying degrees of involvement and responsibility, and commitment to an object, standard, cause, person and/or deity, in which the complete nature of the object of faith is not knowable by reason; an assent, a trust, a gift (of God).

*Ferraiuola* (also ferraiola)—a cape of varying length worn over the cassock.

*Form criticism*—a technique of study of the Bible according to the background cultural forms or styles used in an account. The form critics say the New Testament was handed down piecemeal in different oral forms. The forms are: stories with a moral, miracle stories; sayings; mythical stories when the participants are not human, such as the story of the Transfiguration; and the chronological story, such as the Passion Story.

*Gospel*—glad tidings, usually news of Christ; also the four books or their summary message that tell the story of Christ (viz. Matthew, Mark, Luke, John) (*Anglo Saxon,* good news).

*Grace*—free favor (and spiritual strength) bestowed by God. In Roman Catholic usage: (1) sanctifying grace, bestowed at baptism, can be lost by mortal sin, but regained by repentance, (2) actual grace, temporary help day by day that can serve to lead those in mortal sin to repentance, and also to avoid evil.

*Gradual*—an anthem or Scripture excerpt (in Latin Mass, usually verses from the Psalms or other Scripture) sung or said after the epistle of the Mass (*Latin, gradus,* step—in early times this was said from the step of the altar).

*Historicity*—the state of being historical or present in history.

*Homily*—a short sermon, usually at Mass, in a Catholic Church, based on the Epistle or Gospel reading for the day.

*Icon*—non-dimensional Byzantine-style painting or other representation on wood or metal, used in place of statue by Eastern churches (*Greek, eikon,* image).

*Impediment*—that which prevents or hinders, e.g. the lawful marriage of two persons, or an ordination (e.g., being a soldier, illegitimacy, slavery, guilty of a public crime, etc.) (*Latin, impedimentum;* hindrance; plural; baggage).

*Indulgence*—remission by the Church of temporal punishment for sins which have already been forgiven. Plenary indulgence is a remission of all the temporal punishment and a partial indulgence is a remission of part of the temporal punishment (*Latin, indulgere,* to be kind to).

*Intercession*—a prayer on the behalf of others; Protestants: an intercessory prayer is one that is prayed for the welfare of another; Roman Catholics: in the Mass there are two intercessions, one for the living, one for the dead; Catholics also pray for saints to intercede for them.

*Interconfessional*—pertaining to relations between groups and particularly between denominations and their groupings (see "Confession").

*Interdenominational*—a going between and among several denominations a scope greater and involving more than one church group.

*Intervention*—a Vatican Council speech or communication during debate of a document.

*Introit*—Anglican: a hymn sung as the minister enters the sanctuary; Roman Catholic: first prayer read by priest as he ascends the alter after praying at the foot of the altar. However, with the introduction of a new liturgy resulting from the Vatican Council, the introit is now being said or sung by the congregation; with or without the priest, as he begins Mass.

*Investiture*—Once the act by which one was appointed, usually a priest or prelate, by a medieval ruler, also, vice versa. Today it largely refers to presenting or putting on vestments for Mass and other rites.

*Justification*—*by faith*—salvation is granted not by any special endeavor or good work, but by faith alone.

*Kairos*—plural, *kairoi*—a Greek word for a special kind of time in the New Testament; the breaking of the eternal into the temporal; points of contact between deity and the earthly scheme of things; meanings in different contexts in the New Testament: a limited time, a short season, a point of time (such as the Incarnation and other junctures of God with man).

*Kerygma*—the proclamation of the Good News; the proclamation of faith in general; also the core or essence of the proclamation (*Greek*, proclamation).

*Kiss of peace*—an ancient gesture, still practiced, particularly among Eastern churches, symbolizing brotherly love and general good will toward one another.

*Know Nothing*—in 1852, a third party, the American party opposing immigration and threat of immigration and minorities, and strongly anti-Catholic, arose and flourished for several years; a rule of this secret organization was to "know nothing" when questioned.

*Koinonia*—a fellowship in the New Testament shared community; a group in which one participates and experiences a sense of a group personality and meaning (*Greek*, fellowship, partnership).

*Kyrie eleison*—an ancient Greek exclamation, "Lord, have mercy," that was retained in the Catholic Mass and in some Protestant rites.

*Laity*—the general group of people not ordained as clergy in a church (*Greek*, laos, people).

*Lector*—in the new liturgy outlined by Vatican II, a reader, other than the priest in parts of the Mass from the parish and not ordained. Formerly, the third of four minor orders related to the Sacrament of Holy Orders; the minor order of lector is still given to candidates to the priesthood.

*Litany*—a solemn prayer, usually of petitions said responsively that is, the priest or leader alternates with the congregation (*Greek*, litaneia, an entreating prayer).

*Magisterium*—the teaching authority of the church invested in the Apostles, with Peter as their head, and their successors (*Latin*, magister, teacher).

*Mass of the Catechumens*—the beginning of the Mass, up to the offertory of the bread and wine by the priest. The early catechumens receiving instruction usually attended only the first part.

*Mass of the Faithful*—the main sacrifice part of the Mass from the offertory to the end. In the early church, only the baptized faithful could attend this part of the Mass.

*Melchite*—An Eastern rite, which during the Crusades, returned to the Roman Catholic Church; See of patriarch is in Antioch; found mostly in the Near East and Egypt; uses Greek and Arabic; name given to Christians in the fifth century who supported the Byzantine emperors and the creeds of the early councils called by the emperors (*Syriac, Melcha,* king).

*Metaphysics*—the study or seeking of basic principles that govern life and faith beyond or after the physical. Concerned with prime laws and causes from which is derived a scheme for the universe.

*Metropolitan*—an archbishop over a number of dioceses; in Eastern Christianity, a metropolitan is generally synonymous with archbishop, even though one may not have a special jurisdiction (*Greek, metropolis,* mother city).

*Ministry*—the duties or tasks or program of one who "serves"; includes in the Christian faith, ministry at the altar, ministry to people, ministry to world and society.

*Mission*—the role of the Church accomplishing God's will in the world; often regarded as reconciliation (by Protestants) and extending Christ through time and history through the Church (Catholic). Once used primarily for overseas (and local) recruitment projects or nuclei of new churches (*Latin, missus,* sent).

*Mitre*—ornamental gold or silk cloth headdress of bishop and abbots, with stiffened sides that come to a point, with two pieces of cloth, or lappets hanging down the back (*Greek,* turban).

*Monsignor*—an honorary title symbolizing papal recognition. Two kinds in the U.S.: Protonotary apostolic and domestic prelate, named for life with title of "Rt. Rev."; papal chamberlain, who is called "Very Rev. Msgr." The monsignori wear violet or purple vestments. In Europe, a bishop is also called a monsignor (*Italian,* my lord).

*Motet*—a choir composition of several tone series or parts progressing simultaneously, usually Scripture words, and sung a capella.

*Nativist movement*—a philosophy that favors native born citizens over immigrants; also applies to any movement of reaction (from Black Muslims to John Birch) in defense of a "pure," unwavering tradition or philosophy.

*Natural Law*—a basic law or understanding found in the nature of things, quite predictable in non-rational creatures, and in intelligent creatures, it is seen as the sum total of ethical awareness in man; the consensus of the human conscience.

*Novena*—a prayer period spanning nine days. Originally, a novena was made for a deceased person and is still regarded as such in the novena of masses that follows the death of a pope (*Latin, novenus,* ninth).

*Oikoumene*—see (*Ecumenical*)

*Oratory*—A small chapel for prayer, or, in canon law, buildings set aside for worship by a group or individual (*Latin, oratorium*, a place of prayer).

*Order*—in regard to faith (cf. Faith and Order Commission of the World Council of Churches), in what order does the Holy Spirit work to bring salvation? Important to Lutherans, for instance, one order is faith, justification, vocation, illumination, regeneration, conversion, mystical union, renovation, sanctification, and good works. Variations of order depends to some degree on whether one is baptized an an infant or as an adult. Another order is a religious group approved by the Vatican with special vows of poverty, chastity, and obedience.

*Ordinary*—one who has ordinary authority over a diocese or other area; usually refers to a bishop or archbishop. Also, ordinary of the Mass: that part which does not change.

*Orthodox*—(Eastern), large body of churches with a catholic tradition, with the same sacraments as Roman Catholics and formerly one with the church of the West (Roman Catholic). Schism developed from 1054 to 1472, with earlier roots. Churches look to Constantinople, the Rome of the East, and an ecumenical patriarch, a first among equals. The name Orthodox (*Greek, ortho*, straight, *doxa*, opinion, teaching) distinguishes the churches from heresies in the East in the early centuries of the church.

*Parish*—a group of people within a community and diocese usually surrounding a central church in which the sacraments are administered, and worship services and rites, such as baptism, marriage and funerals are held.

*Paschal meal*—a Jewish meal commemorative of the passing of the angel of death over the Israelites prior to their escape from Egypt. It is celebrated with unleavened bread (matzoh), similar to the bread prepared in haste by the Israelites before their flight, with other food, symbolic of the bitterness of slavery (*Greek, pascha*, from *Hebrew, pasach*, to pass over).

*Pectoral*—(cross) large cross with precious stones hanging low from chain around neck of a bishop and symbolic of his office. One can distinguish a bishop from other priests who are in street clerics (*Latin, pectus, pectoris*, breast).

*Peritus*—(plural, *periti*)—a theologian advisor, particularly to a bishop at the Second Vatican Council (*Latin*, experienced).

*Perpetual Help*—(Our Lady of) name for a Byzantine picture of Mary painted in the thirteenth century. St. Alphonsus Church of the Redemptorist Fathers in Rome has it enshrined. A number of miracles have been attributed to it.

*Pluralism*—the existence of a number of beliefs, all of which have equal rights before the law; philosophically, the mutual existence of value in all forms and teachings.

*Polemic*—that which is "warlike" in character; thus a hot, no-holds-barred defense of one's belief against another to subdue him intellectually and uncharitably is a polemic (*Greek, polemos*, war).

*Pontiff*—usually refers to a pope, who is supreme pontiff, but also applies to all bishops; some believe the word originally came from "pons" (*Latin*, bridge) and "facere" (to make), therefore a bridge builder;

thus the pope as a vicar of Christ helps to build the bridge between man and God (*Latin, pontifex*, high priest).

*Preface*—a prayer of praise and thanksgiving in the Catholic Mass, introducing the canon or most solemn part of the Mass.

*Prelate*—a church person "set aside" with authority over lower ranks of clergy; includes archbishops, bishops, abbots, monsignori of "domestic prelate" rank.

*Presbytery*—representative group or legislative body composed of clergy and one ruling elder from each church in a Presbyterian denomination; presbytery has power to license, ordain, launch missions, etc. (*Greek, presbuteros*, elder).

*Primate*—the top ranking prelate, by seniority or title, in a country or area (*Latin, primus*, first).

*Pro-prefect*—the temporary president of a Vatican congregation or commission.

*Proselytize*—attempt to convert someone from another religious tradition (*Greek, proselutos*, a newcomer, stranger, convert).

*Protestant*—originally, followers of Luther, who in 1529 protested or pledged their dissent concerning a decree of Charles V and the Diet of Spires, and asked for a general ecumenical council of the church; now refers to any non-Roman Catholic and non-Eastern Orthodox, of a mainline organized tradition, as distinguished from more recently organized groups.

*Pseudepigrapha*—collection of books written between 200 B.C. and 100 A.D. which were either anonymous or had the alias of a Biblical personality; these did not appear in any Old Testament canon. Catholics call the pseudepigrapha the "apocrypha" ("hidden" or "books which have been put aside"). Protestants call the *deuterocanonical* writings the Apocrypha (*Greek, pseudo*, false, *epigrapha*, writing).

*Rason*—long loose black everyday garment with wide sleeves, worn by clergy of the Eastern rites.

*Reciprocity*—mutual result and equal benefit and opportunity for those participating in an endeavor; principle of reciprocity in ecumenical relations: don't ask another to take part in your ecumenical project unless you are willing to cooperate in a similar manner.

*Reconciliation*—bringing together after separation; is now most commonly regarded in ecumenical theology as bringing Christ and world together: "God was in Christ, reconciling the world unto himself" (2 Cor. 5: 19).

*Refectory*—a dining hall in a seminary or monastery or convent (*Latin, reficere*, to refresh).

*Reformed*—a changing and seeking to better conditions with new approaches or restoration of past ideas; in church history, Reformed refers to churches that trace back to Zwingli and Calvin, who emphasized the role of the Bible, a fore-ordination to salvation, and a rejection of the bodily presence of Christ in the Lord's Supper (*Latin, reformare*, to form again).

*Relation*—introductory statement and background of a proposed Vatican Council document presented on the floor prior to debate of document.

*Retreat*—a withdrawing from usual daily activity into a quiet place
for meditation and special direction and spiritual instruction.

*Sacrament*—a visible sign of an inner grace or relation with God insti-
tuted by Christ. There are seven in the Roman Catholic church—
Baptism, Confirmation, Holy Eucharist, Penance, Hold Orders,
Matrimony, Anointing of the Sick. In most Protestant churches,
Baptism and the Lord's Supper or Eucharist are sacraments (some-
times known by other names; Baptists call them ordinances.

*Sacramental*—holy deed or object specified by the church for spiritual
benefit. Called sacramental, because of resemblance to the sacraments in obtaining divine favor, but not to be confused with sacraments given by Christ. Three kinds: (1) blessings, (2) exorcism
against evil spirits, (3) blessed objects, such as crucifixes, medals,
rosaries.

*Sanctification*—act of making a person or object holy or sacred; an act
of setting apart or consecrating.

*Sanctuary*—in Roman Catholic churches, the front or center part of
the church where the altar stands, an area referred to by Protestants
as the chancel (technically, the chancel or "railing," *Latin, cancelli,*
is the area between the altar and the nave, or main seating area);
in Protestant churches, sanctuary refers to the main seating area.

*Schema*—(plural, *schemata*), preliminary draft of document under consideration for approval; name of prepared documents on agenda at
the Second Vatican Council (*Latin*).

*See*—an area, such as a diocese or archdiocese, governed by a bishop
(*Latin, sedes,* a seat).

*Septuagint*—Greek version of the Old Testament translated by seventy
(Greek: *Septuaginta*) scholars third century before Christ in Alex-
andria, Egypt, and contains the deuterocanonical (apocryphal)
books.

*Sodality*—a lay association with special disciplines, devotions, and charitable concerns, often devoted to Mary (*Latin, sodalis,* companion).

*Stole*—narrow band, about 6½ feet long which is worn around the neck
of a priest, but is draped over the left shoulder of a deacon, symbolic of his office during liturgical rites (*Latin, stola,* a garment).

*Surplice*—a vestment of white linen, with wide sleeves reaching just
below the hips, usually slightly longer than the similar cotta worn
by Anglican choirs and acolytes (*Latin, super,* over, *pelliceum,* a
robe of fur).

*Synaxis*—a congregation in the early church, usually brought together
for worship and the Eucharist (*Greek, sun,* or *syn,* with, together,
*agein,* to bring).

*Theistic*—belief in a God who is both immanent (in the world) and trans-
cendent, as compared to deism (*Latin, deus,* God) where God is a
non-participant and an extraneous reality; theism permits personal
experience with God as compared to strictly rational deism (*Greek,
theos,* God).

*Thurible*—see "censer" (*Latin: thuribulum,* from *thus, thuris,* incense).

*Uniate*—term for Eastern rites in union with Rome as contrasted to
Eastern Orthodox and other oriental churches not in union with
Rome (*Russian: uniya,* union).

*Union*—the bringing of two or more groups together to function as one.

*Unity*—state of oneness, concord, agreement, harmony, but some believe not necessarily one organization.

*Venerable*—title of an archdeacon among Anglicans; among Roman Catholics, a title for one whose cause of beautification has been introduced but cannot yet be venerated publicly.

*Veni Creator Spiritu*—hymn to the Holy Spirit by Rabanus Maurus, 776-856, sung at the ordination of priests or wherever the Holy Spirit is solemnly called on; used at Confirmation, opening of a Council or synod (*Latin*, Come Creator Spirit).

*Viaticum*—Eucharist given when there is danger of death (*Latin*, preparation for a journey).

*Vicar*—a clergyman who takes the place of or represents another; the Pope is the vicar of Christ; in Anglicanism, one who has charge of a mission or chapel on behalf of a parish pastor or bishop (*Latin, vicarius*, a deputy).

*Voluntaristic*—pertaining to philosophies of free will; unrestrained; open, in regard to society (*Latin, voluntas*, free).

*Vulgate*—Latin translation of the Bible by St. Jerome around 400 A.D. The Council of Trent approved the Vulgate for public readings and indicated it contained no doctrinal errors. The Vulgate was the basis for the English Douay Bible about 1600 A.D. (*Latin, vulgare*, to make public, publish).

*Witness*—to give testimony or evidence of, legally, or in regard to one's faith; also one who is willing to sacrifice for his faith: word translated witness in New Testament Greek is "martus," from which the word martyr derives.

*Zoe*—Greek for "life"; used of Christ as source of life, John 5: 26: "For as the Father hath life—'zoen'—in himself."

# List of Documents

# Index

513